Praise for previous editions of

How to Open and Operate a
Bed & Breakfast

"Before you start to plan on operating a B&B, or even talk about it to neighbors and friends, get a copy of this book. It may convince you that you're cut out to operate one or it will help you decide this isn't for you. It is an excellent 'how-to' book."

—*New York–Pennsylvania Collector*

"Packed with information on what it takes to run a successful bed and breakfast."

—*Christian Library Journal*

"This is a wonderful, practical guide to starting your own bed and breakfast. Stankus writes with an upbeat style, not only when she helps readers determine if they are suited to this type of endeavor, but also when she gives checklists for the basic needs of bed and breakfasts."

—*Columbia Tribune* (Mo.)

Help Us Keep This Guide Up to Date

Every effort has been made by the author and editors to make this guide as accurate and useful as possible. However, many things can change after a guide is published—establishments close, phone numbers change, facilities come under new management, etc.

We would love to hear from you concerning your experiences with this guide and how you feel it could be made better and be kept up to date. While we may not be able to respond to all comments and suggestions, we'll take them to heart and we'll make certain to share them with the author. Please send your comments and suggestions to the following address:

The Globe Pequot Press
Reader Response/Editorial Department
246 Goose Lane
P.O. Box 480
Guilford, CT 06437

Or you may e-mail us at:
editorial@GlobePequot.com

Thanks for your input!

HOME-BASED BUSINESS SERIES

How to Open and Operate a
Bed & Breakfast

Eighth Edition

Jan Stankus

The
Globe
Pequot
Press

GUILFORD, CONNECTICUT

To buy books in quantity for corporate use
or incentives, call **(800) 962–0973**
or e-mail **premiums@GlobePequot.com**.

Copyright © 1986, 1989, 1992, 1995, 1997, 2000, 2004, 2007 by Jan Stankus

Text design: Mary Ballachino
Cover photos, clockwise from top left: Eric Kamp/Index Stock; © Joel Bernard/Masterfile; © Alison Barnes Martin/Masterfile; Eye Wire

ISSN: 1545-5033
ISBN-13: 978-0-7627-4175-5
ISBN-10: 0-7627-4175-9

Manufactured in the United States of America
Eighth Edition/First Printing

This edition is dedicated to the many hardworking
B&B pioneers who took an idea and developed it into an industry.

Contents

Contents

Contents

Contents

Foreword

At first, hosting a bed and breakfast seems simple enough, a natural extension of what you love to do in everyday life—entertaining interesting people, whose company you enjoy. If you're an excellent cook, accomplished host, and skilled household manager, you may feel you can slip into the role of a bed and breakfast innkeeper with little additional instruction.

However, if you ask any successful host about the skills necessary to operate a bed and breakfast, you'll be rewarded by a long list of items, many of which seem unrelated to hospitality and service issues. Since yours is a small business, you also need to be able to market, sell rooms, maintain a Web site, manage money and people, deal with local authorities, fix anything that breaks, be on call 24/7 . . . and keep smiling no matter what.

To operate a bed and breakfast well and profitably can be a daunting challenge. But help is here in the way of this information-filled book by Jan Stankus. She takes the mystery out of marketing, the frustration out of finances, and the disorganization out of operating a home-based business. Jan offers plans, charts, worksheets, advice from successful innkeepers, industry resources, hints, ideas, and plenty of support as you make the transition from aspiring bed and breakfast innkeeper to accomplished innkeeper. And she shows you how to keep smiling as she tells you *How to Open and Operate a Bed & Breakfast*.

Bobbi Zane
Editor and Publisher
Yellow Brick Road: Insight for Aspiring Innkeepers

Preface

It has been twenty-one years since I researched and wrote the first edition of this book, now in its eighth edition. At that time it was clear from the many letters coming into my office at the Traveler's Information Exchange from people who wanted to open a B&B but didn't know where to begin that a book like this had to happen. Back then there was scant information available to help aspiring hosts. Now there are more resources to make the job easier, but the best information still comes from the people who know the most about bed and breakfast: the hosts who open their homes to guests, the people who travel the B&B way, and the managers of reservation service agencies (RSAs) that help hosts and guests get together.

This book is the product of the combined knowledge, experience, and advice of hundreds of B&B hosts, managers of reservation service agencies, B&B consultants across North America, and guests who enjoy B&B hospitality. Together they offer their combined wisdom for bed and breakfast; individually they show the personal style that makes each B&B a unique experience. All the people who have contributed information to make this book possible have done so freely, with the hope that what they know can help a new host get started.

What exactly is bed and breakfast? This question is at the top of the list for people who are thinking about starting their own B&B but still aren't quite sure how to define this unique accommodation. Many people are familiar with bed and breakfast as it exists in Europe, where B&B has long been a tradition. Or they have other personal experience, seeking out B&Bs wherever they travel. Or they've read about it in magazines, newspapers, or guidebooks. Or they've heard about it from friends or acquaintances who have stayed in bed and breakfasts during their travels as an alternative to hotels. By now we've all heard about "bed and breakfast" somewhere or another. The term has become so commonplace that it's applied to all sorts of things, and that's part of the problem. Some large hotels now offer what they call a "bed and breakfast" package. No wonder there's confusion about what B&B is all about! One of the growing pains of a developing industry is that it must seek definition—what it is and what it is not.

This book makes these distinctions: A bed and breakfast home (also called a host home or homestay) is a private residence or other structure on a homeowner's property (such as a guest house or cabin) that is used to accommodate paying guests overnight. Breakfast (either continental or full) is provided. B&B offers guests a good old-fashioned dose of hospitality in a world that is sometimes a little too impersonal. A bed and breakfast home is not a rooming house. It is not a hotel or a motel. It is not a restaurant. And it is not a bed and breakfast inn or a country inn, although they have some important characteristics in common, including a commitment to providing the best in hospitality. Rather, inns are small commercial enterprises (usually having four to twelve guest rooms) in which breakfast is usually part of the deal, just as it is in a bed and breakfast home. But a bed and breakfast home is in a class by itself.

Who should use this book? If you're thinking about operating a bed and breakfast home or a small bed and breakfast inn, you will benefit from the gold mine of information contained here. It will help you figure out if bed and breakfast is right for you. It will help you start up and run your bed and breakfast. It will put you in touch with reservation service agencies and associations that can help you. It will outline your responsibilities as a host. And it will show you where you fit into the B&B industry as a whole in North America.

If you already operate a bed and breakfast, this book allows you the opportunity to compare notes with other people who share your interests. There is no need to be out there all alone. The more we work together, the better able we'll be to shape the future of bed and breakfast.

In addition, B&B consultants and managers of reservation service agencies can use the information here for easy reference. The book will make their job easier by providing a useful tool for their work in training new hosts.

What comes next? The bed and breakfast industry is still evolving in North America. Even as this book goes to press, changes are taking place that will eventually affect all of us, for better or worse. In twenty-one years' time we have seen more regulation, better-educated guests, the explosion of information-age technology, and even a few bad apples. A book like this must evolve with the industry. Just as this current edition has kept up with the changing times, so too will the subsequent edition reflect any significant changes that occur in the next few years.

And speaking of changes, there is now a companion Web site for the book. Go to my Web site, openabedandbreakfast.com, and check for information about helpful worksheets, checklists, and forms soon to be released in electronic form.

Acknowledgments

This continually evolving book relies on the expertise and friendly help of many people. Special thanks go to the many hosts, consultants, and reservation service managers who freely shared their thoughts and anecdotes to help aspiring hosts turn their dreams into reality. Thanks also go to the folks at the Professional Association of Innkeepers International, The National Network of Bed and Breakfast Reservation Services, and the national organizations that have closed their doors (they are indeed missed but their legacy lives on), whose dedication to the bed and breakfast industry continues to benefit hosts everywhere. More thanks go to specialists who offered their expert advice to help build this book: Gerald Arndt for insurance recommendations; John Sedensky, Arline Pat Hunt, and Paula Deigert for recordkeeping pointers and tax-filing information; John Bujalski, D.V.M., my cat's favorite doctor, for advice on hosting pets; Ron Walters of Great Estates Coffee for pointers on producing the perfect brew; and Dave Elliott from Taylor House Bed & Breakfast for Web site and database advice, which is so important to a host in today's world. Extra special thanks go to my conscientious and tireless editorial assistants. Kudos to Emily Williams, who meticulously researched and documented current information on tourist offices throughout North America and the vast array of available guidebooks. And kudos to Leslie Wittman, who ensured that details relating to the countless B&B associations and reservation service agencies referenced in these pages were up to date.

The companion Web site for this book, openabedandbreakfast.com, was made possible only through the expertise and hard work of Kris Aasmo of Tekright, to whom I owe enormous gratitude. I would also like to thank Anastasia Mathis-Belay for transforming numerous checklists, forms, and worksheets into electronic format.

Chapter One

Should You Become a Bed and Breakfast Host?

Many of us toy with the idea of becoming a bed and breakfast host after a wonderful visit at a B&B during a vacation or business trip, or after hearing about how much others have enjoyed this unique type of accommodation. The life of a host seems so easy, so pleasant, so glamorous.

But before getting completely caught up in the fantasy, it's a good idea to look a little more closely at what it really takes to be a good bed and breakfast host. The following quizzes will help prepare you for the realities of bed and breakfast hosting that are discussed later.

Quiz One

Would You Make a Good Host?

For each of the following questions, choose the one answer that most closely describes your life at the moment, or what you would do in each situation if you were a bed and breakfast host.

1. What do you like to serve for breakfast?
   a. Eggs Benedict
   b. Blueberry waffles made from your own special recipe
   c. Granola with chilled yogurt and strawberries, topped with honey
   d. Leftover chili from last night's poker game

2. What kind of bed is in your guest room?
   a. An antique four-poster double bed with a new, pillow-top mattress
   b. A queen-size platform bed (made of natural pine) and a futon
   c. A king-size water bed with adjustable heat control
   d. An army cot that's been in the attic since World War I

3. What is the oldest item in your refrigerator?
   a. Fruit salad left over from this morning's breakfast
   b. Marinated mushrooms for tomorrow's lunch
   c. An unopened jar of homemade raspberry preserves
   d. The corsage from your junior prom

4. What type of wastebasket do you have in the guest room?
   a. A wicker basket that matches the writing table and the chair near the window
   b. A brightly polished metal container lined with tissue paper that complements the wallpaper
   c. A large, handcrafted ceramic urn made by the same artist who created the lamp base and ashtray in the room
   d. A paper bag that says "A&P" on it

5. When did you buy the shower curtain in the guest bathroom?
   a. It's brand-new.
   b. Six months ago
   c. One year ago
   d. It came with the house.

6. A guest arrives at your door after a long, difficult trip that involved missed connections and lost luggage. How do you greet him?
   a. You show him to his room immediately.
   b. You take his coat, offer him a seat in the living room, and bring him a glass of wine.
   c. You point out the nature trail behind your home that goes through a beautiful wooded area to a peaceful lake.
   d. You yell, "Come on in!" from your seat on the couch in front of the TV.

7. You have to leave for work a half hour before your guests plan to be up. How do you handle their breakfast?
   a. You leave a warm quiche and homemade muffins in the oven.
   b. You prepare a "cold tray" with a selection of fresh fruit, croissants, butter, and jam.
   c. You have a freshly baked coffee cake and an insulated carafe of coffee ready.
   d. You throw a box of cornflakes on the kitchen table and hope that your guests will find the milk and sugar.

Okay, I admit that Quiz One is a bit on the light side. Nevertheless, two major points should have become clear as you looked over the possible answers to each serious question.

The first point is that there is no one "right" answer or solution that makes someone a "good" host and someone else not. Each host is an individual with a unique personal style and brand of imagination. A host should be able to rely on his or her own good sense of hospitality and grace—and common sense, too—to make sure that guests feel welcome and comfortable.

The second point is that there are some things that are clearly unacceptable. I truly hope that you did not, in good faith, choose the letter "d" as the answer to any of the questions. If you did, bed and breakfast hosting is probably not for you. But if you chose a, b, or c as answers for any of the questions, you're ready to try Quiz Two, the *real* quiz, which follows.

If you find that you answer "yes" to all or most of the following questions, it's possible that you are just the kind of person who would enjoy being a bed and breakfast host. Both

Quiz Two

The Real Quiz

For each of the following questions, choose "yes" or "no" as the answer. Remember: This is the *real* test for what it takes to become a bed and breakfast host.

1. Do you like meeting all kinds of people?
   a. yes   b. no

2. Is your house located in an area that attracts visitors?
   a. yes   b. no

3. Do you keep your home clean and neat?
   a. yes   b. no

4. Do you like to cook?
   a. yes   b. no

5. Do you currently have a regular income?
   a. yes   b. no

6. Are you organized?
   a. yes   b. no

7. Do you consider yourself a cheerful person?
   a. yes   b. no

8. Do you enjoy entertaining visitors in your home?
   a. yes   b. no

9. Do you have business experience?
   a. yes   b. no

10. Are you computer literate?
    a. yes   b. no

quizzes cover the major qualities that a bed and breakfast host should have. They are outlined well by the founder of Greater Boston Hospitality: "We look for what we like to call 'The Three C's'—Cleanliness, Comfort, and Congeniality." Combine these qualities with a good location and you could very well have a successful bed and breakfast a short time from now.

The Right Reasons

Before reading any further, get a pencil and write down the reasons you want to become a bed and breakfast host.

Done? Now put a number "1" next to your main reason. Then decide which reason is the second-most important and mark it with a number "2" and so on down the line until each reason has been rated in importance. Now we're ready.

Meeting Interesting People

"I love people!" Does your first reason sound something like this? It should. Anyone who has been a bed and breakfast host will tell you that a genuine love of people is first and foremost in this business. "You must be a 'people person,'" says Marjorie Amrom, who runs a bed and breakfast called Trade Winds in Philadelphia. This is true, and it means that a host must honestly enjoy all kinds of people—and I mean all kinds. Through bed and breakfast, you will meet people from the far reaches of the earth, with different customs, traditions, philosophies, religions, lifestyles, vocations, and fashions. They come in all shapes, sizes, and colors. It takes a special person to welcome all types into one's own home with open arms. You need a good blend of curiosity, tolerance, trust, and respect for others.

The variety of people you will meet should be one of the major rewards of your bed and breakfast. "Life is never humdrum," say the hosts of Valley View Farm in Mathias, West Virginia. "There are always new people to talk to and share what each contributes to the others' culture." Edna and Ernest Shipe have hosted hundreds of visitors from all over the world—most European countries, Bolivia, Chile, Haiti, Hong Kong, Japan, China, "and most states in the good old USA." They make a point of saying that such enjoyable educational exchanges are possible only if you are the kind of person who can "accept people who are much different from what you are."

Some people can't, and they will not make good hosts, plain and simple. They will be uncomfortable; their guests will be uncomfortable. The managers of several reservation service agencies report that they have had to turn away prospective hosts on this basis. Anyone with strong intolerances for certain people, for whatever reason, should not become a host. One reservation service agency handles the issue by placing a notice in its contract, to be read before a new host signs the document. It suggests that anyone who has irreconcilable differences regarding race, creed, color, national origin, or sexual orientation would be well advised not to become a host.

Two hosts were dropped by a reservation service agency (RSA) in Washington, D.C., not because they had strong prejudices, but because they just were not the kind of "people person" you've got to be in this business. "In both cases, they would call us and have some sort of complaint or other about the guests, and we felt B&B wasn't for them," says the RSA manager. "We have many hosts who really enjoy having guests, and those who find fault just aren't worth dealing with." "We get as excited today as the first time a guest came," say Mary and Joe Shaw, owners of the Shaw House in Georgetown, South Carolina. Now *that's* more like it.

Hilary Jones of Inngenium, a lodging management consulting business, tells this story: "A rather argumentative couple attended one of our business-planning workshops a few years ago, then stayed to look at B&Bs for sale in the area. During breakfast one morning, they got into a conversation with one of our regulars, who happens to be a licensed psychiatrist. He proceeded to question our quarrelsome pair as to their motives and suitability for innkeeping. Horrified, I started to intervene, but the interrogation was so cleverly veiled that I could only stand back and listen, intrigued. When breakfast was finished and the twosome went off for the day's appointments, the psychiatrist muttered 'never in a million years.' So did they make it? Yes! The couple bought an inn and have become remarkably successful. It just goes to show that occasionally the experts are wrong and that you shouldn't rely on everything you hear at breakfast! P.S. Business-planning clients fear not: Subversive psychiatry is not routinely offered during, or after, our workshops!"

So, yes, you must like people ("Even those you don't like," say the hosts of Friends We Haven't Met, a bed and breakfast in Westminster, California). But more than this, you must show it easily. Are you a warm person? "Our philosophy of bed and breakfast is that you become an honorary member of our family while you are with us," reads the brochure for Penury Hall in Southwest Harbor, Maine. Its owner, Prentice Strong, says that a host "must like people above all and be willing to treat them as family one has not seen for a year or two." Your guests will *feel* completely welcome only if they *are* completely welcome.

"I love activity and company," says one host in Eureka Springs, Arkansas. "I've never been married and didn't want to be a 'little ol' lady' with no kids or family coming to visit. Now I've created my own family. Each guest who comes through my door—in five minutes they're family."

Do you feel this way about the people who come to visit you now? This is a good test to see whether you will enjoy all the activity that goes with bed and breakfast. Do you love getting company and look forward to entertaining friends and relatives who come to see you? Or do you usually find yourself sneaking a look at your watch, counting the minutes until they will leave you in peace?

If you live alone, are used to being alone, and *like* being alone, ask yourself if the presence of other human beings in your home will make you feel that your inner sanctum has been invaded by hostile forces. A person who really cherishes privacy should think twice about opening a bed and breakfast home. You will end up being uncomfortable in the place you love the most, and guests will sense the strain on you.

Take an honest look at your social skills. "I'm a naturally social being," says Janet Turley, who owns the House of Amacord in Buckland, Massachusetts. Can you say the same about yourself? Do you make friends quickly? Are you able to put strangers at ease immediately? Are you pleasant and polite, no matter what? And most important, is all of this easy and enjoyable for you?

"My folks had taken in tourists when I was growing up, and I thought it was entirely natural to have 'new friends' in and out of the house," says Ellen Madison, owner of Woody Hill Guest House B&B in Westerly, Rhode Island. That's exactly how hosting should feel to you—entirely natural.

Unused Space

Do you have an extra room or two in your house? A suite? Perhaps an entire apartment? Or a separate guesthouse or cottage on the grounds? What about a boat or trailer that you use only a short while each year for yourself and your family? A barn? A lighthouse? All these places were once "wasted space" for people who decided to put them to use for bed and breakfast.

"I had a vacant room after my children grew up and moved out," says a host who lives in Philadelphia. "It is attractive, and our home is pleasant. It seemed to be a great way to make a little extra money and to meet new people from all over the country and the world."

"It provided a way to maintain and share our landmark home," say Cynthia and Charles Whited, owners of Strawberry Castle in Penfield, New York.

"Our big country house just seemed ideal for a B&B, so we decided to try it," says the owner of Anchor Hill Lodge in Rogersville, Missouri.

"After my estranged husband left, it was a way of increasing my income, meeting new people, sharing my son's and my home, and deriving more utility from the house," says a Pennsylvania host.

Many of us find ourselves in this situation as our lives change over the years. The house that served us so well for so long no longer "fits." It's too big. Too hard to keep up. Moving may be out of the question for you because the place holds so many memories, or you just plain love it there! But how do you make that big old place run economically after the kids are gone, or maybe your once near-and-dear spouse has taken off for parts unknown? Bed and breakfast could be the answer. The mayor of a town in New England put it well during his address to a bed and breakfast conference convening in his area for the weekend: "When you have a fifteen-room house, bed and breakfast starts looking pretty good!"

Even some young people who have not yet started their families have turned to bed and breakfast. One single woman who lives in Boston grew tired of having a never-ending series of roommates come and go. Yet she wanted the stimulation of having other people around because she works at home. ("When you live alone and work alone, it's too much," she says.) Her solution was bed and breakfast. Now she can have the company of other people and put the second bedroom to good use, all without losing the extra income that having a roommate had provided.

A suite in your home is an added plus if you want to offer bed and breakfast. A suite consists of a sitting room and one or more sleeping rooms. It usually has a private bath and may contain cooking facilities. Some guests prefer this enlarged space. Bob and Hattie Michalis, owners of Gull House in Avalon, California, have found that having a suite has opened up a market for them with honeymoon and anniversary couples looking for a special getaway.

If you have an extra apartment unit in your house, you might want to consider using it for bed and breakfast as an alternative to renting it to full-time tenants. (Be sure to check any rent-control ordinances that may apply before you do this.) "We had a large sixteen-room house and no longer wanted to be landlords. So we took out the apartments," says Robert Somaini of Woodruff House in Barre, Vermont. "This enables us to have use of the whole house and still have an income."

Apartment rentals to "long-term" guests (who stay a week or more) have been quite successful for a Virginia reservation service. "In big cities this can be a very good idea because of relocating executives who need a place for more than two or three nights and desire an apartment," say the owners.

An apartment differs from a suite in that it typically provides a fully equipped kitchen along with the sitting room and one or more sleeping rooms. A suite may or may not have a private entrance; an apartment generally does, although there could be an exterior door as well that is shared with others in the building.

Other good spaces to use for bed and breakfast are any small buildings that might be on your grounds. These go by different names—cabin, bungalow, guesthouse, cottage. What they have in common is that they are located near enough to the main house (where you live) so that you can easily take care of your guests' needs. These small structures are equipped for housekeeping in themselves, with a bathroom, cooking facilities, a sleeping room, and most likely a sitting room.

Using this kind of extra space for bed and breakfast has worked well for Phil and Joan Blood of Chinguague Compound in San Juan Pueblo, New Mexico. They say: "We have this lovely compound with guesthouses on it, and we thought, 'What a fun way to meet people and utilize the property at the same time!'" Their bed and breakfast by the Rio Grande features guesthouses that are each equipped with a kitchen so that if guests prefer, they may "cook in," plus a library and television. "We have a small house behind our home that had always been rented on a yearly basis," says Carol Emerick of San Diego, California. "We decided to furnish the little house and offer it to travelers on a daily/weekly basis."

Keep in mind, though, that if you do have a guesthouse separate from the main house or an apartment or suite set off from your own living space, you must work harder to establish a "bed and breakfast environment" for the guests. The aspect of bed and breakfast that many guests (and hosts) enjoy the most is the opportunity to meet and talk with one another. So make sure that any guests who are not sharing the same roof with you are invited into your living room for coffee or a glass of sherry and a visit at least when they first arrive.

And remember, too, that their experience is not "bed and breakfast" if there's no breakfast! Do-it-yourself is okay on occasion, if the host's schedule absolutely demands it or if that is what guests prefer and ask for, but as a rule, your hospitality should include a continental breakfast at the very minimum. How to get there is the problem; some hosts prepare the trays in the main house and carry them over to the guesthouses. (You might have to adjust your breakfast menu to rule out the more sensitive delicacies—such as soufflé— that would not survive the journey.) Or you could always invite guests to have breakfast with you back at the main house. That way you can easily prepare and serve everything from your own kitchen. (It also gives the guests more of a chance to get to know their hosts.) Try to find what works best for you, as long as you don't eliminate breakfast altogether! If you do this, you might as well just rent out your extra units as regular short- or long-term housing and forget about bed and breakfast!

Some people have become involved in bed and breakfast by making the decision to use their boats to accommodate guests. Host Homes of Boston, for example, has a 46-foot yacht available to guests. Moored in Constitution Quarters in Charlestown, it is only a short walk from the shops and restaurants of the nationally known Faneuil Hall Marketplace in Boston. It's an ideal spot for out-of-town visitors who want to balance dry land with ocean air.

Some hosts have renovated what used to be a barn, offering a rustic environment for guests. Another redesigned a shed into a cute little guesthouse for those with a bit of adventure in their souls. Still another went to work on an old, unused lighthouse. Needless to say, these all took major-scale operations to convert the unused space into interesting and comfortable accommodations.

So if you identified "unused space" as one of the main reasons for your interest in bed and breakfast, evaluate what you've got and what it would take to make the area livable. You can't just put guests in the shed out back with the lawn mower, in the basement behind the hot-water heater, in the attic up against Grandmother's trunks, or in the barn in Bossie's old stall (may she rest in peace). Ask yourself if the space you have is appropriate and worth the time and expense necessary to transform it into a bed and breakfast facility.

For most of us who have just an extra room or two in our homes, the decision is a little easier because the work that needs to be done to prepare them for guests is not that extensive. (Although if you want to offer bed and breakfast as a full-time business, you've got your work cut out for you to prepare and maintain at least six guest rooms.) If you have attractive space that is now being wasted and you would like to get the most out of your property, bed and breakfast could be a good idea.

The Right Skills

"My husband says I'm a cross between Perle Mesta, Erma Bombeck, and Betty Crocker," says Lisa Hileman, discussing the reason she decided to become a bed and breakfast host. If you're like Lisa, who ran a bed and breakfast called Countryside in Summit Point, West Virginia, for many years, maybe you made a similar assessment of your personal skills and realized that they are well suited to bed and breakfast hosting.

The social skills are first and foremost. A love of people is a good start, but can you translate your natural love of humanity into hospitality, as Perle Mesta did? "It's the ultimate compliment to be compared with her," says Lisa. Perle Mesta arrived on the Washington social scene in 1941 and reigned as its most celebrated hostess for the next thirty years. Her elegant parties were attended by prominent political figures and other notables, including Harry S Truman and Dwight D. Eisenhower. Can *you* make people feel this welcome and comfortable? "Antennae" is what host Crescent Dragonwagon of Dairy Hollow House in Eureka Springs, Arkansas, calls this ability. You've got to have that inner sense of what makes people comfortable.

Are you courteous and tactful, no matter what? There could be times when guests test your patience by inviting someone to breakfast without first clearing it with you, playing the television too loudly late at night, leaving their children unsupervised, trailing mud all over your priceless Oriental rug, or using your best towels to remove mascara. Are you able to talk to the guest about the problem calmly and politely, regardless of how angry you might be? If you lose your cool, even with justification, you could lose business. The owner of one reservation service says she rejected one host wishing to list with her reservation service agency for "lack of friendly hospitality." City Lights Bed & Breakfast in New York City reports rejecting a host for the same reason: "not hospitable by nature." "You will be your guests' vacation planner, adviser, gourmet cook, maid, entertainer, and more, and you have to do it with a smile. Remember—every night is opening night," says Irmgard Castleberry, former owner of a Seattle reservation service. It's sometimes not easy to keep smiling, but in this business you have to.

Are you straightforward? Can you say what you have to say without making a big deal about it? "I wish he would give me some money soon!" said one host about her weeklong guest. She needed at least a partial payment to buy groceries for breakfast all week and meet other expenses. Yet she had never mentioned payment directly to the guest because it made her uncomfortable. She just hoped he would take the initiative and pay before the day he checked out. This was a mistake that could have been easily avoided by establishing a clear policy about payment, or corrected by talking to the guest when he arrived. It need never have caused such distress. No matter how uncomfortable it might make you, if there's a problem, you have to be able to deal with it head on, or it will continue to bother you and possibly affect your treatment of a guest or of subsequent guests.

And what did the late Erma Bombeck, well-known writer and syndicated columnist, have that a bed and breakfast host needs? A sense of humor. Being able to laugh in the face of adversity will get you through those times when the commode overflows, the furnace goes on the fritz, or the soufflé implodes. "Roll with the punches," advise the coordinators of a reservation service agency in Virginia.

The owners of a Pennsylvania reservation service say, "Be flexible and ready for surprises. This is an unpredictable business." A good laugh once in a while is sometimes all it takes to set things right again.

Then, again, sometimes it's not enough. Are you handy around the house? Remember that the plumbing, the electrical system, and some of your appliances will be getting more of a workout because there will be more people using them. Imagine this: While you are cleaning the guest bathroom in preparation for visitors this evening, the water faucet comes off in your hands, and water shoots up like Old Faithful. Now what? It's Sunday, and there's no way you can get a plumber. Would you know what to do as an emergency measure? Do you know how to cut off the water supply, tighten the offending screw, or replace the worn-out washer?

Or what about this: While replacing a burnt-out lightbulb in the guest-room reading lamp, you notice that the wires are frayed. You unplug it to take a closer look, but when you plug it back in again, sparks fly. Guests are arriving tomorrow morning—not enough time to take the lamp to the repair shop. Do you know how to repair the frayed wire temporarily (but safely) with electrical tape or how to rewire a lamp yourself?

A host must be prepared to handle emergencies such as these. Bob and Hattie Michalis, owners of Gull House in Avalon, California, claim that the most difficult aspect of being a host is "doing battle with Murphy's Law"—if something can go wrong, it will. If you have the knowledge and training to take care of minor home repairs, all you need is a good toolbox and some basic supplies, and you're ready for almost anything. For the rest of us, glory be that there are some simple, basic books on the market that take us, step by step, through the procedures for a variety of emergency repairs. Sometimes a Perle Mesta has to turn into a Mister Fix-It very quickly.

Among the many useful tidbits shared in *innkeeping,* the newsletter published by the Professional Association of Innkeepers International (PAII), is one host's delight in discovering the Black & Decker three-in-one cordless detail sander, saw, and drill. Soon enough, you will feel the same joy.

Do you like to cook, and are you good at it? What Carol Emerick, owner of the Cottage in San Diego, California, likes most about offering bed and breakfast is "being able to have a legitimate excuse for trying new recipes." A major part of a host's responsibility is preparing and serving breakfast. Is this *your* idea of a good time? No, you don't really have to be a Betty Crocker in order to become a host. There are plenty of easy-to-make dishes that will delight your guests. But if you do love spending time in the kitchen trying new recipes and whipping up old favorites to share with your guests, it will make hosting all the more enjoyable for you.

"Flair for creating an atmosphere" is a valuable skill for a host, says Elsa Dimick, owner of Longswamp B&B in Mertztown, Pennsylvania. It's important to try to make the environment as special as possible for your guests. This aspect of bed and breakfast appeals to

Roy Mixon, who bought and renovated Rockland Farm Retreat in Bumpass, Virginia. He says he especially enjoys "showing off my decorating skills—we have a Fantasy Island plantation for those who wish to enjoy the fantasy." If you're like Roy and have a knack for developing a "look" for your bed and breakfast home, you can use that skill to attract guests looking for something special.

Robert Somaini, owner of Woodruff House in Barre, Vermont, adds this quality to his list of those needed by a host: "knowledgeable in local history." Remember that many of your guests could be visiting your area for the first time, wanting to explore what it has to offer and learn all about it. If you've watched your neighborhood grow and change over the years, now's the chance to put that knowledge to good use.

Your guests will also want and need information about the here and now. Host Carol Emerick says that a major advantage for her guests is her own "in-depth knowledge of what there is to do in San Diego—not just knowledge about the amusements and expensive attractions." These, visitors can find in any guidebook. Your value to them is what you can tell them about the things that do not appear in any guidebook.

Small-business skills are extremely important for a bed and breakfast host. If you don't have them, either get them somehow (basic books on small-business management, a course or two) or hire someone who has them. Nancy Jenkins, former owner of a reservation service agency in California, says that the biggest mistake that new hosts make is "not being well-enough prepared for the bookkeeping and accounting aspects of the business." You have got to be well organized so that you can keep straight who is coming and going, and when; how much money is coming in and going out; and what it all means when it's tax time. This involves keeping receipts, names, addresses, dates, and schedules. (See chapter 5, "The Business of B&B.") It's all paperwork that might seem as if it has little to do with hospitality, but it's this same paperwork that will tell you whether you have a viable bed and breakfast business.

Not enough can be said about the need to be computer literate in order to establish and maintain a successful business. Get a computer, learn how to use it, and get connected to the Internet. Whatever it takes, do it.

A Home-based Business

What Ellen Madison, owner of Woody Hill Guest House B&B in Westerly, Rhode Island, likes about being a host is "the fact that the world comes to me; I do not have to go to it."

Did you note something like this on your list of reasons describing why you want to become a host? Many people who get involved in bed and breakfast do so because they prefer running their own home-based business to heading out each day to a nine-to-five job.

Parents of children who are not yet old enough to go to school find bed and breakfast a great way of bringing in some income while they stay at home with the family. Some retirees want a part-time venture that does not require going back to the kind of schedule they have happily left behind. Other people have physical disabilities that hinder a lot of travel outside the home. Still others have another home-based business (consulting, writing, farming) that easily makes room for a second business also run out of the home (see "The Working Host" in chapter 2). Then there are those of us who simply enjoy the freedom that comes with being our own bosses.

With bed and breakfast, you can arrange your own schedule—accepting guests or not, as you wish. "We're all booked on New Year's Eve," one Boston host told a prospective guest over the phone. Actually, she wasn't. What she really wanted to do was attend the city's annual First Night celebration with her family without having the responsibility of meeting the needs of any guests. Because she runs her own business, she could make that decision. Of course, it meant losing a booking for that night. But if business is generally good for a host, the trade-off for some personal enjoyment can be worth it. The point is that with a home-based business like bed and breakfast, you make your own decisions.

Perhaps you prefer to work like crazy during the "season" (whatever it may be for you in your location—skiing, football, fun in the sun) and then take the other months off. One couple accepts guests only during the week so that their weekends are free. Or maybe you just want a few guests every once in a while, as it suits your own schedule. One busy New England writer does not publicize her bed and breakfast in any way; rather, she has a special agreement with her local reservation service agency that whenever she has the time to take guests, she calls the RSA to let them know. The RSA then refers guests to her for as long as she wishes. This way, the host does not have to spend her time and energy turning away the many guests that she could never accommodate throughout the year. These choices are all available to a bed and breakfast host.

The idea of running your own show from your own home attracts many of us, but it works best for someone who can honestly say that he or she is a "homebody." Do you love your home dearly? Do you love caring for it? And most important, do you love spending most of your time there and nowhere else? This is exactly where you'll be if you become a bed and breakfast host. If you don't absolutely love it, you'll soon get that cooped-up feeling. Give this fact due consideration. If you're the kind of person who usually relies upon your work to get you out into the world regularly, bed and breakfast should be, at most, an adjunct to another job that does just that.

If you're thinking about starting a home-based business for the first time, realize now that there is a major disadvantage to it—you simply can't punch the time clock at 5:00 P.M. and be done with it. With bed and breakfast, you live right in the middle of your business, and you have to be careful or you'll end up sacrificing too much of your private life in your effort to do well. This might not seem like an issue when you first begin, but as time goes on and you find yourself surrounded by more and more guests, you'll want to set aside a time and a space just for yourself or you'll feel as though you're working twenty-four hours a day.

It's a good idea to decide on a place that is completely off-limits except to you and your family, preferably a room other than your bedroom (the den, library, or family room). Whenever you show guests the house, show them only the rooms that they are invited to use, or show them your private space as well with the comment, "This is where I go when I need a little peace and quiet," so that they know this is *your* space. (Be warned that some guests won't take the hint and will come knocking at your door for the slightest reason. Most guests, though, are very considerate and will respect your privacy.) Then set aside some time each day that you can have just for yourself to relax, watch the soaps, read a book, or have coffee with a friend. It might take some time to establish a pattern of personal time for yourself, but you'll be glad you did. It will help you to better enjoy the advantages of having a home-based bed and breakfast business.

A Community Service

Some people get involved in bed and breakfast because they want to share their home with others as a service to the community and its economy. Perhaps you live in an area in which the only lodgings available for visitors are hotels and motels, or there is no public lodging at all.

A host in Annapolis, Maryland, says that she became a host for the purpose of "providing an alternative to high-cost hotels to guests who enjoy and appreciate B&Bs." Mary Decker, owner of Corner House in Rhinebeck, New York, was motivated to become a host by her "awareness of the shortage of rooms available to village visitors." And Crescent Drag-onwagon, owner of Dairy Hollow House in Eureka Springs, Arkansas, had been "wanting to invest locally, in something socially responsible." She decided on bed and breakfast "to create lodging in keeping with the historic nature of our town. Before us, there were only motels and one large hotel."

A number of hosts reach their decision to open a bed and breakfast after enjoying this kind of hospitality themselves. "I stayed in a B&B and enjoyed it and wanted to do that with my house," says the owner of a bed and breakfast in Atlanta, Georgia. As a guest, you can see firsthand how B&B can be an integral part of the business community, offering lodg-ing where there was none, attracting visitors for a boost in the area's tourism trade, and pro-viding a good old-fashioned dose of hospitality to those travelers who are looking for more of a connection with the area they are visiting and the people in it.

Because B&B is good for the local economy, some chambers of commerce are getting into the act to encourage residents to open their homes. They invite speakers, run work-shops, and provide advice. Steve and Nancy Richards, a Rhode Island couple, got involved when their local chamber of commerce started a bed and breakfast program. And in the hill towns of Massachusetts, chambers are actively reaching out to homeowners to consider bed and breakfast.

Margie Haas is the owner of Marjon Bed & Breakfast Inn in Leaburg, Oregon. A private home built in 1971 on the edge of the McKenzie River, Marjon was planned and constructed with the thought of sharing the beauty of nature for all who came to visit. Over the years, the home and its two acres of landscaped grounds became well known to visitors. In the spring, especially, people came to enjoy the park-like atmosphere as the 2,000 azaleas and 700 rho-dodendrons blossomed. Many visitors suggested to Margie how much more enjoyable the place would be if there were overnight accommodations. Because of so many requests, Mar-jon was opened as a bed and breakfast inn "where hospitality is a way of life," says Margie.

Perhaps your home is such a showplace in your community that opening it as a bed and breakfast establishment, as Margie Haas did, would make a valuable contribution to your area. This is especially true if you live in a historic district or if your home qualifies for the National Register of Historic Places. One Philadelphia woman who has a large home in a historic area eventually succumbed to what she calls "gentle pressure" applied by the local reservation service agency to open her home for bed and breakfast.

You must be absolutely sure that you want to share your home with others. For this, you must have an innate trust of your fellow human beings; otherwise, you'll be constantly worrying that your silverware is going to disappear. "If you are concerned only about having your priceless antiques stolen, do not be a host," says Irmgard Castleberry, for many years the owner of a reservation service agency in Seattle, Washington. Another RSA reports that it rejected a host because "the hostess was too nervous about her 'treasures.'" The manager of a Boston RSA tells the story of one prospective host who had a magnificent home but couldn't bring herself to share it. "She wanted to serve breakfast to guests in their bedroom because she didn't want 'just anyone' in her dining room." Guests would have immediately felt her distrust, so the RSA turned her down.

Of course, you have every right to be concerned about your home and everything in it. Just don't overdo it. You must have an "acceptance that possessions are susceptible to mishap," says Mildred Snee of the House of Snee in Narragansett, Rhode Island. Things happen. But if you're going to worry about it, you'll make your guests uncomfortable. They can't help but notice if your main interest is your home and not your guests.

One couple from Pennsylvania stayed at a bed and breakfast home in the Southwest. They had been originally attracted to this particular B&B because it was especially lovely and had advertised a swimming pool. But the two felt most uncomfortable there because of the host's demeanor. "We felt she really wasn't interested in the guests, only in showing off her home." To them, the bed and breakfast felt like a "showplace" that wasn't meant to be used. The home was all it was advertised to be, but the hospitality just wasn't there.

Think about this when you're making your own decision. You must be careful that you don't bend to community pressure to open your home for bed and breakfast when you know it's just not for you. "Be certain that you feel right about opening your home to guests and then act accordingly," says the manager of a California reservation service. Good advice.

Extra Income

Perhaps you listed "extra income" as one of your reasons for wanting to offer bed and breakfast. This is a perfectly legitimate reason, but the key word here is *extra*. No one can state with complete certainty that it's impossible to make a living solely by using the extra space in your home for bed and breakfast, but it is unlikely. This is true even of those B&B

homes that are well located, have more than one guest room, accommodate a steady stream of guests, and charge a room rate higher than the norm. Why? Because a bed and breakfast business is limited in two very important ways: the number of rooms in the home and the number of nights per year they are in use.

First, let's consider how the number of rooms available for guests' use affects income. How many extra rooms do you have? Let's assume for the moment that you have one room. And let's say that you charge $100 per night for this room. Your immediate inclination might be to multiply $100 by the number of nights there are in a year to come up with a figure showing what kind of income you could expect. So $100 multiplied by 365 is $36,500. And with *two* rooms available for guests in your home, that means $73,000! Not bad. *Three* rooms, that's $109,500. And *four* is $146,000! Wow! Sounds great!

Unfortunately, it just doesn't happen this way. Ask any commercial innkeeper or hotel or motel manager. They will tell you that their establishments are completely booked at some times of the year and practically empty at others. This will also be the case with your bed and breakfast. All your rooms will not be filled each night, every night, for 365 nights of the year, no matter what you do.

So what, then, constitutes "success" for a bed and breakfast? Many consider one hundred nights out of a year filled to capacity a good year. So if you have one room to use for bed and breakfast guests, and you are "filled to capacity" for one hundred nights out of the year, at $100 per night, your income is $10,000. For you, this is success. Can you live on $10,000? Of course not. But for an *extra* income, it might sound just fine. And remember, this "extra" is not clear profit. You'll have expenses to pay out of it.

If you have more than one guest room, projecting your income gets a little more complicated and a little more theoretical. The guideline of "one hundred nights at capacity" does not mean, literally, that every bed available in your bed and breakfast will be in use on the same one hundred nights. What will happen is that guests will come and go throughout the year, more at some times, fewer at others. Perhaps one room will be in demand more than another. Despite these things, you can use the guideline to make an educated guess about the income you could expect.

Understanding this, you can now use the Income Projection Worksheet provided on the following page to give yourself a rough but realistic idea of what "success" would mean for you. One recent industry survey shows many bed and breakfasts enjoy an occupancy rate nearing 40 percent. This figure is used in the worksheet for the third year and beyond.

Should You Become a Bed and Breakfast Host?

Income Projection Worksheet

Here is a formula that will help you figure out a rough projection of income for your "successful" bed and breakfast, based on a 40 percent occupancy rate. The sample here uses typical room rates. (See "Pricing Your Bed and Breakfast" in chapter 3 for a detailed explanation of how to price your rooms.)

Sample

2 double rooms	x	$115 per night	=	$230 x 146 nights	=	$33,580
1 single room	x	$ 90 per night	=	$ 90 x 146 nights	=	$13,140
1 suite	x	$150 per night	=	$150 x 146 nights	=	$21,900

Projected Gross Income for 1 year: $68,620

Your Bed and Breakfast

____ double room(s)	x $115 per night	=	$____ x 146 nights	=	$_____
____ single room(s)	x $ 90 per night	=	$____ x 146 nights	=	$_____
____ suite(s)	x $150 per night	=	$____ x 146 nights	=	$_____
apartment(s)				
guesthouse(s)				
cottage(s)				

Projected gross income for 1 year: $_____

Do not expect too much in your first year of operation; success is something you build toward. "I'm still waiting for my first guest," writes one host who advertised her bed and breakfast in one guidebook last year. Says another, "I had eight guests last year, but I hope for more next year." When you're just starting out as a host, you should be very modest about your financial expectations until you see, from experience, what's possible for a B&B in your area.

Keep in mind that the total amount you calculate on the worksheet represents the possible *gross* income of your bed and breakfast—that is, before taxes and before expenses on breakfast, laundry, new sheets, a paint job in the guest rooms, new towels, fresh flowers, new mattresses, business cards, a new reading lamp, the commission to your reservation service agency, the cost of membership in the chamber of commerce . . . to name just some of the usual expenses that must be incurred to run a bed and breakfast.

One of the biggest misconceptions that some people have is that bed and breakfast is a surefire, get-rich-quick scheme. "Some expect to make a million dollars the first month," says Rita Duncan, the manager of Blue Ridge Bed & Breakfast in Berryville, Virginia. They're wrong.

"Don't expect this to become a large income producer," cautions the owner of a reservation service agency in Portland, Oregon. Anyone attracted to hosting mainly for the money will be sorely disappointed. Guests will see this immediately and feel quite uncomfortable about it. A number of reservation service agencies report that they initially rejected or later dropped hosts because they were overly concerned with money.

"I do not accept hosts who are doing this just for the bucks. It has to be something that the host enjoys!" says the founder of a Dallas RSA called Bed & Breakfast Texas Style. How can you tell? It shows. A Florida host met guests in the driveway and asked for payment in full, right there and then! When her RSA found out about it, this host was listed no longer.

But the question remains: Can someone be involved in bed and breakfast for the *right* reasons and still make a living by doing it? What if you had four or five rooms to offer guests? Would that be enough? "You need at least six to make a living," says Marcia Whittington of Host Homes of Boston. And with a property of that size, we're usually talking about an enterprise the level of an inn, rather than just a bed and breakfast home with rooms to spare. An inn is definitely a full-time commercial venture—with expenses, taxes, and regulations governing its operation in a commercial category. Bed and breakfast homes are not in the same category.

"If a host wants to make a living at B&B, he or she must open an inn," says Susan Morris, for many years the executive director of a trade organization for reservation services. For those who want to operate a bed and breakfast home, "they must realize that by and large it is not a way of earning a living but a way of supplementing income and having a marvelous time meeting all sorts of interesting people and making many friends."

Frequently Asked Questions

Q: Will I make a lot of money?

A: Operating a B&B will probably not make you rich, just happy. Assuming that your B&B is well located and attracts visitors throughout the year, the "I can make a living" point is usually set at five or six guest rooms. Most hosts consider their B&B income as "extra."

Q: What's the worst thing about running a B&B?

A: Depends upon whom you ask. Some say getting up way too early in the morning, others say Murphy's Law, still others point to uncooperative city or town agencies, and yet others say they can't think of anything bad at all about running a B&B!

Q: What is the biggest problem B&B hosts encounter?

A: The answers from hosts over the years have remained the same: guests who don't show up, guests who cancel at the last minute, and guests who won't tell you when they're coming or arrive on your doorstep hours after the designated time. Nobody has managed to solve these problems completely.

Q: Should I list with a reservation service agency?

A: Yes, especially when you are first starting your business. An RSA takes a reasonable commission in return for lots and lots of work that benefits your B&B.

Q: Can I run a B&B and have another full-time job at the same time?

A: Yes, lots of people do it. Keep in mind, though, that you have to be organized enough to juggle your dual responsibilities and still keep a smile on your face.

Q: Can a single person operate a successful B&B?

A: Many single people operate B&Bs. Those who enjoy the most success have a good support system of friends, relatives, neighbors, and reliable contractors.

Q: Will operating a B&B disrupt my family life?

A: All hosts need to find a balance between work and home life. Consult with your spouse and children to identify ways to carve out quality family time.

Q: Do I need to have e-mail and a Web site?

A: In this day and age, yes. An increasing number of guests research bed and breakfasts on the Internet and then either make a reservation request by e-mail or book reservations online.

Chapter Two

What Does It Take to Run a Successful Bed and Breakfast?

Location

"Location! Location! Location!" No one can phrase it any better than this host did, or any more emphatically. Your success with bed and breakfast depends primarily upon where your home is located. People must have a reason to visit the area where you live or you simply won't get any guests, no matter how nice you are or how clean and comfortable your home may be. You must carefully assess the location of your home before making a decision to offer bed and breakfast.

If you live right in a major city, you're in a prime spot. "Where the people are is where the people want to be," says the founder of the reservation service agency called Greater Boston Hospitality. Cities draw visitors throughout the year for myriad reasons. Homes in pleasant, low-crime neighborhoods with easy access to different parts of the city (by walking or public transportation) are most certainly in demand.

First of all, cities attract tourists who come to explore, visit the museums, see the sights, do some shopping. Then there are those who come to see a special exhibit or attend a particular performance—Star Wars at the Museum of Science, Andrea Bocelli at the Met, Reba McIntyre at the Grand Ole Opry. Business travelers come for meetings, to make sales, to go to job interviews, to relocate the family. And some people come to visit friends or relatives who are undergoing medical treatment in a local hospital, or to have tests or outpatient treatment themselves.

Any city or town will have visitors coming in for weddings, graduations, funerals, and holiday celebrations of one sort or another. These are all potential guests for bed and breakfast hosts located in more densely populated areas.

Rural areas also have their attractions. One successful independent bed and breakfast is Valley View Farm, owned by Edna and Ernest Shipe in Mathias, West Virginia. It is located near Lost River State Park, so visitors here can hike, play tennis, go horseback riding, or swim—that is, if they get bored with the beautiful farmland and all the animals (even chinchillas) right out the front door.

Another possible source of people to stay in your bed and breakfast is any national or international corporation near your home. A large company with branch offices is likely to have personnel shuttling among its different locations. One New England host offers bed and breakfast solely for business executives associated with a computer company a short distance from her home. She has as many guests as she wants from just this one company.

Consider, too, that each year thousands of people make special trips to see where the Pilgrims landed, where Custer made his last stand, where Hawthorne once lived, and where Elvis Presley is buried. Proximity to any kind of tourist attraction is a plus for a bed and breakfast.

A notable success story comes from Green Meadow Ranch in Shipshewana, Indiana, which is the location of one of the largest flea markets in the country (held twice a week in the summer) and an antiques auction (held once a week, year-round). Living in a tourist area has helped bring a high number of visitors to the home of Paul and Ruth Miller, who hand out their B&B card at the flea market.

A bed and breakfast home in New Jersey called Cozy Acres B&B is just 10 miles from Atlantic City's beaches and casinos. "We are in a safe, rural setting," says Cecelia Swezeny. "The best of two worlds—the excitement of the casinos and the relaxation of the country."

A home situated near a college, university, or private school can benefit from the considerable amount of traffic that always surrounds an institution of higher learning. Students come to scout the school or attend conferences, parents come to visit, alumni come back for reunions, visiting professors come to lecture—and they all need places to stay.

Take note of any short-term programs offered by schools of any type near you. People often come from all over the country to attend workshops or short sessions of intense study. One example is the summer program that takes place at Jacob's Pillow in western Massachusetts. Aspiring professional dancers are in residence here for several weeks; friends and family coming to visit or attend their performances must seek overnight accommodations.

Do not overlook the popularity of sports, either college or professional, in your area. A contending team has a large following, and its fans will be looking for accommodations when they come to attend the games. The biggest season for Rest & Repast Bed & Breakfast service in central Pennsylvania? "Football!" says founder Linda Feltman. This reservation service agency's homes near Penn State fill up for the home games, especially so in years when the team is doing well. "Everybody and their uncle wants to come to a game," says Feltman. The result is that more bed and breakfast homes are needed to accommodate all those football enthusiasts. Remember, though, that sports are seasonal. Your home could be in great demand for several months—but only for those months, unless there is some other attraction for visitors. If you are planning to operate a full-time bed and breakfast with no other income (which is difficult, as explained in chapter 1), you'll need to have guests for more than one season in order to make a living. A nearby beach could draw guests to your home year-round if you live in Florida, but if you're in Maine, you don't need anyone to tell you that the beach season is far too short. The same thing goes for hosts in ski country. During a snowy winter, visitors will literally tramp a path to your door, but you'll be very lonely in winters that get little snowfall, and you can count on all your guests being long gone by spring, when the slopes have turned to mud.

If you are lucky, you already live in a home in an area that draws visitors for more than one season. If not, as long as bed and breakfast hosting is a part-time project for you, you might find that you actually prefer the seasonal nature of your B&B business. It will be easier to plan ahead from year to year.

If you would like to purchase a home with the intention of starting a bed and breakfast (see "Real Estate" in chapter 4), one crucial point to investigate is what brings people to the area and for how many months out of the year. Look for a place that draws visitors for three seasons. Many New England hosts, for example, can take advantage of the fact that people come in summer to go to the beach, in fall to see the foliage, and in winter to ski.

Make the effort to find out about any major events that will take place in your area in the near or distant future, as these could turn the site where your home is located into a tourist attraction virtually overnight. Events like the World's Fair and the Olympics have certainly done this in the past. Find out, too, about natural events for which your location might be a key vantage point. For the coming of Halley's Comet and the most recent total eclipse of the sun, remember how so many people were drawn out of fascination to certain parts of the world to better view these uncommon events. Being in the right place at the right time means knowing what's coming and planning for it.

Some events are thankfully more common and more frequent, so the influx of visitors is not as short-lived and unpredictable. Such annual events as the Boston Marathon and the hot-air-balloon festival in Albuquerque, New Mexico, attract countless visitors from out of town each year. Is your home located near the site of activities like these, or near a fairground, a racetrack, or a civic center where other kinds of activities are scheduled on a seasonal or year-round basis? Just one of these could provide the bread and butter for your bed and breakfast.

A good location also makes your home more attractive to reservation service agencies that are looking to increase the number of host homes registered with them. RSAs will be much more interested in you if the number of guests they will be able to place with you will be high.

There are some areas where RSAs can't seem to get enough hosts. Downtown Boston is a good example. What a joy it is for a tourist to leave a host home in the Back Bay or in Beacon Hill and walk along the Freedom Trail without having to hassle with public transportation or taxis. But what a task it is for RSAs covering the Boston area to find enough "downtown" hosts to meet the demand at certain times of the year.

The best advice to help you determine whether your home is in a good location is this: Identify the reasons people come to your area and in which months of the year. Use the checklist included here as a guide. The more reasons you can find, and the more months of the year they cover, the more potential your home has to become a successful bed and breakfast.

Location Checklist

Following is a list of attractions that draw visitors to any particular area. A large number of visitors from out of town can mean a large number of guests for a bed and breakfast home near any of these sites. How well located is your home for a bed and breakfast business? Use this checklist to find out.

Neighborhood
- ☐ Downtown area
- ☐ Retail district
- ☐ Historical district
- ☐ Business district

Businesses
- ☐ Major corporation
- ☐ Research facility
- ☐ Government offices

Academic Schools
- ☐ College or university
- ☐ Junior college
- ☐ Technical school
- ☐ Boarding school
- ☐ Summer programs
- ☐ Religious school

Schools for the Arts
- ☐ Dance
- ☐ Art
- ☐ Music
- ☐ Photography
- ☐ Theater

Military Bases
- ☐ Army
- ☐ Navy
- ☐ Air Force
- ☐ Marines
- ☐ Coast Guard

Group Residences
- ☐ Retirement home
- ☐ Nursing home
- ☐ Hospital
- ☐ Convent/monastery
- ☐ Retreat
- ☐ Summer camp

Transportation
- ☐ Airport
- ☐ Train station
- ☐ Bus station
- ☐ Major highway
- ☐ Local public transportation

Houses of Worship
- ☐ Church
- ☐ Temple
- ☐ Mosque

Cultural Sites
- ☐ Theater
- ☐ Museum
- ☐ Observatory
- ☐ Music hall
- ☐ Art gallery

Beaches
- ☐ Ocean
- ☐ Pond
- ☐ River
- ☐ Lake

Recreational Sites
- ☐ Sports arena/stadium
- ☐ Concert arena/stadium
- ☐ Convention center
- ☐ Civic center
- ☐ Racetrack
- ☐ Casino
- ☐ Fairground
- ☐ Amusement park
- ☐ Carnival

Natural Sites
- ☐ Mountains
- ☐ Desert
- ☐ Nature preserve
- ☐ Wildlife sanctuary
- ☐ Park
- ☐ Glacier
- ☐ Volcano
- ☐ Hot springs
- ☐ Caves/cavern

Special Attractions
- ☐ Historical site
- ☐ Architectural site
- ☐ Tourist attraction
- ☐ Well-known restaurant
- ☐ Archaeological site

Shopping
- ☐ Auction
- ☐ Flea market
- ☐ Wholesale outlet
- ☐ Specialty store
- ☐ Antiques store
- ☐ Regional arts/crafts/food

Animals/Wildlife
- ☐ Zoo
- ☐ Exotic animal farm
- ☐ Wildlife preserve
- ☐ Major animal hospital
- ☐ Aquarium/oceanarium

Recreational Activities
- ☐ Swimming
- ☐ Hiking
- ☐ Climbing
- ☐ Nature walks
- ☐ Foliage walks
- ☐ Bicycling
- ☐ Boating/sailing
- ☐ Waterskiing
- ☐ Fishing
- ☐ Hunting
- ☐ Golfing
- ☐ Car/motorcycle racing
- ☐ Running
- ☐ Bird-watching
- ☐ Whale-watching
- ☐ Cross-country/downhill skiing
- ☐ Ice-skating
- ☐ Tobogganing
- ☐ Snowmobiling
- ☐ Gambling

Comfort

Remember how you managed to get used to that banging radiator back in your first apartment? (After a while, you didn't even notice.) And those cold, cold nights every fall before the landlord turned on the heat for the winter? (You dealt with the problem by wearing two sweaters.) And your roommate's white cat, which always wanted to cuddle whenever you were wearing black? (You started wearing white clothes for the first time in your life.)

We're all adaptable to an extent. If we are subjected to a minor irritation long enough, the noise and the drafts and the cat hair don't bother us at all. We learn to live with them, even forget about them. But it takes a while, right? New annoyances can still drive us up a wall. A dog barking. A baby crying. Cigar smoke. To a large extent, comfort depends on what you're used to. As a bed and breakfast host, you will find that one of your most difficult responsibilities is providing for the comfort of a vast diversity of people who all have their own ideas about what "comfort" is really all about.

Noise

To assess how comfortable your home might seem to other people, first identify how much "noise" there is on a normal basis. Tonight, after everyone else has gone to bed, listen to your house. What do you hear? The clock ticking? The faucet dripping? The dog scratching at the door? The cat batting around its catnip mouse? The furnace kicking on? These are normal nighttime sounds to you; they make your home feel cozy. But some bed and breakfast guests might not agree. Go into a guest room, close the door, and listen for how many sounds you can still hear. If you're on the first floor and you can still hear Grandpa snoring in his room up on the third, your guests will surely hear him, too.

There are commendably few criticisms from people about the bed and breakfast homes they have visited. Some that have been made, though, deal with the very issue of noise. A couple from Alabama loved their stay at a B&B in North Carolina—except for a shower that dripped all night long, disturbing them with its continual *thunk! thunk! thunk!* Asked what they would change if they could alter one thing about this B&B, they immediately said (you guessed it), "The dripping shower!" A guest at another B&B found it more than a little disconcerting to be startled awake each morning by the bloodcurdling screams of the resident cockatiel.

And I remember all too well my unpleasant nocturnal experience at a bed and breakfast home that had a grandfather clock. Lots of people can sleep right through the bonging and chiming that come at regular intervals with this type of clock. I'm not one of them. I most unhappily greeted the night, all night, every hour on the hour, and again on the half hour. Morning couldn't come soon enough. At the time I was convinced that my restless night was my own fault, a product of an unusual sensitivity to "normal" sounds, so I never mentioned that infernal clock to my hosts. I realize now that I should have. To this day I have visions of unhappy guests counting the minutes (in half-hour intervals) until morning, when they can get up, check out, and end the torture.

The point is that there are some unnecessary noises that you can do something about. Get the shower fixed, even if you've gotten used to the continual dripping. (The North Carolina host later did just this, according to the Alabama couple.) If you're so fond of that grandfather clock, by all means keep it, but move it well away from the guest room, or just don't wind it on the nights you have visitors. Any kind of noise that *can* be eliminated *should* be eliminated.

For sounds that might annoy but must remain, do your best. "When I am doing dishes late at night, I turn on fans to drown out the clatter," says Donna Tanney of Gates Hill Homestead in Brookfield, New York.

There will always be the normal household sounds of conversation, the furnace or air-conditioning system, the radio or television, the telephone ringing, doors opening and closing. So that these do not disturb guests after they retire for the night, any home intended for bed and breakfast should be large enough, and the walls and doors solid enough, to give everyone in it the freedom to sleep and wake at will and to go about their activities without bothering anyone. Think about your home. Is it roomy enough to handle the presence of a few more people with sufficient quiet and privacy, or will it feel cramped, crowded, and noisy every time you have guests? Are the rooms arranged in such a way that they are somewhat insulated from one another? Do your walls and doors do a good job of blocking out the sounds from other parts of the house?

One couple visiting a bed and breakfast home felt unduly chastised for making excessive noise. Here, another guest complained that she was bothered by the couple's conversation (which they insisted was held in low tones in their own room, with the door shut). This occurred at about 10:00 P.M., which the couple considered an early enough hour to be having a conversation instead of sleeping. The other guest's sleep was disturbed by this "noise," even though the two guest rooms were separated by two doors and a hallway. The couple was so upset at being shushed when they were sure they were being totally considerate that they checked out a day early, vowing never to return to "the B&B with paper-thin walls."

Now whether the walls were indeed paper-thin or whether the complaining guest was just overly sensitive to noise, we don't know for sure. But you know your own home. How soundproof is it? Do you need to take measures to prevent sounds from carrying? Buying and installing soundproofing materials, such as sound-absorbing tiles or panels, can be costly. You can take lesser measures that will help to an extent. Heavy drapes and rugs (with rug pads) help absorb the sounds within a room. And wallpaper adds an extra insulating layer that muffles sound better than bare walls covered only with paint.

Rooms that share a common wall are likely to share sounds as well. If you have a choice, do not set up your home so that you have two guest rooms side by side. (In fact, you might not want your own bedroom, or those of other household members, adjacent to a guest room.) If one room is above another, you can also expect some sounds to carry. Again, rugs with rug pads will help, but you might have to take stronger action. One host who was renovating a small apartment in her Boston town house to be used for bed and breakfast knew that noise would be a problem because the apartment was on the ground floor, and above it were three more floors of solid activity. Her first order of business? Calling in a contractor to complete a professional soundproofing job on the ceiling.

Unfortunately, what goes on inside your home is not your only worry. There's a whole noisy world out there that you can't do a thing about. (Ever try to tell a rooster to ignore the rising sun?) Consider whether there is some sort of recurring activity outside your home that could disturb your guests. Does loud music come from the club down the street until late at night? Do irate commuters lean on their car horns at the intersection right outside each morning? Does the dog next door get vocal at an early hour? Do church bells call the faithful to sunrise services faithfully every morning? Does the guy next door play the trumpet? Again, heavy drapes will certainly help, but they can't perform miracles. If the problem is bad, you might finally want to install those thermal windows you've been thinking about. Double-paned windows not only do a terrific job of insulating your home from the weather, they also help cut down on that outside noise that could affect your guests' comfort.

Children

The presence of children in a host home raises the question of noise and general disruption as well. There are travelers who have the idea (often a misconception) that their quiet and privacy will be marred by the antics of any youngsters in residence. If you have children, you will most likely lose some business because of them, regardless of how well behaved and considerate your kids might be. Some people have made up their minds in advance, and that's that. But know that for any potential guests that you lose, there are other travelers who will be attracted to your B&B for the very same reason. Parents traveling with their own kids actively seek out bed and breakfast homes where the hosts will gladly accept them. (Who's more understanding than a host who already has a few of her own?) And some travelers who are not parents themselves simply adore children and would find it a privilege to share the company of yours.

So take heart: The fact that you have children need not crush your plans to start a bed and breakfast business. You do have to be concerned, however, about how your kids behave around company. What are they like now when your friends come to visit or when strangers come to the door? It could be that they will take quite naturally to having guests in the house and go on about their business without disturbing the normal amount of privacy and quiet that guests will expect. But you know if your kids are basically unruly. If you can predict that they'll be jumping up and down on the guests' beds and throwing hot cross buns at breakfast, you might want to wait until they're older before offering bed and breakfast at your home. And if you have an

Chinguague Compound is a quiet, secluded bed and breakfast located on the banks of the Rio Grande in San Juan Pueblo, New Mexico. Joan Blood, its co-owner, recalls a couple who came down from the city of Denver for several days and stayed in one of the small adobe cottages surrounded by cottonwoods. When Joan asked the couple the first morning how they had slept the previous night, the woman hesitated and then said, "Well, I had to turn on the fan before I could get to sleep." Since the temperature that night had been down in the fifties, Joan's husband, Phil, commented, "I didn't realize it was that warm." The woman then replied, "Oh, no, it wasn't that it was too warm . . . I couldn't get used to all this quiet!"

infant who gets you up several times a night (and keeps you up sometimes the whole night through), you can't expect to inflict the feeding and the teething and everything else that goes with infancy on your bed and breakfast guests. You should wait at least until that stage is over.

Pets

For the amount of controversy that they can cause, pets are right up there with children. Reservation service agencies consider the presence of both in a host home carefully before deciding to include it in their listings. "Pets and small children in a host home can be a negative," says the owner of an RSA in Florida. If a large number of guests are automatically going to rule out any host home that contains either, this means that the RSA won't be able to place as many guests there as in other B&B homes. Some hosts have been turned away by reservation service agencies because of this. If you are hoping to list your home with an RSA, ask the manager to be candid with you about whether the presence of your children or pets is an issue.

Why would any guest object to staying in a house guarded by old, faithful Rex? Allergies. Once you start hosting, you'll find out quickly that there are many people out there who are allergic to animals. To stay in your home would be misery for them, as hard as that might be to believe. So if you do have a dog or a cat that is allowed inside the house, note this fact on all literature that you print, on your Web site or other online postings, and in all information that you send for listing in directories. And make sure that any reservation service agency that refers guests to you knows all about your pets. It will absolutely make a difference to the comfort of some travelers looking for bed and breakfast.

Smoking

Smoking is another major issue in the bed and breakfast industry—whether you do or whether you don't, whether you allow it or whether you won't. No matter what you choose, your decision will affect your business. If you are a nonsmoker and prefer to host nonsmokers only, you have a lot of company. An informal survey shows that this is the case with most hosts. If you smoke or there are smokers living in your household, you've got to assess the effect that this has on your home. To give yourself a more objective view, try this: Go outdoors for at least five minutes (do *not* have a cigarette while you're out there), then come back in and let your nose tell you a few things. Put it to work on the upholstered chairs, the drapes, the bedding, and the rugs. Do they all smell like Sunday morning after the Saturday-night poker game? If so, you've got a problem, and it has nothing to do with the surgeon general's warning.

One manager of a reservation service agency recalls a couple who applied to become hosts. The manager found the home lovely—except for the strong odor of stale cigarette smoke that permeated everything. The two were very heavy smokers, a fact that would hinder their efforts to develop a bed and breakfast business. Fortunately, they decided soon after the manager's visit that they weren't quite ready to open a B&B (for other, personal reasons), so she was spared the necessity of turning them down as hosts. The following year they contacted her again when they felt they were "ready." The manager went back to their home to see if there had been any changes and found that they had both quit smoking. Their lovely home no longer had that disagreeable odor. They were, indeed, ready.

The owner of a reservation service agency in Georgia also had a problem with an applicant because, she says, "The cigars he smoked were too smelly!" She turned him down.

True, there are smokers who travel and who would like to enjoy the privilege of smoking while staying at bed and breakfast homes. You can always gear your B&B business to these people if yours is a smoking household. Recognize, though, that you cannot expect nonsmokers to stay there as well and be happy about it. Someone is bound to light up at the breakfast table, and before you know it, a nice breakfast could turn into an episode of *The People's Court.* Some hosts have chosen to have a "limited smoking" household, in which those guests who wish to smoke may do so only outside, in their rooms, or in another designated area. This way, the comfort of other guests, and perhaps of the hosts themselves, is not affected. If yours is a smoke-free household and you intend to keep it that way, advertise it as smoke-free to attract the type of guests you want.

Temperature and Ventilation

Other elements key to your guests' comfort are the temperature and ventilation of the bedrooms where your guests will sleep. How much or how little heat and ventilation there should be is a highly personal matter. One guest will need the window open a crack at night (no matter what the temperature outside may be) or he won't be able to sleep; another will need the window sealed tight in even the hottest weather or *he* can't sleep. Some abhor air-conditioning; others can't live without it. Ideally, the answer is to have the heating, cooling, and ventilation all adjustable within each room so that guests have some control over the environment. But often this is just not possible (especially with central heating or central air-conditioning).

You can address individual differences among your guests by having available a portable heater (make sure that it has automatic shutoff and other safety features), a window or ceiling fan, or an air-conditioning unit that can be used or not, as a guest wishes. If any of your guest rooms is a "problem room," though (sweltering in the summer or freezing in the winter when the rest of the house is just fine), more drastic action might be recommended for everyone's comfort. Here, insulation or double-paned windows could offer a permanent solution.

Ellie Welch Ramsey, founder of a Boston reservation service, tells the story of a host who was visited by a gentleman from Egypt. Accustomed to the warm, dry climate of his own country, he found the chilly, damp October weather hard to take. The host, a hardy New Englander, was, of course, quite comfortable. Not wanting to turn on the furnace at this early date, she gave her guest a stocking cap to wear around the house. The Egyptian placed it on his head and there it stayed, but he was still cold. So the host went out and bought a portable space heater and put it in his room. "Ellie, I might have spent every penny I got from this visit on the heater, but it made everybody happy," said the host.

Neighborhood

Once you're confident that your home can provide the kind of comfort that your various guests will need, there's one more consideration before you're through with your checklist. This is your neighborhood. Take a stroll around the area where you live. If you're located in a rural area, fine; your guests should enjoy the outdoors as much as the indoors.

But if your home is located in a city or town, ask yourself if all your visitors will feel comfortable when they walk out the front door. Is your neighborhood "safe," with a low incidence of crime? (Or are you always looking over your shoulder?) Is it pleasant, picturesque? (Or is it somewhat run-down?) Is it integrated? (Or is it so exclusively ethnic that anyone else would feel out of place?) Some very lovely people with very lovely homes have been turned down by reservation service agencies because they are located in neighborhoods where many guests simply would not feel comfortable for various reasons. What your neighborhood is like is definitely a factor when it comes to developing your bed and breakfast business.

Atmosphere

The overall atmosphere in a home has a lot to do with whether visitors will feel comfortable. Is the host friendly and warm? Does the home look as though someone cares about it? The feeling of being totally welcome when a guest walks through the front door can often override any minor problems with the heat, the ventilation, the pets, the kids, the neighborhood, the smoking, and the noise. When inspecting the homes of people who wanted to become hosts, the founders of a Rhode Island reservation service let this govern their decision: "The basic criterion we used was this one simple question: Would I choose to stay there?"

Ask yourself this same question. Come in through your own front door as if you're doing it for the first time and take a look around. Is this the kind of place you would like to stay in if you were traveling? If it is, you're in business.

Cleanliness

If someone were to ring your doorbell right now, would you have to shove a few newspapers into the hall closet and kick a pair of shoes under the couch before answering the door? And would this do the trick, or (be honest) would it really take a bulldozer and a half-dozen blowtorches to clean out your home before it is ready for company?

If you want to be a host, you've got to take a long, hard look at how you keep your house. Some of us might be perfectly comfortable surrounded by clutter in our homes (the lived-in look) and feel moved to wash the kitchen floor only once a year (it will only get dirty again anyway), but we cannot expect guests in our home to feel the same way. You must meet *their* standards, or you will undoubtedly be faced with refunding money to dissatisfied guests and being dropped by any reservation service agency that sends you referrals.

At this moment you might be saying to yourself, "Of course my house is clean!" But how clean is it, really? (A good test is to ask yourself if your mother or in-laws would think so.) I once knew a woman who washed her kitchen and bathroom walls every week, without fail. I thought she was obsessive; she thought this was just normal housekeeping. Personal standards do vary. Because the highest level of cleanliness is a requirement for a host home, following is a step-by-step discussion of the standards you will have to meet to make your home "guest ready."

First of all, go outside and pretend that you are seeing your home for the first time. Do you like what you see? Or do your windows need to be washed? Is the paint chipped or peeling? Are there fingerprints or smudge marks around the doorknob? Are there papers or cans strewn around the yard or spilling over the trash barrels? Does the grass need to be cut or the hedges pruned? Does your teenager keep an old Ford in the driveway "for parts"? One reservation service agency in Pennsylvania reports that a host home was rejected not because the inside was unclean, but because the exterior was in such shabby condition that guests did not want to go inside. You want your guests' first impression to be a good one, so do whatever is necessary to make the outside of your home inviting.

The Bathroom

Next, take a look at the bathroom that your guests will be using. Does the room need a fresh coat of paint or new wallpaper to brighten it? When was the last time you had the curtains cleaned? Does the shower curtain need to be replaced? (If the idea of running your hands over it doesn't appeal to you, it probably does.)

How much cleaning you do before and during a guest's visit depends on how much traffic the bathroom will see. If it is one that visitors will share with you or your family or with other guests, you have to be extra conscientious to make sure that the bathroom gets clean and stays that way during a visit.

Clean the room initially by washing the floor, scrubbing the sink, wiping the mirror and any counter space, removing dirty towels or laundry or reminders of previous guests, and cleaning and disinfecting the toilet bowl, the bathtub, and the shower. All this must be done after each guest's visit to prepare the room for the next guest who comes to stay at your home. If you or other members of the household also use this bathroom, find a way to keep personal items in a certain area, in a cabinet, or on separate shelves. Your family's personal items (such as shampoo, toothpaste, and razors) should be returned to their designated space after each use and not left in view.

Using at least one bath rug (two or more in a larger bathroom) will help keep the floor clean while guests are in residence. Have several sets, or more, of matching rugs so that you can change them often. It's a lot easier to throw a set of dirty rugs into the laundry hamper and replace them with clean ones than it is to repeatedly wash an exposed floor that is destined to get dirty every time someone trails water across it. The rugs will also help soak up any spillage from the shower, tub, or sink. It's not pleasant to discover that the cuffs of your trousers or hem of your bathrobe has gotten wet from being dragged through a standing puddle left after someone's shower. Make sure the rugs have a nonskid backing to avoid accidents.

While a guest is in residence, you should empty the wastebasket daily and perform touch-ups to keep the room fresh—straighten towels, sponge the sink, wipe the mirror. Keep a new sponge visible so that if a guest is so inclined to clean up after using the bathroom, he or she can take the initiative to make a few swipes at the sink or tub before leaving the room to others. If you have a long-term guest (a week or more), wash the floor and clean the sink, toilet, tub, and shower whenever necessary. And empty the clothes hamper before the dirty towels start pushing their way out.

The Kitchen

The kitchen, too, must be immaculate. There should be no dirty dishes in the sink or stacked on counters. The floor must be washed often, and anything "turning" (or turned) in the refrigerator must be removed. Most hosts invite guests to put their own food in the refrigerator and to get ice from the freezer compartment whenever they wish. A three-week-old head of lettuce could scare them right out the front door.

Equally scary are those unwelcome creatures that sometimes decide to take up habitation in our homes, no matter how clean we are. Most of us can usually make short work of a mouse, but the more common, and more tenacious, household nuisances are those bugs—cockroaches, ants, flies, mosquitoes, and fleas. If you have any kind of problem with insects, there is no way you can expect a guest to stay in your home and be happy about it. As with many homes in rural areas or in hot and humid climates, yours may be destined to get an occasional bug just passing through. (Rita Duncan, manager of Blue Ridge Bed and Breakfast in Virginia, says, "Show me a country home that doesn't get spiders!") Still, take precautions to ensure that some little traveler won't surprise a guest pattering to the bathroom with bare feet in the middle of the night. Find the source of the problem and fix it. Repair the broken window screen, fill the crack in the cellar door, use flea powder on the dog, hire an exterminator if you must.

The Living and Dining Rooms

Consider your living room and dining room next, along with any other common area (perhaps a library or television room) that you will be sharing with your guests. The biggest problem these rooms ever seem to present is clutter—things that should have been put away or thrown away long ago. The first place to look is on the coffee table. If it holds an accumulation of newspapers that go back to the Clinton administration, it's time to clear out the clutter. From the coffee table, move to the mounds of jackets from last season and the forgotten toys. Once a room is neat, all it takes is a quick vacuuming and dusting to prepare for company.

It might not be easy to keep your home in this state of readiness. Cleaning is noted as the

A woman from Massachusetts noticed that among the information included in one directory of bed and breakfast homes is the length of notice that each host requires before a guest's arrival. This makes sense, of course, considering that a host needs time to prepare the home to receive guests. But the woman was intrigued by the note for the bed and breakfast home where she would be staying. "The host listed '15 minutes,'" she says—obviously not much notice at all. What can you do in fifteen minutes? When the guest arrived, the host explained the reason behind the extremely short notice: "Then I am excused for not putting everything in apple-pie order!"

least favorite aspect of bed and breakfast by hosts across the country. They basically agree with Carolyn Morrow of Leftwich House in Graham, North Carolina, when she says the most difficult aspect of being a host is "keeping a clean house all the time."

The Guest Room

The guest room (or rooms) should be your main concern. Guests' quarters must be spotless—vacuumed, dusted, and free of anything that is not there specifically for a guest's comfort. The owner of a Pennsylvania reservation service agency rejected a host because the guest room contained cartons of old shoes and soft drinks. "These had no place in a guest room," she says. But when she pointed this out to the homeowner, he said that he thought there was nothing wrong with storing these items there. He kept saying, "Well, that is cosmetic."

This "cosmetic" problem caused the RSA to refuse to list his home. Imagine how you would feel if you checked into the Ritz and someone's old shoes were in the corner of your room. A guest room in your home should be treated as if it were a room in the Ritz; remove anything that is not for guests' use exclusively. Of course, this means the closet, too. It is undeniably tempting to place some boxes of memorabilia on the shelves (what can a few hurt?) or hang up that extra coat (who will notice?), but don't do it. You do not want your guests to feel as if they are staying in a storage room.

If you would like to list your home with a reservation service agency, you can expect the RSA to inspect your home before making a decision. "If someone won't clean for me, I know they won't clean for a guest," says the founder of Greater Boston Hospitality. RSAs go to each prospective host home with a checklist for the basics, even to those places that are out in the boondocks. If you meet the standards for cleanliness, along with other requirements, an RSA will most likely list you as one of its host homes. If your home falls below the standards, an RSA will find out soon enough through complaints. And that will be the end of referrals to your home.

The ultimate question here is whether meeting the high standards of cleanliness required is a big deal for you. Ask yourself if cleaning your home is going to be a major undertaking every time you expect a guest. It shouldn't be. Hosting will not be fun if every phone call for a reservation throws you into a panic to prepare your home.

Ask yourself, too, whether the other members of your household will do their part in keeping the house clean, or will this become a continual source of friction among you? Their willing cooperation is essential. You don't want to greet guests in a spick-and-span house full of grouchy faces.

Cleanliness Checklist

Bathroom

☐ Floor scrubbed
☐ Clean bath mat
☐ Clean, nonskid rug
☐ Walls/ceiling clean and bright
☐ Clean shower curtain
☐ Tub/shower scrubbed
☐ Toilet cleaned/disinfected
☐ Sink scrubbed
☐ Mirrors wiped
☐ Clean towels
☐ Windows washed
☐ Light fixtures clean
☐ Cabinets wiped, polished
☐ Clean sponge visible
☐ Family items removed
☐ Medicine cabinet free of personal items
☐ Wastebasket emptied
☐ Paint free of chips
☐ No loose edges on wallpaper
☐ Grout between tiles free of mildew

Common Areas

(Living Room, TV Room, Library, Hallways)

☐ Paint/wallpaper in good repair
☐ Walls/ceiling clean and bright
☐ Rugs vacuumed
☐ Clutter removed
☐ Furniture dusted, polished
☐ Floors clean, polished
☐ Windows washed
☐ Curtains clean
☐ Light fixtures clean

Guest Room

☐ Floor clean, polished
☐ Windows washed
☐ Walls/ceiling clean and bright
☐ Rug vacuumed, free of stains
☐ Furniture polished, dusted
☐ Mirrors wiped
☐ Closet empty of family items
☐ Room free of storage items
☐ Clutter removed
☐ Light fixtures clean
☐ Curtains clean
☐ Bedding clean
☐ Paint/wallpaper in good repair
☐ Wastebasket emptied
☐ Under bed clean, no storage

Kitchen/Dining Area

☐ Floor washed, polished
☐ Cabinets wiped, polished, dusted
☐ Refrigerator/stove wiped
☐ Counters wiped/free of clutter
☐ No dirty dishes
☐ Trash/wastebasket emptied
☐ No old food in refrigerator, in pantry, on shelves
☐ Table cleared off, wiped
☐ Windows washed
☐ Walls/ceiling clean and bright
☐ Light fixtures clean
☐ Curtains clean
☐ Rug vacuumed
☐ Paint/wallpaper in good repair

House Exterior and Yard

☐ Windows washed
☐ No trash barrels visible
☐ No litter on grounds
☐ No chipped or peeling paint
☐ Grass cut, hedges pruned
☐ Leaves raked
☐ Snow shoveled from walk, porch
☐ Finger marks removed from door

Lifestyle

Before making that final decision to open your home to guests, remember that this is your *home* we're talking about here. This is the place where you run around in your bathrobe, argue with your spouse, and have the gang over to watch *Monday Night Football.* Do not make the mistake of assuming that having strangers around will not affect how you can act in your own home. It will. So think seriously about your living habits and routines before deciding to go ahead with bed and breakfast. Ask yourself whether the presence of guests will be disruptive to your household and, just as important, whether the way your household runs will be disruptive to your guests.

Consider your own daily routine. What time do you get up in the morning? Some of your guests will be early birds out of necessity (to get to appointments on time or to make travel connections) or just because they enjoy that hour of the day. Beth Kinsman, former manager of a New York reservation service agency, said that she got a lot of fishermen from Rhode Island who wanted to get up and going at 5:00 A.M. That's what they were used to, and they brought business to the hosts registered with her reservation service agency. If you are used to getting up later than Rhode Island fishermen do, will you be able to adjust to an earlier schedule when you have to? Or will you be cranky all day because you couldn't get enough sleep?

As a guest in a bed and breakfast home in West Hyannisport, Massachusetts, I had to be up before dawn to catch a bus that left for Boston at 6:00 A.M. This meant that my hosts had to get up when I did (around 5:00 A.M.) to prepare coffee and the oatmeal I had requested (the only food I could face at that hour). My hosts did indeed roll out of bed before the sun was up, make breakfast and keep me company while I ate (or tried to), and drive me to meet my bus. Could you do all this as graciously and cheerfully as my Cape Cod hosts did? This is what it takes. Gloria Belknap, owner of the Terrace Townehouse in downtown Boston, says she always gets up at 5:30 A.M. whenever guests are in the house, which is most of the time.

Some hosts never get used to it. When asked what he liked least about being a bed and breakfast host, Robert Somaini of Woodruff House in Vermont did not have to think twice: "Getting up early in the morning!"

One guest who enjoys staying in bed and breakfast homes says he could never take on the role of host: "Imagine having to be polite to people at that hour!" And a young man who attended a workshop for aspiring bed and breakfast hosts became distressed as he realized that he couldn't stay in bed late on weekend mornings when he had guests in the house. "Saturday is my day to sleep in," he lamented.

The same consideration goes for going to sleep at night. Do you retire early? Earlier than most people? You can always make arrangements with your guests for the "last one up" to shut off the lights in the television room and ask them to please be quiet. But will this be enough? Does the sound of the television, radio, or conversation at normal levels generally prevent you from sleeping? If it does, you could be in for problems as a host. You can't expect your guests to go to sleep just because you do.

Another point to ponder is what you look like in the morning. I don't mean that dazed look that afflicts many of us for a time after rising; we're talking about your overall appearance. Can you make yourself presentable for company in the morning? Can you be dressed for the day? Your hair combed? Your face washed? Your teeth brushed?

This might sound like so much common sense, but some hosts have actually offended their guests because they simply didn't look "ready" for them when they came down for breakfast. A couple from Pennsylvania were asked if there was anything they didn't like about a bed and breakfast home they visited during their trip to the Southwest. They responded: "Rollers in hostess's hair at breakfast!"

Think about it. As a guest, you come to a bed and breakfast because you want something special, an experience that transcends what you would find in a hotel or motel. Yes, you know that it is a private home and the hosts live there, doing what they do in their daily lives. Eating and sleeping are among their normal activities. Yet they are supposed to want you there. They are supposed to be ready for you. So you go down to what you expect will be a treat for breakfast in a lovely setting—and your host greets you, bleary-eyed, in her housecoat and rollers. Suddenly, you feel as if you're imposing. Perhaps she would rather be in bed than fixing your breakfast and attempting polite conversation with you over a cup of coffee. The breakfast might be absolutely magnificent, but somehow the magic is gone.

Now I must admit that one host did greet me at the breakfast table in her housecoat, and, to be completely honest, I couldn't have cared less. I was her only guest, it was very early, and I felt bad enough knowing I was the reason she was up to begin with. I would have felt worse if I knew she had gone to the trouble to get dressed just on my account. To this day, I hope she went back to bed after I ate breakfast and checked out.

The point is that there may be times when it seems perfectly natural, and comfortable, for you to be seen in your housecoat. (What host is going to get fully dressed just to go down the hall to the bathroom in the middle of the night?) But you must be tuned in to when it is inappropriate. For instance, when you are hosting single travelers of the opposite sex, you should dress appropriately. (The guest might get the wrong message.) And by no means give a houseful of guests something to talk about by showing up in bedroom attire at a breakfast table where there is standing room only. (We're all dressed. Why isn't she?)

What we wear throughout the day, of course, depends upon what we normally do during that time. If you work on a farm, it's not likely you'll be donning a three-piece suit to bale the hay. If you refinish furniture at home, nothing but the biggest, oldest shirts will do. Don't feel that you have to dress in a way other than what you need to just because there are guests in residence. But *do* take the time and trouble to clean up your act when all the dirty work is over. Casual clothes (T-shirts and jeans) are fine, as long as they're clean. Just be aware that there are limits to how casual a host can be. "If you are in the habit of running around in your skivvies, change your habits," says the former proprietor of a reservation service agency in Massachusetts.

If there are other members of the household besides you, recognize that *their* lifestyles will also be affected by your bed and breakfast business. A married couple who opened a B&B in Annapolis, Maryland, advises new hosts to "be certain that your spouse is 100 percent in support of the project and willing to do all duties if needed." Nothing breeds dissension faster than one person's bearing all the responsibilities and doing all the work.

It is interesting to discover, though, that several women who offer bed and breakfast found their husbands lukewarm about the idea at first. But after they started accepting guests, more or less on a trial basis, the husbands so enjoyed the company of the guests that they not only pitched right in and did their share of the work, it was hard to tear them away from conversation with guests at the breakfast table.

Special consideration should go to your children. Do they have a place to play and to do their homework that will not interfere with guests and where guests will not interfere with them? Or will you be constantly shushing them and chasing them out of the living room whenever guests are in the house? Remember, too, that they will have to be presentable for company, with clean clothes and scrubbed faces. Is this more than you (and they) can handle?

It's a good idea to have an official family meeting to discuss the idea of bed and breakfast before taking steps to open one. "It is a family business; make sure the whole family is for it," says the founder of one reservation service. If not everyone can agree to at least try it (and this includes your three-year-old child who is determined to keep her duckies in the guests' bathtub), then you should probably shelve the idea, at least for the time being. All the members of the household must be in complete cooperation. If they're not, it will show.

This was certainly the case when a couple from Boston stayed in a bed and breakfast home in Newfoundland that was run by a married pair. It was the husband who greeted the travelers upon arrival. "He welcomed us as though we were long-lost friends," they recall. "He showed us around the whole house and told us all about his home repairs, his B&B business, and his day job." The couple went to bed that night with a warm feeling of being totally welcome in the home. But when they got up the next morning, they found that the friendly host they had met the night before was gone for the day. In his place was his wife. Suddenly, the atmosphere was different. "She kind of begrudgingly served us breakfast," the couple remembers. The remainder of their visit was marred by how impersonal the woman continued to be toward her guests. She gave them the distinct impression that she did not want them there.

Try to evaluate objectively how everyone gets along in your household. There will always be disagreements, but are they few and far between and resolved with a minimum of broken dishware? One Louisiana reservation service reports that it found it necessary to drop a host (one who had previously enjoyed a great deal of business) because family problems developed there that were most distressing to the guests. If your home life is stormy, don't even *consider* bed and breakfast.

Many of us are fortunate to have a happy home life and a comfortable home where guests would add to the pleasure of our daily lives. If yours is such a lifestyle, bed and breakfast hosting could very well enrich your life beyond your expectations.

The Working Host

Bed and breakfast is a good project for those people whose careers or other responsibilities do not take them outside the home a great deal of the time. For this reason many retirees welcome the opportunity to meet interesting people right in the home they at last have the time to enjoy. By offering bed and breakfast, a retiree can also bring in a supplemental income without having to go back to the rigors of even a part-time job that involves keeping strict schedules and commuting to an office.

Parents of small children, too, want and need to spend time at home. For the spouse who minds the infant or toddler, bed and breakfast hosting can instill a gratifying element of social activity into his or her life, as well as add to the family income without the necessity of leaving the home to work.

But the question comes up about the working host. Can someone who has a career and works either full-time or part-time make a go of bed and breakfast? The answer is yes.

For hosts who already have home-based businesses, bed and breakfast is a natural; it integrates easily into their daily routines. Let's take, for example, hosts who work the land for their livelihood. The owners of Lakeside Farm in Webster, South Dakota, of Sycamore Haven Farm in Kinzers, Pennsylvania, and of Valley View Farm in Mathias, West Virginia, all successfully combine full-time work on their farms with bed and breakfast hosting. Having guests is "no trouble," says the ranch manager of Anchor Hill Lodge, a bed and breakfast in Rogersville, Missouri, "I have good ranch help and considerate guests." The only occasional problem, according to Edna Shipe of Valley View Farm, is "keeping yourself tidy the day you have dirty garden work." Some hosts have found that guests actually like to help with the chores. For many visitors from the city, farm life is a new and wonderful experience. It's a joy to pick apples and feed the animals, a refreshing change from their usual activities.

Hosts with other types of home-based businesses have also fared well with bed and breakfast. Carol Emerick of the Cottage in San Diego, California, does antique-furniture restoration on a part-time basis. Because she does this at home, she is available if her guests need her for any reason.

Another host is a full-time, self-employed writer, who meets the needs of her guests this way: "I set my hours to theirs, and I hire help. I accept being 'inconvenienced' in one business as the price for having another one thrive," says Crescent Dragonwagon of Dairy Hollow House in Eureka Springs, Arkansas.

There are other hosts who are fortunate to be in a line of work that they can relate to their bed and breakfast hosting, even though the work itself is outside the home. Pat Hunt, owner of Hunts' Hideaway in Morgan, Vermont, is an income-tax and business consultant.

Among her clients she now counts some area bed and breakfast hosts. To have the assistance of a professional who is experienced with bed and breakfast can be a definite advantage to a host when it comes time to prepare tax returns.

Another host works for a company that offers walking tours. Her daily contact with visitors from out of town through her job is an excellent way to publicize the bed and breakfast option available at her home. Also, she has a call-forwarding service from her home to her office so that telephone calls from prospective guests will not be missed. (Of course, any host involved in some sort of venture that is naturally complementary to B&B must be careful not to pressure clients of either business to use the other.)

Some working hosts are lucky enough to have flexible schedules. The owner of B&G's B&B in San Diego, California, for instance, works full-time in real estate sales. The nature of the business allows the host this leeway: "I can plan my own work hours to fit them into the schedules of my guests."

If one spouse works and the other does not, the responsibilities of bed and breakfast hosting can be shared. A host registered with a Philadelphia reservation service is a full-time social worker, but her husband is retired. Cynthia Whited of Strawberry Castle in Penfield, New York, is a clinical microbiologist. She works full-time, but her husband does not. In both cases the husbands' flexible schedules allow for the duties of a bed and breakfast host to be carried out easily.

Other bed and breakfast hosts work as teachers in kindergarten, elementary or high school, or college. There are also financial advisers, librarians, artists, nurses, counselors, accountants, salespersons, lawyers, economists, media specialists, interior designers, doctors, therapists, travel agents, pharmacists, real estate agents, and musicians. One is a full-time town manager, another a retired television personality, still another a minister. Reports have also come in from an electrician, a carpenter, an acupuncturist, a graphic designer, and a court reporter. Though busy, they all find ways to make bed and breakfast work for them.

As a working host, you will have to plan ahead to arrange an arrival time for each of your guests that works with your own schedule. Inform prospective guests in advance that you work and that you must agree upon an arrival time. If they tell you that they will be arriving at your door at 7:00 A.M. next Thursday and you know that you have to leave your house by 8:00 A.M. to be at work on time, make sure that you tell them this (nicely, of course) so that they know you will not just "be there" whenever they choose to arrive. Because bed and breakfast is so new in this country, sometimes guests do not understand just how much inconvenience they can cause a host by arriving late; they must be educated.

There will be times when a guest will not be able to adjust his or her arrival time to your schedule. One Boston host leaves a cell phone outside along with a friendly note and a neighbor's number. A Philadelphia host who works as a teacher and business consultant says, "Usually, I make arrangements to have the guests arrive when I will be home. If this is not possible, I ask someone to be here to let my guests in." This is a workable alternative, but make sure that the "someone" is a neighbor, relative, spouse, or close friend who can be trusted to greet your guests with the same warmth as you would yourself and who will get them comfortably settled until you can return home.

A host who works part-time in retail management instructs guests that they may check in after 6:30 P.M., the time she arrives home from work. And because she works afternoons only, preparing breakfast is never a problem.

Breakfast can be a problem that has to be solved for some working hosts. A teacher in Westhampton Beach, New York, works full-time. Her solution to conflicting morning schedules is "I have someone come in to make breakfast." Another host with the responsibilities of a contract administrator found this answer to serving breakfast to her guests: "I ask if they can be seated to eat prior to my leaving if it's on a work day. If they can't eat before I leave, my husband can finish up where I leave off."

Most bed and breakfast guests are, in fact, usually flexible enough that something can be worked out to the mutual satisfaction of both the host and guest regarding breakfast. Many working hosts find that guests are just as happy waking up to a table already set, a coffeepot ready to plug in, and a breakfast that has been prepared in advance and left for them in the refrigerator or the warming oven. Some guests don't even mind making their own breakfast. (This is especially true of those who don't consider themselves "morning people" and who might be thankful for the chance to wake up a little more slowly and in private.) As long as a special arrangement for breakfast is not a surprise to guests and is not inconvenient for them, your working schedule should not be a major problem.

Departure time must also be established in advance. When guests are making a reservation with you, find out when they would prefer to check out. Then try to settle on a time that is agreeable for both of you so that you can be home if possible. Some working hosts publish in their literature definite arrival and departure periods that coincide with their own schedules. This way, they don't have to negotiate each individual guest's coming and going; guests automatically know what is expected of them.

Setting certain times for arrivals and departures helped Lisa Hileman organize the various aspects of her busy life better when she first opened Countryside in Summit Point, West Virginia. "I ran a B&B, went to college two days a week, did freelance writing and lecturing, and took care of a husband and child," she says. "Check-in time was set between 4:00 and 7:00 P.M., checkout at 11:00 A.M. This kept our costs down and gave me and my family our private time."

What about other times of the day when guests are in residence but the host is at work? To date no one has reported this to be a major concern. One host finds that her full-time work as the director of a language arts program in Philadelphia's school system does not interfere with guests' wants and needs very much at all. "Most people come to the city for recreation or business," she says. "They are not in the house to see me."

Even though bed and breakfast can go smoothly for a working host most of the time, you must be ready to turn away prospective guests, referring them elsewhere when possible, if it seems clear that your individual schedules will collide in a big way. One Kentucky host explains her schedule immediately to people who contact her for bed and breakfast—before the reservation is made. "I talk it over with them when the call comes in," says the owner of Bowling Green Bed & Breakfast. "They can then decline if they feel they'll be inconvenienced. If I cannot fit in a reservation, I say so."

This is good advice. You do not want even one guest to feel as if the bed and breakfast experience has been less than what he or she expected. Some guests will simply not be able to fit their lives into your schedule—or would be unhappy trying. Sure, a guest can get up at 6:00 A.M. to eat breakfast, but does he want to? And, yes, a guest can put off arrival time until 7:00 P.M., but if she's planning to be in town at noon, why should she? Learn to recognize that scheduling conflicts like these are potential sources of dissatisfaction. Some people would be happier elsewhere, so be honest about it. They will thank you in the long run and perhaps think of you if they are ever coming to your area again. It's much better for you to take fewer guests than to run the risk of anyone feeling neglected or inconvenienced.

And be ready to turn away guests if there will be too many all at once for you to handle. "Be careful not to overschedule," cautions a host from Graham, North Carolina. Trying to juggle your schedule for one or two guests at a time is difficult enough; for a houseful of visitors, perhaps all with different arrival and departure times, it's impossible.

Like many other working hosts across North America, you can happily integrate bed and breakfast into your life. But you must be very well organized and much more specific about what you expect from your guests and what they can expect from you. Most guests will be able to adjust their plans to fit your schedule if given enough advance notice. The main thing to remember is that you should enjoy hosting, and you want your guests to feel relaxed and comfortable about all the arrangements.

Chapter Three
Getting Started

I f you were living in Ireland, there would be no question about what basics you would be expected to provide for your bed and breakfast guests. The Bord Fáilte (the government-run Irish tourist board) regulates bed and breakfast operations in that country, and it has developed a precise list of requirements. There, for example, hosts must install a full-size sink of specified dimensions with hot and cold running water in each guest bedroom in order for their bed and breakfast to be included in the board's approved accommodation list.

In the United States no such sweeping government regulation exists. What takes its place are state and local government regulations and standards developed by the original American Bed & Breakfast Association and Bed & Breakfast Reservation Services World-Wide (national organizations now out of business); Bed & Breakfast, The National Network of Bed and Breakfast Reservation Services (TNN); the Professional Association of Innkeepers International; and individual reservation service agencies and B&B associations across the country. Hosts who list with an RSA or join a B&B association must adhere to its guidelines. Unaffiliated hosts must strive to maintain the same high standards in order to remain competitive. In recent years the American Automobile Association and Mobil have been including bed and breakfasts in their travel guides; those B&Bs are subject to inspections and ratings according to requirements set by these organizations.

There is a general agreement about what basics should be provided in any bed and breakfast home. What follows is a discussion of these based on information provided by numerous RSAs throughout the United States and Canada. The combined information results in invaluable assistance for new hosts.

The Basics

Bedroom Basics

Providing an inviting, comfortable bedroom is your most important priority. First, consider how to best accommodate the variety of guests who will be staying with you—single travelers, couples, friends, groups, families with children. They all require different sleeping arrangements. How versatile can you make your guest rooms? Some hosts vary the sizes of beds to better accommodate the various types of travelers they see—for example, outfitting one guest room with twin beds (perfect for friends or for a parent traveling with an older child) and furnishing other guest rooms with queen beds, which are comfortable for single travelers as well as couples.

"Queen-size beds are the most popular," reports the manager of a Boston reservation service agency. Not only are queen-size mattresses roomier in width than full-size mattresses by 6 inches, but at 80 inches long (6½ feet), they are also 5 inches longer than a regular twin-size or double-size mattress. The extra length is a plus for accommodating those guests who are more than 6 feet tall. If you decide to furnish some guest rooms with twin or full-size beds, consider purchasing the extra-long variety, with 80-inch-long mattresses.

If you're not buying new beds, measure what you've got so that you know if there will be a potential problem meeting the comfort needs of your statuesque visitors. If all of your mattresses fall into the regular-length category, one of the questions you should add to your list when taking a guest's reservation should be, "Are you over 6 feet tall?" Then let the guest decide what's best for his or her comfort; it's better for someone to go elsewhere than to stay at your B&B and not be able to get a good night's rest. A special warning for antiques lovers: Antique beds are typically shorter than modern ones, making them potentially unsuitable for certain guests. One tall woman staying in a charming Victorian B&B in Cambridge, outfitted with period furniture, was asked if her bed was comfortable. "Yes," she said, and then added, "except my feet hang off the bed so I have to sleep on a diagonal."

Once you've determined the sizes of beds your B&B will have, your next task is selecting mattresses. The best advice is to do your homework first before heading out to a retailer with checkbook in hand. Mattresses are high-ticket items with a cost that reaches into the hundreds of dollars, so choose wisely. What follows is a discussion of the basics.

When considering any new mattress, you need to know all about what's in it, what's on it, and what's under it. Spec sheets provided by the manufacturers (most have Web sites) or a salesperson should help clear up any mysteries. Inside the mattress you'll find any number of metal coils, usually ranging from 300 to 700 in number. These coils can be made of

For a mattress buying guide, visit www.whatsthe best-mattress.com

thick- or thin-gauge wire and are attached to one another with interconnecting wires. A durable mattress with a long comfort life depends largely on how all the innards work together over time. In its simplest terms, a higher number of coils offers firmer support; thicker coils offer firmer support; and the more interconnecting wires the better, helping to prevent future sagging and lumpy spots.

What's on top of the mattress core—the upholstery—is also crucial to comfort. Here, you have some tough choices to make. Because people sleep in various positions (on their backs, sides, or stomachs), the surface of the mattress can make all the difference, even if the core mattress doesn't change. Those who sleep on their sides or backs often find the extra padding provided by a plush-top (also called a pillow-top) or foam mattress the most comfortable (because the padding gently supports the hollow in the back and the crook in the neck). Stomach sleepers, though, typically find a flatter surface more comfortable (because it puts less strain on the back).

You can expect that you will be welcoming all kinds of sleepers into your B&B. Unfortunately, there is no easy answer when it comes to choosing mattresses. Ask the salesperson a lot of questions, and try the various mattresses yourself in a showroom, including those that offer firmness combinations in the same mattress. You might want to take a friend or two (of differing body types) along with you to help try out the stock, shifting to various positions. (Take friends who do not get embarrassed easily. You'll all have to do your thinking lying down.)

The foundation under the mattress—the box spring—is another key element in your purchase decisions. Selecting the right foundation can increase the life expectancy of your mattress dramatically. The best advice is to purchase a whole set, mattress and box spring, together rather than buying them separately. Manufacturers design their bedding systems to work together for optimum comfort and longevity. You would be wise to purchase a "premium"-quality set (rather than a "promotional"-quality set) to ensure the highest durability. This information should be printed on the label attached to the mattress.

Ordinarily, a mattress should last about ten years. With a bed and breakfast, though, you can't realistically expect your mattresses to last that long. There are some things you can do, however, to prolong a mattress's life as much as possible. First, make sure that there is a comfortable chair in the room to discourage guests from sitting on the edges of the bed. Nothing wears down a mattress quicker than constant sitting on its edge. Air the mattress each day by pulling back the bed covers (for at least twenty minutes) so that moisture is not trapped beneath the covers. (Also, make sure that you remove the wrapper from a new mattress before use to avoid trapping moisture inside.) A mattress pad and cover will protect it from stains, but wash these often, stripping the bed completely to air it out. A mattress should be turned around (and over) once a month or so (depending on use) so that it doesn't tend to "settle" in certain spots.

Other Kinds of Beds

What about other kinds of beds—hide-a-beds, sofa beds, water beds, hanging beds? Can these be used to accommodate bed and breakfast guests? Yes and no. Yes in some situations if the bed is of high quality; no if the bed does not offer the comfort that a guest is entitled to expect.

"Once I had a hide-a-bed that I had to make for myself, and it was not comfortable," says a woman from California who included this note in her evaluation of a bed and breakfast home she had visited on the West Coast. There are folding beds that slide one under the other (for a twin-bed or bunk-bed arrangement) or that disappear into a wall. These are great space savers (and sure solve the problem of making the bed in the morning). They can indeed be used to accommodate guests—but only if they are well made and comfortable and if you don't expect the guest to find it, make it, unmake it, and hide it again.

A sofa bed or a cot is not acceptable unless there are unusual circumstances. A cot is terrific, for example, whenever parents prefer that their child share their room or whenever three or four economy-minded friends would rather share the cost of bunking in one room instead of two. And a sofa bed can come to the rescue whenever a group of friends really want to be together in the same bed and breakfast home and they explicitly state that a sofa bed would be fine as a way to accommodate everybody. As a rule, though, a cot or sofa bed should not be substituted for a "real" bed in a guest room.

A water bed can be a great adventure for people who have never experienced its ebb and flow with their nocturnal activities. You can make it as "firm" as you (or they) wish by just adding more water, and the accompanying heating unit ensures a cozy welcome for skiers or anyone who is visiting your area in the colder months.

A hanging bed, too, with its slight swinging sensation, can be a unique experience for guests. This is a platform suspended from the ceiling with a mattress placed on top. Like a hide-a-bed, it can disappear into the ceiling if you wish by use of a pulley system. It should be installed only by a good carpenter or builder. Where the bed will be placed in the bedroom depends on the location in the ceiling of the structural beams that will be able to support the weight of the bed and your guest, safely and securely.

Bed Linens and Coverings

Now that you've decided on the perfect bed, you will need to first encase the mattress in a protective covering made of tightly woven material (which helps to control dust mites), and then dress it in upper and lower sheets and matching pillowcases. (If color-coordinated with the room, these can make the bed especially attractive.) Always wash new sheets before using them. Buy good-quality sheets and avoid totally synthetic fabrics, as they tend to trap moisture more than cotton or cotton blends do, or buy the more expensive linen. Change the sheets after a guest checks out and before the next one arrives to use the same bed; if a guest is staying awhile, change the sheets at least every three days—every two days in hot, humid climates.

The life of your sheets depends in part on how clean you can manage to keep them. Never outfit a guest's bed in sheets that are stained in any way. Attack a new stain as soon as you can before it sets (you'll see them all—coffee, tea, juice, soft drinks, wine, chocolate, perfume, lipstick, mascara, blood, ink). Then at least you have a fighting chance to prolong the life of your sheets, but expect that you will have to replace them more often than you do for those on your own bed. As a bed and breakfast host, you'll soon find yourself waiting with keen anticipation for each annual January white sale.

A guest's bed should be equipped with at least one blanket, even in very warm weather (some people will be cold no matter what the temperature is), and extras should be stored right in the guest room so that your visitors can help themselves if they want an additional cover for the night. A quilt or electric blanket is a wonderful amenity in colder months. If you do supply an electric blanket, always inquire of your guests whether they understand how to use it. If they haven't used one before, you might have to explain its special features—how to set the temperature, whether or not the ends of the blanket can be tucked in, and the fact that other blankets should not be piled high on top of it while it is heating.

Wash or dry-clean your blankets periodically (before they look as though they need it) and air them out frequently to keep them in good shape. The first thing to go is usually the binding along the edges. You can buy binding separately and give older blankets a fresh look by sewing the new over the old. Once the blankets develop worn spots or holes or become stained, however, they can no longer be used on a guest's bed.

If you furnish a quilt for your guests, this can take the place of a bedspread. A quilt used in conjunction with matching sheets, and perhaps dust ruffles to hide the base of the bed, can create a pleasing, total look for the bed. (A wall hanging of the same quilted material or a color-coordinated roll blind or canopy can easily extend that look to the rest of the room.) If you choose to place a bedspread on the bed, there are a number of attractive possibilities made of chenille, lace, or yarn that has been crocheted or knitted. To help keep a bedspread clean and in good repair, consider providing the "amenity" of turning down your guests' beds at night, removing the spread to a safer place such as the shelf in the closet or the top of the cedar chest at the foot of the bed. Again, the presence of a chair in the room will help to discourage guests from lounging on the bed (and the spread).

Pillows

Good pillows, offering support and adjustability, are essential to a good night's rest. Any guest waking up with a stiff neck or sore spine will probably not be inclined to return in the future or to recommend the B&B to others. A good pillow offers a supportive core (which does not totally collapse under the weight of a person's head), plus adjustability (just the right amount of soft fill that can move around to conform to an individual's specific comfort needs). Pillows made with down or a down and feather combination are favorites for their comfort and versatility.

When purchasing pillows, the best advice is to make your selection in person, where you can squeeze the merchandise. Try pushing the ends of a pillow toward its center. If the pillow retains the new shape, then it's probably a winner. And remember that bigger may not be better. You want pillows that will accommodate the widest range of guests, large and small, from stomach sleepers to side sleepers. Are down pillows expensive? They are certainly more costly than polyester fill, but keep in mind that your guests' comfort is one area where saving money on up-front expenses will not work to a host's advantage. In the long run, the higher cost of a good pillow pays off.

A good pillow can last five to ten years, a so-so pillow two or less. (Enclose your pillows in both a slipcover and a pillowcase for their protection, and fluff them frequently.) To tell if your pillows are "dead," put them to this test: Fold natural pillows (made with down or feathers) in half, press out all the air, then release. The same goes for a synthetic pillow, but put a shoe on top. If the pillow unfolds itself and returns to its original shape, then it still offers the support it should. If the pillow doesn't unfold, it's time for it to go to its final resting place.

Every bed should be supplied with two pillows per guest, and it's a good idea to put an extra in the closet for those who need more than two to get them through the night. A small percentage of the population (one statistic says as small as 1 percent) is allergic to down or feathers; more are allergic to dust mites, which live in mattresses and pillows. Because of this, hosts are advised to use tightly woven encasings on down pillows and to offer a choice of a synthetic, hypoallergenic pillow.

Floor Coverings

Getting out of bed should be as pleasant as getting into it. Your guests' feet come into contact with waking reality before any other part of their body—so make that first step as inviting as possible by providing some kind of covering on the floor next to the bed. If you prefer not to furnish the guest room with a room-size carpet (perhaps to show off your beautifully maintained hardwood floors), at least place a good-size scatter rug (with a nonskid backing) next to each side of the bed.

Other Furnishings

Other than the bed, there are a few pieces of furniture that you will need in each guest room as well. A comfortable chair has been mentioned several times already as an enticement away from the expensive mattress that was not designed to support a person's weight except in a prone position. If there is an alternative to the bed—a big, comfy armchair, a rocking chair, or a straight-back chair with a padded seat—it will not only help lengthen the life of your mattress but will also preserve the good condition of the bedspread. And having a chair in the room is also most considerate of guests who might want to write letters or read without having to resort to the only other place to do either of these—the bed.

A suitcase rack is also a practical addition to a guest room. Guess where the suitcase goes if there's no designated place to put it? Right—on the bed. Again, think of the mattress and the spread and then either buy a rack designed expressly for this purpose or put together your own improvised version—an old trunk, perhaps, or a low, flat table. Be careful about positioning it in the room so that the edge of an open suitcase will not rub against your favorite painting or scrape against the wall.

You can discourage your guests from continual foraging in their suitcases (which, in turn, cuts down on the rubs and scrapes) by supplying ample clothes hangers in the closet. For each guest, plan on at least six, more if a guest will be staying longer than two or three days or if the weather is chilly and there are more layers that need to be dealt with. Padded hangers are an especially nice touch for finer garments. It's a good idea to include special hangers for trousers or skirts as well. Install a few hooks on the bathroom door or the inside of the closet door so that guests can use these for their robes or nightgowns.

The closet should be completely empty of any items except those that guests have brought with them and the extra blankets, pillows, and sheets that are intended for their use. In addition to this space to temporarily store their clothes, guests should also have access to at least two drawers each in a bureau. Line the drawers with paper and change the lining often.

People have lots of things that they like near them at night—eyeglasses, a book they want to finish, a glass of water, their dentures. To hold these kinds of personal items, there should be a night table next to the bed. If the guest room has a double, queen-size, or king-size bed, you'll need two—one for each side. On the table, place a box of facial tissues, an alarm clock (one that runs quietly), and a radio if you have an extra. If you allow smoking, it's best to place the ashtray elsewhere in the room so as to discourage smoking in bed.

It's a good idea to have another small table in the room besides the night table, as that can get cluttered quickly. You'll need to provide several glasses per guest for water and other beverages, plus a pitcher of water (which is optional but a nice touch), a basket of goodies to eat in case your guest wants a snack (some hosts provide a minifridge), maybe some of your business cards or stationery, a vase of flowers, and perhaps a phone extension. The top of the bureau can hold some of these items, and a writing desk is also an option, but a separate table can be arranged to hold these items in a more attractive way.

There should always be a reading lamp near the bed because many people do like to read before going to sleep. This can be placed on the night table or above the bed. If your guest room has a double, queen-size, or king-size bed, you'll need two reading lamps, one on each side of the bed. That comfortable chair that you hope your guests will be using also needs a good source of light. Use lightbulbs that provide adequate light for reading; three-way bulbs allow a guest to choose the wattage.

Your guests will be preparing to meet the outside world from the confines of their room, so provide a large mirror to help their efforts. A full-length mirror is best, but any large mirror (positioned so that it can accommodate the widest range in heights) is fine. A hand mirror is a considerate addition to the items on top of the bureau.

Place a wastebasket in a convenient location in each guest room. Lining the baskets will protect their surfaces from the more messy discarded items, such as banana peels and old cigarette butts. Some surfaces (like wicker) are harder to clean than others, and some (like metal) will discolor. The lining will make your job easier and the baskets will last longer. Still, resorting to that durable plastic bag from Stop 'n' Save somehow breaks the tone you've tried so hard to establish. Old newspapers, too, don't give the right impression, and neither do plain brown paper bags. Some hosts have found this solution: They stock quantities of tissue paper (the kind used for wrapping gifts), either in white or in a color that coordinates with the color of the room, and arrange a few sheets inside the wastebasket. These make an attractive accent in the room and, at the same time, provide some protection for the basket's inside surface. While a guest is in residence, empty the wastebasket each day, clean the inside if necessary, and line it with new tissue paper.

The furnishings in your guest room do not have to be new, but they do have to be in good repair. "Old" furniture sometimes looks drab, and maybe you should consider a new upholstery job on that faded chair, a new finish on that night table, or a new shade on that lamp to get the room "guest ready." If any piece of furniture detracts from the charm of the room, it will be noticed—so take care of it.

Heat and Ventilation

The overall comfort of a room depends, in large part, on adequate heat in the cooler months and adequate ventilation or a cooling system in warmer months. If there is a problem with too much or too little heat or air-conditioning in any of your guest rooms, you have to take steps to alleviate the problem. (See "Comfort" in chapter 2.)

Windows and Doors

All windows in the guests' bedrooms must be screened in good weather, have storm windows in cool weather, and have some sort of window covering for privacy—even if the nearest possible Peeping Tom is the neighbor's cow that sometimes wanders out of the pasture and into your yard. "Don't laugh," say the owners of a reservation service agency in Pennsylvania. "Many of our hosts live in woods, and so shades are not necessary, but guests don't know that!" Anyone used to living in a more densely populated area is accustomed to guarding personal privacy more carefully. Draw curtains or window blinds will help assuage the concerns of city dwellers traveling to more rural areas. They also keep the morning sun from streaming through windows, awakening weary travelers far too early.

If your bed and breakfast home is in an urban area, you should have not only curtains or window blinds on bedroom windows but window locks as well.

A privacy lock for the bedroom door is also recommended regardless of the location of your B&B. Some people just don't sleep well in a strange place (no matter how nice it is) knowing that someone can just walk in through the door at any time. A hook-and-eye type of lock is fine, unless you intend to undergo an inspection for a listing in the American Automobile Association's Tourbook publications. The AAA requires all guest room doors to a common hall or the exterior to be equipped with a lock that permits a guest to lock the door when leaving the room, along with a deadbolt that a guest can lock from the inside. Doors to connecting rooms must also have a deadbolt. Each sliding door must have a locking device as well. A secondary security lock is required on all ground-floor doors and those accessible from walkways and common balconies.

Harry and Elaine Dickson, owners of the Captain Ezra Nye House in Sandwich, Massachusetts, decorate their restored historic home with treasures from around the world that reflect the personalities of the innkeepers. Still, not every guest appreciates everything in their collection, as Elaine relates in this tale. "Just last night we had guests in a room that has a brass gargoyle door knocker on it from Canterbury Cathedral. The husband asked if we could remove the knocker as his wife thought it would bring ghosts into the room. Solution: Harry removed it."

Bedroom Basics Checklist

☐ Reading lamp	☐ Encasings on pillows
☐ Night table(s) next to bed	☐ Pillowcases
☐ Suitcase rack	☐ Privacy lock on door
☐ Comfortable chair	☐ Window screens in warm weather
☐ Bureau with at least two drawers	☐ Storm windows in cold weather
☐ Wastebasket	☐ Window locks (if on first floor)
☐ Closet free of personal items	☐ Box of facial tissues
☐ Six hangers or more per guest in closet	☐ Alarm clock
☐ Hooks to hang robes	☐ Ashtray (if smoking is allowed)
☐ Large mirror/hand mirror	☐ Two glasses (for water/other beverages)
☐ Rug next to bed	☐ Ventilation (fan/air-conditioning)
☐ Drying rack (if bathroom is shared)	☐ Heat in cold months
☐ Window covering (blinds/draw curtains)	☐ Mattress in good condition
☐ Bed base with good support	☐ Clean, fluffy blanket on bed
☐ Mattress pad	☐ Bedspread or quilt
☐ Mattress encasing	☐ Extra sheets and pillowcases available
☐ Two clean sheets (upper/lower)	☐ Easy access to extra blankets
☐ Two pillows	☐ Hypoallergenic pillow
☐ Guest refrigerator	☐ Snack/beverage tray

One final note about the door: Make sure that you have for each guest room a proper door that is solid and closes into a frame. An accordion door might be serviceable for your own purposes, but it gives a less private feeling to a room and should be avoided when it comes to outfitting a guest room with the basics.

A Final Test

So now you've got it all—the bed and the right mattress, a comfortable chair, a rug, the sheets and pillows, the blankets, the reading light. Are you ready for guests? There's one sure way to find out—try it out yourself. Spend a night in the guest room. Read in bed, write a few letters you've been putting off for a while, have a glass of wine, eat a snack. Then go to sleep. There's no better test than to see how you like your own hospitality. Sweet dreams.

Bathroom Basics

For the bathroom that your guests will be using, your initial concern should be whether the current plumbing and fixtures are in good working order and can handle the increased demand on them that bed and breakfast hosting will cause. A host who has only one or two guests every once in a while should encounter no problem. If you've got big plans to fill the five extra rooms in your home every night of the week, however, you might have to do some renovations.

Each guest bathroom must have an adequate supply of hot and cold running water. Does your hot-water tank have the capacity to produce all the hot water you'll be needing when you open the doors to your bed and breakfast? (If you will be able to accommodate eight people, that means a potential of eight hot showers in a row, plus your own, plus those of any other household members.) If yours can't, here are your options: Buy a new, larger tank; install an auxiliary tank or individual water-heating unit; take fewer guests per night; or schedule your own showers around those of your guests.

Consider, too, whether your present sewage system can handle greater use. More than one host reports having to finance a completely new sewage treatment system before being able to open for business. Be advised that all sanitary facilities must meet the regulations in force where you live and that water must be from an approved source.

A bed and breakfast home need not provide a private bath for each guest room. There are many flourishing B&B homes in which bathrooms are shared among guests or with the host and other household members. Guests generally understand that they are staying in a private home, and many are not uncomfortable about this arrangement. One gentleman visiting a bed and breakfast farm in South Dakota had a "half-bath" (without tub or shower) adjoining his room. For a shower, "I had to use the family's improvised shower facility in the basement, off the family rec room," he says. No problem.

One couple staying at a bed and breakfast home in Nova Scotia was accommodated in the one guest room that happened to have an adjoining bathroom. Although the place did have another bathroom for guests to use, that one had no shower. Only the bathroom that was accessible through the couple's bedroom contained a shower. "We were prewarned and asked if we minded the traffic through our room," the couple reports. "We often had folks who wanted a shower tiptoeing through our room in the early morning." An inconvenience, yes, but the couple looks back on their visit there as one of the most enjoyable vacations they've ever taken. For some, sharing a bathroom is just not an issue.

Others are more private people and would truly be happier with a bathroom to themselves, no matter what you do to make their stay comfortable. A New Jersey woman wrote a rave review of the bed and breakfast home she visited in Rhode Island—how helpful, nice, friendly, and generous the host was; how "terrific" breakfast was; and how she would absolutely love to stay there again. Yet, when asked if she would like to change anything about this wonderful place, her comment was "private bath."

A Pennsylvania couple had a similar reaction to a bed and breakfast ranch in Arizona. They loved it. They even had a private bath, but they had to go downstairs to use it. This was an inconvenience that they noted in their report in spite of their answer to whether or not they would want to stay at the ranch again: "Definitely!" "Private baths are still the choice for Americans. Europeans are not as fussy," observes the founder of Greater Boston Hospitality. "When I hear the words 'private bath,' I shudder," says Ellen Madison, owner of Woody Hill B&B in Westerly, Rhode Island. "I know my chances of hooking that caller are slim." This is in spite of the many other amenities she offers—swimming pool, porch swings, gardens, and French toast with homemade raspberry sauce over fresh peaches.

The truth is that some people will never be completely happy about the bathroom arrangements (too small; too distant from the bedroom; it's upstairs; it's downstairs; it's shared), but a good measure of hospitality can often outweigh someone's idea that a private bathroom adjoining the guest room is the ultimate in comfort.

This is true, however, only when the inconvenience is indeed minor. With a shared bath, people have different schedules and can usually work things out. But one woman stayed in a bed and breakfast home in the White Mountains of New Hampshire where the sole bathroom had to accommodate eight people. And it could be reached only by going through the kitchen to the back of the house. She was uncomfortable, for good reason, and so will your guests be if your home does not offer a proportionate number of bathrooms for the number of guests it accommodates. Four people sharing one bathroom is plenty; more can manage, but the risk of a traffic jam at the bathroom door is greater.

For the privacy of your guests (especially where there is a shared bathroom), make sure that there is some sort of lock on the door (hook-and-eye type is fine), a door or curtain on the shower stall, and blinds or draw curtains on windows.

For the safety of your guests, any rugs placed in the bathroom should have a nonskid backing, and there should be a nonskid bath mat or strips in the tub. A grip rail for the tub and the shower is also recommended. (A towel rack cannot substitute for this; it isn't made to support the full weight of a person needing to steady himself or herself getting in or out of the tub or shower.)

For the comfort of your guests, the bathroom should have ventilation, either an extractor fan or a window that can be opened. The addition of some live plants or a vase of flowers here can also help make the room more pleasant. Keep a new sponge and cleaning supplies handy, along with air freshener or deodorizer so that guests who wish to do so can freshen up the room a bit after use. (Burning a match is a simple but effective way to deodorize a bathroom; a small box of matches left out for guests is a considerate touch.) There should be a wastebasket in the room—emptied on a daily basis.

Place a box of facial tissues in both the guest room and the bathroom. Many of us have discovered that the "generic" brands of tissue are often just as soft and serviceable as the name brands. It makes economic sense to supply these for your guests, but the austere packaging might give the impression that you are cutting corners instead of seeking the best for your guests' comfort. Still, if the idea of spending one-half more for a brand name just because the tissues are packaged in attractive boxes doesn't set well with you, consider the purchase of a few decorative tissue-box holders (they come in wicker, ceramic, plastic, and fabric). If you use these, you need never advertise what brand you're using.

Where the economy brands do not seem to contain the quality of the more well-known products is in toilet tissue. For this item you're probably better off watching for sales on the brand you favor and stocking up. There should always be a roll of tissue on the holder in the bathroom, along with a second roll (and a second box of facial tissues as well) located on a shelf or in another convenient spot in the room. Avoid dyed and perfumed toilet tissue. Some people are sensitive to these things and would be happier with a good brand of soft, plain white, unscented tissue that will not trigger chemical sensitivities.

Each guest should be given a bath towel, a hand towel, and a washcloth, preferably a matching set. It's not a bad idea to include a medium-size towel or a turban towel, as some people like the luxury of this extra to dry their hair after washing it. The towels must be clean (no stains) and in good repair (no holes, tears, frayed edges, or worn spots), preferably thick and fluffy, and of high-quality material. Change them as often as needed. For a guest there's nothing worse than coming back to the bed and breakfast after a long day of sightseeing to clean up for a night on the town and finding used towels still damp and dirty from the morning's post-jogging shower. Some hosts show guests where the stacks of clean towels are stored and invite them to help themselves to fresh ones as needed. If you prefer this method, also explain to guests where they should deposit their used ones. For this you might want to place a small clothes hamper or laundry bag in the bathroom (also a good idea for those sandy beach towels that guests bring back to the house after swimming and sunning).

If there will be more than one person using a bathroom, the best way to help guests keep their towels separate is to give everyone a complete towel set in a different color. This works especially well when the colors of the towels are coordinated with the colors of the guest rooms (blue for the Blue Room, yellow for the Sunshine Room, and so forth). Some hosts put a towel set for each guest inside a large basket and place it inside the bedroom. Guests can also use this basket to transport their own toilet articles back and forth to the shared bath. (Do make some shelf space available in the bathroom for those guests who wish to leave their own toothpaste, toothbrush, shampoo, and the like there.)

If a bathroom is shared, placing a drying rack in each guest room will allow guests to bring their own towels back into their room and spread them out there to dry. (A drying rack will also save your bedposts and chair backs from discoloration as a result of guests' resorting to the most convenient makeshift rack for their wet towels.) Do this only if the moisture will not damage your floors or floor covering. In the bathroom install enough towel racks so that guests can hang up their towels while bathing and leave them there to dry afterward. (Heated towel rails connected to the hot-water system are a nice touch in colder climates. They not only give your guests warm, comfy towels after their bath or shower, but they also facilitate the drying of the towels.) And make sure that there are a few hooks in the bathroom where guests can hang their robes.

Include a small, individually wrapped bar of soap in each guest's "bathroom basket" if the bathroom is to be shared, or place some liquid soap at the sink. If guests have a private bath, a new bar of soap at the sink is also an option (but sometimes a more expensive one, as bars used by one guest really shouldn't be left for the next one who checks in). If you do choose to stock bar soap instead of liquid soap, make sure that you have soap dishes on hand; either place one in the guest's basket along with the soap and towels or set out a few in the bathroom. Supply some liquid soap at the tub or shower. And a bowl or basket of small, wrapped scented soaps, packets of bubble bath, lotions, and shampoo set out in the bathroom are a nice touch. (Sample sizes of toiletries are usually available at discount drugstores.)

Each guest will need a water glass. These may be placed in the bathroom or, if the bathroom is shared among three or more people, on a small tray in each guest room. Disposable paper cups are fine and are probably the most sanitary solution. Some hosts have installed a cup dispenser in the bathroom; other hosts feel that this device detracts from the decor of the room. Remember that you will also be providing a glass for each guest to use for soft drinks or wine. Either keep the water glass clearly separate from the other—by placing it in the bathroom or on its own tray with a water pitcher—or set out several glasses for each guest in his or her own room. Change or wash the glasses every day.

If you decide that renovations are necessary in order to accommodate your guests, consider the following alterations. If there is not already a good light source by the mirror, have a qualified electrician install one. And if your bathroom does not already have an electrical outlet where guests can plug in a shaver, curling iron, or hair dryer, you might want to have this added as well. (Note that there are building codes that govern the use of electricity in bathrooms. A bathroom outlet should have a GFCI (ground fault circuit interrupter), be positioned high and at least 5 feet from the tub, and be fitted with a waterproof plastic cover plate. Ask your electrician if any other regulations apply.) You might decide that it's best to pass on the bathroom outlet as a safety measure; as long as there's an outlet in the guest's bedroom that can be used for a hair dryer, this should be fine. Placing a supply of disposable razors and a can of shaving cream in the bathroom should satisfy anyone who finds that he cannot use his electric razor there.

You might think that you need to add an additional bathroom to meet your guests' needs. Before you go ahead and do this, be advised that there are alternatives. One is to remodel an existing bathroom (if it's large enough) so that the toilet and bathing areas are partitioned off from each other, with separate entrances. This allows others who share the bathroom to visit the toilet area while someone else is using the bathing facilities. Remember, too, that showering usually requires less water than does a nice soak in the bathtub. If you need to conserve your hot-water supply, you might want to establish a "showers only" policy. (One other advantage to this is that showers are usually quicker than baths—which means that the shared bathroom will be tied up for less time.)

Another possibility is adding a sink with hot and cold running water in one or more of your guest rooms. This would relieve the demand on the main bathroom when all that the guests want to do is wash their hands or brush their teeth. Individual units (electric or gas) for heating the water can be installed right under the sink so that there is no extra demand on your central water-heating unit. You should consider this alternative only if the plumbing in your home can be extended easily into a guest room. (If a guest room shares a wall with the bathroom, for example, or is positioned directly above the kitchen, additions to pipes can be made more easily than if a plumber has to burrow through a couple of walls to install the sink.)

These alternatives to financing a new hot-water tank and building a second bathroom could be less costly, but in the words of a plumbing-supply dealer, "nothing's cheap." It's best to give some thought to various alternatives, get estimates on all of them, check appropriate health and building regulations, and then decide what's best for your situation. Because new pipes and electrical cables may have to be laid to provide adequate bathroom facilities for your guests, be warned that walls, ceilings, and floors could suffer some damage in the process. So make no other major renovations anywhere in the house (such as laying down new linoleum in the kitchen or repapering the walls in the guest rooms) before taking care of this priority.

Now that the tradition of bed and breakfast has crossed the Atlantic, hosts in this country can better appreciate the experiences of our fellow hosts across the way. During its years of operation, a bed and breakfast home in Dublin, Ireland, offered only showers (no baths) so as to use the hot-water supply more efficiently. "This arrangement—of showers only—never gave us any problems . . . that is, until two Englishmen stayed with us who wanted to have a bath together," says Patrick Boland, former proprietor of the Linden Lodge. "We would not have agreed to it anyway, because one of them was carrying a very dangerous-looking toy submarine already armed with two dangerous-looking toy torpedoes that, had they struck the other fellow amidships, would certainly have caused damage."

Bathroom Basics Checklist

- ☐ Sewage system adequate
- ☐ Well-lighted mirror at sink
- ☐ Shelf space for toiletries
- ☐ Nonskid bath mat in tub
- ☐ Box of facial tissues (plus one extra box)
- ☐ Wastebasket
- ☐ Roll of toilet tissue (plus one extra roll)
- ☐ Nonskid rug on floor
- ☐ Water glass for each guest
- ☐ Curtain or door on shower
- ☐ Hooks for robes
- ☐ Window covering (blinds/draw curtains)
- ☐ Privacy lock on door
- ☐ Plenty of hot water

- ☐ Liquid soap in tub/shower
- ☐ Liquid or unused bar soap at sink
- ☐ Soap dishes if needed
- ☐ One bath towel per guest
- ☐ One hand towel per guest
- ☐ One washcloth per guest
- ☐ Separate towel racks for each guest
- ☐ Drying rack for towels/hand washables
- ☐ Air freshener
- ☐ Fresh sponge and cleaning supplies
- ☐ Plumbing/fixtures in good working order
- ☐ Ventilation (fan/window that opens)
- ☐ Extra bath mats and rugs (if bath is shared)

The Amenities

Rita Duncan, manager of a reservation service agency in Virginia called Blue Ridge Bed & Breakfast, has this to say about the hosts who list with her agency: "I fully trust their good taste and graciousness." As long as the requirements of cleanliness and a good, hearty breakfast are met, "the rest is left to the hosts' discretion," she says.

What Rita is referring to here are the amenities—extras that hosts provide to make their guests comfortable. Just what these might be is a highly individual matter, depending on a host's own interests, hobbies, likes and dislikes, and location. From the amenities you decide to offer, your bed and breakfast home will take on its own character and make the B&B experience exactly what it's supposed to be for your guests—special. No two bed and breakfast homes are alike. And this is a large part of the attraction.

The discussion of amenities that follows shows what different hosts throughout North America do to add that extra-special character to their bed and breakfast homes. You should look at them as food for thought. How do they spark your own imagination?

An "amenity" is anything extra that goes beyond the basics. A host is not obligated to provide more than a clean, comfortable accommodation, but the finer touches will make the bed and breakfast experience special for the people who stay with you. The basics are what guests expect; the amenities are what they remember.

There are some amenities that are easy to provide and cost little or nothing but make quite an impression. A couple visiting the 3B's Bed & Breakfast in Spring Valley, Ohio, reports that they came back to their room in the evening to find that their host had "turned back our bed while we were out—nice touch!"

A woman staying at Shir-Will Farms in Bloomfield, Ontario, was delighted to find a single rose in a vase on her bedside table. Fresh flowers or a few plants always add a special something to a guest room.

Gloria Belknap, owner of the Terrace Townehouse in Boston, invites guests to place their shoes outside the door of their room when they retire. In the morning the shoes will be right where they left them—polished and shined.

A host is expected to furnish breakfast for guests. Nothing more than this is actually necessary, but it's very thoughtful to offer drinks, and sometimes food, at other times as well. People arriving at your home at night might be hungry after traveling, but because of the late hour they might be unable to go out to a restaurant. A bedtime snack to help latecomers get through the night is an amenity offered regularly at Leftwich House in Graham, North Carolina; the Shaw House in Georgetown, South Carolina; and many other bed and breakfast homes. A Cape Cod couple brings out a platter of homemade peanut butter cookies in the evenings. One Massachusetts reservation service agency suggests to hosts that they make popcorn as a snack or offer apples in season.

The manager of a reservation service agency in South Carolina called Historic Charleston Bed & Breakfast recommends to its hosts that they place a "goody basket" containing fruit and candy in each guest room so that visitors can help themselves.

At the Brinley Victorian Inn in Newport, Rhode Island, guests will find mints on their pillows. An RSA in the state of Washington takes this idea one step further. The manager sends a supply of gold labels to each of its hosts so that they can affix them to paper doilies. These are then placed on guests' pillows with a chocolate "kiss" that is wrapped in foil. The labels say, "A Kiss to Build a Dream On"—a touch that is "very popular with guests," says the manager.

Boston host Gloria Belknap makes a hit with her visitors by offering an "afternoon tea" at which she serves her own special homemade scones, hot from the oven. Some guests enjoy this amenity so much that they ask if they may invite friends over to join them for the occasion. A number of B&Bs now offer an optional afternoon tea or evening social hour.

Phil and Joan Blood, co-owners of Chinguague Compound in San Juan Pueblo, New Mexico, are more informal about providing extra food for guests. "In season, we encourage guests to go out and pick fresh fruit from the trees."

Some guests will bring their own snacks and drinks. Linda and David Nichols, owners of Hidden Brooks Bed & Breakfast in New Hampshire, allow guests the use of their refrigerator to store cold drinks and any food they might have brought with them. A Boston host offers to put any food that guests are carrying in their own cooler in her refrigerator when they arrive, then fills the cooler with ice when the guests are ready to check out.

A host should always make sure that there is ice available for guests to use with drinks they have bought themselves. One reservation service agency recommends placement of a full ice bucket, along with several glasses, in each guest room. Some hosts prefer to simply let guests know that they are welcome to get ice from the freezer compartment of the refrigerator whenever they wish.

Providing complimentary drinks is a nice touch. Greater Boston Hospitality encourages hosts listed with this reservation service agency to place a few cans of soft drinks or mineral water in an ice bucket or small refrigerator for each guest room. (You might want to ask guests what they prefer and then supply the drinks of their choice.) One B&B in Annapolis, Maryland, stocks a refrigerator with complimentary soft drinks and wine. A glass of sherry or other nightcap before bed is an amenity usually welcomed by guests. Hosts listed with one RSA will supply a complimentary bottle of champagne for newlyweds.

Some hosts extend kitchen privileges to those who ask for it, especially guests who are staying longer than two or three days and would like to make their own meals rather than eat out all the time. Others invite guests to join the family for lunch or dinner (usually with an adjustment to the final bill). Still others have found that the best solution is to prepare meals together. A woman from Pittsburgh who was staying in her first bed and breakfast home ate all her meals with her hosts. "We discovered that we were all into vegetarian cooking, and we tried a new recipe or two," says Lauren Schneider, recalling her weeklong visit with a young Canadian couple. They relied on fresh vegetables from the garden, split the cost of beer, and "shared things like cooking and washing dishes," she says.

If a guest is celebrating a special event, take the opportunity to acknowledge it in some way. The owner of a B&B in West Virginia says, "We make birthday cakes, give birthday gifts, anniversary gifts, wedding gifts—all at no extra charge." If it seems appropriate, a remembrance of a special occasion—a card, a small gift, or a cake if you want to take the time to bake it—is a wonderful personal touch that your guests will never forget.

Transportation is another amenity that is often needed and always appreciated by travelers. Some of your guests will be coming to the area by means of bus, train, or plane. Without their own car, they must rely on taxis or other public transportation to get to and from your home. Pickup at airports and bus and train stations is offered by a number of hosts as a courtesy to their guests. If providing this service is convenient for you (sometimes hosts can't arrange to do this because of work or family responsibilities), it's a good amenity to offer. One guest writes that she was met by her host at the airport, which was an hour's drive from the bed and breakfast home. The drive itself turned out to be one of the highlights that she remembers the most about her trip: "We spent about three hours driving along the shore and stopping at various small museums," she says. Some hosts will give their guests tours of the area if they wish; others have negotiated agreements with local car-rental companies to provide their guests with discounts on rentals.

A supply of reading material is a good idea. Travelers often look for a relaxing diversion before they retire for the night, want to read up on the area they're visiting, or just want to keep up with the news of the day while they're away from home. At Corner House in Rhinebeck, New York, there is a bookcase full of books in each room, along with magazines and brochures of local attractions and interests. Catherine Hatala, a host registered with a Philadelphia reservation service, subscribes to a variety of current periodicals (*New York Times, New Yorker, Prevention, Reader's Digest, U.S. News & World Report*) to satisfy the different reading tastes of her guests. A morning paper is always available for guests at the Shaw House in Georgetown, South Carolina. (Subscribing to a local paper, as well as to any magazine devoted to your city, state, or area, is also recommended. Note that these subscriptions are tax deductible; see chapter 5.)

Some magazines may offer you or your guests discounted subscriptions. If you find that you host a large number of people who fall into one or two main categories (business executives, anglers, bird-watchers, musicians), contact the offices of any magazines directed to these special audiences and inquire about any amenity program currently offered to hotels and discuss such an arrangement for your bed and breakfast.

Some hosts offer additional diversions for their guests' enjoyment. At Gates Hill Homestead in Brookfield, New York, guests will find a card table and some decks of cards waiting for them. A Massachusetts reservation service suggests to its hosts that they put up a dartboard game in the yard or the family room. There's a piano at Leftwich House in Graham, North Carolina, and at Woodruff House in Barre, Vermont. (For guests who prefer the more meditative diversions, there are also rockers on the porches of both of these establishments.) In each guesthouse on the Chinguague Compound in New Mexico, there is a television set. These days, many hosts supply guest rooms with televisions and DVD players and offer a selection of DVDs. Some provide a CD player and a selection of CDs.

Depending on the area where you live, other amenities might come to mind. One couple from New Mexico were pleasantly surprised that their host in Bodega Bay, California, had thought of a way to help them enjoy the scenery even more. "There was a large telescope, so we could look over the bay," they recall. Some hosts lend guests a fishing pole if they want to try their luck. Other hosts offer the use of binoculars for bird-watching, golf clubs, volleyball and net, tennis racquets, sleds, toboggans, surfboards, water skis or snow skis, canoes, bicycles, and weights and exercise equipment.

There are some hosts who even allow guests the use of their personal memberships in social or athletic clubs, museums, and libraries. The owner of Singleton House in Arkansas invites visitors to join her on Sunday mornings for a jaunt with the local hiking club. Cozy Acres B&B in New Jersey provides beach badges during the summer; Spindrift Bed & Breakfast in Oregon offers rain gear for the beach to those who can't resist a walk on the sand, despite the weather. At High Tide in Orleans, Massachusetts, guests are supplied with beach umbrellas and towels. Visitors to the state of Maine have a chance to go sailing with one of the bed and breakfast hosts.

As many guests will be unfamiliar with the area, you can do them a favor by helping to arrange their entertainment. If visitors are coming for the specific purpose of attending a play, concert, museum opening, or festival, offer to reserve tickets for them through your local connections. Strawberry Castle Bed & Breakfast in New York will arrange horse-and-buggy rides for its guests. Dairy Hollow House in Arkansas will set up guided fishing trips (and then cook the catch for the guests' dinner!). If guests decide to take a side trip, it's a nice gesture to store their unneeded luggage for them. Consider what attracts people to your area and think of ways you can be helpful to your guests as they explore it.

Daily activities that seem quite ordinary to you could, in fact, be quite exciting to someone from a different environment. Watching cows being milked is greatly enjoyed by guests at Sycamore Haven Farm in Kinzers, Pennsylvania. Take stock of your own situation. Do you live in an area where you could offer horseback riding, hayrides, hiking, or jogging? These special features can attract visitors to your bed and breakfast.

Do you have a special skill that you could offer guests as an amenity? The owner of a bed and breakfast in Atlanta, Georgia, offers to type reports and letters for guests and to make translations from Spanish and French. A New York reservation service lists some hosts who offer their services as interpreters. "I board cats," says New York host Elaine Samuels. Among the amenities she extends to her guests is "a cat to sleep with, if desired."

"We believe in your own uniqueness," says the manager of one reservation service agency. Take a close look at your own skills and lifestyle and how you can draw from these to make your guests' visit special. Be creative.

There are more common amenities that will enhance the overall comfort of your guests. The climate will dictate some of these extras—suntan lotion or sunscreen for beachgoers; insect repellent in humid areas; umbrellas for rainy days. Shop around for a supply of small sample-size containers of lotions, shaving cream, shampoo, hair conditioner, and toothpaste. Other items that guests appreciate are disposable razors, bath salts, scented soaps, toothbrushes, cotton swabs, and disposable shower caps. Some hosts place a pin cushion with needles and thread in every guest room and make available a hair dryer, curling iron, makeup mirror, iron, and ironing board.

Guests will find robes at the Beach House in Huron, Ohio. At Marjon Bed & Breakfast Inn in Leaburg, Oregon, they may help themselves to a pair of multicolored "soxlcts" from a large wooden bowl in the living room to wear around the house.

You can expect that guests will have their own individual needs beyond the things that you have thought to provide for their comfort. "Bandages, rags for cleaning bicycles, safety pins—you name it, and I've been asked for it," says Ellen Madison, owner of Woody Hill Guest House in Rhode Island. At times Lona and George Smith, owners of Summerwood in New York, have loaned sweaters, boots, and scarves to guests who came unprepared for

Amenities Checklist

- [ ] Turn back bed covers
- [ ] Shine shoes
- [ ] Flowers/plants in guest room
- [ ] Bedtime snack
- [ ] Fruit bowl/ "goody basket" in room
- [ ] Mints/candies on pillow
- [ ] Afternoon tea
- [ ] Complimentary soft drinks/ tea/coffee/mineral water
- [ ] Complimentary wine/beer/liqueur
- [ ] Ice bucket/small fridge
- [ ] Complimentary champagne for special occasions
- [ ] Kitchen privileges
- [ ] Lunch/dinner with host
- [ ] Cards/gifts/cakes for special occasions
- [ ] Pickup at airport, bus, or train station
- [ ] Tours of area
- [ ] Car-rental discounts
- [ ] Reading material
- [ ] Magazine subscription discounts
- [ ] Games
- [ ] Piano/other musical instruments
- [ ] DVD player/library
- [ ] Television/cable
- [ ] Telephone
- [ ] CD player/music
- [ ] Radio
- [ ] Hot tub/Jacuzzi/sauna

- [ ] Swimming pool/pond
- [ ] Suntan lotion/sunscreen
- [ ] Air-conditioning
- [ ] Newspaper
- [ ] Weights/exercise equipment
- [ ] Use of membership in clubs/museums/libraries/ gym
- [ ] Sailing/boating excursions
- [ ] Fishing/lobstering excursions
- [ ] Horseback riding
- [ ] Insect repellent
- [ ] Hand cream/lotions
- [ ] Shaving cream
- [ ] Shampoo
- [ ] Hair conditioner
- [ ] Toothpaste/toothbrushes
- [ ] BBQ grill
- [ ] Disposable razors
- [ ] Bath salts
- [ ] Scented soaps/bubble bath
- [ ] Cotton swabs
- [ ] Disposable shower caps
- [ ] Pincushion with needles/ thread/safety pins
- [ ] Hair dryer
- [ ] Curling iron
- [ ] Makeup mirror
- [ ] Iron and ironing board
- [ ] Laundry privileges/service
- [ ] Arrange tickets to events
- [ ] Restaurant discounts
- [ ] Store luggage

- [ ] Beach badges
- [ ] Beach umbrellas/towels
- [ ] Sunglasses/straw hats
- [ ] Umbrellas/slickers
- [ ] Earmuffs/hand warmers
- [ ] Robes
- [ ] Slippers/socks
- [ ] Sports/recreational equipment:
  - [ ] Telescope
  - [ ] Fishing poles
  - [ ] Canoe/boat
  - [ ] Binoculars
  - [ ] Golf clubs
  - [ ] Volleyball and net
  - [ ] Tennis/badminton racquets
  - [ ] Sleds/toboggans
  - [ ] Surfboards
  - [ ] Water skis
  - [ ] Snow skis
  - [ ] Bicycles
- [ ] Hayrides
- [ ] Hiking/jogging trails
- [ ] Bicycle paths
- [ ] Business services
- [ ] Foreign-language translation; interpreter services
- [ ] Farm animals
- [ ] Note paper/envelopes and pen
- [ ] Use of fax machine/ computer
- [ ] Internet connection
- [ ] Off-street parking

the local weather. Blue's Bed and Breakfast in Cambridge, Massachusetts, keeps extra down jackets on hand.

More and more B&Bs are providing telephones in their guest rooms. B&Bs catering to business travelers also offer use of a fax, Internet connection, and sometimes a computer. For business travelers who stay several weeks but return home on weekends, some B&Bs store personal items over the weekend for their guests' convenience.

The subject of laundry is bound to come up. If you wish, permit guests to use your washer and dryer, or run a load of laundry for them. (Most hosts add on an extra fee for this privilege.) Or you might want to provide some liquid laundry soap and a drying rack, or clothesline and clothespins, for hand washables.

Some amenities should be free of charge, as part of the hospitality provided by your bed and breakfast. Most of these are obvious—turning down the bed at night, flowers in the guest rooms, mints on the pillows, a complimentary glass of wine in the evening, a bed-time snack.

Other extras cost a host time and money—traveling a great distance to pick up someone at the airport, spending half a day sailing, doing laundry, baking cakes. The next section, "Pricing Your Bed and Breakfast," will help you determine how to cost your rooms, taking amenities into consideration. In preparation look at the list of possible amenities that appears in this chapter. Check off the ones that you can and want to offer your guests. Remember that you need not try to do more than what is possible for you. Just a few extra touches here and there are enough to let your guests know that they are special to you. The personal touch is what they're looking for, and they'll be sure to find it with the opportunity to visit with you in your home. According to Robert Somaini, owner of Woodruff House in Vermont, this is the greatest amenity that any guest can receive: "a chance to meet an eccentric native—me!"

Pricing Your Bed and Breakfast

How much should you charge your guests? "There is no strict answer to this question other than to say, 'Be sensible,'" says the manager of one reservation service agency. Being sensible means not charging too much or too little. Following are guidelines that will help you price your bed and breakfast. (If you list your B&B with a reservation service agency, the price is usually reached by compromise between the individual host and the agency.)

First, categorize your rooms according to the classifications that follow, which are based on a survey of rates charged by B&Bs across North America. While the overall average room price is around $142, individual B&Bs may charge more or less due to geographic region and amenities offered. When setting your prices, be sure to reflect a combination of prevailing B&B prices in your area and your B&B's individual features.

> *Modest to Average:* Rooms are clean, comfortable, and pleasant. Some amenities are included. Single range $55–$150; double range $65–$160.

> *Above Average to Luxury:* Outstanding to extraordinary accommodations in a good location. Superior aesthetic features. Rooms are tastefully furnished. A variety of amenities are included. Single range $85–$260; double range $95–$300.

Whether your bed and breakfast rooms should be at the low end or the high end of the suggested price range in your category depends in part on the amenities that you make available to your guests. It is best to adjust the price of the room to include the cost of providing the amenities that will be enjoyed by the majority of your guests. True, some guests will not watch the television in their bedroom, and some won't care to ride the bicycle you provide. But for those who do, you can make them feel a lot more comfortable by making these amenities part of the whole package deal. (Charging a separate fee for each typical amenity could make your guests feel as if they're on the meter every time they make a move to enjoy what your B&B has to offer.)

Typical amenities, such as an in-room television or guest refrigerator, should be included in the overall room price. (Also check the section "The Amenities" earlier in this chapter.) The more amenities you can offer, the higher the price you can charge.

If your bed and breakfast offers extras that are above and beyond the typical amenities, you should charge for these separately. Some hosts arrange tours and entertainment for an additional fee. Some allow guests to use the washer and dryer for their personal laundry. Others offer to babysit for guests' children. And still others rent out sports equipment (skates, skis). Then there are those hosts who offer to put their own special skills to work for guests (such as yoga instruction or foreign language translation). All these are services that go beyond what a guest normally expects in a bed and breakfast situation.

Because many of your guests will not want babysitting services or yoga instruction, these types of unusual amenities should not be included in the room price.

For your overall room price, there are times when the rate should be adjusted: a third adult staying in the same room on a cot (usually $10–$20 extra); a child under twelve years of age staying in the same room with parents ($10–$20 extra); a pet ($10–$20 extra). If your bed and breakfast is located in a resort area, your off-season rates should be lowered 20 to 25 percent. And hosts usually add a surcharge ($10–$15) for a guest who is staying one night only.

Now you should have an approximate amount calculated for your guest rooms. The next thing you should do is compare your prices with those of area hotels and motels. A survey of hosts and reservation service agencies throughout North America shows that an overwhelming majority of B&B accommodations cost less than those of nearby hotels and motels. So if you find that the estimated prices you have just come up with exceed what local commercial establishments are charging, you are probably asking too much and need to rework your prices.

It's also wise to take a look at what other bed and breakfast hosts in your location charge and compare your estimated prices with their rates. If your prices differ greatly, you should have very good reasons to justify them. Before guests make reservations at a bed and breakfast, they usually shop around to see what's available for the best price. That is only good sense. If your prices seem too high or even too low, you can expect that they will wonder why.

Coming up with the right price is never an easy task because it depends on such a variety of factors. Some new hosts tend to price their rooms too low. "My bit of advice to new hosts is to make your fee high enough to cover the service you give," says an experienced host from West Virginia. "I did not. I started too low and gave so much. Our house is one of West Virginia's grand old houses, and my guests walk on my Oriental rugs and use my best china, crystal, and silver. I serve a good, big home-cooked breakfast. Not only do they have my house, but 225 acres to wander over with my ducks, cats, dogs, and cows to feed, my garden to enjoy. They can also fish in my two ponds." After a time she adjusted her prices to better reflect the quality of accommodation her guests were receiving. "Print prices

To check rates of local B&Bs, go to:
www.bbonline.com
www.bedandbreakfast.com

on a separate rate sheet or put a range on your brochure," suggests Betsy Grater, owner of Betsy's Bed & Breakfast in Baltimore, Maryland. That way, if you do change your prices, you won't have to throw away hundreds of brochures and go to the expense of printing new ones with the adjusted prices. And keep the rates on your Web site current.

One reservation service manager offers new hosts this advice for pricing their rooms: "Don't charge so much as to shut yourself out of any business. But don't charge so little that you are giving away your time and effort." After all the calculations are done, this is the best test of your prices.

Chapter Four
Getting Connected

Reservation Service Agencies

"Join a reservation service." This advice comes from a host registered with a reservation service agency in Philadelphia. "I could not have started without it," she says.

It's good advice. For new hosts, getting connected with a local or national reservation service agency (RSA) has enormous advantages. RSA personnel have the experience, know-how, and resources to help new hosts set up and run their bed and breakfast homes. Most local RSAs do practically all the nitty-gritty work that an individual host would have to do if he or she were to go it alone. As the owner of an RSA in New York puts it: The reservation service agency takes care of "everything that is necessary except hosting the guest."

The primary function of a reservation service agency is just what the name indicates—it's an agency that makes reservations for guests in bed and breakfast homes. A host pays a membership fee (usually), plus a commission to the RSA for each guest referred through the service. Some RSAs represent hosts in a particular city or town exclusively; some are statewide; others are regional, covering a certain area of a state or several neighboring states. As a new host, you will find that one of your biggest problems will be getting guests to come to your home. If an RSA does no more than solve this problem for you, it's worth the amount that you pay the agency, especially in the early stages when your bed and break-fast is essentially unknown. Beyond the very valuable service of connecting guests with your B&B, an RSA generally offers other kinds of assistance helpful to both new and experienced hosts.

"We handle all the bothersome details," says the manager of a Massachusetts RSA. These include confirmations and deposits and local, regional, and national advertising. "Descriptions and directions and requirements are forwarded to guests without troubling the hosts," says the manager of a Connecticut reservation service. "Hosts don't have to do the telephone and administrative work of arranging reservations," says the manager of an RSA in Massachusetts. "We do all the paperwork for them and supply them with receipts, booklets, pamphlets, etcetera," says the manager of a Philadelphia reservation service. "Hosts have the advantage of our careful screening and ability to match guests with hosts," say the managers of a Virginia reservation service. The manager of a New York RSA cites anonymity as a major advantage to hosts who wish to protect their privacy; RSAs will give out a host's home address and telephone number only when a reservation is confirmed. The list goes on. A good reservation service agency can make the life of a host much, much easier.

So if an RSA is the answer to your prayers, you might be wondering why some hosts choose to stay independent. They give different reasons. Some hosts have the time, the desire, and the know-how to do all the work themselves; they enjoy being totally self-reliant. Some hosts are located in areas where no local reservation service agency exists. And some hosts are reluctant to list with an RSA because their prices are so low that once they deduct the percentage that goes to the RSA for a commission for placing each guest and then deduct their expenses, there's just not much left. And the Internet offers an enticing way for hosts to market their B&Bs directly to guests with little trouble or expense.

So, yes, a host can survive, even thrive, without ever connecting with an RSA. The question is: What's best for you? Are you willing and able to answer all the inquiries you will be receiving by telephone and e-mail (including those that do not result in reservations), to print and distribute your own brochures, to do your own advertising, to create and maintain your own Web site, to handle the reservations yourself, to send out confirmations? Some hosts just don't have the time, energy, and skill to take care of all these details, and some honestly do not enjoy these aspects of bed and breakfast, although they love the actual hosting. Consider your own situation, your likes and dislikes, your skills. Do you want and need some help? If so, contact local RSAs to see what they could do for you. Consult the listing of reservation service agencies in appendix 2 to locate those near you. Be aware that an RSA in your area might not be looking for new hosts in your particular location. This is due mainly to the law of supply and demand. If there are not enough hosts in a certain location to meet the demand from prospective guests for lodging there, then the RSA manager will look for more hosts. But if there are too many hosts and not many guests, then the referrals from the RSA will be spread among them. For this reason some RSA managers try to maintain an optimum number of hosts to make the referral system work to the hosts' advantage.

There could be more than one RSA in your area. Check them all out according to the guidelines given in the following section. Use the "Checklist for Interviewing Reservation Services Agencies" on the following page to help you in the interview process. Talk with the manager, ask a lot of questions about how the RSA operates, check the RSA's Web site, and then make the decision that's best for your bed and breakfast.

Does the RSA Do Its Job Well?

For a reservation service, doing its job well means having a fully operational office that can handle all aspects of making and confirming reservations, plus outreach, networking, promoting good community relations, and more.

When you interview various reservation services to represent your B&B, find out about office hours and staffing. Does the RSA have regular weekday business hours? Additional hours on evenings and weekends are a plus for your business. Does a staff member answer the phone? Is there an answering machine or voice-mail system that offers a warm and friendly greeting to callers? How promptly are telephone and e-mail messages returned?

A reservation service that is represented on the Internet allows potential guests instantaneous access to information about the B&Bs it represents. In this day and age, a well-maintained Web site is a must for an RSA. Here, reservation services can profile the individual B&Bs they represent, including photos and descriptions, post a room availability chart, and invite potential guests to fill out an inquiry form or request a reservation online.

A reservation service with a fax machine can send a detailed description of your B&B, complete with an illustration, to potential guests who do not have Internet access, giving it an edge over competitors. A fax machine can also facilitate the application process and allow the reservation to be confirmed within minutes after it has been made.

Inquire how other business operations are handled, and use that information to evaluate how efficiently the RSA can do its job. For example, does the staff use the latest computer software to track reservations and keep accounting records? Overall, look for a highly organized, friendly office with state-of-the-art technology.

Checklist for Interviewing Reservation Service Agencies

RSA's name _____

Contact person _____

Address _____

_____

Telephone number _____

E-mail address _____

Web site _____

Number of staff members _____   Office hours _____

Office services:

_____ Answering machine/voice mail   _____ Live telephone coverage

_____ Fax machine   _____ Prompt reply to messages

_____ E-mail

Professional affiliations:

_____ Professional Association of Innkeepers International (PAII)

_____ State/Regional B&B association

_____ The National Network of Bed and Breakfast Reservation Services (TNN)

Business affiliations:

_____ Chamber of commerce

_____ Tourist board/visitors bureau

Outreach:

_____ RSA brochure (current)

_____ RSA directory of host homes (up-to-date)

_____ Web site

_____ Telephone directory listing (White Pages and Yellow Pages)

_____ Listed in online B&B directories

_____ Newsletter

Guidebooks in which RSA has a listing:

_____

_____

_____

_____

Recent articles in which RSA is mentioned:

_____

_____

_____

_____

Recent advertising placed by RSA:

_____

_____

_____

_____

Host arrangements:

Commission: _____

_____Inspection fee for new hosts ($_____)

_____Annual membership fee ($_____)

_____Host contract required

_____Booking fee ($_____)

New host assistance:

_____

_____

_____

_____

What Assistance Does the RSA Offer New Hosts?

Someone who is just starting out as a host needs advice about how to do it. The manager of a local RSA will usually come to your home to see if it has the right kind of setup for accommodating guests, and he or she will talk to you about bed and breakfast hosting. Some RSAs provide this initial consultation for free; others charge a fee, usually between $20 and $50. If you pass the inspection and interview to the RSA's satisfaction and your home is located in an area where it will attract guests, the RSA will be interested in listing your home. What you need to know now is what kind of help you can expect from the RSA to get ready for that first guest. At the very least the RSA will provide you with a listing of the standards you are expected to meet and the guidelines you are expected to follow. Some RSAs, however, provide more than this.

"We offer one-on-one training, a beginner's manual on hosting, and Monday-through-Friday office hours for new hosts to call with questions," says the manager of a Boston RSA. The owner of a reservation service agency in the Northwest offers "an initial two- to three-hour session for training, then ongoing help and assistance, including copies of books on hosting." A number of RSAs, in fact, have developed their own booklets or host packets on how to be a host.

The manager of a Philadelphia RSA likes to give new hosts a good example. "First, I show them my B&B," she says. Then she spends time with them discussing how to turn their own home into what a B&B should be. If you wish, an RSA manager will usually give suggestions for making your guest rooms more comfortable and attractive and will offer opinions about decorating, both minor and extensive. "I have just signed on a couple who have just poured their foundation, and we worked out their B&B from blueprints!" says the manager of a reservation service agency in Massachusetts.

To help new hosts get ready to handle various types of situations that they can expect to encounter with their guests, a Cape Cod reservation service agency arranges role-plays so that hosts can practice typical scenarios. Then when it's time for the real thing, they're ready. The manager of one reservation service in Boston has even been asked by a new host to be at her home when she greeted her very first guest. "She was nervous about it," she says. Having a representative of the RSA with her made the first time easier.

New hosts also need to be apprised of the local regulations governing zoning and fire and safety guidelines, as well as tax and insurance information. A reservation service agency has already had to investigate these, so the agency can give you the guidance you need to have in order to operate a bed and breakfast home in your community.

What Kind of Ongoing Assistance Does the RSA Provide?

There are some responsibilities that automatically go along with the RSA's job of making reservations for guests at its bed and breakfast homes. These include answering telephone, e-mail, and mail inquiries; screening and matching guests with hosts (see "Screening Your Guests" in chapter 7); sending confirmations to guests who make reservations; and promoting bed and breakfast through the distribution of brochures and advertising.

You should expect these services, done well, from any reservation service agency that you choose to join. It's not unusual, though, for an RSA manager to go above and beyond the call of duty. Some send regular newsletters and reprints of helpful information to hosts and help hosts with recordkeeping and tax preparation, and some supply year-end cumulative records of reservations. A Connecticut reservation service offers "listening, guidance, and sympathy" to hosts who need to talk about a problem. And the manager of Blue Ridge Bed & Breakfast in Virginia says that she's even helped a host clean at the last minute to get ready for a guest!

Any "extras" a host receives from an RSA really depends on the person who is running the service, and is determined by that person's strengths and total time commitment to RSA activities. Where these extra benefits are concerned, there can be wide differences among RSAs. So do not expect them, but feel lucky if you find that your RSA manager is the kind of person who can and will go beyond the basics needed for your bed and breakfast business.

How Does the RSA Publicize Its Services to Potential Guests?

For an individual host, one of the main advantages of joining a reservation service agency is that the agency takes the responsibility for drumming up business. While the individual host remains comfortably anonymous, the RSA reaches out to the public in search of potential guests, doing all the work and bearing all the expense.

If you are considering joining an RSA, take a look at the available bed and breakfast guidebooks to see if the RSA is listed in them, and with the correct address and telephone number. Many people looking for a bed and breakfast use guidebooks as a source of information. An RSA manager has to be conscientious about supplying the authors with all the necessary up-to-date information for each new edition. (Otherwise, an RSA could be listed with an out-of-date address or phone number, or not included at all.) A new RSA especially has to make sure that the information gets into the right hands at the right time. If your area RSA is listed in a selection of guidebooks, you can be assured that prospective guests will be able to find and contact the RSA easily—and your bed and breakfast, in turn, will benefit.

Check the Yellow Pages of your phone book under the section headed "Bed and Breakfast" to see if the reservation service agency is listed there. Inclusion makes the RSA readily accessible to people seeking a bed and breakfast.

The literature that the reservation service agency prints and distributes will be representing your bed and breakfast home, so examine it closely. Does the RSA have a brochure that is attractive and professional? Is the artwork appealing, well executed, and appropriate? Is the information easy to read and to understand? Are the name, address, and telephone number of the RSA printed clearly, with office hours included? Does the brochure explain how to make a reservation?

Find out where the RSA distributes its brochures. One Virginia reservation service, for example, supplies brochures to all welcome centers run by that state. A Louisiana reservation service agency makes special rack cards to be placed in the literature display racks located at all the state visitors information centers. Bed & Breakfast Atlanta reaches out to local institutions, businesses, and special-events coordinators.

Ask the RSA manager where the agency places advertisements to let travelers know that bed and breakfast accommodations are available in the area. A reservation service in New England, for example, advertises in magazines and travel guides that profile that geographical area. Five Pennsylvania RSAs advertise jointly in such publications of national interest as *Better Homes & Gardens,* the *New York Times,* and *Country Magazine.* The managers of one of these RSAs, called Rest & Repast, have found it worthwhile to advertise in publications directed to Penn State University alumni and parents because so many of its host homes are located near Penn State. Such specific advertising that targets the travelers who come to your area frequently can be very effective.

A lot of great publicity comes not from paid advertisements but from articles written about bed and breakfast. Does the RSA make it a point to get in touch with writers for local and national publications to try to interest them in doing a story about bed and breakfast? "Say yes if we ask you to give a travel writer a free night," a New York reservation service tells its hosts. Outreach to the press should be part of the promotion plan undertaken by an RSA.

Find out whether the RSA has a Web site. As more and more people search the Internet for the information they want, a reservation service agency that advertises in this medium has an edge over the competition. Consider the advantages of being a host listed with one of the following reservation services:

"I have developed an Internet page that lists all the B&Bs that I represent along with a description, prices, and a picture of each one. There is also a map with all the B&Bs' general locations on it," says the manager of a reservation service in Arizona.

"We have moved aggressively into the Internet as a vehicle to have a wider audience worldwide. We now have all our hosts on the World Wide Web, where we also have either pictures or line drawings of their properties. This has made a big hit with hosts who cannot afford to list individually but are seen on our Web site. Many guests have complimented us on the extensive and complete listings," says the manager of Bed & Breakfast Cape Cod.

"Our hosts have an option of purchasing a Web site within our site for a onetime fee with no rent. We pay the rent. They get their own Internet address to use, too," says the owner of a Pennsylvania reservation service.

Try an Internet search to find out how savvy an RSA manager is about listing it with the search engines that potential guests are sure to use. Type the RSA's name into the search box provided by www.google.com or www.dogpile.com, and see if the search engine locates the RSA. Another approach is to type the words "bed and breakfast reservations" plus the name of your town, region, or state into a search box and see if the RSA is among those located.

It makes sense that the publicity done by your reservation service agency will affect the number of guests that your bed and breakfast will receive. If the RSA's overall promotion and publicity are good, a host who decides to list with the RSA will be at a definite advantage.

Is the RSA Affiliated with Any Organizations?

Just as an individual host can benefit from joining with other hosts, so can an RSA increase its effectiveness by affiliating with appropriate organizations. If you are considering joining an RSA, investigate what affiliations the RSA has that could benefit your bed and breakfast.

There is only one existing organization just for RSAs—The National Network of Bed and Breakfast Reservation Services (TNN). This organization has criteria that members must meet to enforce high standards within the bed and breakfast industry. The National Network is made up of members who work together to promote bed and breakfast, to maintain high standards, and to deal with problems as they arise. The National Network selects one RSA per geographical area as its representative. Each member RSA is responsible for inspecting every individual B&B it represents. Visit TNN's Web site for more information (www.go-lodging.com).

In addition to bed and breakfast associations, membership in the local or state tourist bureau can be extremely beneficial to a reservation service agency and the hosts it represents. Through literature, referrals, and their own Web sites, tourist bureaus promote bed and breakfast as a way to encourage tourism in their jurisdictions. Many tourist bureau Web sites now offer links to reservation services' Web sites, making it easy for potential guests to locate accommodations. And very often the bureau will provide maps, calendars, and sightseeing brochures free of charge or at a low cost to its members. "We are an active member of the Worcester County Convention & Visitors Bureau, and it has sent us the major portion of our business," says the owner of an RSA in central Massachusetts. "It is the best investment I could have made. They provide me with all the information about the area, which I distribute to my host homes. Tourism is booming in this part of our state, and my host homes are reaping the benefits."

The chamber of commerce is also an important affiliation for a local RSA. A number of chambers are cooperating with local RSA managers to help new hosts set up their bed and breakfast homes. An RSA that becomes a member of the chamber of commerce can establish important ties in the community where the bed and breakfast homes operate.

From more guests to free maps, a new host can directly benefit from joining an RSA that is well integrated into the community and in touch with the national bed and breakfast scene. Finding out what affiliations an RSA has will tell you about the resources that agency is in a position to offer its hosts. The more an RSA networks, the better off you'll be.

Does the RSA Encourage Communication among Its Hosts?

Remember that once you join a reservation service agency, you become part of a network of bed and breakfast homes, usually sight unseen. Yet every one of these hosts who belong to the same RSA as you do automatically affects your bed and breakfast business. It's important for you to be confident that all your "brothers and sisters" are as conscientious about hosting as you are, working hard to keep up the standards of comfort, cleanliness, and congeniality set by the RSA. You have a reputation to maintain.

In recognition of this, some RSA managers are making an effort to give their hosts the opportunity to meet one another and to establish a support network among them. Some arrange "house tours" in which hosts can visit one another's homes not only to get acquainted but also to compare notes and share ideas about hosting. Some RSAs organize annual get-togethers that are part business and part social. One New York reservation service gives awards at these events: An "Honored Host" award goes to the member who hosted one hundred nights during the previous year. The "Preferred Host Award" goes to the member who received the highest percentage of compliments from guests' letters and evaluations. "We have an annual host ice cream festival, where we gather, have fun, meet one another, trade ideas, and get ready for the upcoming season. It is a fun, productive time for all of us. Attendance is always excellent," says the manager of a Pennsylvania reservation service.

By encouraging communication among its hosts, an RSA can play an important role in developing the kind of personal commitment among them that will work to the benefit of all members. This is the kind of RSA a new host should look for.

Does the RSA Keep in Touch with Former Guests?

Many hosts report that a large percentage of the guests who stay with them are repeat customers. Some say that up to *50 percent* of their guests have visited before! This means that once your bed and breakfast has established itself, it could be largely dependent on people who have already enjoyed your hospitality. But be warned: Your guests cannot be trusted to remember your name or your B&B's name, let alone your address and telephone number. And if they have trouble finding you again, they could end up somewhere else instead of at your B&B. To refresh their memories every once in a while, either you or your RSA has to keep in touch with former guests. (See "Memories" in chapter 8.)

Find out if the RSA has any method for communicating with former guests on a regular basis. An RSA in Massachusetts, for example, sends an updated host-home directory to former guests. A reservation service in Florida sends pictures, cards, and brochures to people who have made reservations in the past. A Rhode Island reservation service provides a discount coupon to returning guests.

One RSA in central New York sends out notes on holidays and lets former guests know in advance about special seasonal attractions in the area. Rest & Repast in Pennsylvania places a large number of football fans in host homes near Penn State University. Many come back each year because the RSA has a follow-up plan. "Football guests who have booked at least two seasons and two games each year get a letter in December telling them that they have priority booking until March 1 for next year's football season," says the RSA manager. Another manager also ties her notes in with the special interests of former guests. "If I know someone is interested in, for example, the Bach Choir, I will send information about the next time they are performing in the area," she says.

Some RSAs rely on their hosts to maintain communications with former guests, or they offer a newsletter distributed via e-mail or posted on their Web site. It is an added bonus for a host to list with a reservation service agency that can, and does, follow up on guests who have made reservations through that agency sometime in the past.

What Obligations Does an RSA Have to Its Hosts?

Beyond the assistance that an RSA provides to its hosts, there are a number of professional courtesies that the RSA manager should extend to the hosts as part of a good business relationship. These are outlined here by Ellen Madison, a host who grew up in a home that accommodated tourists and who is now the operator of her own bed and breakfast home in Westerly, Rhode Island, called Woody Hill Guest House.

Accessibility is at the top of the list. "RSAs should be available to their hosts as much as possible," says Ellen, "particularly in the evenings and on weekends when the need for an immediate clarification or a referral is probably the greatest. If nothing else, an answering machine should be in use and calls returned as quickly as possible." E-mail and a fax machine are also musts to facilitate good communication between a reservation service agency and the hosts it represents.

Ellen goes on to say that RSAs should get back to hosts as soon as possible in the event of cancellations or deposits that never arrive. If the host is not notified of a change in plans, he or she will go ahead and make all the necessary preparations for a guest's arrival—cleaning the house, clearing the schedule, and buying food. For an RSA to let the host know at the last minute that no one is coming doesn't mean much when you've got a refrigerator full of honeydew melon. Now you've either got to eat it or let it go to waste. "And honeydew melon for a week is very boring," Ellen says.

Ellen advises RSAs to be aware of their hosts' financial situations when determining their rates. "They should be aware of the costs to a host for operating a B&B, which will be different depending on all sorts of conditions—whether the host is single or married, whether he or she is trying to earn a living by operating a B&B, how much investment the host had to make initially." Room rates that are too low might not cover a host's costs; and a commission that is too high might take away the possibility of making a profit. And, too, if payment in full is made directly to the RSA, prompt remittance to the host is in order.

It is only fair to mention that there have been a few (and thankfully only a few) complaints about certain reservation service agencies because they did not pay the host promptly, they did not remit the total amount due, or the check issued by the RSA manager bounced. One of these RSAs is now out of business. Then there was the disagreeable fellow who managed to alienate an unusually large number of associates within the short span of time he was operating an RSA—which is now in good hands. As a host, you should insist on the professional treatment due to you and your guests by your reservation service agency. Report any problems to the associations with which the RSA is affiliated. On the whole, RSAs operate efficiently and to the benefit of the hosts they represent. We can expect that they will stay that way if people involved in the bed and breakfast industry continue to safeguard the high standards that have been set.

What Obligations Does a Host Have to His or Her RSA?

Just as you can expect professional courtesies from your RSA, so should the RSA be able to expect certain courtesies from you as one of its hosts, beyond your responsibility to maintain the standards set by the RSA for comfort, cleanliness, and congeniality.

Again, accessibility is very important. "Have an answering machine and check it often," says the manager of one reservation agency, stressing the importance of responding quickly to phone calls from your RSA. "Travelers want to make their reservations *now,* not the day after tomorrow or even tomorrow. The hosts most often available are naturally booked first and most," adds the owner of a reservation service agency in Louisiana. Remember that most RSAs will check with a host first before confirming a reservation. This means that a prospective guest is usually waiting to hear via a return phone call or e-mail whether the bed and breakfast he or she wants is available. If a definite answer is too long in coming, there's nothing to stop the person from making a few more calls to other places to try to confirm a reservation. The manager of Bed & Breakfast Hawaii offers this advice for speeding up the booking process: "Many hosts have added fax machines and e-mail, allowing for instant booking confirmations."

If you list with an RSA, the agency will expect your bed and breakfast to be available for guests unless there is an emergency situation or if you are scheduled to be out of town for a vacation or some other reason. Some reservation services even note availability on their Web sites. "If a host is almost never in or turns down a request to take guests too often (we keep records), we tend to call hosts who are reachable and who will take guests even though it may be an inconvenience," says the owner of a Canadian reservation service. "If their personal life is not to be interfered with—such as on long holidays, or when personal guests or family members are home (the list goes on)—I ask the hosts if there is any point in continuing to offer B&B on a whenever-it-suits-me basis." If you really want to be a host, you can't take your responsibility lightly. An RSA may drop you in favor of hosts who are more reliable.

Being organized is almost as important as being accessible. "Keep a good calendar," advises the manager of an RSA in Boston. If you've booked guests, you've got to remember that they're coming, and you've got to be careful not to double-book your rooms! If you're disorganized, get organized fast or you're in for problems, and so is your RSA.

One of the major concerns of many RSA managers is that some of their hosts try to go around the agency when former guests want to stay at their homes again. Sometimes a guest will contact the host directly because he or she happens to have the name and address handy and feels like an old friend. The host, in turn, tries to keep the arrangement a secret from the RSA so that he or she can avoid paying the commission. This is unprofessional behavior that undercuts the very structure within the bed and breakfast industry that allows individual hosts a measure of the privacy and protection they want and need. The owner of a reservation service in Hawaii identifies this as the biggest problem RSAs face: "It causes the reservation service to constantly search for new clients. Hosts don't understand if the service is not there, the new customers will dry up." So if a former guest contacts you directly, do the right thing: Contact the RSA that originally processed the reservation and route the guest through the procedure that you and the RSA have agreed on.

Does the RSA Require a Host Contract?

You can expect that any RSA with which you wish to list your bed and breakfast home will ask you to sign a host contract that outlines certain obligations on your part and explains the services that the RSA will provide to you.

Items that a host contract usually covers are the membership fee and the commission to be paid to the RSA, the procedure for handling reservations and confirmations, deposit and cancellation policies, and the duration of the agreement and renewal and termination procedures—as well as any other items that might be desired by the RSA, such as insurance requirements for individual hosts or the right of the RSA to make periodic inspections of its host homes. Some contracts stipulate that a host must list with that agency exclusively, ruling out referrals from any other agency. Other RSAs have no such stipulation, and hosts are free to list with more than one RSA if they wish and to do as much independent business as they feel like. The ones that require an exclusive arrangement have their reasons. According to the owner of one California RSA, one of the main reasons is that the RSA needs to be almost certain that a room is available before taking the time, the trouble, and the expense to describe it to a potential guest, interesting the person in one particular bed and breakfast, only to find that the reservation is refused by the host. Then it's back to square one—more time, more trouble, more expense. For this reason RSAs generally prefer that a host list with them exclusively even if the host contract does not require it. "Be an exclusive member so that I can confirm a reservation on the first call," says the manager of one Midwestern reservation service agency.

Some B&B hosts choose to list with more than one reservation service. LesLee Solberg, owner of Denali View B&B in Talkeetna, Alaska, finds that the biggest problem she has encountered with this practice is the bookkeeping that goes along with it. "Everyone seems to be different. With competition as it is, I try to use my B&B philosophy and make it as easy as I can for an RSA to use our service. If it means bending a little to accommodate an RSA's payment schedule, we will do so; however, we do have some rules about payments that we adhere to until they have established a business relationship with us (one season). Then we can go onto their payment schedule."

What Fees Are Paid to the RSA for Its Services?

You can't get something for nothing, of course. If you wish to take advantage of the services that a reservation service agency will provide for your bed and breakfast, you must support the effort. Most RSAs have a payment structure that involves, first, an annual membership fee and, second, a commission for each guest that the agency places with a host. Fees vary. A recent survey of reservation service agencies across the United States showed that about 50 percent charged an annual membership fee of between $25 and $100, while a third charged no fee at all. Many reservation service agencies charge a commission equal to 25 percent of a guest's bill.

Fees collected by a reservation service agency from its hosts go to pay for advertising costs; telephone expenses; printing and copying literature; postage; any city, county, or state licenses that might be necessary; professional fees for membership in tourist bureaus, the chamber of commerce, and bed and breakfast associations; and, of course, the time the manager and other staff spend on the work. There are long hours. "My phone rings until 11:00 at night," says the manager of a reservation service in Massachusetts. Others answer e-mails in the wee hours, an experience not unusual at all, based on reports from RSA managers throughout North America.

"When our hosts open the door to greet their guests, they will know the following: when the guests are expected, how long they will stay, how much deposit was paid, how much hosts should collect, their reason for coming, what their age group is, their interests, their food preferences, their allergies, their jobs or backgrounds. We do have a fully staffed office year-round with regular office hours to take calls and make reservations. We work very hard for our commission, and we earn it," says the owner of one reservation service.

More than one RSA manager has pointed out the low profit margin from their activities on behalf of hosts. This is because of the relatively low fees charged hosts and the high expenses that the RSA has. Be aware that many RSA managers are also bed and breakfast hosts who established reservation service agencies in their areas because they saw a need for it. "My B&B room supports my RSA business or I'd be out of business," says the owner of a Florida RSA. So before you balk at paying a membership fee and commissions to an RSA, consider how much it would cost you otherwise if you were to take care of all the advertising, mailing, printing, and telephone bills yourself. In the vast majority of cases, the fee structure is quite a bargain for what your bed and breakfast will receive in return.

Special-focus B&B Groups

One way to attract larger numbers of guests to your bed and breakfast is to reach out to people who share your special interests. Already a number of reservation service agencies and specialized programs have been established for the purpose of providing bed and breakfast accommodations to people who have a common interest. Some are national organizations, others are regional. Some advertise widely, some publicize exclusively among their own memberships. Listed in this section are some bed and breakfast organizations that have a special focus. If you believe that your background, interests, or affiliations qualify you for listing your bed and breakfast with any of these, write or call for more information.

After checking this list, it's a good idea to set out on your own trail of discovery for others. Check with any social or professional group to which you belong to learn if it might already have a bed and breakfast program for its members. (If not, you could take the initiative to organize one.)

It is important to note that B&B groups of this type generally operate according to the true bed and breakfast spirit—in which money is not of the utmost importance. You can expect that any income that you receive as a result of affiliating with a special-focus bed and breakfast organization will be minimal, and you will have to pay a nominal membership fee. The value for you lies in the goodwill that you will have the opportunity to establish among a number of people, as well as the good word that will spread about your bed and breakfast as a result. And if you are not entirely sure that you want to open your own B&B, participating in a special-focus group for a time can give you some perspective.

Hosts who are fifty years of age or older may join a membership club that provides bed and breakfast accommodations for one another:

Evergreen Bed and Breakfast Club
201 West Broad Street, #181
Falls Church, VA 22046
(815) 456–3111
www.evergreenclub.com

Some bed and breakfast groups were founded in the spirit of brotherhood and sister-hood. Homecomings is for Unitarian Universalists and others of like mind.

UU're Home
43 Vermont Court
Asheville, NC 28806
(828) 281–3253
www.uurehome.com

Teachers and others in the field of education are invited to participate in a worldwide network of members who offer accommodations to one another through opportunities for hosting, guest visits, home exchanges, and house-sitting.

Educators Bed & Breakfast Travel Network
P.O. Box 5279
Eugene, OR 97405
(800) 956–4822
www.educatorstravel.com

National Bed and Breakfast Associations

New hosts can benefit considerably by connecting with one or more of the national bed and breakfast associations in existence. The guidebooks and directories published by these organizations, and their Web sites, are directed to prospective guests to help them find the kind of bed and breakfast accommodations they are seeking. As a member, your B&B would be included in these well-known publications and Web sites, enabling you to easily reach thousands of potential guests. The national bed and breakfast associations are listed here.

Professional Association of Innkeepers International

The Professional Association of Innkeepers International (PAII) is a trade association for country inn and bed and breakfast innkeepers with additional membership categories designed for aspiring innkeepers and those associated with the industry. Members receive the monthly *innkeeping* newsletter, discounts on industry publications and products, and an invitation to an annual conference that features a session specifically for aspiring innkeepers. For information, contact:

> Professional Association of Innkeepers International
> 207 White Horse Pike
> Haddon Heights, NJ 08035
> (856) 310–1102
> www.paii.org

Select Registry: Distinguished Inns of North America

Someone who has owned or run an inn with at least six guest rooms for a minimum of three years is eligible to apply for membership in the Select Registry. This association requires mandatory inspections as part of its quality-assurance program. The registry publishes a directory and maintains a Web site with profiles of member B&Bs.

> Select Registry
> 501 East Michigan Avenue
> Marshall, MI 49068
> (800) 344–5244
> (269) 789–0393
> www.selectregistry.com

African American Association of Innkeepers International

The stated mission of the African American Association of Innkeepers International is "to provide a standard of excellence in the industry and serve as a resource for aspiring innkeepers of color." Dedicated to increasing public awareness of African-American–

owned inns, the association acts as a support and networking group for current and aspiring innkeepers. The association also holds conferences with sessions devoted to the process of securing loans and other start-up concerns.

African American Association of Innkeepers International
(no mailing address)
(877) 422–5777
africanamericaninns.com

State and Regional Bed and Breakfast Associations

Many bed and breakfast hosts join together to form state and regional associations for mutual benefit and support, to set guidelines for bed and breakfast operations and ensure quality control through periodic inspections, to share ideas and solve problems, to act as a lobbying force when necessary, and to increase community awareness of bed and breakfast. A number of state associations publish booklets containing descriptions of their member B&Bs. Booklets are distributed free at state welcome centers. Most also have Web sites with an individual posting and/or link for each member. Many associations hold conferences and trade shows and offer workshops on various topics, including starting a B&B. Some sell packets of information for aspiring innkeepers, compile cookbooks, and maintain listings of B&Bs for sale. Some associations participate in group buying to purchase items at bulk rates (such as paper towels, soap, and sheets) and engage in group advertising in newspapers and magazines.

Listed in appendix 3 are some of the state associations that have been established. For regional associations, ask your state contact for a referral, or check the Web sites noted below. If one exists in your area, find out its criteria for membership, how it operates, and its benefits to you as a host. Some groups restrict membership to those hosts whose bed and breakfast operations qualify as full-time commercial "businesses"; others welcome membership from owners of small commercial inns as well as from hosts who use only one or two rooms in their private homes for bed and breakfast. A few limit their membership to bed and breakfast homes that share a specific characteristic, such as historic homes. Most associations have standards that a B&B must meet before joining, along with an inspection program.

Be advised that association members often rotate responsibilities among themselves, so contact information changes frequently and may not always include a phone number and/or Web site. Because of this, some of the listings may be outdated by the time you try to reach the association in your area. To find current information, check the lists provided on the Web sites indicated in the box on this page.

For lists of B&B associations, visit:
www.bbonline.com
www.bedandbreakfast.com
www.bbcanada.com

Internet Discussion Groups

"I had a lot of trouble getting started. It was hard to get information, and there was no one to talk to," says one host about her experience in trying to set up a bed and breakfast home. This is not uncommon. There are resources out there, but you have to know where to look. Once you connect with a reservation service agency, you can rely upon the RSA for information and guidance. But maybe there is no RSA in your area. Or maybe you're just beginning to think about the idea of hosting. Where can you turn if you just want to ask a simple question? What if you want someone's honest opinion about the advantages of getting involved with a reservation service agency? What if you want to find out if joining a tourist bureau or chamber of commerce has paid off in guests for anyone else before you go ahead and do it? What if you want to quietly investigate local rules and regulations concerning home-based businesses and don't know how to go about it? One of your best sources of information is another host, someone who has already done what you're about to do, or another aspiring innkeeper who is doing his or her B&B "homework," just as you are.

The need of new or aspiring hosts to talk to someone experienced with bed and breakfast was the inspiration behind the Helping Hands Network, established by this book's first edition in the mid-1980s. For more than ten years, this informal network of hosts gave advice through phone conversations and letters to those new to the B&B field. But times have changed. Communication is now much faster and easier via cyberspace. So, starting with the sixth edition, the Helping Hands Network was disbanded. Taking its place are Internet discussion groups specifically for aspiring innkeepers.

The best discussion group for aspiring and active innkeepers is called B&B Talk, which

> For the B&B Talk forum, visit:
> http://forum.thebandblady.com

is moderated by three top experts in the hospitality industry: Kit Cassingham, owner of Sage Blossom Consulting and editor of *Innfo eZine,* an electronic newsletter devoted to B&B; Bobbi Zane, editor of *Yellow Brick Road,* an electronic newsletter for aspiring innkeepers; and Steve Wirt, owner of Inngenious B&B Web Site Design and Promotion. Discussions cover buying or selling a B&B, marketing, daily operations, and more—offering an invaluable resource for any aspiring host.

Resources

Whether you are just beginning to think about offering bed and breakfast or are already an experienced host, it is always worth your while to check out the available resources so that you can keep up with what's happening within the bed and breakfast industry. The Professional Association of Innkeepers International sells a variety of educational materials and reports. And don't overlook personal experience as a good way to learn about what's going on in the industry. "Too many prospective hosts have never been in a B&B," says Mary Hill of Guesthouses Bed & Breakfast, Inc., in Charlottesville, Virginia. "Stay in B&Bs every chance you can."

Newsletters

To keep abreast of new ideas and developments that could affect you, subscribe to newsletters directed toward current or aspiring innkeepers. Listed here is a selection of these publications, which are offered in electronic format.

Yellow Brick Road, devoted to those planning to open a B&B, offers an array of topics that could include anything and everything from parking concerns to inspections, how to answer a phone properly, time management of housekeeping chores, and recordkeeping. *Innfo eZine* provides in-depth educational articles on nitty-gritty topics of interest, such as ADA compliance, insurance, environmental concerns, and finances. *Innkeeping* is circulated to members of the Professional Association of Innkeepers International (PAII). Information could include tips on processing guests' credit cards, simplifying life in the kitchen, and sample bookkeeping tables. *Arrington's Bed & Breakfast Journal* offers informative articles and lists of useful resources, including vendors of quilts, soaps, robes, and other products. Selected information is posted online on the *Journal*'s Web site.

> For electronic newsletters devoted to innkeeping, visit:
> www.yellowbrickroadnl.com
> www.thebandblady.com/ezine.html
> www.paii.org
> www.bnbjournal.com

Internet Research

A recent search on the Internet called up more than *three million* references to bed and breakfast! More and more B&B associations, reservation service agencies, guidebook authors, and individual B&Bs are posting Web sites with information that could be of benefit to a new host. If you don't already have Internet access, *get it*—and learn how to use search engines to help you do research. Keep in mind, though, that the Internet has sometimes been likened to the Wild West, where anything goes. Anybody can say just about anything, but that doesn't mean that it's accurate or up to date. On the other hand, there are numerous well-maintained Web sites, and you could very well find credible information to help you build your B&B business.

Real Estate

If you intend to purchase an existing bed and breakfast (also known as a turnkey operation) for sale or a property suitable for conversion to a bed and breakfast, start by looking at the major online B&B resources for listings and information. In addition, contact B&B associations representing the area or areas that interest you. A number of associations list B&Bs for sale on their Web sites. (To locate associations, see list in appendix 3).

Understand that local real estate agents may or may not have a sense of what your needs are, so if you choose to enlist the help of an agent to locate property to convert into a

> To find inns for sale, visit:
> www.bbonline.com
> www.bedandbreakfast.com
> www.oatesbredfeldt.com
> www.bnbfinder.com
> www.bedandbreakfastforsale.com
> www.bbcanada.com

B&B, be sure to make your own checklist, putting zoning regulations and location as top priorities. Do not take the word of a real estate agent on zoning regulations; contact the zoning or planning department yourself to be sure a B&B operation is permissible; then get it in writing before you buy. And if a real estate agent is pushing a property as suitable for B&B, insist upon a clause in your purchase agreement that allows you to withdraw if permissions from all necessary city and state regulatory agencies (such as fire and health departments) are not forthcoming. After locating a property that you think has potential, it can't hurt to engage the services of a bed and breakfast consultant who specializes in real estate to help you evaluate its pros and cons. (See list of consultants in appendix 1.) If purchasing an existing bed and breakfast operation, for your own protection, be sure to ask for proof of permissions before finalizing the deal.

Innsitting/Interim Innkeeping

For aspiring hosts who would like a taste of what it's like to run a B&B, or who are not yet ready to make an investment in their own B&B business, innsitting (also called interim innkeeping) may offer a good answer. There are a small number of innsitting services that connect personnel with inns that need help. Before placement, some services run instructional workshops where participants first experience the actual day-to-day routine of a host—everything from processing reservations to doing laundry. Innsitters are expected to have the skills and knowledge they need to run a B&B, and they get paid for the service they provide.

For more information about innsitting, first contact the Interim Innkeepers Network, a "not-for-profit" association that offers information about training and apprenticeships, as well as networking and assignment referrals. Other sources of information include the Professional Association of Innkeepers International, which is developing a master innkeeper certificate appropriate for innkeepers and innsitters alike. Check out New England B&B Consultants, who teach innsitting seminars and maintain an innsitters database.

> For a network of interim innkeepers, visit:
> www.interiminnkeepers.net
>
> For innsitter training, information, and directories, visit:
> www.paii.com
> www.nebbc.com
> www.bbinnstitute.com
> www.innsitting.com

Instruction is also offered by the Bed & Breakfast Innstitute of Learning. And take the time to check out the résumés posted on innsitter directories. These individual listings provide great examples of the kinds of qualities innkeepers look for when hiring an innsitter.

Consultants, Workshops, and Apprenticeships

For new hosts or for people thinking about hosting someday, attending an introductory workshop can be a valuable experience. Here you can become more acquainted with what is happening with bed and breakfast on a local level, meet others with the same interests, and get your specific questions answered face to face by someone knowledgeable about bed and breakfast. Check your local adult education center for current offerings as well as listings of evening classes or weekend seminars held at nearby colleges (especially those that work with the Small Business Administration to foster local businesses). In some areas the chamber of commerce helps organize workshops to inspire interest in hosting.

But your best bet is to check with any reservation service agency in your area. Often it is the manager who is arranging workshops locally, so he or she can let you know when and where the next one will be held. And of course, the manager might be happy to help a new host get started by visiting the home and making suggestions, assuming that the host plans to list with the RSA. Some RSAs charge a small fee for this service; others do not. B&B associations also sometimes offer workshops appropriate for aspiring hosts.

Some bed and breakfast consultants operate independently and are not affiliated with a particular reservation service agency. Of these, some prefer to work with hosts within their own geographic area; others are willing to travel or will arrange private consultations by mail or phone. (If you decide that your best alternative is to hire a consultant to come to you from out of town or even out of state, consider first assembling a small group of people who are interested in hosting to attend the workshop in order to cover the costs of the consultant's time and travel expenses.) A few consultants provide online instruction. Longtime B&B consultant Kit Cassingham of Sage Blossom Consulting offers online seminars covering the money, business, and hospitality aspects of operating a B&B. The course can be completed by students at their own pace. An online course offers a great convenience for an aspiring innkeeper—just be sure to check the credentials of anyone offering this form of instruction. As a start, look for professional affiliations on the instructor's Web site.

To locate B&B consultants,
visit:
www.yellowbrickroadnl.com
www.bbonline.com

If you think that running a B&B is the right thing for you but aren't completely sure, there's one way to find out: Try it. Sign up for one of the B&B apprenticeship programs. "It is a perfect opportunity to try on the innkeeper's hat before taking the plunge," says Barbara Gavron, who offers apprenticeships at her B&B, Singleton House, in Eureka Springs, Arkansas. For apprenticeships, check the consultants list in appendix 1 for the code letter "A."

What would an apprenticeship program cover? Handling incoming calls, booking guests, preparing and serving breakfast, and doing housekeeping chores, among other things. After coaching by an experienced innkeeper, prospective hosts have a chance for hands-on experience, then honest feedback. Programs like these, which usually run from five days to two weeks, offer a real taste of what it would be like to run your own bed and breakfast.

Appendix 1 contains a select, state-by-state listing of established, well-known consulting services. You may find others through your research with local reservation services agencies and B&B associations. Many offer consulting services for new or aspiring hosts, or they can refer you to local consultants. Some consultants operate nationally as well as locally. Some have specialties, such as marketing or real estate. Always inquire about fees for services; most are reasonable. Additional information about consultants appears on the Web sites noted in the box on this page.

Chapter Five
The Business of B&B

S ome hosts view their bed and breakfast activities as a hobby. They accommodate only a small number of visitors each year and like it that way, despite the fact that the income from their B&B effort is minimal. They keep a low profile in the community by not advertising openly; rather, they work only through a reservation service agency, which safeguards their personal privacy. Other hosts look at their bed and breakfast activities as a business venture. They go public with advertising campaigns, take out memberships in community organizations, and work to develop a home-based, income-producing business. (Some of the more ambitious bed and breakfast hosts then decide to go on to the next step, opening an inn, which moves them into the realm of a commercial enterprise.)

When it comes to legal matters, what's important is not so much how *you* view your B&B activities, but how they are viewed by the agencies invested with the responsibilities of regulating small businesses or protecting the health and welfare of the general public. Your level of hosting is just one consideration that may come under the scrutiny of federal, state, or local agencies that take an interest in your bed and breakfast. Because bed and breakfast is still a relatively new concept in some localities, be advised that you may encounter confusion or contradiction when dealing with representatives of various regulating agencies. Therefore, it's advisable to be as well informed as possible before you open your B&B.

Following is a discussion of some of the main aspects of the business of bed and breakfast that every host must be concerned with—zoning laws, insurance coverage, health and safety, record keeping, and taxes. The information and suggestions given here are intended as background for the individual bed and breakfast host. They are no substitute for the professional advice of an attorney or an accountant, and they cannot reflect the differences in regulations from community to community or new developments in the bed and breakfast industry as a whole that take place after the publication of this book. Each host has to take personal responsibility for gathering the information that pertains to his or her own bed and breakfast activities.

If you run into problems, free counseling about business matters is available from the U.S. Small Business Administration (SBA) office in your area or its affiliate called SCORE (Service Corps of Retired Executives). The SBA and the Internal Revenue Service both offer informative publications and free counseling dealing with a variety of aspects of small-business management. Of particular interest are SCORE's e-mail counselors, who have skills in a wide range of specialties that include taxes, record keeping, marketing, computers, the Internet, Web site design, and even bed and breakfast operations.

For small-business information, visit:
www.sba.gov
www.business.gov
www.score.org

And don't overlook one of the best sources of information about operating a bed and breakfast home in your particular locality—the local reservation service agency. If you choose to list your home with an RSA, that organization can be enormously valuable in helping you set up your B&B in compliance with established guidelines.

Do your homework. Explore regulations that could apply to your bed and breakfast activities, get advice if you need it, and take steps to comply where necessary. Understand what your B&B is and what it is not: Be ready to explain the differences if the occasion arises that your B&B is mistakenly classified as an inn, a hotel, or a restaurant. Regulating agencies are still catching up with the bed and breakfast movement, so it's to your advantage to be armed with as much information as you possibly can as the process continues.

Also crucial to your success in opening and running a B&B is the often ignored but very important planning stage. To get where you want to go, you need to look at where you are now and draw yourself a road map. This is the business plan. The information throughout this book can be used for writing a business plan that applies to your unique situation. This chapter includes direction on how to develop this essential part of your start-up process.

Zoning

Back in 1916 the first zoning regulations were enacted in the United States as a way to plan the growth and development of neighborhoods. Because of zoning, you won't see a shoe factory opening across the street from your home or a large luxury hotel going up next door. Simply, the idea was that businesses and residences should not mix; they needed separate "zones" within a community in order to safeguard the quality of life for the people living there. The early zoning codes did not clearly address the conflicting idea of a home-based business—a person working out of a residence. Home-based businesses in some areas were prohibited by law, largely because of efforts to do away with "sweatshops," where working conditions were poor, wages were exceedingly low, and young children far below working age were employed.

Such regulations were intended to protect people from exploitation in the workplace and to improve living conditions in general, but they were adopted before the concept of bed and breakfast took hold in this country. A B&B is not a factory, a hotel, or a sweatshop. But what is it? The lack of a clear-cut definition or precedent on the books has caused confusion in more than one community. At times local zoning board officials mistakenly apply existing regulations to bed and breakfast, even though B&B does not fit neatly into categories that have already been defined. In some communities, however, zoning codes have been updated to allow for the operation of bed and breakfast homes. (Owners of a Maryland B&B report that they even worked with the mayor to include bed and breakfast in that city's zoning code.) Even so, in some communities the issue has not yet been addressed at all on an official level.

The additional problem that "not all B&Bs are alike" was noted in an article appearing in the *Zoning News,* published by the American Planning Association. It states: "Traditional B&Bs—a single-family home with one or two guest rooms—are compatible with and can even enhance established residential neighborhoods. Bed and breakfast inns with over a dozen guest rooms are primarily businesses and would be quite disruptive in residential settings." The "disruptive" impact on a neighborhood is judged by looking at the primary function of the home as either a family dwelling or as an inn; a low-occupancy versus high-occupancy rate; and the number of bedrooms offered to travelers. Noise and parking are two key concerns.

Zoning codes have been known to do any, and all, of the following:

- *Limit the number of guest rooms or guests allowed.* In a residential area, a bed and breakfast home may be required to restrict its accommodation of guests to five or fewer rooms, even if there are additional guest rooms on the premises. Some codes base the number of guest rooms allowed on the square footage of the building; the bigger the building, the more guest rooms allowed. A more uncommon regulation limits the number of overnight guests.

- *Limit the length of stay for guests.* Those zoning codes limiting length of stay will typically do so for seven, fourteen, or thirty consecutive days, although some codes go as high as sixty. This is done primarily to prevent guests from becoming tenants.

- *Require off-street parking.* The parking situation is always a major concern of zoning boards, especially in urban areas where parking space is limited. As a result, off-street parking for guests is often a requirement for a B&B. Typically, a B&B will need one space per guest room, plus sufficient space for residents of the dwelling. Some codes permit parking in a yard (preferably screened from view of neighbors) or in a nearby location.

- *Forbid or restrict signage.* In a residential area it is not uncommon for a zoning board to forbid a small B&B operation from identifying its location by means of a sign. When signs are permitted, sometimes they must be as small as 1 foot square and affixed directly to the building at a typical height of 6 feet or placed atop a post in the yard. Illumination is sometimes regulated as well as the wording of the sign itself.

Zoning codes may permit only minimal exterior modification of the home and sometimes interior modification as well; restrict food service to breakfast only, with a further restriction to continental breakfast; require permits to operate; require a B&B's owner or manager to live on the premises; establish how many B&Bs can operate in a given area and set minimum distances between them; and more. In a recent survey, about 20 percent of reservation service agencies reported that their hosts were required to have business licenses, although in some cases this applied only to B&Bs with a certain number of guest rooms.

Because zoning boards make their decisions independently of one another, a favorable resolution in one city or county unfortunately does not mean a favorable resolution in another, even within the same state. Still, zoning boards will at times look to one another for guidance, so a collective body of favorable zoning rulings does work to the advantage of the bed and breakfast industry as a whole. For example, a 1983 New York court ruling that defined bed and breakfast as a "customary home occupation" has been helpful in clarifying zoning laws within that state as well as in other states. According to a report on bed and breakfast issued by the New York State Sea Grant Extension Program, "Customary home occupations typically are exempted from certain residential zone limitations."

Before proceeding with your plans to open a bed and breakfast home, it is vital that you obtain accurate information about the zoning regulations in your community, along with any permits or business licenses that may be required for B&Bs. (If you're looking to purchase a house specifically for the purpose of opening a B&B, make sure you check out zoning codes *before* you buy.) The best advice is to explore regulations cautiously, gathering as much information as you can from other sources before you have direct contact with anyone on the zoning board. "Some unprepared potential hosts have tried for zoning approval and have been rejected because they failed to educate the zoning people properly," reports the owner of a New Jersey reservation service. A good first step is to talk to other bed and breakfast hosts in your immediate neighborhood (if there are any), the manager of any local reservation service agency, and any B&B association representing your area. Also get in touch with friends and acquaintances who run home-based businesses in your area—hairdressers, accountants, graphic designers, tailors. Their experience with local ordinances will help you get a perspective on the situation.

Once you've used your network to get the lay of the land, you're ready to contact the zoning board or planning department in your city or county. "I tell all potential hosts to visit zoning offices and health inspectors whether they are opening a couple of rooms for the summer or buying, renovating, or restoring an existing home," says the manager of an RSA in a rural area. First find out the zone designation of the property and ask for a zoning verification letter explaining what is allowed in that zone and any conditions for development. (It's important to get everything in writing in case you need to document your case for any reason in the future.) Sometimes B&Bs are already addressed, but often they are not mentioned at all. This means you have to fit your operation into existing regulations, obtain a variance, or try to change the regulations. If you're looking to buy, you might want to consider buying in a community where zoning has already been approved for

B&Bs. Also take the time to investigate any neighborhood covenants that might restrict home-based businesses.

If you decide to go the route of changing existing regulations to permit the operation of B&Bs, Pam Carruthers, manager of Bed and Breakfast Cambridge and Greater Boston, recommends that you do not go it alone. "You have to be willing to be politically active," she says. "Join with others." Together you will have a stronger voice. A San Diego host reports that this city incorporated B&B accommodations in the zoning code as of January 2000. B&Bs had been working with the city on this issue since 1986! A number of B&B associations get actively involved in zoning issues. Find out if your local association will join you in your efforts.

To obtain approval for your B&B operation, it's possible you will have to go before a zoning-board hearing or speak out at community meetings. Be prepared to address the noise and parking concerns that are certain to come up. Surveys show that most guests are middle-class, educated, married professionals—not exactly the profile of a rowdy bunch. And determine in advance how you will meet the parking needs of your guests. Speak to the benefits of introducing bed and breakfast to your community. For example, guests will typically purchase meals at nearby restaurants and make purchases at local shops, which is good for the area's economy. Or perhaps you plan to restore an older structure for use as a B&B, which contributes to the historic preservation of the neighborhood.

Be ready to distinguish your B&B from a "rooming house" that accommodates "tenants," as there may be a precedent excluding boardinghouses, inns, hotels, or motels from residential areas. A bed and breakfast home that accommodates occasional guests, displays no signs, and in no way diminishes the quality of life enjoyed by the residents is very different from any of these commercial establishments.

Insurance

As a bed and breakfast host, you are of course concerned about the safety and well-being of your guests, just as you are about that of your family, your property, and yourself. A host's concerns about possible fire, theft, personal injury, or property damage should take two forms—prevention and insurance.

As a host, you have to be keenly alert to possible hazards and take whatever precautions necessary: Remove throw rugs that don't have a nonskid backing; put up gates at the top and bottom of staircases if you plan to host children; restrict the use of your swimming pool to daylight hours and remove the diving board; install grab bars for support at the bathtub and in the shower; require guests wishing to make use of your sailboat, weight-lifting equipment, or toboggan to sign a liability disclaimer; install smoke alarms and carbon monoxide detectors; provide fire extinguishers in strategic places; install sprinklers if your house is three or more stories high; require guests traveling with pets to sign a statement of liability in the event that the animal causes damage; install a burglar alarm and a double-lock system for front and back doors; add emergency lighting; install handrails and slip prevention on stairs. To be on the safe side, you might want to serve nonalcoholic drinks only. Serving alcohol could also affect your eligibility for insurance coverage, as it is considered an additional risk. For each host there is a unique set of circumstances that could require other preventative measures as well. (See the next section, "Health and Safety.")

Although you may already carry some form of homeowner's insurance, it would be a mistake to assume that your current policy automatically covers your bed and breakfast activities. It is absolutely essential that you contact your insurance agent before opening your home for B&B to discuss, first, exactly what your policy does cover as far as your bed and breakfast is concerned and, second, additional insurance where necessary. Be assured that rates are usually quite reasonable because there are so few claims within the industry, many believe due largely to a genuine concern for the property by both hosts and guests. Do ask about credits—reductions in your premium—for precautions you have taken for the safety of your guests, because they make you a better risk.

It is not unusual for a host to find that his or her insurance agent has no experience with bed and breakfast. Be ready to explain the nature of what you plan to do as well as the level of hosting you realistically expect. Find out what exactly your current homeowner's policy would cover if you opened your home for B&B. Be sure the business exclusions are removed from the policy. Ask for the confirmation *in writing,* from the carrier rather than the agent, just in case the occasion does arise in the future when you need to rely on a favorable interpretation of your existing policy. Be advised, however, that a homeowner's policy alone is not considered sufficient for your B&B's insurance needs. According to one agent specializing in insurance for B&Bs and inns, an "unendorsed" homeowner's policy has too many exclusions to be the proper way to insure your business. The agent recommends an "all risks" policy with the broadest coverage available.

If your regular insurance agent is not helpful to you in securing the extra liability, fire, or theft coverage that you want (and that your attorney recommends), or an umbrella policy to boost your current liability coverage, then talk to another agent, preferably one recommended by B&B hosts who have already gone through the insuring process. B&B is new ground for many insurance agents, and they are cautious, sometimes to the point of not being helpful at all. Some hosts have found it necessary to go to more than one agent before they were able to obtain the kind of insurance they wanted. Other hosts have resorted to purchasing a commercial insurance package covering the items they were most concerned about, and this is probably the best way to go. Your goal is adequate coverage on buildings and contents, personal effects, loss of income, food spoilage, commercial and products liability, personal injury, personal liability, full liquor liability, medical payments to guests, workers' compensation (for hosts who have employees), and innkeepers' liability.

If you join a reservation service agency, check to see if your membership makes you eligible for general liability insurance. Some RSAs have an agreement with an insurance company to provide their hosts with $1 million bodily injury and property damage coverage, which includes premises/operations, products liability, personal injury liability, advertising injury liability, and host liquor liability (not regular liquor liability—you cannot charge for a drink).

For B&B insurance information, visit:
www.jameswolf.com
www.bandblady.com
www.paii.org

It is important to note the distinction between "host liquor liability" and "regular liquor liability" in your coverage. Anyone who sells liquor—a full-service inn with a liquor license, for example—needs *regular* liquor liability coverage. So take extra care to clarify this point of your insurance coverage with your agent. If you plan to serve alcohol to your B&B guests, even if you don't charge for it, be forewarned that you could be held liable for any bodily injury or property damage that may result.

And be sure to check your automobile insurance coverage as well. Many hosts will use their own vehicles to transport guests to and from the airport, train station, or bus station, or will offer a ride at other times if it is convenient (usually without a fee attached to the service). If you plan to offer this amenity to your guests, find out to what extent your current policy covers passengers and if that coverage extends to those who have a business connection to you, or who pay a fee for transportation to you. If you charge a guest for transportation, you have no coverage under your personal policy. You might have to make adjustments either in your policy or in the transportation services you provide to your guests. Or consider switching to a commercial policy—it may even be cheaper.

Mike and Annette Endres, owners of Ahinahina Farm Bed and Breakfast in Hawaii, offer this suggestion for obtaining medical insurance now that you will be operating your own business: "Don't forget to visit your local chamber of commerce." Chambers often offer their members medical insurance at competitive group rates.

Before making a final decision about overall coverage, you might want to read through the helpful publication called *Insurance: That Nine Letter Word,* which is available for a fee from the Professional Association of Innkeepers International. Also, read the series of insurance articles written by Kit Cassingham of Sage Blossom Consulting and posted on her Web site, www.thebandblady.com.

Also recommended is the informative Web site for James Wolf Insurance (www .jameswolf.com), which provides an excellent discussion of what to look for in an insurance policy tailored to the needs of bed and breakfast operations, with straightforward explanations and examples. This agent specializes in providing insurance to bed and breakfasts, with no minimum room requirement—insuring operations with only one or two guest rooms, as well as full-service country inns with many guest rooms and a restaurant.

Health and Safety

When it comes to the safety and well-being of your guests, make it your first priority to comply with regulations that govern the operation of your bed and breakfast, and be prepared for periodic inspections. (In a nationwide survey, 64 percent of the B&Bs contacted reported that they are regularly inspected by state or local officials.) If there are no regulations specific to the operation of B&Bs in your area, the manager of an Arkansas reservation service suggests picking up the free copies of state regulations governing the operation of hotels, motels, boardinghouses, and restaurants. "Then use common sense in your own situation," she says. In addition, heed recommendations made by reservation service agencies, B&B associations, and experienced hosts.

Environmental Hazards

Start with inspections for environmental hazards. A bed and breakfast home built a century ago has considerable charm, but it might also harbor toxins that could be dangerous to yourself and your guests. Have your property inspected for lead-based paint (banned in 1978 but still present in many structures built before that time). It is especially important to remove or encapsulate areas with lead paint if you expect to host children younger than twelve years of age. Also, check for carbon monoxide, especially if you have working fireplaces. Install carbon monoxide detectors according to recommended guidelines. If you plan to renovate the basement for guest quarters or for your own living space, be sure to test for radon, mold, and asbestos, as well as contamination resulting from oil or gasoline tanks. If you are purchasing a property with the intention of offering bed and breakfast, ask the real estate agent to disclose any available information about these potential hazards, and then contract for your own inspection.

Fire Prevention

Fire prevention and early detection should be major concerns. Check with your local fire department for regulations and recommendations. The owner of a reservation service agency in Maine advises hosts to have smoke alarms and fire extinguishers on each floor of the house. One of each in every guest bedroom is not too many. Post evacuation procedures on the back of the door in each guest room. Easy exit to outside from every guest bedroom is also essential. Two means of egress are recommended, if not required. One Philadelphia host reports that she purchased a fire ladder to keep inside one guest bedroom located on the second floor. The owner of an RSA in Tempe, Arizona, called Mi Casa Su Casa tells hosts to make sure that all windows can be opened to allow escape or rescue in the event of fire. In general, a bed and breakfast home should conform to local and state fire codes.

The manager of an RSA in New York advises hosts to prohibit guests from smoking in bedrooms. (Some hosts prohibit smoking in their homes altogether because of the fire hazard.) And although it's wonderful to be able to provide guests with the amenity of a fireplace in their bedroom, be sure to explain how to use it properly and how to extinguish the fire completely. Conduct a house check in common rooms before retiring to check fireplace embers and cigarettes in ashtrays if you do allow smoking.

Some insurance companies now require that doors on guest rooms close automatically and meet fire safety codes. The automatic door closer that is least expensive and easiest to install (and least intrusive on the decor) simply replaces a hinge pin on the door.

Note that a number of states and communities apply to B&Bs in their jurisdictions the Life Safety Code recommended by the National Fire Protection Association as a national standard. B&Bs that operate on a minimal level of activity usually have few modifications to make. Those that exceed a given number of guest rooms or accommodate more than a certain number of guests, however, could be required to have enclosed staircases, more exits and egress windows, additional smoke detectors, or possibly a sprinkler system. The Department of Inspections and Appeals for the state of Iowa, for example, requires B&Bs hosting two or fewer families at one time to have a working smoke detector in each sleeping room and a fire extinguisher on each floor. But B&Bs exceeding this volume of guests must be licensed and inspected as a hotel with the stricter regulations.

Alaska is one state that requires a notarized certification from each host assuring minimum life-safety precautions in order to qualify for an annual permit to operate a B&B. In addition to smoke detectors and egress windows in each guest room, the state requires fire-resistant coverings in storage spaces under stairs and a thermal barrier separating foam-plastic insulation from livable space. It also prohibits use of electrical wiring that is in deteriorating condition or is open to casual contact. And to avoid injury to someone escaping from a fire, neither stairs without handrails nor ladders (instead of stairs) are allowed.

Another state with strict fire regulations is Maine. "Under Maine law, B&Bs are considered commercial establishments subject to the same health- and fire-safety laws as hotels and motels. We are licensed by the state and subject to inspection twice a year. The fire-safety laws are very stringent with respect to alarm systems, fire doors, and exits when you exceed a certain number of guests. Requirements should be carefully verified before committing to alterations to increase guest capacity," report Merrit and Barbara Williams, owners of 71 Park Street Bed and Breakfast in Ellsworth, Maine.

These states offer only a few examples of how fire regulations can be applied to B&Bs. It is imperative that anyone planning to open a B&B find out about fire regulations beforehand. They could dictate the need for renovations before you start to operate and determine the level of hosting you decide to do.

Accident Prevention

The few insurance claims made so far in the bed and breakfast industry as a whole have been reported as the "slip and fall" variety, so take care to safeguard against accidental injury. The founder of Bed & Breakfast Associates Bay Colony in Boston instructs hosts listed with that agency to remove obstacles from hallways and stairways so that no one can trip over them. "Look around your home for situations that may cause falls or injuries—for instance, slippery, highly waxed stairs or floors and small scatter rugs. Decorative items or plants should not be on the floor where they will intrude on a hallway or block an exit," advises Pam Carruthers of Bed and Breakfast Cambridge and Greater Boston. A California reservation service requires its hosts to tack all carpeting and rugs securely. Any broken steps should be fixed immediately. If young children will be visiting your bed and breakfast, it's a good idea to put gates across open stairways. Safety plugs in electrical outlets and locks on lower cabinets will also help prevent hazards to children.

Bathrooms should be of special concern when it comes to guests' safety and health. The owner of an Atlanta bed and breakfast recommends that hosts guard against falls by installing grab bars next to the tub and shower. The managers of an RSA in Massachusetts tell their hosts to put nonskid strips in the bathtub. Bed and Breakfast Cambridge and Greater Boston's safety guidelines state that hosts should use unbreakable drinking glasses only and avoid placing hooks at eye level.

Be sure any electrical outlets are well grounded. An inexpensive device designed to prevent electrocution is a GFCI (ground fault circuit interrupter). Available in hardware and electrical-supply stores, the GFCI comes either as a portable adapter for plugging into an outlet or as a replacement for the outlet itself. The state of Alaska requires its B&Bs to have a pressure-relief valve on any hot-water heater, along with a drain to direct steam from the valve down away from a person's face to the floor.

Be aware of possible hazards out of doors. "In wintertime keep walks and stairs clear of ice and snow," says the owner of a Massachusetts RSA. The owner of a Canadian reservation service recommends a hand railing on steps leading to the front and back doors, and a railing around porches. "We have a huge deck on the ocean side and have had a safe railing installed," say Robbie and Don Smith, owners of Spindrift Bed & Breakfast in Bandon, Oregon.

Good lighting out of doors is important for your guests' safety. The owner of Bed & Breakfast Hawaii suggests that driveways be lighted. The owners of an Ohio reservation service tell hosts to make sure that the parking area where guests leave their cars is secure and well lighted. If guests are out at night, the porch light should be left on until their return. One Boston B&B owner installed a photoelectric floodlight that comes on whenever movement is detected outside the house.

Good lighting inside the house is especially important because your guests are unfamiliar with the layout of your home. At night they can become disoriented easily. It's advisable to have a night-light on in the hallway for the entire night. You might even want to make a night-light available to guests to use inside their bedroom or private bathroom if they wish. Make sure that there is a lamp or other light switch right next to the bed. "A good safety item that happens to be cheap to operate—only pennies a month—is the little two-pronged low-wattage night-light. We've had some for fifteen years, and they are a must for people stumbling around in the night trying to locate a bathroom in a strange house," report the managers of a Massachusetts B&B. Light switches that illuminate in the dark also make nocturnal travels safer. Emergency lighting is recommended.

Security

Be sure that you have good, solid locks on exterior doors, ground-floor windows, and bedroom doors. The owner of the Arizona RSA Mi Casa Su Casa recommends to her hosts who happen to have sliding glass doors that they use metal screw pins or key-controlled window locking devices as a burglary prevention. Once you have the appropriate locks, use them. Do not leave your front door open at night for late arrivals or other guests' convenience. Security measures are important, even if the perception of your community is that it is crime-free. Inadequate security can provide the basis for a lawsuit against you should that one-in-a-million robbery, assault, or other crime befall one of your guests. If your B&B does happen to be situated in a high-risk neighborhood, be sure to alert prospective guests to this fact before they arrive so that they will not be tempted to walk when a taxi is advisable. Or offer to pick them up at the train or bus station.

New hosts always wonder whether it is safe to give a house key to guests. Although bed and breakfast guests do seem to be cut from the best cloth, it's always best to take normal precautions. It is not recommended that you give a house key to guests. Try, as much as possible, to arrange your schedule around their comings and goings. But when this is not possible, you might decide that lending a house key is necessary. Use your good judgment about this. Some hosts have a double-lock on exterior doors, then they lend guests the key to only one of the locks and collect it immediately after the schedule conflict is over. The owner of a Rhode Island RSA recommends that any key lent to guests be stamped or tagged "Do Not Duplicate." A locksmith will think twice about making a copy if asked. Some hosts favor a "keyless" lock with changeable combinations.

Depending on the layout and amenities of your home, you might need to institute other safety measures. If you have a swimming pool, for example, you might want to enforce a rule prohibiting swimming after dark. The manager of one reservation service agency recommends that hosts who have pools ask guests to sign a release if they wish to use the pool. If children will be visiting your B&B, there must be an enclosure around the pool to prevent them from wandering up to the edge. If you don't have such an enclosure, you should restrict the children you accept at your B&B to twelve years of age or older. One host who lives near a river used to supply a raft for guests but discontinued this amenity upon the advice of her insurance agent.

Food Safety

It is very possible that your state's department of public health has adopted some type of regulation concerning food service at bed and breakfasts in its jurisdiction. Because you serve a complimentary breakfast to guests, you must meet any state or local guidelines for health and safety in food preparation, storage, and overall kitchen operation. Generally, all food and drink must be handled in such a manner as to prevent contamination; sanitary facilities must meet local code; and the water supply must be from an approved source and possibly subject to periodic testing.

The National Restaurant Association Educational Foundation (NRAEF) operates a food-safety training and certification program called ServSafe, which is recognized by most federal and state regulatory agencies. In some states, ServSafe certification is required for innkeepers. Contact your state or local health department for requirements in your area. Training classes and exam administration are usually offered through the health department or a community college, although some states allow training via CD-ROM or online.

For food-safety training and certification, visit: www.nraef.org/servsafe

"A bed and breakfast operation currently is not considered a restaurant, and a commercial kitchen is not required," concluded a study conducted by the New York Sea Grant Extension program at Cornell University, regarding considerations in starting a bed and breakfast business. This is generally true from locality to locality, but there has been sporadic confusion in certain areas about whether the "commercial" guidelines for the health and safety of customers in a restaurant should be applied to bed and breakfast homes. One Washington host tells the horror story of being required to install a dishwasher that cost $10,000 because that's what the local restaurant code called for. In some cases the confusion resulted when hosts offered lunches or dinners for an extra fee—that is, they were "selling" food. (Breakfast, on the other hand, is "free"—included in the price of the room.) Check with your local reservation service agency to find out if there has been any confusion about this issue in your area.

Some states have taken steps to clear up the confusion by addressing the unique nature of B&Bs in new legislation tailored to the industry. Where this has happened, smaller B&B operations and those serving only a complimentary continental breakfast are usually exempted from the more stringent regulations and the need to obtain a residential or commercial kitchen permit. Check regulations in your state to determine how bed and breakfasts are categorized.

The U.S. Food and Drug Administration for Food Safety and Applied Nutrition sums up basic sanitation precautions in four steps: "clean, cook, separate, and chill." Clean your hands, fresh produce, preparation surfaces, and utensils properly. Cook food at the appropriate temperatures, especially meat, poultry, seafood, eggs, and leftovers. Separate raw meat, poultry, and seafood from all other foods in the shopping cart and in the refrigerator, and use separate cutting boards. Chill food in a refrigerator

For information on food safety, visit: www.foodsafety.gov www.fightbac.org

Health and Safety Checklist

General

- ☐ Emergency numbers by telephone
- ☐ Handrails on all staircases
- ☐ No broken steps
- ☐ Obstacles removed from stairs, hallways, exits, and outside walkways
- ☐ Nonskid rugs only; carpeting tacked securely
- ☐ Railings around porches
- ☐ Parking area, porches, and outside walkways lit at night
- ☐ Outside walkways and stairs clear of snow and ice
- ☐ Night-lights in hallways, bathrooms, and guest rooms
- ☐ Smoke alarm in each guest room
- ☐ Fire exit from each guest room
- ☐ Fire extinguisher on each floor
- ☐ Evacuation procedures posted in each guest room
- ☐ Enclosed staircases, fire doors, sprinkler system, if required
- ☐ Fire inspection, if required

- ☐ Electrical wiring in good condition, not exposed to guest contact
- ☐ Water from an approved source
- ☐ Water, plumbing, sewage system inspected, if required
- ☐ Pool, sauna, whirpool inspected, if required
- ☐ Locks on exterior doors, ground-floor windows, and bedroom doors
- ☐ House inspected for environmental hazards— lead, asbestos, radon, mold, carbon monoxide
- ☐ No hooks for clothing/towels at eye level
- ☐ Insects/rodents exterminated if necessary
- ☐ Additional precautions taken for guests with children, such as gates across stairways, locks on lower cabinets, and safety plugs in electrical outlets
- ☐ Carbon monoxide detectors

Bathroom

- ☐ Cleaned thoroughly and disinfected in advance of each new guest's arrival
- ☐ Daily cleanups while guests are in residence
- ☐ Towels changed often

set at 40 degrees F, and set your freezer temperature at 0 degrees F. Never thaw food at room temperature. Detailed information about these four steps can be found on the USFDA's Web site. In addition, educational information is available from the Partnership for Food Safety Education. A helpful brochure can be downloaded from its Web site.

Emergency Plans

A host must be prepared to deal with any medical emergency that arises. Keep a first-aid kit on hand and some common medicines for reducing fever, but use common sense about

- ☐ Sprayed for mold and mildew
- ☐ Unbreakable glasses or paper cups only
- ☐ Grab-bars next to tub and shower
- ☐ Electrical outlets well grounded
- ☐ Liquid soap or individually wrapped soap for each guest
- ☐ Medications removed from guest bathroom or kept in locked cabinet

Kitchen

- ☐ Sparkling clean
- ☐ Inspected and licensed, if required
- ☐ No use of laundry facilities during food preparation or service (if located in kitchen)
- ☐ Pets kept out of kitchen and dining areas when in use
- ☐ Toxic substances such as insecticides and detergents, medicines, first-aid supplies, and other chemicals stored separately in closed cabinets
- ☐ Garbage containers lined and covered
- ☐ Hands washed with soap and hot water prior to preparing or serving food
- ☐ No smoking or eating during food preparation or serving
- ☐ Rubber gloves used if cook has cut on hands
- ☐ Food preparation surfaces washed and sanitized
- ☐ Two cutting boards for separated foods
- ☐ Food items wrapped or covered until serving
- ☐ Perishables refrigerated at 40 degrees F until serving
- ☐ Fruits washed thoroughly
- ☐ Butter and jam presented in single-serving amounts
- ☐ Two sinks, or sink and basin, and rack used for hand-washing of dishes
- ☐ Internal temperature of dishwasher at least 150 degrees F
- ☐ Dishes sanitized with bleach solution after washing and rinsing in hot water, then air-dried
- ☐ Utensils cleaned/sanitized
- ☐ Microwave cleaned daily
- ☐ Food cooked to recommended temperatures
- ☐ Dishcloths used instead of sponges
- ☐ Paper towels used for cleanup
- ☐ Food defrosted in refrigerator only

supplying them to guests. The manager of a Rhode Island reservation service recommends no dispensing of medications at all. You may decide to leave the purchase and use of medications entirely up to guests themselves. Do not leave medicines in the guest-bathroom cabinet or near food items in the kitchen. Bed and Breakfast Cambridge and Greater Boston suggests that medications be kept in a locked cabinet.

It's good practice to get the name of a close relative or friend during the reservation process or upon a guest's arrival. "We obtain emergency numbers and names for guests when making reservations," say the owners of an Atlanta reservation service. And near the telephone, keep a card that contains a listing of emergency numbers: fire department, police, nearest hospital, a local physician, ambulance, poison control center. In the event that an emergency does arise, you or your guests will be able to move into action quickly. And be sure guests know how to reach you in an emergency, twenty-four hours a day, especially if work takes you away from your B&B for much of the day or guests are staying in unhosted accommodations.

Develop a well-thought-out emergency plan, including evacuation procedures, and post it in your B&B. Evacuation procedures should be posted in every guest room. If you have others working at the B&B with you, make sure that they all have copies of the emergency plan and know the location of fire extinguishers and how to operate them. If you work outside the home, keep an extra copy of your emergency plan, with emergency phone numbers, in your workplace.

For disaster preparation and recovery for small businesses, visit: www.sba.gov

For disaster planning, visit: www.ibhs.org

For food and water safety after disasters, visit: www.foodsafety.gov

In the past few years, too many of us have learned the hard way that disasters will happen—fires, floods, hurricanes, power outages, even terrorist attacks. In these instances, a B&B host is responsible for protecting both the guests and the business to the best of his or her ability. Know how to shut down your utilities, and keep a supply of bottled water and have emergency lights ready. Figure out a basic backup system for your computerized records; a zip disk you can carry with you during an evacuation is one easy solution to what could be a difficult recovery period. Check the Small Business Administration Web site for advice on preparing for and recovering from a disaster. After the crisis is over, your primary concerns about reopening your B&B may revolve around health and safety issues. Information about food and water safety after disasters can be found on the U.S. Food and Drug Administration Web site.

A "Green" B&B

Surveys indicate that a majority of travelers, as high as 83 percent, favor accommodations that are environmentally responsible. Some earth-friendly strategies are easy to implement, such as switching detergents; recycling bottles, cans, and paper; installing low-flow shower heads and faucets; turning off lights in unoccupied rooms; using programmable thermostats; providing soap dispensers instead of packaged soaps; and encouraging guests to reuse towels and linens for a second day.

Other strategies are more costly initially but will be cost-effective in the long term, such as installing double-paned windows, adding insulation to the house, landscaping with local, easy-care plants that require a minimum of watering, and replacing older, energy-guzzling appliances. Some B&B owners who have purchased energy-saving products or undertaken carefully thought-out renovations report saving a thousand dollars or more per year.

For advice on purchasing and using environmentally friendly products, plus product ratings, visit: www.greenerchoices.org

For information about energy-efficient products and practices, visit: www.energystar.gov/smallbiz

For environmentally friendly products, visit: www.greenhotels.com

For "Green B&B" information and an online forum, visit: www.thebandblady.com

The best source for information about specific products comes from the Environmental Protection Agency (EPA), which offers free and low-cost energy-saving ideas through its Energy Star program. There is even a category for small businesses in the lodging industry (which includes bed and breakfast). The Energy Star Web site provides information about energy-efficient equipment in a number of product categories, including windows and doors, computers and other office equipment, heating and cooling systems, and major appliances such as washing machines, dishwashers, and refrigerators. In addition you'll find tips, success stories, and lists of companies that provide various products and services. You are invited to download a free one-hundred-page guide called *Putting Energy into Profits*, and you may call Energy Star's toll-free number for advice about energy efficiency: (888) 782–7937. At the very least, look for the Energy Star sticker whenever you are making new equipment purchases. In addition, check with local energy providers to learn about rebates they may offer for purchasing energy-efficient hot-water tanks, gas fireplaces, solar electricity systems, and other products.

More on the subject of earth-friendly products, practices, and vendors is available on the Web sites for *Consumer Reports* Greener Choices and the Green Hotels Association. In addition, Kit Cassingham of Sage Blossom Consulting provides articles and links on her Web site, plus a "Green B&B Forum," an online discussion of related issues open to everyone.

Keeping Records

As a way to advise prospective hosts about the realities of running a bed and breakfast, managers of reservation service agencies across North America were asked to identify the biggest mistake made by new B&B hosts. The manager of a California reservation service said this: "Not being well enough prepared for the bookkeeping and accounting aspects of the business." Too many new hosts tend to focus solely on the fun part of hosting—meeting guests and making their stay a wonderful experience. (After all, that's why they got involved with B&B in the first place.) But they pay too little attention to their finances, so when it's time to give Uncle Sam some facts and figures, it's nearly an impossible task to re-create an entire year of receipts and disbursements and to produce records that were never kept.

No matter how much or how little hosting you plan to do, it is absolutely essential that you keep accurate records of your activities. First of all, your bed and breakfast income is subject to taxes. (See the section on taxes later in this chapter.) You need good records in order to determine how much you do or do not owe and to substantiate your figures to the satisfaction of the federal and state governments. Just as important, you need to give yourself the benefit of understanding your own business and planning for its future. Are you making or losing money? Has the volume of guests increased or decreased over the past year, compared with the year before? Where do you want your bed and breakfast operation to be a year from now? Three years from now? Five years? If you want growth, you have to plan for it. To devise an intelligent business plan, you need a way to assess where you are now, how your situation compares with those of previous years, and what it will take to reach your goals. Good records are the key.

When it comes to setting up a record-keeping system for your bed and breakfast, there's only one rule to follow: Choose a system that you understand thoroughly and control completely. Yes, you can hire a bookkeeper or an accountant to handle the books, and you should seek professional advice. But a big mistake some hosts make is relying solely on someone else to take care of this important aspect of the business! Never forget that you, as the owner and therefore the one ultimately responsible for the accuracy of your records, should know what's going on at all times—even if a financial professional is helping you.

Basically your job is to keep track of what's coming in (receipts) and what's going out (disbursements), along with keeping an accurate record of reservations. There are various methods designed to help you fulfill these functions, from a simple ledger to a sophisticated software package. Computerizing your records is recommended. Check industry newsletters and magazines for listings and ads of companies that market software developed specifically for B&Bs.

Look at the options available and then decide what works best for you. Use the recommendations and sample forms in this section to set up your own record-keeping system; ask a financial professional to work with you on this project if necessary. Don't overlook the help that may be available to you if you list your B&B with a reservation service agency. "We provide bookkeeping forms," says the manager of a reservation service in New England. "We explain our record-keeping procedures and our forms. We also will assist our hosts in setting up their own records for reservations and accounting," says the manager of a Maryland reservation service. "We show them how to keep a simple journal for a home B&B," says the manager of a New York reservation service. Not all RSAs offer this kind of help, but it certainly doesn't hurt to ask.

Calendar

First order of business: "Keep an accurate calendar," says the manager of an Arizona reservation service agency. Start with a datebook to log reservations for the coming weeks and months. Make its home in a convenient place—next to the phone, perhaps—and keep it accurate and up to date. "Immediately write down bookings as they come in, so as to avoid mistakes and overbooking. We never overbooked in our ten years of business. Constantly check and recheck and write down and be careful. Don't be lazy or disorganized, or you don't belong in the business. Good business management is as important to B&B as good housekeeping," says Lisa Hileman, who owned and operated Countryside in Summit Point, West Virginia. Jeanne Gilbert, owner of Gilbert's Bed and Breakfast in Rehoboth, Massachusetts, keeps a record of bookings in two places. One datebook goes with her everywhere—just in case. "You never know when someone at the bank or grocery store wants to book an out-of-town relative," she says.

Guest Register

Next comes a guest register. This is a large ledger-type book where a guest signs in upon arrival with his or her name, address, and dates of visit. It is a good way to keep track of how many guests visit over a period of time and how many nights your rooms are booked per month or per year. The contents can be used to identify the extent of your best "seasons" out of the year (when large numbers of guests visit because of the fall foliage, skiing, sunning, cherry blossom time, or tulips in bloom, for example). The register can show you when you should go easy on the advertising because you'll already be operating at capacity and won't be able to accommodate any more guests anyway, and when you should do some creative marketing to bring guests to your door in the off-season. You can purchase an attractive ledger for use as a guest register in most stationery stores.

Guest Record

In addition to a datebook and a guest register, both of which supply you with valuable chronological references, you should keep an information record for each guest who visits your home, filed alphabetically by the guests' last names. The information can be computerized, but it can be just as easily recorded on sturdy 4" x 6" or 5" x 8" cards. Or adapt the sample form provided here for your own needs, make copies, add three-hole punches, and then place the finished forms inside a binder that is divided alphabetically. (Note that the Sample Guest Information Record in this section includes a space for calculating the commission owed by a host to his or her reservation service agency for booking the guest. If you operate independently and do not use the services of an RSA, you will, of course, want to delete RSA references on your own form.)

The guest information record should include the guest's name, address, telephone number, and e-mail address, along with the dates of arrival and departure, total number of nights stayed, number of people in the party (write down all their names), which room or rooms were occupied, city/state or other taxes collected, and total amount paid to you and how it was paid (cash, personal check). Some hosts also like to record the license number and make of a guest's vehicle, pertinent information from the screening form you used when the guest first made the reservation (for example, whether a guest is a smoker or has allergies; see "Screening Your Guests" in chapter 7), and personal notes that will help jog their memories later when it's time to send follow-up notes to former guests (such as someone's interest in stamp collecting or the date of a birthday or an anniversary). Also write down how the guest heard about your bed and breakfast; a review of the sources at the end of every year can help you identify the advertising strategies that are working and those that aren't.

Computer Database and Reports

If you choose to use a computer to keep your records, select a software program that allows you to create reports and spreadsheets easily. Dave Elliott, a co-owner of Taylor House Bed & Breakfast in Boston and a teacher of computer courses, created a database with easy-to-use software. His database entry screen contains information that a host needs for both the calendar and the guest record. (Please see "Sample Database Entry Screen" in this section.)

By using information contained in the database, a host can generate a weekly occupancy chart that shows at a glance which rooms are booked and which are still available. A chart like this can help a host respond quickly to a room request from a prospective guest. "We keep the chart by the phone," says Dave Elliott. (Please see "Sample Weekly Occupancy Chart from a Database.")

Another valuable report that can be constructed from a database shows the room sales for each month. This report lists the number of people booked on each day of the month and the number of nights they stayed. For a new host, a monthly report like this provides valuable information to help predict the peaks and valleys of an annual business. (Please see "Sample Monthly Room Sales Report.")

Taylor House B&B owners also use information in their database to prepare a day-by-day calendar that gives them an overall picture of the comings and goings of guests. For this they use a floor plan created in Microsoft's Powerpoint graphics program, printed out four on a page. The four floor plans are dated by hand. Then, using red ink, they write the name of an arriving guest, number of people in the party, number of nights booked, and arrival time, in the designated room. Using black ink, they write the name of any guest who already occupies a room. (Note that the sample shown in this section uses a double underline instead of red ink.) One look at the color-coded floor plan tells the hosts which rooms

Sample Guest Information Record

Guest Name(s) ___Mary and David Jones_____

Address ___100 West Garfield Street_____

City ___Cambridge_____ State _MA_ Zip ___02138____

Phone ___(617) 555-1001_____ Fax ___(617) 555-1002_____

E-mail address _manddjones@earthlink.net_____

Arrival date __7/8/06_____ Departure date ____7/10/06_____

Method of payment:

Deposit: ___Personal Check____ Balance/other charges: _____Cash_____

Number of persons in party___2___

Room(s) booked ___The Blue Room_____

ACCOMMODATIONS FEE

Room rate $___100____

Multiplied by number of nights ___x 2____

Accommodations fee $___200____

Plus _5_ % room/occupancy tax $___+10____

Total $___210____

Minus deposit in advance $___-100____

Received by host on date ____——____

or collected by RSA __√__

Balance due upon arrival $___110____

(Date paid ___7/8/06_____)

RESERVATION SERVICE AGENCY FEE

Accommodations fee $ _____200_____
(from above)

Multiplied by __25%__ RSA commission   _____x .25_____

Amount owed RSA by host $ _____50_____

(Date paid _____ — _____)

Deposit collected by RSA $ _____100_____

Minus commission due $ _____– 50_____

Amount owed host by RSA $ _____50_____

(Date received_____7/16/06_____)

OTHER CHARGES

_____Postcards_____ $ _____4.00_____

_____ $ _____

Total due at checkout $ _____4.00_____

(Date paid _____7/10/06_____)

Car description & license _____Red 2005 Toyota, Mass. #243978_____

Heard about us from _____Mary's Mom (Sue Smith) - guest last fall_____

Reason for visiting _____15th anniversary (7/9/06)_____

Notes _____Mary - English professor at Boston U.; jogs in a.m._____

_____David - jazz musician, Red Sox fan, loved my strawberry jam!_____

For reservation software,
visit: www.rezstream.com

must be thoroughly prepared for new arrivals. "We keep these posted on clipboards in our dining room. When everything is black, we have no prep work!" says Dave Elliott.

A reservation software program called RezStream Professional has been gaining popularity among B&B hosts. The program allows easy input of reservations, generation of occupancy reports, and more. Go to the company's Web site to request a demonstration of how a reservation process works. Some hosts who have created their own databases and used them for a while find the RezStream software a logical next step.

Checking Account

The next order of business is to set up a checking account strictly for your bed and breakfast business. According to Liza Roman, owner of a Boston-based bookkeeping firm called Roman Numerals, which services some bed and breakfast clients in the area, one of the best aids for keeping track of all funds that go into (receipts) and out of (disbursements) your B&B operation is a checking account set up separately from your personal account. Such an account provides clear documentation of how much money you process for your B&B business during any month or any year. Trying to untangle this information from your personal account can be quite a chore. Furthermore, according to financial-services expert John Sedensky, the Internal Revenue Service does not look favorably upon the commingling of personal and business funds. He recommends separate bank accounts and credit cards as well.

When making purchases, ask for separate receipts: one for items intended for guests and another for items intended for personal use. Of course, there will be times when this is not possible to do at the checkout counter. (A clerk is unlikely to separate out the cost of the one apple you intend to eat on the way home from the total cost per dozen, for example.) In this case, pay for the items out of one account, then reimburse the other account, making sure to leave a "paper trail" that can be easily tracked to avoid confusion later. Do this by writing a check from one account to the other and noting on the check what the payment is for. Paula Deigert, financial-services expert and former reservation service manager, recommends making the bank the focal point of your accounting system: "When

Sample Database Entry Screen

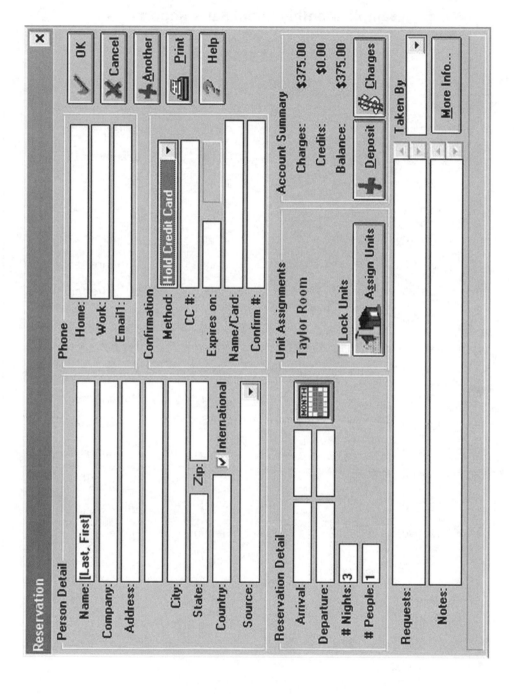

Sample Monthly Room Sales Report

ROOM ASSIGNMENTS

Month	Date	Days	People	Last Name	Room Requested
12	12/2/06	4	2	Barnes	Taylor
	12/3/06	5	1	Phillip	Beaumont
	12/5/06	2	1	Sikes	Beaumont
	12/9/06	3	2	Allen	Taylor
	12/11/06	4	2	Crosby	Beaumont (Twin)
	12/11/06	1	2	Jones	Haffenreffer
	12/13/06	1	1	Klein	Haffenreffer
	12/15/06	2	2	Malone	Taylor
	12/18/06	11	1	Fleming	Taylor
	12/19/06	4	2	Lee	Beaumont
	12/20/06	1	1	Simpson	Haffenreffer
	12/21/06	2	2	James	Haffenreffer
	12/23/06	4	2	Stewart	Haffenreffer
	12/23/06	4	2	McKay	Beaumont
	12/29/06	1	1	Ward	Taylor
	12/30/06	3	1	Fleming	Haffenreffer
	12/31/06	2	2	Colson	Beaumont
	12/31/06	4	2	Sears	Taylor
TOTALS		58	29		

Sample Weekly Occupancy Chart from a Database

Taylor House Bed and Breakfast Occupancy

Room	Sunday	Monday	Tuesday	Wednesday	Thursday	Friday	Saturday
	10/01/06	10/02/06	10/03/06	10/04/06	10/5/06	10/06/06	10/07/06
Taylor				Kim	Kim	Kim	Lee
Beaumont				Jones	Simpson	Olive	Olive
Haffenreffer	Radner	Klein	Brennan	Brennan	Michaels	Michaels	Michaels
	10/08/06	10/09/06	10/10/06	10/11/06	10/12/06	10/13/06	10/14/06
Taylor	Greco					Marks	Marks
Beaumont	Garner	Garner				Phillip	Phillip
Haffenreffer	Michaels					Ward	Ward
	10/15/06	10/16/06	10/17/06	10/18/06	10/19/06	10/20/06	10/21/06
Taylor	Marks		Speigleman		Colson		Anderson
Beaumont							Klein
Haffenreffer	Ward	Ward	Ward	Ward		Sears	Sears
	10/22/06	10/23/06	10/24/06	10/25/06	10/26/06	10/27/06	10/28/06
Taylor	Bieber	Bieber	Bieber	Bieber	Bieber		Brown
Beaumont	Bieber	Bieber	Bieber	Bieber	Bieber	Fleming	Fleming
Haffenreffer	Sears	Sears	Sears	Sears	Sears	Sears	Brown
	10/29/06	10/30/06	10/31/06	11/01/06	11/02/06	11/03/06	11/04/06
Taylor	Fleming				Shea	Shea	
Beaumont		Stewart	Stewart	Stewart	Stewart		Doan
Haffenreffer			Langston	Langston	Langston		

Taylor House Bed & Breakfast

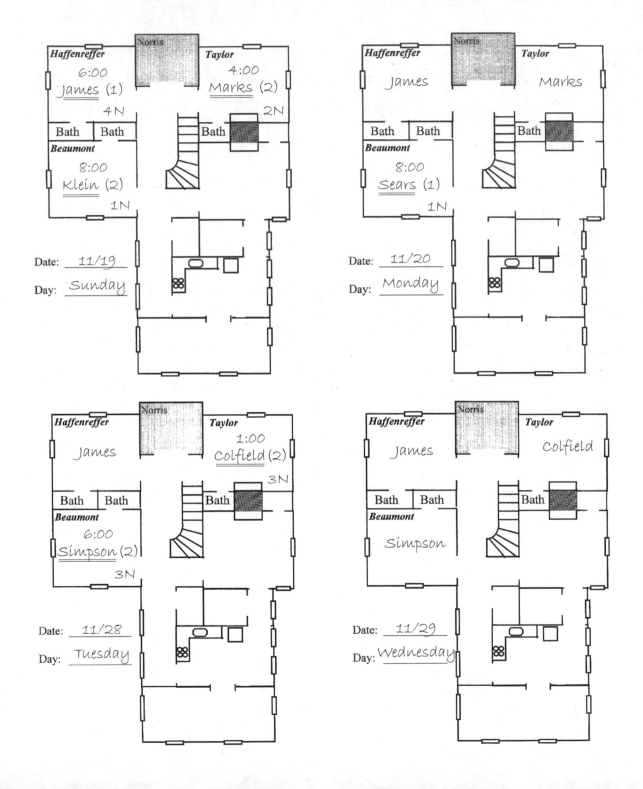

you reconcile your monthly bank statement, that means you agree with the bank on the amount of money that has been paid out by your business in your check register and the amount of revenue you have taken in from your deposits."

A good type of checkbook to use is the ledger style, which provides space for you to make clarifying notes for all transactions. The more documentation you have for money coming in and going out, the better off you'll be at tax time. Some business-style checkbooks come with stubs or carbon copies for your easy reference. Paula Deigert recommends using a check register to record all transactions: deposits, bank charges, payments made and to whom, and balances. A check register, which can be purchased in any office-supply store, is set up to record information in a more detailed way than a regular checkbook format allows.

Start-up Expenses

The next step in setting up a complete record-keeping system should come before you ever start hosting. Examine your home in terms of its readiness to provide all the basics necessary to accommodate your future guests. Will you have to make some changes or improvements before you can accept guests? (Refer to the checklists for bedroom and bathroom basics in chapter 3, as well as the insurance and the health and safety requirements noted in this chapter.) To get your home ready, you will most likely have some start-up expenses. Make a list of items you will have to buy and renovations you will have to make (if any), along with approximate costs. The following list includes some typical examples of start-up expenses that some new hosts find necessary.

New mattress	Membership fee for RSA
New sheets	Membership fee in B&B association
New pillows	Insurance
New towels	Legal advice
Extra towel racks	Brochures
Soap dishes	Night-lights
Clock for guest room	Repairing broken step

Painting bathroom	Installing railing around porch
Shampooing rugs	Air conditioner
Refinishing bedside table	Ice bucket
Smoke detectors	Serving tray
New locks	Computer software

Once you've totaled the estimated costs for all the items you would like to buy and improvements you would like to make, go back over the list and see if there's anything that can be omitted as not absolutely essential. Heed the advice of Carolyn Morrow, owner of Leftwich House, a bed and breakfast in Graham, North Carolina: "Spend as little as possible. You'll need capital until your business is established." You should be ready to make necessary expenditures for your guests' comfort, but you must know where to draw the line.

"I recently renovated my bathroom, which was in poor shape; at least I thought so," says the owner of RMF Bed & Breakfast in Atlanta, Georgia. "I am very proud of it and for a while I was showing it to everyone. One of my guests, who was a repeat guest from before the renovation, said, when shown the room, 'It's very nice. It was okay before, too.' At first I was a bit disappointed, but upon reflection I felt very good. Perhaps the defects of the rest of my home, like the bathroom, aren't so apparent to others. It may be that I am more disturbed than anyone else by the imperfections."

(A new shade for the lamp in the guest room might be nice, but will the old one do for a while?) Trim your start-up costs as much as you reasonably can without sacrificing the quality of the accommodations your B&B offers.

Operating Expenses

After determining what you need to open your home for bed and breakfast, and figuring a total amount for them, consider what your ongoing expenses would be for day-to-day operation of your B&B. Such expenses might include these:

Food	Stamps
Beverages	Envelopes
Coffee filters	Telephone calls
Hand/face soap	Electricity
Sample sizes of lotion/shampoo	Heat
Laundry	Cleaning supplies
Use of automobile (gas and mileage)	Cleaning help
Facial/toilet tissue	Internet access

At first it's difficult to come up with a daily, weekly, or "per guest" figure on operational expenses. Once you've hosted for a while, you're in a much better position to predict how many boxes of facial tissue or cans of cleanser you will go through in a typical year. Having this information can certainly help you budget for the long term. But for now, concentrate on making as complete a list of operational expenses as possible so that you can plan to document them in your records.

Chart of Accounts

Now that you have your lists of anticipated start-up expenses and ongoing business expenses, use them to develop a chart of accounts, which is nothing more than a list of categories for the different types of expenses your business will incur. Assign numbers to the categories in your chart for easy reference. When categorizing expenses, combine items where it makes sense to do so. "Beverages" and "coffee filters" could go under the general category of "food items and supplies," for example. A category for "miscellaneous" is also very useful. (Note that your first year of business will probably include more categories because of start-up expenses. Put categories referring to start-up expenses such as "porch railing" or "air conditioner" last so that they can easily be deleted from the bottom of the list in the monthly records that follow.) Your chart of accounts will probably look something like the sample that follows.

101   Telephone
102   Postage

103   Linens/bedding/towels

104   Food items and supplies

105   Advertising/Promotion

106   Commissions to RSA

107   Utilities

108   Office supplies

109   Dues/subscriptions

110   Auto

111   Insurance

112   Bank fees

113   Maintenance/repairs

114   Accounting and legal fees

115   Business fees/taxes

116   Housekeeping supplies

117   Outside services

118   Miscellaneous

Cash Disbursement Journal

Now you are ready to set up your Cash Disbursement Journal. Purchase a ledger from an office-supply store designed for this purpose; it will be divided into narrow columns. Across the top write headings for each column starting with the date of transaction, who was paid, and check number; then list each item noted in your chart of accounts. Record each expenditure in the journal using the sample that follows as a model. Don't forget to record the commission automatically deducted by your reservation service agency when it collects the deposit from guests that the RSA booked for you.

At the end of each month, add your columns and you will have—to the penny—the amount that you spent during the past month on your B&B business. Then start a new month in the journal's pages. At the end of twelve months, you can build a comprehensive picture of your B&B operation's expenditures for one year's time by totaling the transactions for every month. You can also use the results for figuring your income taxes. Harry and Elaine Dickson, owners of Captain Ezra Nye House in Sandwich, Massachusetts, rec-

Sample Cash Disbursement Journal

July 2006

Date	Paid To:	Check #	Phone 101	Postage 102	Linens 103	Food 104	Adv. 105	RSA 106
7/1	A&P	351				32.75		
7/2	AT&T	352	58.45					
7/5	P.O.	353		29.00				
7/7		354				12.35		
7/16	RSA	deducted from deposit						24.00

ommend using Part II, "Expenses, Profit or Loss from Business," on Schedule C, Income Tax Form 1040, as the model for expense categories. "At year's end we total the expenses line by line. Voilà, the hardest part of our income tax is done!" say the Dicksons. (See the section on taxes later in this chapter.)

For each disbursement you should use your B&B checking account and always get a receipt. To store receipts (such as cash register slips and confirming invoices marked "paid"), a simple but effective method is to buy an accordian file with twelve compartments or twelve large manila envelopes at the beginning of each year. Label each compartment or envelope by month. Place all receipts you collect for a particular month in the designated envelope or slot. It's very helpful to write on the back of each receipt what the expenditure was for—envelopes, stamps, food—along with the account number from your chart of accounts. (So the back of a cash register receipt from the A&P, for example, should say "food, #104.") You have the choice of recording each expenditure in the Cash Disbursement Journal as soon as it's made or waiting until the end of each month to record all expenditures in the order in which they occurred. (Don't forget to place a checkmark on each receipt after it's recorded to give yourself an easy way to see whether or not it's been entered into the journal.) For your own sanity choose one method or the other. Recording some receipts as they come in but leaving others until later will just be cause for frustration.

Cash Receipts Journal

Now that you have your Cash Disbursement Journal, you will also need a Cash Receipts Journal. First, follow the same procedure for setting up a chart of accounts, this one for money coming in (receipts). Most of your income will be from accommodations fees for B&B, but you might also find that your business includes, for example, running a B&B workshop at a nearby adult education center a couple times a year and providing babysitting services for guests upon request. Then your chart of accounts will look something like the sample below.

201   Accommodations fee for B&B
202   B&B workshops
203   Babysitting

Use your chart of accounts to set up your Cash Receipts Journal according to the model given here. In your journal record all money coming in. (Note that some hosts elect to keep just one journal and use it for both receipts and disbursements. Because most—or all—of the income that bed and breakfast hosts receive comes from one source, guests paying an accommodations fee for B&B, one column can be set aside for this.)

If your B&B is listed with a reservation service agency, ask the RSA to provide a statement of bookings on a monthly or quarterly basis to help you with your record keeping. Many RSAs already offer this service. "Our hosts receive a copy of each reservation for their records," says the manager of a California reservation service. "We supply a monthly activity statement," says the manager of a Florida reservation service.

Sample Cash Receipts Journal

July 2006

Date	Received From:	Method of payment	B&B 201	B&B Workshops 202	Babysitting 203
7/8	Mary Jones	Cash	Bal. Due $66		
7/9	Sam Smith	Traveler's Checks	$120		
7/10	Sam Smith	Cash			$15
7/11	Jeff Black	Personal Check	Deposit $60		
7/15	Adult Ed. Center	Business Check		$100	
7/16	RSA	Business Check	Deposit Mary Jones $36		

Petty Cash

It's advisable to pay for all B&B expenses out of your B&B account so that you'll have that documentation in the checkbook and check register, and your canceled checks, but sometimes there are small expenditures for which you cannot realistically write a check. What you need to handle these inexpensive but necessary items is a petty-cash fund for your B&B operation. Write a check out of your B&B account in the amount of $40 or $50, cash it, and keep that money in a special envelope or box. Draw from it whenever you need to pay for a small item—a pen for 99 cents, a loaf of bread for $2.89. Keep all the receipts in the envelope or box with the remaining money. At any time the receipts and cash on hand should total the petty-cash fund amount. Whenever the cash needs to be replenished, write a check for the total amount of receipts. Then place the receipts in a small envelope with the check number and date written on the outside. If you write the check in January, place the envelope in the January receipts file. "Petty cash" will be recorded as a disbursement for that month.

Personal Log

In addition to everything else, it's a good idea to keep a personal log, almost like a diary, of your day-to-day bed and breakfast activities. An appointment calendar that provides lots of space for notes will do nicely. Here, record what you do that does not show up in your other journals: "cleaned guest rooms (2 hours), made breakfast for guests (half an hour), took them to airport (12 miles round-trip; 1 hour), and did laundry (45 minutes)." This personal log can help you substantiate what your bed and breakfast activities involve if the occasion ever arises. (For example, some hosts have found it necessary to prove to local authorities how a B&B differs from a landlord-tenant situation.) It will also provide a basis for determining your total hours of work spent on B&B activities and will help you figure out deductions for the business use of your car and utilities.

Getting Help

If the idea of setting up a recordkeeping system by yourself still seems overwhelming, seek help. Consult a bookkeeper or an accountant, ask for advice from your local Small Business Administration office, take an adult education course in bookkeeping basics for home-based businesses, purchase self-help books on the subject, talk to other hosts and reservation service managers, or hire a B&B consultant. There are good options for taking care of the record keeping for your business. The choice is up to you, but one way or another you must make sure that you put just as much effort into this aspect of your business as the "fun" parts!

Business Planning Resources

The U.S. Small Business Administration (SBA) offers an extensive library of free publications designed to help owners of small businesses master business planning skills. Most helpful to B&B hosts are the following publications: *The Business Plan for Homebased Busi-*

ness, Budgeting in a Small Service Firm, Record Keeping in a Small Business, Business Plan Workbook, and *Marketing for Small Business.* Publications are available online at the SBA Web site. If you do not have Internet access, call the SBA answer desk (800–827–5722). In addition,

For small-business publications and resources, visit: www.sba.gov

For free small-business counseling, visit: www.score.org

the SBA conducts free online courses in business subjects, and the Service Corps of Retired Executives (SCORE) offers free counseling in a variety of specialities.

Taxes

Before you open a bed and breakfast in your home, make it your business to educate yourself thoroughly about the tax laws that would apply to your operation. A heart-to-heart talk with an accountant or a representative of the Internal Revenue Service (or both) during the early planning stages will help you understand what your legal responsibilities are. And once you know what your obligations are and the options available to you, you will be in a better position to devise an intelligent business plan for the start-up and growth of your bed and breakfast operation over its first three to five years. This is true even if you expect your venture to start small and perhaps stay small for some time. You can make tax laws work to your advantage if you have good counsel. Make sure you get it.

Following is a discussion of some of the main concerns that you will have as a "sole proprietor" of a bed and breakfast operated out of your own home. If you are involved in a business partnership or if you run a commercial enterprise—rather than a home-based business—you will need to gather additional information; in this case, it is recommended that you consult a financial-services professional to help you. Note also that tax laws have been known to change from year to year, and they can differ from state to state. Because of this, the information given here is intended as background only for the owner-occupied B&B business, designed to familiarize you with the basics. One of your responsibilities as a bed and breakfast host is to identify the tax laws that do apply to your particular set of circumstances and then take the steps necessary to comply with reporting requirements and payment of any taxes due.

Running a bed and breakfast out of your own home is considered a "sole proprietorship" for federal tax purposes. Earned income from your B&B activities is reported on Schedule C, which is filed in addition to the usual Form 1040. Schedule C is the place to report the total income you received from B&B (the "gross income") and deductions for the expenses you've paid for your B&B operations. When you subtract the total amount for expenses from the gross income, the result is your "net income," or the taxable portion of your income from B&B. Sometimes your expenses and the other deductions you want to take can exceed your income, but be warned, says B&B host and financial consultant Arline Pat Hunt, that "you cannot show a loss on the business caused by use of the residence. You can show zero income. For instance, if your income from B&B is $6,000 and your operating expenses (such as advertising, food, car, and supplies) amount to $2,000, you cannot take more than $4,000 toward your house expenses (insurance, interest, taxes, and utilities) and depreciation of the house. Those amounts not used, however, can be carried over to future years when the income might be greater."

Business Expenses

There are guidelines for determining legitimate business expenses. All the expenses that you claim must have been incurred in connection with your business (that is, they were not personal expenses—such as the purchase of a hot tub that is not intended for guests' use). The expenses must also be ordinary and necessary for the business. (For example, printing brochures to advertise your B&B is a very common, "ordinary" thing to do—but taking an around-the-world trip to distribute them could be viewed with suspicion.) And finally, the amount declared for any expense must be reasonable. (Five dollars spent on the economy size of laundry detergent is "reasonable," but $5,000 spent on a washing machine would more than likely come under scrutiny.) Use the chart of accounts you prepared for record keeping as a reference (see "Keeping Records" earlier in this chapter). Typical deductible business expenses for your B&B operation are those for:

Business cards	Commission to RSA	Postage
Brochures	Laundry	Food
Advertising	Ledgers	Coffee

Accounting fees	Business insurance	Soap
Membership dues to chamber of commerce	A course in bookkeeping	Facial tissue
	Magazines/newspapers	This book

One host—who is also an accountant—comes up with a "per guest" figure each tax year for how much it costs him to host each guest. He calculates this amount from total costs for paper products, water usage, postage, telephone, food, laundry, and other B&B-related expenses, as compared to the number of guests he has accommodated during the year. Then he uses the "per guest" figure for tax reports. The "per guest" calculation is optional for the purpose of tax reporting, but it is very helpful in determining your profit margin and in making projections for the coming year.

Depreciation

Costly items that will have long-term use over several years' time or more can either be immediately written off for their full purchase price or be depreciated for a percentage of their cost over a period of time. The amount is calculated and reported on Form 4562. Be sure to get expert advice before depreciating items for the home, or the home itself, when use is shared by guests and yourself, because the IRS targets this in B&B audits. Typical expenditures that can be depreciated are those for:

Furniture	Washing machine
Air conditioner for guest room	Fixtures
Computer	Major repairs

Prorated Expenditures and Deductions

Expenditures that are partly for bed and breakfast and partly personal can be prorated so that the business portion is either deducted as a business expense or depreciated. Business use of your family car is one of these. For her own B&B business, Hunt's Hideaway, Arline Pat Hunt estimates one shopping trip per week for B&B-related activities such as buying groceries and banking and then multiplies the mileage by the IRS standard rate (which changes every year).

Deductions can also be made for the portion of your home that is used exclusively and regularly for bed and breakfast, so utilities, insurance, and repairs can be prorated. Note that for an owner-occupied B&B, this would not include areas such as the kitchen or living room, which are shared by the family. And in terms of taxes, the sale of a home that has been used for a business is more complicated than the sale of a residence only. If you see a possible sale of your B&B home in the future, be sure to discuss with your accountant the best way to fulfill your tax obligations with this in mind. According to Arline Pat Hunt, you may not qualify for the rollover into another residence or for the exemption on the capital gains tax that applies to homeowners who are over fifty-five years old. (The capital gains represent the difference between the purchase price and the selling price.) If this is an issue, one way to call the whole house a "residence" when selling is to not use any part of it for business in the year of sale. "However, this may not be practical if the business operation is a selling point," says Hunt.

Self-employment Tax

If you make a net income of more than $400 from your bed and breakfast, then you must also file a self-employment tax on Form SE. This is Social Security tax for people who are self-employed. The self-employed must also take the initiative to pay quarterly taxes based on income they expect to earn in the coming year, because no employer is withholding part of their earnings for this purpose. IRS Estimated Personal Tax Form 1040 SE is used for these quarterly payments. If you hire anyone to help you run your B&B (for example, someone to clean on a regular basis or do yard work or secretarial tasks), you are also responsible for Social Security and unemployment taxes on employees.

State Taxes

Check the tax laws of your particular state carefully to determine whether your state requires some form of income tax on home-based businesses. (Some do not.) If yours does have a reporting procedure that you must follow, do not assume that the rules are the same as those for federal income tax. In most states they are similar to an extent, but there are usually some exceptions. Some states are satisfied with a photocopy of the federal Schedule C, but others have their own separate set of calculations that must be completed according to a separate set of rules. And be aware that some states have what's called a State Gross Receipts Tax that is levied in addition to regular income tax; find out if your state is among these. Some states also require a room occupancy excise tax for bed and breakfast establishments operating above a minimum number of rooms; find out if your B&B falls into the taxable category.

Sales Tax

Any sales tax due is also collected by the state. Sales tax laws vary from state to state. In some states, so far, sales tax is not collected for bed and breakfast activities in one's home. To find out if you should be paying sales tax for B&B or for items that you sell as a sideline to your B&B operation (such as quilts or other arts and crafts), contact the state department of taxation. Be prepared to meet with some confusion; some states have established definite policies about sales tax where bed and breakfast is concerned, but many more have not. If you're given a decision, ask for it in writing so that there is no confusion later on. If you are required to collect and remit sales tax, find out what percentage your state requires, add the tax to each guest's bill, and pay the tax due according to the schedule set up by the state (usually four times a year). Do not ignore this obligation. Upon learning that some B&B operators were not collecting and remitting sales tax, the State of New York's Department of Taxation threatened to subpoena information about guest bookings. The penalty for failure to remit sales tax can rise to an additional 50 percent of taxes due plus interest.

Property Taxes

Property taxes represent another area where you could have obligations beyond your current residential taxes. Find out if there has been any determination about taxing B&Bs in your area at commercial rates. If so, your property taxes could be three or four times what they are now. In recent years there have been attempts made to tax B&Bs at commercial rates, even though the payment of thousands of dollars per year threatens to drive many out of business. If this kind of effort is under way in your area, your best defense is to join with other B&B hosts and reservation service agencies to launch a legislative battle to exempt small B&Bs from the higher taxes. This was the case in Massachusetts, where an organized effort helped pass legislation that protects B&Bs having three or fewer guest rooms from the higher commercial property taxes.

Help from the RSA

In general, don't overlook the help that is available from your local reservation service agency. The RSA manager is familiar with the tax laws as applied to your locality and can most likely be counted on for a few pointers or other assistance if you are listed with the agency. Whereas some RSAs leave sales-tax collection to individual hosts, others take responsibility for collecting sales tax whenever reservations are placed through the agency. "We file sales tax for all hosts who do not solicit business outside the reservation service," says the manager of a Georgia RSA. "We collect the state sales tax on behalf of our hosts and send it in monthly," says the manager of a Pennsylvania reservation service. A service like this relieves the host of the sales-tax worry as long as guests are accepted only through the RSA; otherwise, the host still has to remit taxes for those guests who do not book through the agency.

When income tax time rolls around, there are some RSAs that supply documentation and advice. "At the end of each year, we send hosts an accounting of all the guests that they have had. We do not help them with the actual tax preparation, but we do suggest to them what can and can't be considered a deduction, such as free-room nights given as promotion, cleaning supplies, etcetera," says one RSA manager. Another offers "an easy-to-use record-keeping system that is maintained on the host's check register and provides monthly and year-to-date income and expense computer printouts. As a result, the host has current financial information for management of his or her operations and the documentation needed to easily complete all tax forms." "We give income-tax-time reports to each host on their gross and net receipts for the year," says the manager of a Texas reservation service. "Our RSA gives us a monthly summary of transactions, which helps enormously in preparing the Schedule C," says Catherine Hatala, owner of Rodman Renaissance in Philadelphia.

Records in Relation to Taxes

If you have kept good records (see section on "Keeping Records" earlier in this chapter), meeting your tax obligations will be that much easier because detailed information on your income and expenses is at your fingertips. Hold on to records for up to seven years in the event of a tax audit or your desire to take out a loan or sell the business. Banks usually want to see financial statements for the last two or three years of operation. It is advisable to retain a second set of records (an extra copy of tax returns or a backup disk or hard copy of financial statements) in a secure location outside your home, perhaps at work or in a safe-deposit box at the bank.

Although it will reduce your expenses to maintain your own records and file tax reports yourself, do not try to single-handedly produce quarterly and year-end statements and tax reports unless you truly understand what you're doing. If you're determined to do it all yourself, you might find it helpful to first enlist the counsel of an accountant.

Financial-services expert John Sedensky recommends first having an accountant review your record-keeping methods and make suggestions for improvement; then hire a financial professional to prepare tax returns from your records. Hiring an enrolled agent—a licensed tax specialist who functions in tax areas—is typically less costly than hiring a tax attorney or an accountant. (Call your state chapter of the National Association of Enrolled Agents for referrals. Look under "Tax Return Preparation" in the Yellow Pages.)

An IRS Audit

No matter who does your taxes, always remember that *you* are the one responsible for the accuracy of the reports. If you hire someone to take care of this for you, make sure you know exactly what he or she is doing. One former host sadly reports that she had to go out of business after an IRS audit assessed $8,000 in back taxes. It seems that she had been too trusting in leaving everything in the hands of her CPA, who had taken inappropriate deductions on her tax reports. In the end she was the one who suffered.

A word to the wise: You cannot be too obsessive about keeping good records or too honest about reporting accurate information on your tax returns. The reason? The IRS targets cash-basis businesses (such as B&Bs) for audit because there is more of a tendency for business owners not to report all their income. The audits are conducted according to recommendations made in an IRS training document called "Market Segment Specialization Program: Bed & Breakfasts," first published in May 1993. An IRS audit of a B&B business involves an interview and close scrutiny of your records.

The IRS audit interview focuses on a detailed description of your B&B business and its history, which includes date acquired, loans obtained for purchase, date opened for business, condition of structure, cost of any renovations, number of guest rooms and types of baths, common areas used by guests, room rates, seasons operated, meals served, fees for pets and children, liquor license, types of credit cards accepted, advertising, gifts and crafts sold, tips and gratuities, special events (such as weddings or meetings), transportation fees, insurance carrier, and employees.

The IRS agent will want to see the following documents: federal and state income tax returns for several years; prior revenue agent's reports, if any, including previous audits; city or county bed-tax returns; your business partner's tax returns; payroll tax returns; W–2, W–4, and 1099 forms; journals detailing cash disbursements, cash receipts, voucher payables, sales, and purchases; guest registration book and guest cards; chart of accounts; bank statements, both business and personal; savings and investment statements; and loan documents.

The areas where the IRS will look for possible unreported income are charges for any extras beyond room rental fees. These include reservation and cancellation fees as well as income from referrals, catering, gifts and crafts sold, special events held at the B&B, and "taxi" service provided to guests.

Areas of abuse the IRS is looking for in particular are personal expenses deducted as business expenses on Schedule C, such as bank charges for personal accounts; family portion of food expenses; the basic rate of a sole telephone used in both business and personal calls; repairs and maintenance to areas other than the specific rooms held for business; as well as disproportionate deductions of utility costs, interest, taxes, and insurance.

The IRS permits no deductions for a B&B business in a personal residence if rooms are rented for fewer than fifteen days during a taxable year. Such a small scale of operation places the activity into a hobby category so that income from it is not taxable and related expenses are not deductible. Take note, however, that small, home-based businesses are reviewed for tax purposes over a five-year span. A B&B owner must show a profit in two out of five years to take the B&B effort out of the hobby category.

Tax Information Resources

For information to help you meet your tax obligations, the best sources are the user-friendly IRS Web site for tax forms and publications and its companion Web site specifically for small businesses. And check out the IRS-sponsored online classroom, "Small Business/Self-Employed Virtual Small Business Tax Workshop", designed to help small-business owners understand and meet their federal tax obligations.

Helpful publications can be downloaded from the IRS Web sites and are also available by calling 800–TAX–FORM (800–829–3676). Publications of particular interest to small-business owners include a tax calendar (#1518), *Small Business Talk* (#1853), *Your Rights as a Taxpayer* (#1), *Your Federal Income Tax* (#17), *Tax Guide for Small Businesses* (#334), *Self-Employment Tax* (#533), *Starting a Business and Keeping Records* (#583), *Business Use of Your Home* (#587), and *Guide to Free Tax Services* (#910). The IRS also offers the *Introduction to Federal Taxes for Small Businesses and Self-Employed* CD-ROM (#3693*), *Small Business Resource Guide* CD-ROM (#3207), and *A Virtual Small Business Tax Workshop* DVD (#1066c).

> **For tax forms and publications, visit:** www.irs.treas.gov
>
> **For tax information and tools specifically for small businesses,** visit: www.irs.gov/smallbiz

Writing Your Business Plan

Ever write a term paper in high school or college? Of course, who hasn't? At the time you might have complained about it, but now you will find out just how valuable the experience can be. If you think about it, you will remember that your term paper project forced you to analyze your thoughts about a particular subject, write them down in a logical way, and communicate them to others. This is what you want to do in your business plan.

What exactly is a business plan? Some call it a road map to lead you to your goal. Others call it a blueprint for success. You wouldn't build a house without a blueprint, would you? Neither should you try to build a business without one. Basically, your business plan contains your vision of what you want your B&B business to become and shows how you intend to make it happen.

There are two reasons for developing a sound business plan. The first is for your own benefit. A lovely fantasy is one thing, but figuring out how to get from fantasy to reality is entirely another. Writing a business plan will help you analyze your strengths and weaknesses and choose strategies to overcome challenges. And it will help protect you from nasty surprises that you hadn't anticipated.

The second reason for developing a business plan is to communicate your vision in a concrete way to other key people. Who are these people? Perhaps a potential business partner, a vendor with whom you would like to establish credit, your accountant, the banker who is considering making a small-business loan to you, and maybe even your somewhat skeptical spouse, who isn't sure that opening a B&B is such a good idea.

What does a bed and breakfast business plan contain? While each is tailored to reflect the unique nature of the individual B&B, there are elements common to all. Following is a basic guide to use when preparing your business plan.

For now, concentrate on collecting and organizing all the information, seeking help if you need it. As you finish various sections, insert them into a binder, which allows for updates and additions at any time. Prepare the finished product on a computer to achieve a polished, professional-looking format. Aim for a total length somewhere between thirty and fifty pages. On the following page is a basic outline to help you construct your B&B business plan. Additional information can be found on the Web sites operated by the American Express Small Business Exchange and Palo Alto software. If you wish, you can build your plan on-line at the Web site for the Canada Business Service Centers. Its helpful interactive planner will even prepare financial projections for you based on the information that you input.

For business-planning information and tools, visit:
www.americanexpress.com/smallbusiness
www.cbsc.org/ibp
www.bplans.com

Cover Page

If you intend to show your business plan to others, you need a cover page with a title and date, plus your name, the B&B's name, address, telephone and FAX numbers, and e-mail address. Add your business logo if you have one. The title should include the words "business plan," for example, "Business Plan for Opening and Operating the Dew Drop Inn."

Summary

Here is where you explain what your overall plan is, in one hundred words or less. I'm not kidding. You will need to be able to explain your plan succinctly again and again for the benefit of a variety of people you meet, so write this paragraph carefully and memorize it.

Prepare all the other parts of the business plan first, then use the information here. Include a brief description of your future B&B (lovely colonial with five guest rooms), location advantages (near the beach, a university, and a hospital), competition (only one other B&B in a 10-mile radius), financial health (mortgage paid off, need small-business loan to start up), time line (expect to open in ten months), marketing plan (first-year outreach includes guidebook listings, special events, and using community resources), community support (the mayor and town council agree we need a B&B in this location), and other relevant information about your ability to manage the business. Then condense, condense, condense.

Objectives

Ever been to a job interview where somebody asks where you see yourself a year from now? Five years? Ten years? I must admit, the first time I heard the question I thought the interviewer must be kidding. But now I know better. In business, those who plan ahead often end up where they want to go.

In this section, state your objectives both for the short term (to open a B&B by June of next year), the long term (to build my B&B business into a successful, three-season operation with a 95 percent occupancy rate in five years), and the interim (to increase the percentage of visitors by 20 percent every year for the first three years).

Market Analysis

Who will your customers be? In this section list the attractions that regularly draw people to the area (the nearby beach, the university, and the hospital, as well as the flea market in the summer and the town festivals). Find statistics wherever you can to include (call the local tourist board, the chamber of commerce, local reservation service agencies, B&B associations). Good sources for bed and breakfast statistics are the Professional Association of Innkeepers International and the *Yellow Brick Road* newsletter.

Business Plan Contents

Cover Page
Summary
Objectives
Market Analysis
Competition
Time Line
Marketing Plan
Marketing Projection Worksheet
Management
Finances
Appendix

Competition

Check out the competition. Where do visitors to your area stay now? The hotel in town? The motel on Route 6? The B&B that just happens to be next door to your house? Make a list of other accommodations in the area and estimate how many guests they draw per month and per year. Find out as much as you can through phone calls to local B&B associations and reservation service agencies and annual reports from area hotels. Are there too many or too few B&Bs? Do hotels sell out during certain times (college graduation, the annual road race) and need a place to send the overflow?

Time Line

Opening a new B&B requires a time line (also called a Gandtt chart) that puts the activities involved into perspective. Included in this section is a basic time line for anyone thinking of opening a B&B to use as a guide. Of course, some activities should happen before others—such as collecting information. Buying new furniture should come at the very end, after everything else—financing, marketing strategies, and so on—is already in place. The sample time line provided here assumes that you will take ten months to make your plans and shows when you should focus your energy on certain activities. Be advised, though, that many aspiring hosts take longer than ten months to make their plans. Some take several years.

One word of caution—none of the activities are ever really "done." For example, you will be collecting new information continually, well after you have opened your B&B. When the time line shows your focus should turn to another activity, the previous one should never disappear altogether. Chart your progress on the Activity Worksheet that appears in appendix 6, making a note of those activities that still need action. A sample Activity Worksheet is included here to show how it might be used to track your activities. The sample shows two of the ten activities listed on the worksheet.

Annual Marketing Plan

Why do you need a *plan* to market your B&B? There are plenty of activities that can help increase the number of guests booking rooms with you. (See chapter 6, "Publicizing Your Bed & Breakfast.") Can't you just go from one marketing activity to another whenever you feel like it?

Sample Activity Time Line for Opening a B&B

Activities	Sept.	Oct.	Nov.	Dec.	Jan.	Feb.	Mar.	Apr.	May	June
1. Collect information	■									
2. Examine your lifestyle		■								
3. Evaluate your home and surroundings		■								
4. Identify your market			■	■						
5. Develop a business plan				■	■					
6. Comply with regulations					■	■	■			
7. Prepare a budget						■	■			
8. Prepare a marketing plan						■	■	■		
9. Set up business systems							■	■		
10. Refurbish and decorate								■	■	
Opening Day!										✳

Sample Activity Worksheet for Opening a B&B

Activities	Task Done	Action Items	Progress Notes
1. Collect information Publications Workshops / apprenticeships Consultants Associations / reservation services Internet	 ✓ ✓ ✓ 	• Sign up for workshop at community college. • Buy book on developing a marketing plan. • Call local reservation service. • Search the Internet for B&B resources. • Contact local association.	Workshop full—reserve next one in advance. Can't find local association—contact PAII for info.
2. Examine lifestyle Personality Skills Work Family Support network	✓	• Write down pros & cons of current lifestyle. • Make a list of combined skills in household. • Make a list of skills we need but don't have. • Chart out a schedule for a week balancing work & B&B hosting and evaluate. • Talk to the family about the idea of B&B!	
(Note: There are ten activities, all of which appear on the blank worksheet in appendix 6.)			

Sample Marketing Plan

Three Primary Objectives:

A.   To promote my B&B in guidebooks and online directories

B.   To use community resources to promote my B&B

C.   To plan and hold special events to introduce people to my B&B

Month	Type of Marketing Activity	Projected Expenses	Actual Expenses
January	A. Buy three regional guidebooks. B. Make a list of community resources (examples: local tourist office, chamber of commerce, bridal shop, hospital, university, flea market). C. Write down ten ideas for events (examples: murder-mystery weekend, Halloween hayride, apple picking, shop-till-you-drop weekend).	3 books @ $20 = $60	
February	A. Read guidebooks and write down three reasons each author would be interested in my B&B (example: authors prefer country settings, resident pets, and gourmet breakfasts). B. Target one community resource as a priority (example: local university). C. Select one event to plan (example: Halloween hayride) and make a list of everything needed (examples: hay wagon, cider, cookies).		
March	A. Draft letters to guidebook authors containing three reasons each should visit my B&B. B. Call local university to find out which departments often have visitors coming from out of town (example: alumni office). C. Research costs for each item on event list (example: rental of hay wagon with horse, hay, and driver).		

Month	Type of Marketing Activity	Projected Expenses	Actual Expenses
April	A. Print error-free letters to guidebook authors on B&B stationery and mail with brochure and pictures of B&B, along with an invitation for a complimentary night's stay. B. Make friendly telephone contact with key person in each university department and ask if I can stop by with brochures. C. Make budget for event and write down ideas for cutting costs (example: ask hay wagon owner if he will donate rental in exchange for placing his business name on my promotional flyers as a co-sponsor of the event).	$10 postage $30 film and developing	
May	A. Research online directories and select three with high traffic and affordable fees. B. Visit key people in university departments (examples: receptionist and alumni events coordinator) and invite them to a complimentary breakfast at my B&B. C. Identify market (example: romantic couples) and plan scope of event (example: refreshments and B&B tour 6:00 to 8:00 P.M., moonlight hayride 8:00 to 10:00 P.M.).		
June	A. Write advertising copy and take digital photos of B&B for online listings. B. Entertain receptionist and alumni events coordinator from university with breakfast, a B&B tour, and offer of a discount for one night; send them home with brochures. C. Draft flyer for event and ask friends to proofread, solicit help for the event.	$30 food 2 discount coupons @ $30–$60	

Month	Type of Marketing Activity	Projected Expenses	Actual Expenses
July	A. Contact the three selected online directories to place my listings. B. Target second community resource as a priority (example: hospital). C. Prepare final version of flyer and call printers for comparative prices.	$400 listing fees	
August	A. Entertain guidebook author with a complimentary night's stay while she is on tour doing research for her next guidebook. B. Call local hospital to find out which departments refer people coming to visit patients to convenient lodging. C. Get flyers printed and call local newspapers for prices on calendar listings and ads; call local radio station.	Complimentary night and breakfast @ $100 $60 printing	
September	A. Send follow-up note to guidebook author. B. Visit key staff people at local hospital to drop off brochures and invite them to a complimentary breakfast at my B&B. C. Distribute flyers to local businesses, churches, and community organizations, and post on bulletin boards; place ads and listing for event in local papers.	4 ads @ $30 = $120	
October	A. Send e-mails to guidebook authors inviting them to Halloween hayride. B. Entertain key personnel from hospital (examples: receptionist and coordinator of patient services) with breakfast and B&B tour, along with a discount for a future one-night stay. C. Prepare for event, appear for interview on local radio show, and entertain all who come, sending them home with a brochure and small gift (example: small ceramic jack-o'-lantern with B&B's name and address on it).	$30 food, 2 discount coupons @ $30–$60 Event costs (food, extra staff, gifts, etc.) $400	

Month	Type of Marketing Activity	Projected Expenses	Actual Expenses
November	A. Send follow-up notes to guidebook authors who attended Halloween hayride. B. Target third community resource as a priority (example: bridal shop). C. Send follow-up notes to all who came to event.	$15 notepaper and postage	
December	A. Evaluate responses to date from online directory listings. B. Call bridal shop and find out who the owner and key salespeople are. C. Look at original list of event ideas and target one as a priority for the coming year.		

Well, sure, if you want to leave such an important aspect of your business to whim, but it's not the best way to ensure an increase of guests over time. Preparing an annual marketing plan helps you focus on your main goals. By charting your marketing activities month by month in advance, you can use the plan as a calendar to make sure that the necessary follow-through happens.

The marketing plan itself is also an indication to others of how seriously you take your business and should be included in your business plan.

Your first task is to select three primary marketing goals for the upcoming year. This won't be easy for a new host, who has so much to do. Resist the temptation to try to do everything all at once. Instead, select one goal that will have immediate payback (such as a special event) and one with long-term benefit (such as a guidebook listing); the third is your choice. You can always add more goals once you have had a chance to evaluate the time and energy you are spending on the first three in relation to the results.

The best time-management consultants give the same advice: Break large tasks down into smaller ones. A series of small tasks done over time will surely lead you to your goal faster than a huge task that seems so overwhelming that you just keep putting it off. This is exactly what you need to do with your three goals. For each, write down twelve steps and assign one to every month of your annual marketing plan.

You will find that some tasks (like a phone call) take no more than a few minutes, while others (such as designing a new brochure) may take hours. It's important to keep making the time to complete your tasks every single month if you expect to reap the eventual rewards.

The sample marketing plan given in this chapter shows how owners of a five-room B&B will work to increase the number of "room nights" sold in the coming year. You can use the blank form in appendix 6 to write your own annual marketing plan.

Marketing Projection Worksheet

Marketing is very much like spinning a few plates, then a few more, and a few more. For a while, they all continue to spin nicely, then a few slow down and eventually stop spinning altogether unless they get a good shove to get them going again.

From year to year, as you focus on different marketing goals, you will find that you are still reaping good results from some activities in previous years (such as joining a B&B association that lists members on its Web site), while others are not generating guests at all anymore (perhaps that nice hotel clerk who used to send the hotel's overflow to you has gone back to graduate school, leaving in her place a stranger who knows nothing about your B&B). The marketing activity that was once spinning merrily along needs a good shove.

Making an annual marketing projection worksheet for yourself will help you determine which activities need attention and forecast the results from various types of outreach. The sample worksheet in this chapter lists a variety of activities that a typical five-room B&B located in a rural area near a beach and a college might undertake, plus some local activities that draw visitors. Note that the worksheet has a column for projected room nights sold—what the B&B owner hopes the activity or attraction will generate. There is also a column for actual results. Completing this column month by month gives a host valuable feedback for the future. If the Halloween hayride you worked so hard to organize was a bust, that tells you not to try it again next year. But maybe that murder-mystery weekend left guests clamoring for more. That makes it a good activity to repeat.

Use the sample worksheet as a model; of course, your own worksheet will include items that are unique to your own B&B and its location. A blank worksheet appears in appendix 6 for your use.

Sample Marketing Projection Worksheet

Calendar	Marketing Activity or Local Attraction	Projected Room Nights Sold	Actual Room Nights Sold
January			
Second weekend	Winter festival in town	20	
Third week	New guidebook listing appears	10	
February			
First week	New guidebook listing	10	
Feb. 14 & 15	Valentine's Day special	20	
March			
First weekend	Learn-to-quilt weekend	20	
Third week	State tourist office's pamphlet appears	10	
April			
Third Monday	Road race & weekend festivities	10	
All month	Distribution of state tourist office's pamphlet continues	6	
May			
Third week	College graduation and festivities	40	
Fourth week	B&B association links to your Web site	20	
June			
First week	Wedding	30	
Third week	New-student week at college	50	
Fourth week	Beach season begins	50	

Calendar	Marketing Activity or Local Attraction	Projected Room Nights Sold	Actual Room Nights Sold
July			
All month	Beach season	150	
July 4th week	July 4th festivities	50	
August			
All month	Beach season	150	
September			
Labor Day weekend	Labor Day festivities	30	
Third week	Fall college semester begins	30	
October			
Second weekend	Homecoming festivities	40	
Third week	Fall foliage	50	
October 31	Halloween hayride special	20	
November			
Third week	Thanksgiving vacation	30	
December			
First weekend	Shop-till-you-drop special	30	

Management

How you intend to operate your business is a key element in your business plan, and it will be scrutinized carefully by your banker and potential investors. Do you have the know-how to manage the business? Include highlights of your impressive résumé here (graduate of gourmet cooking school, degree in hotel management, refinish furniture for a hobby). Identify other operations staff here as well (spouse is an accountant and computer consultant, part-time office assistant will be hired).

Finances

Using information from the "Keeping Records" section earlier in this chapter, develop a budget for the first year (your start-up year), then the following four years. The best advice is to work with your accountant to develop a realistic picture of where your finances will be for each of the next five years. List your start-up expenses (B&B association fees, smoke detectors, new towels, repairs) and estimate ongoing expenses (part-time office help, telephone calls, food, laundry), and then show your accountant these preliminary figures along with your marketing plan and anticipated numbers of guests.

Together, draft a final budget and discuss the overall picture. Do you need a small-business loan now to cover start-up costs? Will you be operating in the black after the first year? The second year? The third? Your financial picture is a crucial part of your business plan. To help you figure out what your projected financial needs are for your start-up year, use the Projected Expenses Worksheet in appendix 6.

Appendix

The appendix should contain reference material that supports the observations or conclusions stated in your business plan (such as part of a statistical analysis of the demographics of your region) as well as letters of support or commitment for your endeavor (such as a letter from an area reservation service agency stating that a B&B is desperately needed in your location).

Chapter Six

Publicizing Your Bed & Breakfast

You may have the loveliest bed and breakfast in the world, but if you wait until someone "discovers" it, you could be waiting a long, long time. Hosts who choose to list their bed and breakfast homes with a reservation service agency can expect that the RSA will do the outreach needed to bring guests to their homes. (Be aware, though, that no RSA can guarantee a certain number of guests as a result of its efforts.) You can do some extra public relations yourself if you wish to host more guests than the number you receive through your RSA, or you can choose to list with several RSAs (provided that you don't have an exclusive contract with one of them) as a way to attract more guests. But if you choose to be independent and not list with any RSA at all, you've got to go out there and get those guests yourself.

Understand that doing all of your own publicity means several things. One is that the anonymity that hosts listed with a reservation service agency enjoy is not possible for you. An RSA protects the names, addresses, and phone numbers of its hosts; there's no reason to use such specific information in its advertisements, brochures, Web site, or press releases because the RSA uses its own. An independent host, on the other hand, has no choice but to use this information on his or her Web site or literature. (The guests do have to have a way to get in touch with the host to make a reservation.) So before you start an all-out campaign to have guests beating a path to your door, be aware that they might do just that. You must be ready to take on all the phone calls (day and night), to handle all the mail, answer e-mails promptly, and even deal with occasional visitors who arrive on your doorstep after seeing your address listed in a guidebook. And to make it even more appealing for prospective guests to make a reservation with you (rather than with another nearby B&B), consider getting a toll-free telephone number and an e-mail address.

Because your bed and breakfast will be in the public eye, make sure that you know where your B&B stands in terms of local zoning ordinances, health and safety regulations, fire codes, and insurance coverage. (See chapter 5, "The Business of B&B.") It's not a bad idea to consult an attorney about your responsibilities in these areas before you start publicizing your bed and breakfast. When you've satisfied these conditions, you're ready to go public.

Creating Your Literature

Your literature represents your bed and breakfast. Prospective guests will see your brochures, your business cards, and your stationery (and also your Web site, discussed later in this chapter) long before they ever set eyes on you and your bed and breakfast. The decision to visit—or not—will be made on the basis of the literature they see. How well it's done, or how poorly, will have a direct effect on your business. The literature does not have to be expensive, but it must entice visitors to your bed and breakfast, and it must give all the information necessary for prospective guests to follow through on reservations. Literature that is attractive and functional is essential for the success of your bed and breakfast business.

Your B&B Brochure

The brochure is your most important piece of literature. You will be sending it out in response to requests for more information, leaving it in strategic places to generate interest in your bed and breakfast, and giving it to anyone who will make referrals to you. Everything about it—the content, the colors, the paper stock, the artwork, the typography—should work together to create an appealing image for your bed and breakfast.

Your B&B's Image

First consider the sort of image you want to create. How would you describe the ambience of your bed and breakfast? What is special about it? What is appealing about it? Does it have a distinctive architectural style? What colors predominate in the guest rooms, or perhaps in the whole house? What type of furnishings do you have? Are you located in the country, city, or suburbs?

Taking all these things into consideration, what would you say is the most salient feature of your bed and breakfast? Is it that your home is listed in the National Register of Historic Places; that it is surrounded by apple orchards; that you are a purple freak, and all your rooms are decorated in shades thereof? You can use the prominent feature of your bed and breakfast to build an image for your brochure.

"If your establishment is Victorian, you obviously do not want your logo or brochure to have a rustic cabin feel. People paint a mental picture in their mind long before they make a decision where to stay. The advertising materials you provide them will make all the difference on just how appealing that picture is," says one graphic designer who specializes in B&B promotion.

Choosing Colors and Paper

The colors you choose for your brochure can add to or detract from that image. Certain colors carry certain connotations. If you want to emphasize a nature theme because your home is located in the country, then green is a good choice as a color, either for the ink or the paper stock. Other earth colors could work well, too. The use of warm brown, burnt orange, or deep red can evoke an image of the beauty of autumn in the country—which will be to your advantage if you're located in an area to which tourists come in droves to enjoy the fall foliage. If your B&B is in the heart of ski country, you might want to use white and blue ("cold" colors) as a way to suggest winter. If your guest rooms are decorated in a particular color or if there is a predominant color in your home, then that color is a natural one to use in your brochure.

Be aware that the cost of a brochure goes up if you want to use that all-important color to create your bed and breakfast's image. Colored ink costs more than black ink. Colored paper stock costs more than white paper stock. Other cost factors are the weight of the paper and its surface. The thicker (or "heavier") the paper, the more it costs, but this is a necessary expense. Brochures are generally printed on heavier paper stock so that they will hold up well. A brochure printed on paper that is as flimsy as copy paper (20-pound paper) will wrinkle and rip far too easily. You need something more hardy to withstand all the handling, mailing, and even storage. Having your brochures printed on 60-pound paper will be worth the investment. The cost goes up if you want paper that has been specially coated (for a slick and shiny look) or that has a special texture. Smooth but uncoated paper is less expensive.

Cutting Costs

You should always ask for prices before ordering. Sometimes you can reach a compromise with a printer to get closer to what you really want without paying full price for it. For example, the printer might be willing to use colored ink on your brochure at no extra charge if another client has ordered colored ink for another job. If the ink will already be on the printing press (so that the printer doesn't have to clean the press and change the ink just for you), then there is no setup cost involved. True, you might be asked to accept a color other than the one you had in mind, but the savings could be worth the compromise on your part. Also, sometimes a printer will have in stock a lot of paper that he or she would like to sell and thus be willing to discount it to you. This usually occurs with specialty papers (the coated and the textured and the unusual colors that are not ordered by large numbers of people), the kinds that cost more than plainer papers, so you could pick up quite a bargain. It can't hurt to ask. So what if the off-white you wanted turns out to be an elegant eggshell color? No big deal if you can save a significant amount of money and maybe even make your brochure look better than you thought your budget would allow.

Naming Your B&B

The image of your bed and breakfast that you want to present to prospective guests can be captured well by choosing a name for your B&B. Printed right on the front of the brochure, a good name will leave no question in a prospective guest's mind what the main feature of your B&B is. (Naming your B&B will also help former guests find you again when they are planning a return trip to your area or want to recommend your B&B to friends. See "Memories" in chapter 8.) Are you trying to entice visitors to your B&B on the basis of your location in the country? Peeping Cow Inn sure does a good job of it. Do you have animals, and rather exotic ones at that? Camel Lot is not only a B&B but also a breeding farm for unusual animals. Do you offer a refuge from the hustle and bustle of city life? Hunt's Hideaway sounds good.

Trademarking Your Business Name

Now that you've gone to all the trouble of choosing just the right name for your bed and breakfast, it's crucial that you protect it so that it remains yours and yours alone. Trademarking your name, along with your logo, ensures that potential guests will be able to find you easily on the Internet, that satisfied guests can locate you again, and that your B&B will not be confused with another business using the same name!

How do you protect your chosen name? There are two levels of trademark protection: statewide and nationwide. It is wise to register with both. One B&B owner reports that she registered her business name only in her state, to find later that another B&B operation had registered the same name nationwide. Now, time and again, the two B&Bs are confused.

> To trademark your B&B's name, go to: www.uspto.gov

To register your B&B's name as a local trademark, contact the secretary of state's office for your state. For a nationwide trademark, you must register with the U.S. Patent and Trademark Office. The USPTO Web site provides a search engine (TESS) to help determine if your selected name has already been claimed by someone else. The site also gives applications and procedures for registration.

Using Artwork Effectively

While you're thinking of a name, imagine the type of logo that could go with it. A logo is a small, uncomplicated illustration that acts as a symbol, in this case, of your bed and breakfast. (Sometimes thinking up a logo first can help you with the name.) The two do not necessarily have to echo each other, but it helps. Countryside, a bed and breakfast in West Virginia, uses a drawing of an apple tree, its branches laden with enormous apples. "We use the apple tree logo because we are surrounded by apple orchards," says its owner. Meadow Spring Farm in Kennett Square, Pennsylvania, uses a cow standing next to a farmhouse. Mayflower Bed and Breakfast in Belmont, Massachusetts, uses a logo of the *Mayflower* ship.

Longswamp Bed and Breakfast in Mertztown, Pennsylvania, uses cattails. The Wild Rose of York, located in York, Maine, uses a wild rose.

Tying in your logo with your location, as the owners of the Wild Rose of York do, can be effective. The logo for a bed and breakfast located in Bear Creek, Pennsylvania, shows three little bears contentedly asleep in a bed, a quilt pulled up to their fuzzy chins. The House of Snee, located on Ocean Road in Narragansett, Rhode Island, uses an anchor partially submerged in water. Anchor Hill Lodge in Rogersville, Missouri, also uses (guess what?) an anchor. Mrs. K's Bed & Breakfast is in Kennett Square, Pennsylvania's "mushroom capital." Her logo? A mushroom.

Many hosts also like to use an illustration of their home on their brochure in addition to, or instead of, the logo. "People like to see what they're getting," says Boston host Susan Naimark, a graphic designer who has produced some literature for bed and breakfasts. An illustration showing your B&B to its best advantage can give prospective guests a good idea of what to expect. The likeness must be a good rendering, clean and precise. It should also emphasize something about your B&B that is visually appealing. A drawing done from any old angle is not nearly as impressive as one that focuses on an interesting feature

For an affordable logo design, visit: www.logoworks.com

of the house. The brochure used by Betsy's Bed and Breakfast in Baltimore, Maryland, for example, uses a lovely illustration of the home on the cover. The drawing exaggerates the height of her three-story town house (built in 1871). A lamppost of the same period and a flag streaming from an upper window saying "Betsy's Bed & Breakfast" give a prospective guest a clear image of what this place is like. Inside the brochure, guests find out through a short description what it's like inside the house.

Another bed and breakfast that uses an illustration of the house well is Spindrift Bed & Breakfast in Bandon, Oregon, which is located right next to the beach. The drawing shows a peaceful, pleasant home right next to the waves and the sand, exactly what beach lovers want to see.

Locating Illustrations

So if you do want to use an illustration of your home in the brochure, and a logo as well, what's the best way to go about getting the artwork you need without spending your life's savings? Know that you can't just cut out a drawing that you like from a magazine or newspaper or book and start using it on your literature. Most artwork that has already been prepared and used has been copyrighted; you can't use it unless you obtain permission from the owner. But the good news is that there are some copyright-free illustrations, commonly known as clip art, available to anyone who wishes to use them. It's possible that you can find something ready-made that is right for your purposes. These illustrations are printed in books, and the king of free art is Dover Publications, which prints a whole line of books containing various types of artwork that you can cut out and use. Such artwork includes monograms, floral designs, food and drink illustrations, Art Nouveau and Art Deco graphics and borders, and designs from numerous countries. There's even a book containing ready-to-use teddy bear illustrations. Using something from one of these books (if it fits into the image you're trying to create) is one of the least expensive ways to obtain your artwork. Be aware that these book illustrations may not come in the exact size that you want (a

> For clip art, go to:
> www.clipart.com
> www.doverpublications.com

lot of them are printed larger than your needs will require). So if you do locate an illustration that would be perfect as your logo, you will probably have to reduce or enlarge it to obtain a usable size. Clip art is also available for purchase on CD-ROM, but note that some collections could cost hundreds of dollars. A better source may be a Web site that offers free or economically priced clip art.

One other inexpensive way to obtain artwork is to have a talented friend or relative help you out. Sometimes art students are more than happy to create a custom-made logo for clients for a small fee because they know that the resulting literature can be used to enhance their portfolios. So don't hesitate to contact the art department of a local college.

If you want to have a professional artist design your logo (and perhaps even the whole brochure) the way you want it, the best advice is to shop around for the right person to do it. "Insist on seeing sample work," says graphic designer Susan Naimark. Even if the artist has not produced anything similar to what you have in mind, you can still get a sense of that artist's style by looking at other work he or she has done. Then talk price and get a figure in advance for the work you want done. Be warned that some artists will want to charge you an arm and a leg; others will ask for so little that you'll wonder how they make a living. It's a good idea to get several bids if you're talking about the design and production of the whole brochure. One Internet company called LogoWorks allows a customer to choose a budget for a stated number of designs from which to choose.

One very good way to locate an artist to do the job you want is to look at the literature that other hosts use. If you see something that you really like, get in touch with the host and ask if you can get a referral to the artist, even if that person lives in another part of the country. Note, too, that graphic designers who specialize in B&B literature often advertise in industry publications or on Web sites devoted to innkeeping. Is there a problem doing literature long distance? Not really. It's nice to be able to get together, face-to-face, as the project progresses, but it's not absolutely necessary. Let the artist know exactly what you want through e-mails and telephone conversations. Supply photographs of your home or your own sketches if you wish. From these the artist can sketch out ideas for you to look at. The process can work if you've contracted the services of an artist you know you want.

Using Photographs

A good photograph of your B&B can be your best advertising tool if used effectively in your materials. The results depend largely upon the quality of the photo—its composition, its clarity, and the atmosphere or image it imparts. If you can obtain photos that meet this high standard, publishing them in your materials can only benefit your B&B business.

One B&B that uses photographs effectively is Denali View Bed & Breakfast in Talkeetna, Alaska. The brochure and postcard each contain a collage of photos of the B&B both inside and out, plus scenes from the area. The business card is an attractive picture of the B&B itself with its name, address, and phone number printed on the back. Owner LesLee Solberg planned to order a large quantity of materials, so she put out forty bids to printing companies in six states. The one she chose had the best price for the high-quality product she wanted, but turnaround time was four to six months. Although she had to wait, she is very happy with the result. The lesson here is shop around, ask questions about prices and turnaround time, and do not make a decision without first seeing samples of other work similar to yours that the printer has done.

If you prefer to produce do-it-yourself materials on your computer, you can use images produced by a digital camera, scan printed photos yourself (converting them to digital images), or have a photo-processing service handle this for you. Once you have digital images, you can easily place them in your homemade brochure or newsletter, and place them on your Web site.

Doing It Yourself

A graphic designer can provide you with knowledgeable advice about the colors, paper, type styles, and layout that would be most effective for your brochure. Still, no host has to rely on a graphic designer to produce a brochure, especially if economizing is an issue. You can design a brochure yourself, formatting the contents on a computer, adding an illustration where you want it, and then getting it copied. Mike and Annette Endres, owners of Ahinahina Farm Bed and Breakfast in Hawaii, for example, produced an attractive brochure and business card right on their Macintosh. You can print a supply of brochures, too, by purchasing high-quality paper from an office supply store and using it in your laser printer.

For digital images, cards, calendars, and keepsakes, visit: www.photoworks.com

If you want to do as much as you can yourself, without the help of a professional graphic designer, there are a few basics you should keep in mind for the best results. The main rule is to keep everything simple, clear, neat, and clean. Your brochure should not look cluttered. Use headings for the various pieces of information you include so that readers don't have to hunt for anything. If you're telling people how to make a reservation, put a title on it that says "How to Make a Reservation." And stick to one typeface for the body copy. For the headlines you can either use the same typeface (except larger, in bold), or you can choose a different face altogether. But don't use more than two typefaces in your brochure or it will take on a confused appearance. Be sure that the grammar, spelling, and punctuation are correct.

The Content

The look of your brochure is, of course, very important, and you should do whatever is necessary to produce one that is as attractive as possible within your budget. The importance of the content of your brochure, however, can't be emphasized enough.

This might sound obvious, but don't forget to include the name and address of your bed and breakfast and your telephone number! Sometimes hosts get so wrapped up in the other aspects of designing their brochure that they forget to include the most important information. And remember that most of your calls will be coming from people outside your locality, so make sure that you include your area code. One Michigan bed and breakfast printed literature without this detail. Yes, it's a little thing. But it's an inconvenience for the guest to have to call directory assistance for that crucial piece of information. If you have a toll-free number, e-mail address, or Web site, list these as well. Proofread your copy closely before it goes to the printer to be sure that you put *all* the necessary contact information in the brochure—and this includes the zip code, too!

Somewhere in your brochure you should explain how to make a reservation. If you have certain "office hours" when you will be available to answer your telephone, write them down in the brochure. "Evenings and after 6:00 P.M. weekends" reads one brochure. Right away a guest knows that calling during the day might not result in a connection. Maybe you prefer that people call you only during certain hours. Say so. Many hosts also include a reservation form on one part of the brochure so that guests can mail it back to make a reservation. Don't forget to include room prices and cancellation-fee information. (Note that some hosts publish a separate price list so that a new brochure doesn't have to be printed every time prices change—and they will.) If you wish to accept reservations through the mail, then take a look at the screening checklist provided in chapter 7 for a listing of the information you should obtain on your reservation form.

In your brochure it's wise to give a brief description of what bed and breakfast is (not everyone who sees the brochure will know) and to explain why a guest should come to your bed and breakfast home. Are you near the beach? Are you right downtown? Do you offer a romantic hideaway? Is there great hiking nearby? If there's something especially attractive about your bed and breakfast, mention it in your brochure. Some hosts who are terrific cooks like to lure guests to their homes by describing the goodies that will be theirs to enjoy. If you serve a mean blueberry blintz, it can't hurt to mention this fact in your brochure.

There are other helpful items that can be included in the brochure if you wish. For example, Gwen's Guest Home in Ottawa, Ontario, prints a street map on the inside of her brochure, with the B&B clearly marked. The back of the brochure contains a listing of useful telephone numbers that a visitor might have occasion to use—everything from a dentist and a barber to an optician, dry cleaners, and florist, as well as emergency numbers. The brochure even includes a place for guests to make their own notes. Now there's a useful brochure!

As you begin to work on your own ideas for your brochure, collect some from other bed and breakfast hosts to spark your imagination. Translating the uniqueness of your bed and breakfast home into a piece of literature is no easy task, but sometimes seeing how other hosts have approached the job can help you do your own even better.

Your B&B Stationery

You might decide to make your brochure a self-mailer so that you don't need an envelope every time you need to mail a copy to anyone. (In your brochure design you'll have to set aside a portion of space for the return address, the address of the person you're mailing the piece to, and the stamp.) Still, it's unlikely that you'll be able to exist without ever using paper and envelopes. You will want to write business letters or notes to guests on different occasions. This raises the question of whether you should have your own special bed and breakfast stationery, in addition to your brochure, designed and printed.

It's nice to have your stationery custom-made, with the name and address of your B&B and your logo imprinted on the envelopes, note paper, and perhaps even business cards and postcards. If your budget can handle it, by all means have a designer work with you to create stationery that complements the image you've worked on for the brochure, coordinating colors and style. But if you've got to economize (as most hosts do until their businesses get rolling), there are ways to keep costs down.

One good way to minimize your expenses for stationery is to purchase plain paper and envelopes (preferably during sales) and use either a custom-made rubber stamp or stickers to imprint your bed and breakfast's name and address on them.

A rubber stamp involves the least investment, and one can usually be ordered through copy centers, print shops, or an online company. The cost starts at around $15 and goes up the larger the size of the stamp, or if you wish to include some sort of design with the address. You might want to consider having just your logo made into a separate stamp so that you can repeat the image more than once on the paper you're using for letterhead. Using different-colored inks can produce attractive though inexpensive results.

The alternative to rubber stamps is to purchase a quantity of address stickers. These are inexpensive, in the $20–25 range for a roll of 1,000 self-stick labels. The price fluctuates slightly, depending on the colors, type styles, or optional symbols you choose, but it's an economical solution nonetheless.

For address labels and rubber stamps, go to: www.affordableaddress labels.com

If you like the idea of labels but want to see samples or want more of a choice in what you're getting, check with print shops or copy centers in your area to see what they offer and check companies doing business online. Prices are competitive, but the selection increases. Self-stick labels come in a variety of shapes and sizes—ovals, circles, squares, rectangles. You can get them in gold or silver, with just about any ink color you can imagine. You can have your logo printed on them with your name and address if you wish. The more elaborate the design, the more they cost. A roll of 1,000 can cost in the $100 range or more, depending on the size, shape, ink, paper stock, and length of the message imprinted. Still, this amounts to only pennies per label. If you find that the price is near enough to the printing costs of customized stationery, you still might want to go with the self-stick labels because of their versatility.

Self-stick labels work well not only on envelopes and note paper—they're also great to label other items as well. You can affix them to wrapped soaps that you put in the guest bathrooms. You can also wrap some cookies in plastic wrap and place a sticker on the wrapping—a nice addition to a complimentary snack tray for your guests in the evening. Place them on the covers of magazines that are left out as reading material for guests. Place them on the covers of guidebooks that you lend to your guests but don't want to lose—the label is a good reminder of ownership. And you should place the labels on any brochures that you give to your guests about area sightseeing. If you like to give your guests a gift when they leave your bed and breakfast, put the sticker on the small jar of rhubarb jam you made yourself, the section of honeycomb from your own beehive, or the recipe card that goes with those muffins for the road.

When you're first starting out, any unnecessary expenditure is unwise. For a time you might want to use just plain stationery on which you print out your B&B's name and address from your computer. The important thing, of course, is to communicate with your guests. Once your B&B is regularly accommodating a good number of guests, it's time to think more seriously about upgrading your stationery.

Distributing Your Literature

Once you've gone to the trouble and expense to have a brochure designed, it's not going to do you any good if the copies you ordered sit in the closet. You have to make sure that the brochures get into the right hands.

Local Distribution Sources

For local distribution of your literature, there are various avenues you can explore. Sometimes the tourist bureaus or chambers of commerce will make available to the public brochures for those bed and breakfasts that are members of their organizations. If you join either of these organizations, inquire if this is a practice. In addition, take brochures to area hospitals, senior citizen homes, real estate agents, houses of worship, and colleges (especially alumni offices and offices that deal with new students or parents). All these places come into frequent contact with people visiting from out of town for various reasons—to see a patient at a hospital, to spend some time with a relative who lives at a residence for senior citizens, to check up on a son or daughter at college, to look for a house, to attend a wedding. And contact the directors of local performing arts centers that bring in talent from out of town. More than one performer who is "on the road" has preferred the quiet, homey charm of a bed and breakfast to a hotel. (One host reports the pleasure of providing accommodations for actress Cloris Leachman. Another talks of hosting singer Mary Travers of Peter, Paul, and Mary. Others name Peggy Fleming, Brooke Shields, Robert Redford, Barbra Streisand, Ben Affleck, and Meatloaf among their guests.)

Keep your eyes open for other possibilities in your neighborhood for distribution of your literature. One very successful bed and breakfast owner gives out her brochures at an area flea market. Some hosts leave a few brochures with the clerks at nearby hotels in the event of an overflow situation. One host reports that she takes literature to bridal shops and stores that rent tuxedos; obviously the clientele will know people coming to town for the big event, and they'll need places to stay. Another host who doesn't mind making last-minute arrangements leaves brochures at gas stations to help out people who are stranded because of car trouble.

Keep in mind, though, that you should be selective about where you leave your literature. You want to attract guests who fit the model of a "bed and breakfast person," and ideally, you should have enough advance notice of a reservation to check their personal information. It's not a good idea, for example, to leave a stack of brochures on the bar at the local watering hole. The last thing you want is a guest who has had one too many stumbling to your front door in the middle of the night.

If there is a local company that offers walking tours or bus tours of your area, try to establish a working relationship with the owner or tour operators. Sometimes tour companies will make information about lodging available to their clients. You might also want to talk to the owners about arranging package deals that include bed and breakfast lodging for clients. It's no coincidence that some tour operators became bed and breakfast hosts when they discovered that one activity so naturally complemented the other.

Another avenue to explore is any car-rental company in your area. The more well-known chains offer discounts to members of certain groups; a local representative might be very interested in providing discounts to your guests if your bed and breakfast regularly accommodates visitors who are interested in renting cars. So find out if you can offer discounted car rentals to your guests as an amenity and, at the same time, see if the company will make your brochures available in its literature display rack. You might also want to check out possibilities with any local office connected to a national moving company. The people who come and go in your area are bound to need the services of either one of you at one time or another. Perhaps your bed and breakfast and the moving company could cooperate in filling the needs of these people.

Innovative Methods

Some hosts undertake more innovative measures to publicize their bed and breakfast homes. One host has found an approach that has been quite effective for her business. She puts on her Victorian red-and-white pinstriped maid's costume with its ruffled apron, which is embroidered with the name of her B&B. Then she walks downtown with a basket full of brochures. "Those who are interested come to me and ask for a brochure. It's loads of fun."

No, you don't have to follow her example in order to be successful. But don't close your mind to new ideas for distributing your literature. Maybe you can think of your own unique method for spreading the word that would be a good addition to the suggestions made here.

How to Use Your Community Resources

If you join your local reservation service agency or B&B association, you can rely upon the their membership with the local tourist bureaus and the chamber of commerce as a way to take advantage of these organizations' resources. But if you're going it alone, you're going to have to seriously consider joining these organizations yourself.

Your local tourist bureaus can be an enormous help to you if you are a member. They publish current information directed toward visitors, including listings of recommended lodging. Because local tourist bureaus generally operate on a membership system, these listings tend to be restricted to those hotels, motels, and bed and breakfast homes or RSAs that are members. The lesson is that it's worth the price to join because the tourist bureau is the first place that people contact for information to help them plan a visit to the area. So check membership guidelines and fee requirements for local tourist bureaus.

In addition, tourist bureaus publish a variety of information that they make available to their members in bulk for free or at a low cost. You want to be able to orient your guests to the area as best you can, so having copies of sightseeing brochures, calendars of events, and maps will help you give your guests a better introduction to the community. (See "Orientation" in chapter 8.)

Every state's department of commerce or tourism also has an interest in meeting the needs of visitors to the state. So in addition to contacting your local or regional tourist boards, get in touch with this state agency as well. Some print and distribute their own guides to bed and breakfast in their own states or will stock member B&Bs' brochures in visitor centers. Web sites maintained by state tourist offices frequently offer B&B listings, advertising opportunities, and direct links to regional tourist bureaus. Some also link to the Web sites of B&B associations, reservation services, or individual B&Bs. Some even offer online reservations or a virtual tour of area B&Bs. (Consult appendix 4 for state and provincial tourist offices.)

Membership in the chamber of commerce can also be helpful to an independent bed and breakfast owner. Chambers are concerned with developing tourism in their areas and work to promote their members. It's not uncommon for someone planning to visit the area to contact the local chamber of commerce to ask for specific referrals to bed and breakfasts. Your membership will put you in the right place at the right time.

"We have found it useful to list with the chamber of commerce and advertise in the regional guide that it publishes. It also includes our flyers in the informational packets it mails out to inquirers," report Merritt and Barbara Williams, owners of a B&B in Ellsworth, Maine.

"Often your chamber of commerce will maintain an inquiry log of people who contact them prior to visiting or moving to your local area. This inquiry log is usually available for the cost of copying or a small subscription fee at most. It will provide you with a perfect direct-mail list to use in spreading the word about your B&B to pre-interested people. Mail them a brochure and include a small personal note to 'Come stay with us!' The response will surprise you!" say Mike and Annette Endres, owners of a B&B in Hawaii.

Because your relationship with tourist bureaus and the chamber of commerce is so important, why not invite their staffs to visit your bed and breakfast? Inviting the director or president of each organization for one of your gourmet breakfasts and a tour of your B&B is a great idea—but so is asking the receptionist, the secretary, the administrative assistant, and regular volunteers. These are the people who end up answering most of the inquiries from the public; they are the ones who will be responding to questions about bed and breakfast and making referrals. It's to your benefit to get to know them personally if you can, and to familiarize them with your bed and breakfast. You might even want to offer a free weekend stay to some of the staff to introduce them to your B&B.

How to Get Listed in B&B Guidebooks

Print guidebooks are an important source of information for people as they make their travel plans. To have your bed and breakfast described in even one guidebook will benefit your business because thousands of people will see it. So how do you go about getting this terrific publicity? Your job is to bring your bed and breakfast to the attention of the people who are writing the books and make them want to include you.

First you've got to identify the books in which you would like to have your bed and breakfast included. There are a number of guidebooks on the market that are devoted exclusively to bed and breakfast; become familiar with all the ones that would be appropriate for your bed and breakfast's location and features. A listing of selected books that focus on bed and breakfast appears in appendix 5. For an exhaustive listing (more than 1,300 titles), visit www.amazon.com and enter the keywords "bed and breakfast" for a search in the book category. While the listing will include everything remotely related to B&B (including cookbooks and novels), it will give you an excellent starting point for your research.

For mail-order B&B guidebooks, visit: www.amazon.com

Study the preface or introduction of each book you decide to purchase to see if the author explains how she or he selects the bed and breakfast homes for inclusion. Some authors also have Web sites with helpful information about their selection process. Note that some bed and breakfast associations publish their own guidebooks to publicize their members, such as the Select Registry. To be added to the next edition of such books, you must be a member of the association, so it makes sense to join if you qualify.

Other guidebooks are not associated with any B&B group. They are researched independently by the author, and the author makes the decision about which bed and breakfasts to feature (or not). Some of the books are general guides, but many have a special angle. Some are regional guides; some focus only on luxury bed and breakfasts; some are cookbooks. You will find that a number of these books will be appropriate for promoting your bed and breakfast, and others will not. A book devoted to B&Bs that have live-in cats, for example, will not list your B&B if you have no resident feline, so there's no point in trying to get information to the author for an upcoming edition. And if you live on the East Coast, you can't expect that a guide to West Coast bed and breakfasts will be likely to mention your B&B. So ferret out the ones for which your B&B might qualify.

Now you've got to convince the authors that the omission of your bed and breakfast in the next edition of their books would be a great loss indeed. Writers look for something special about any B&B that they include in their books. Maybe you make baked apple pancakes according to a recipe that has been handed down for five generations in your family, and no one else knows the secret ingredient except the last of the line (you). Now you want to share the secret with the world, via a bed and breakfast cookbook. Now that might interest an author. Is your bed and breakfast an architectural oddity? Was it remodeled into a B&B from a lighthouse or a barn? Was it designed by a well-known architect? Does it have historical significance—part of the Underground Railroad during the Civil War, for instance? Details like these will interest a reader in coming to your B&B, so therefore an author will be interested in you.

Write to the author explaining the feature of your B&B that you think makes it special. (Sometimes the author will give an e-mail or snail mail address for reader correspondence or include an application in the back of the book. If not, write in care of the publisher.) In your correspondence offer to answer the author's questions by telephone (inform the author that you would be more than happy to accept a collect call) and extend an invitation to visit your B&B on a gratis basis. Be aware that authors must research many, many bed and breakfasts—which can involve a lot of time and expense—so these courtesies will be appreciated. Send a brochure, a copy of a newspaper or magazine article that mentions your B&B (if one is available), and a photograph that makes a good impression of your home (this is optional). Do not—repeat, *do not*—just stuff a brochure in an envelope and mail it with no explanatory letter enclosed. There's a very good chance it will just end up in the circular file. If you have a Web site, be sure to include the address in your correspondence.

Don't overlook guidebooks that are not devoted to bed and breakfast exclusively but, rather, describe your city, state, or region in a more general way for tourists. If you see that an author recommends lodging for tourists, it can't hurt to send the writer information about your bed and breakfast. Do it now while you are thinking about it. It is better to send information early for a new edition than too late for the one that has just gone to press, because usually a year or more elapses between updates. And remember, if anything at all changes—such as the addition of a toll-free number or a Web site—be sure to inform the author of the change immediately.

Be advised that some authors will ask you to pay a fee for your B&B to be listed in the next edition. According to a past survey, fewer than 25 percent of authors charge a listing fee, while others charge nothing at all. Some authors who charge a fee give first-timers a break. You've got a choice to make. Should you pay for the publicity? If a particular guide-book is popular (ask the author how many copies were sold last year before agreeing to pay), the fee could be a good investment. This is especially true if the author has a Web site that promotes the book or even lists some of the recommended properties online. A selection of books that feature bed and breakfast accommodations appears in appendix 5.

How to Get Press Coverage

One of the best kinds of publicity you can get for your bed and breakfast is free. Articles written about your B&B in local, regional, or even national newspapers and magazines cost you virtually nothing, but the benefits continue long after the articles have been written. Once you've been operating a bed and breakfast for a while, writers might come to you looking for a story, but don't sit too long by the telephone waiting for the calls to come in. If you want an article written about your bed and breakfast, you need to convince a writer that readers would like to hear about it, that it's "news."

To get the process under way, the first thing you must do is identify those newspapers and magazines that would be likely to do a story on your bed and breakfast. Your hometown newspaper is a good bet because your B&B is local news; if you live in a large city, it'll be harder to get an article into print because there's a lot more competition for the available space. Still, it's not impossible. The larger newspapers have major sections on lifestyle, business, food—all of which could have good reason to publish an article about bed and breakfast. Magazines devoted to your city, state, or region are also good possibilities.

Keep in mind that an article in a local paper will not really pay off in a big way in terms of guests. (After all, why should people who live where you do stay in a B&B in their own community?) It's true that local people have friends, relatives, and business acquaintances who might be interested in your services at some point, but the real advantage of local coverage is that you can use the article to generate more articles that could attract considerably more visitors to your bed and breakfast. To get national press coverage, it helps if you've got a reprint of a local article to spark some interest. Somehow, the fact that your B&B has already been written about shows that someone thinks it's news (one point in your favor), and it also lends a certain "legitimacy" to your operation (another point in your favor). That reprint of a local article could open a few doors, so it's usually best to work on obtaining local coverage before you contact national publications.

When it comes to national publications, you're going to have to pick and choose carefully to try to tie in a certain aspect of your bed and breakfast with the focus of a particular publication. Is your B&B used as a base by people who come to the area for bird-watching, skiing, sunning, sailing, hiking, rock climbing, spelunking, or other special interests? It's a good bet that whenever a number of people follow a particular interest, there's a magazine devoted to it somewhere. If you don't already know what it's called and what it looks like, find out. (The reference librarian at your public library can help you locate guides to periodical literature, which will tell you what you need to know.) You can also do your own Internet research by entering relevant keywords in the search field at Google.com. Then get a copy of the magazine. Subscribe. Look at the publication's Web site. Become familiar with the types of articles it prints and the various writers who work for it.

For whatever publication that you're targeting, get to know the writers through their work. Identify one who would be likely to cover the subject according to the angle you're thinking about. You'll want to direct a press release to this person.

Quite simply, the press release will explain "the story." Writing one is no big deal if you know what you want to say. First, you'll need a title that pinpoints the significance of the story. "Historic Home Opens Its Doors to Bed and Breakfast Guests" should interest a writer who deals with historical subjects. "A Bed & Breakfast for Bird-Watchers" should interest someone who writes about birds for a nature magazine. Tailor your press release—and its title—to the publication and the writer.

In the first paragraph explain the meaning behind the title by answering, briefly, the questions of "who?" "what?" "where?" and "when?" This is the place to give the name of your bed and breakfast, its special feature that makes it news, its location, and some indication whether this is a new business or has been in operation for a while.

In the second paragraph give some details on how the B&B came about, quote someone who has enjoyed your hospitality or is an expert on the special feature you're promoting (skiing, architecture, sailing), or just discuss the special feature a little more specifically. In the last paragraph give your name, address, Web site, e-mail address, and the telephone number of your bed and breakfast for further information. And that's it. You've written a press release. Check the spelling, grammar, and punctuation and print it double-spaced on your letterhead. It's ready to mail.

Along with the press release, send a cover letter directed to the individual writer. Invite the writer to e-mail or call you (collect if the call will be long distance) if he or she has any questions and to spend a few days at your bed and breakfast on a gratis basis. In addition, include a brochure for your B&B, with a good photograph if you have one. (Do not ask for it to be returned.) And if you have a reprint of any article written about your B&B, send it along as well.

Don't get discouraged if nothing happens right away. Information that you send out might not result in a story for months and months. And sometimes a writer will take you up on that free visit, but no story is published until quite some time later. Recognize that it's all part of the process. For now the important thing is that you get that process under way.

Advertising Your Bed and Breakfast

While you're doing your best to get some free publicity, you might find it necessary to buy space in newspapers or magazines to advertise your bed and breakfast. (At the very least buy a listing in the Yellow Pages under "Bed and Breakfast.")

If you haven't discovered this already, you soon will: Advertising is not cheap. If you think that a full-page ad in the *New York Times* is just what you need to bring those guests to your door, you'd better be prepared to mortgage your home to pay for it. Fortunately, there are ways to beat the typically high cost of paid advertising.

One solution is to participate in joint advertising with other bed and breakfast homes. If you belong to a national or regional bed and breakfast association, a tourist board, or a local chamber of commerce, find out about joint advertising opportunities through those organizations. Together with other bed and breakfast hosts, you can purchase an ad that's large enough to be noticed, but you pay only a percentage of the total cost. You might also want to talk to other independent bed and breakfast operators in your area to see if they would be interested in purchasing an ad with you in a national or regional newspaper or magazine.

Ads in local papers can pay off in guests, too. There are always area residents who will be needing accommodations for out-of-town friends, relatives, or business associates. Ad rates in small community papers are usually quite reasonable, and the more times you run the same ad, the better deal you get on the cost. Remember the "law of frequency" when deciding upon an advertising schedule. You can't run an ad just once and expect the inquiries to come pouring in. A smaller ad run a number of times is more effective than a large ad run just once.

Susan Morris, an experienced reservation service manager, offers this word of caution about advertising in general: "Don't advertise in every publication approaching you or you'll go broke. Decide what markets you want to reach, then advertise to do that, but find out before you make a final decision what the circulation of the publication is."

You should try to get an article written about your bed and breakfast in any type of specialty magazine that is of interest to visitors to your area, but one way to be sure to reach aficionados is to buy an ad in that specialty magazine. For example, the owners of Fireacre Farm in central New York started their bed and breakfast business by hosting rock hounds who came to the area on mineral-collecting trips. The best way to let rock hounds know about Fireacre Farm? Advertise in mineral collectors' magazines.

One type of advertising that is inexpensive but often overlooked is the placement of an ad inside a program for a particular event taking place in your area. Does your area host events for which a number of people come from out of town? Chamber music concerts, art shows, dance performances, flower shows, state fairs, plays, sports competitions—all of these have programs that are distributed to the people who attend. And most of them print advertisements from local businesses as a way to fund the events. Buying an ad in a program is not expensive, and it reaches the people who will most likely be returning to your area for similar events in the future. In addition, there's no greater public relations for your bed and breakfast than to support a community event by means of your advertising.

Camille Harris and Patrick Foster of the Foster-Harris House in Washington, Virginia, recommend that hosts "note the source of each referral and keep careful cumulative records so that you can determine if advertising is paying off." Jeanne Gilbert, owner of Gilbert's Bed & Breakfast in Rehoboth, Massachusetts, adds, "Ask every guest, and even those just calling for information, how they learned about you. Keep track of this information so that you'll know the best places to spend your advertising dollars."

Creative Marketing for Off-season Business

Inevitably, every host faces empty rooms during the off-season. So what can you do to fill those rooms? First survey your own lifestyle and identify your talents. Do you have a degree from a culinary school? Try offering a "culinary arts" weekend where you introduce guests to the secrets of making exotic desserts. Do you have expertise in quiltmaking, knitting, embroidering, or woodworking? Offer a package deal where registrants can learn a craft as they enjoy your hospitality. And don't be too quick to discount your talents as nonmarketable! Come March and early April, I can easily envision scores of feet beating a path to the door of any accountant host who offers a weekend of tax consultations!

If your B&B is large enough to accommodate a group and has meeting space, go after businesses that might use your B&B for weekend retreats or weekday seminars. If cost-effective, hire someone to offer a special fun weekend. Some larger B&Bs hire community actors to present a "Murder Mystery Weekend" complete with murder victim, suspects, detectives, and witnesses. The guests all play a part, and everyone has a great time. Another idea for the slow season was launched by a Rhode Island reservation service—a weekend of ballroom dance instruction. Guests stay in any of four participating B&B inns and enjoy dancing in the ballroom of a Newport mansion.

Hidden Brook B&B in Cummington, Massachusetts, supplies customers with a monthly calendar highlighting theme weekends and local events. Who could resist a January getaway to enjoy a combination of skiing, country dancing, bread making, and wood stove cookery? One Pennsylvania host offers theme weekends for holiday shopping, music, romance, Thanksgiving, and St. Patrick's Day.

Hidden Brook worked with other New Hampshire B&B owners to devise a way to entice visitors to come to the area during the month of September—a scarecrow contest with prizes donated by local merchants. "For some reason September is a slow month," says Jody Kerssenbrock, owner of Hidden Brook B&B. "Folks are waiting for October to see the foliage. We needed a way to 'scare up' tourism during the off-season."

Other imaginative ideas devised by hosts include a weekend showing of old movies, complete with a lecture by a local professor; workshops in wildflower identification, watercolor painting, and photography; classes in wine making, fitness, meditation, and yoga; finding and cutting your own Christmas tree; sleigh rides; horseback riding; picnics; breakfast in bed; "Fantasy Island" weekends . . . and more.

Some hosts use the off-season to get more connected with their community by offering to host special events or fund-raisers for local charities, youth groups, and other non-profits. Whatever investment that is made by the B&B is more than paid for in goodwill and future referrals.

Marketing in Unsettled Times

"One of the biggest challenges you will face as a new innkeeper will be keeping occupancy during difficult times such as economic downturns and man-made or natural disasters," says Bobbi Zane, editor of *Yellow Brick Road*. "Each of these occurrences can have a detrimental effect on tourism and your bottom line." In difficult times some people forgo vacations. Others stay closer to home, choosing not to fly or cross international borders. This means fewer guests visiting from other countries—for some hosts, the backbone of their business.

What can you do? First, recognize the fact that fewer people will be beating a path to your door. You can't just sit back and wait for guests to find you, even if that happened in the past. You must be proactive because now there is greater competition for fewer guests.

Start by going back to basics. In a brisk market, too often simple courtesies are overlooked. It's sad to say but, yes, hosts can get lazy when things are going well. These days, it's a cold, cold world out there—or it can seem so to a potential guest who receives a curt e-mail reply from a host or connects with an answering machine instead of a live human being. In a shrinking market, courtesy wins. Be polite, friendly, and helpful, in every way you can. Answer the phone yourself (instead of allowing your answering machine to pick up). Reply promptly to e-mails using a warm, personal tone (instead of dashing off a brief phrase or two with no greeting or signature). "Make it easy to book your inn," says Bobbi. "Although not for everybody, online booking is easiest. Return phone calls promptly, within minutes if possible. And can you be more flexible about check-in and checkout times? taking credit cards? accepting children and/or pets?"

And don't stop there. Step up your marketing efforts. Be creative. Reach out to new markets. Relax your policy on a two-night-stay minimum—take one-nighters. Contact loyal guests and offer specials, such as a free night or room upgrades. Do what you can to become more savvy about marketing. Look at competitors' Web sites and brochures. What features do they have that outshine your own? Keep information on your Web site and brochures accurate, up to date, and inviting.

During a guest's visit, be extra-attentive to the person's needs and comfort. A satisfied guest will return and refer—this idea can't be stressed enough. "Focus on what guests really want," says Bobbi. These days more people are looking for a quiet, peaceful, safe haven. Market those qualities, and offer to help guests plan their stay, complete with itinerary. Give guests more for their money, including small, custom-made gifts, which are also good marketing tools: a sweatshirt, T-shirt, or coffee mug with your logo on it.

For custom-made gifts, visit: www.cafepress.com

Take this time to make friends. Network with other hosts and brainstorm ways to help each other through bumpy times. If you're operating independently, set up a system for "overflow" referrals among other independent B&Bs. In those now too often rare times when one B&B has too much business, others in the network can benefit.

"Be a joiner," says Bobbi. Network with local businesspeople, volunteer, serve on committees, make strategic alliances in the travel and tourism industry, and work with local attractions to draw customers. Arrange to offer your guests a discount, complimentary wine, or dessert at a few select restaurants.

Rethink your space. You are set up to accommodate overnight guests, yes, but can your B&B offer additional services? One Boston host renovated his space in order to carve out a function room that can hold up to thirty-five people comfortably. He now rents out the space for events that include business meetings and wedding rehearsal dinners. He can offer a continental breakfast, if desired, or arrange catering for lunches and dinners. (*Note*: Be sure to check local regulations regarding the preparation of meals other than breakfast.) Does your property have a large space that could serve as a function room, or a large garden where tables and chairs could be set up? If so, you can use the opportunity to derive some income from hosting events, while at the same time introducing new people to your B&B and what it has to offer. (You might want to suggest a tour of your B&B as part of the package.) And think about connecting with local adult education centers. Perhaps they might be interested in contracting with you to use your function-room space for classes or workshops. "Hold an open house and invite everyone in town," suggests Bobbi.

Marketing on the Internet

Step 1: Getting Started

If you don't already own a computer, buy one. If you don't know how to operate a computer, learn. And get online, whatever it takes. There was a time when a B&B host could manage just fine without ever touching a computer, but no longer. Recent statistics indicate that more than a billion people worldwide now have Internet access. In North America an estimated 68 percent of the population is online, and increasing numbers of people throughout the world are plugging in, too. Overall, the volume of Internet traffic continues to expand at triple-digit rates.

One survey places B&B Web sites and online B&B directories ahead of word of mouth and print guidebooks when it comes to attracting new guests. Some innkeepers report that more than 80 percent of their reservations come from the Internet. Indeed, some in the industry say that the Internet is rapidly replacing the print medium as the most effective method of advertising and that word of mouth no longer rules. Others say that the Internet provides an important, interim step in the process, one that reflects evolution of the times. "When we entered the world of innkeeping at the Wedgwood Inn of New Hope,

Pennsylvania, in the spring of 1982, word of mouth referrals from satisfied inn guests were our number-one source of new business," says innkeeper Carl Glassman. Then, prospective guests would do research by reading about the inn in guidebooks and travel publications and then call for a brochure and rates. Now, prospective guests tend to do their research via the Internet, checking online directories and the inn's own Web site, and then send an e-mail. "The more things change, the more things sometimes remain the same about innkeeping," says Carl. "Two hundred years ago, guests arrived by horse and buggy. Today we still cater to the 'carriage trade,' but now they arrive by different modes of transportation and learn about us and contact us in new ways, too."

What does this mean for today's B&B? Clearly, hosts who get online will benefit in many ways, including research, advertising, and efficient communication. And for innkeepers with new or small businesses, the Internet offers a way to compete on a level playing field with larger and more established B&Bs. Welcome to the twenty-first century.

Computer System

Because technology is changing rapidly, the best advice is to purchase a newer computer system rather than acquire one secondhand. You will see the difference in terms of speed and compatibility with changing technology. If you don't know what you're doing, do not attempt to purchase parts of the system separately—the computer, the monitor, the printer, the keyboard. Instead, research a package where everything comes together at a good price. Most systems also come loaded with software for word processing and other uses. Select a computer that you find easy to use. If you don't know how to operate a computer, seek out a course at a community college or adult education center, or visit your local library, which may offer use of computers with Internet access to its patrons. Often, a one-day workshop can get you started with the basics. After that, it's playtime—learning by doing.

Internet Connection

Most computers now come equipped with an ethernet network port and a built-in wireless card as ways to connect to an Internet service provider. While it's still possible to connect to the Internet using a 56K modem and a regular telephone line, these will not serve you well in today's fast-paced world. Many innkeepers prefer a faster connection, opting to use a DSL line or cable connection, or they choose wireless Internet service, which allows them to offer easy Internet access to their guests as well.

Internet Service Provider

An Internet service provider, or ISP, is your gateway into cyberspace, connecting your computer to the vast web of computers in the world. The ISP will also provide your e-mail address and, if you wish, your Web site address. Selecting an ISP should be done carefully. You cannot keep your e-mail and Web site addresses if you change ISPs (unless you have purchased your own domain name), so you will face the problem of changing and disseminating new contact information, which could cut into your business.

How do you find an ISP? Look for ads in the business section of your newspaper or in computer magazines. Or get onto the Internet any way you can—use a friend's computer, install a diskette with a free introductory offer on your own computer, go to the library, barter with your kids to get them to allow you to use their computer—whatever it takes. Then take a look at Web sites and e-mail addresses of other B&B hosts, noting which providers are used most often. The provider name is always imbedded in the e-mail address after the user name, such as *YourB&Bname@providername.net*. Contact the most utilized ISPs and ask questions.

Next, clarify access privileges. Will you have unlimited access to the Internet, twenty-four hours a day, at a flat monthly rate? Or is there a limit on the number of hours you can be on the Internet, and you are charged an additional hourly rate for any time that exceeds that number? Do not sign with an ISP that does not have a flat-rate plan with unlimited access.

Finally, find out what minimum requirements your computer needs to meet in terms of operating system and memory in order to use the ISP's services. An ISP will usually send you a CD to insert into your computer's CD-ROM drive, then the software will instruct you how to properly load it. You don't want to sign with a provider that requires, for example, System 9.2 when all you have is 8.0. Then you'll have to upgrade your system before you can get online, which may not be an easy matter if your computer also needs more memory to handle the revamp.

Phone Line

If you will be using a telephone line to connect to the Internet, this means that anyone trying to call you on that line may experience either a busy signal or go directly into your voice mail, or the call may kick you off-line, depending on the type of telephone service you

For Internet call waiting, visit: www.pagoo.com

For details about how Wi-Fi works, go to: http://computer.howstuff works.com/wireless-network have. While it is possible to purchase a service that will alert you whenever a call is coming in, the best choice may be to choose a cable or DSL connection.

Wireless Fidelity (Wi-Fi)

Another option is to install wireless Internet (Wi-Fi), which offers state-of-the-art Internet access from any room in your B&B (including guest rooms). Basically, a Wi-Fi setup uses radio waves to allow any equipped computer in the vicinity of a "hot spot" to connect to the Internet. For any host attempting to attract business travelers, offering Wi-Fi can be an added advantage.

Step 2: Creating a Presence in Cyberspace

If your first step is setting up a computer system and getting online, your second should be purchasing the invaluable book *Marketing Guestrooms Online,* originally by Steve Demarest and revised by Scott Crumpton. Newly updated in 2006, this manual explains everything you need to know, not only to establish a presence in cyberspace but also to become successful in using the Internet as a marketing tool. For the price, you will receive a well-rounded Internet education specifically geared toward the needs of innkeepers.

The Fast, Easy Way to Enter Cyberspace

For a novice, the fastest, easiest way to launch your B&B into cyberspace is to give the pertinent information to an online directory service and let its staff do it for you. You supply information and graphics typically used in a printed brochure, and the service transforms it into a listing or even a Web site. Some services do it for free, others for a fee usually ranging from $100 to $250 for a basic package (more for extras), which includes posting your listing in the online guide for a specified period. The advantage is that you can start using this type of service immediately, without having either a Web site or an e-mail address of your own. While it's better to include an e-mail address in the listing for a potential guest's immediate follow-up, this can always be added later. Hosts who choose well can enjoy almost immediate results. "I created the listing, paid my money, and within two hours a guy from South Carolina called and booked four nights," reports the owner of Blue's Bed and Breakfast in Cambridge, Massachusetts.

Selecting Online Directories

How do you choose among the dozens of online guides or directories that offer an opportunity to post a listing about your B&B? First of all, anything free is a no-lose situation. Go for it. After that, pick and choose. To acquire an overview of available guides, start by checking the online rating services. INNSTAR offers reviews of more than 150 online guides primarily for the benefit of bed and breakfast guests. The value of this five-star rating system to innkeepers is obvious for the useful information it provides. Bill Wayne, founder of INNSTAR and owner of Cedarcroft Farm Bed & Breakfast in Missouri, bases his evaluations on six categories, including depth of descriptions provided, quality assurance, and how easy it is to find and navigate the site. More ratings can be found on the Web site for "INNTELLIGENT Advice for Innkeepers." Here, guides are ranked in part on how visible they are on key search engines.

Some of the top-ranked online B&B directories that have general appeal are listed in the box on this page. Others appeal to specific audiences. The helpful Web site bbonline.com, for example, has a variety of categories—for B&Bs that are romantic, historic, pet-friendly, kid-friendly, have access for people with disabilities, specialize in weddings, or are located on the shore or in the mountains. Another Web site, the International Bed and Breakfast Pages, lists B&Bs throughout the world, attracting an international audience to the B&Bs included in that directory. Gay-owned and gay-friendly B&Bs are invited to list in the Purple Roofs Travel Directory.

Many online directories offer basic listing services for a reasonable annual fee, usually under $125. Examine your advertising budget closely and determine whether you should try one, two, or more for your first year in business. Then keep track of how many guests result from your listings as a way to plan for future advertising in online directories.

For evaluations of online B&B directories, check out:
www.innstar.com
www.inntelligent.com

For highly rated online B&B directories, visit:
www.bbonline.com
www.bedandbreakfast.com
www.bbcanada.com
www.lanierbb.com

For online B&B directories that target specific audiences, go to:
www.bbonline.com
www.purpleroofs.com
www.petsonthego.com
www.ibbp.com

Step 3: Creating Your Own Web Site

If you want to acquire some perspective on just how pervasive the Internet is, go to the Web site www.google.com (it's a search engine that searches the Internet for keywords), and enter the words "bed and breakfast." Then take a look at what comes up. A recent Google search located more than *fifty-six million* references.

At this point you might ask yourself why you should bother trying to compete with the countless other B&Bs on the Internet for the attention of prospective guests; it's so overwhelming. Here's a good answer: According to a travel industry report, about 64 million Americans research their travel options online. And it's a level playing field: A search engine will pull up your B&B just as quickly as it will another. Individual B&Bs have reported good news from establishing a presence on the Internet. Dave Elliott of Taylor House, among the first wave of B&Bs to use the Internet for marketing, reports that more than 80 percent of his bookings now come from the Internet, compared with 50 percent five years ago.

Given these statistics, it makes sense for a host to utilize the Internet to fullest advantage. While advertising through online directories (where listings look pretty much the same) is advisable as a component of your overall marketing strategy, consider creating your own Web site as well, unique to your B&B. Designing and controlling content on your own Web site and using it as your primary outreach tool will help exude your B&B's unique charm to attract guests.

Select a Domain Name

Start with securing a name for your Web site, called a domain name. Let's say the name of your B&B is the Yellow Rose Inn. A good choice for your Web site, then, would be www.yellow roseinn.com. Hopefully, no one else has claimed this name before you thought of it, but you will need to confirm the name's availability. Use an online service to conduct a search. If your first choice is taken, try some variations: How about www.yellowrosebnb.com? Your next step will be registering the name, which you can do online for a fee in the $70 range. This fee will buy you the rights to the name for a period of time, usually two years, with an annual fee after that for continued ownership. Once you have your Web site up and running, include the domain name on your brochures, business cards, stationery, and in guidebook listings.

To search for and register a domain name, go to: www.domainit.com

Constructing Your Web Site

To help you figure out what you should include on your Web site, start with the basic information typically included in a brochure. Then do some research. Browse through various Web sites advertising B&Bs, and make a list of what you like and what you don't like. What do others include? Photos, illustrations, online reservation request form, e-mail address and phone number, room descriptions, layout of the house, history of the B&B, host bios, and availability chart, along with recipes, map of the neighborhood, and a weather link? Is the layout of the Web site confusing or easy to navigate? Are the pages cluttered or pleasingly organized? Are the colors garish or boring, or tasteful and appropriate to the B&B's ambience? Is the type too large or too small for easy reading, or is it presented in easy bites with clear headers? Is the site too cutsey with smiley faces or other childish clip art or animations, or are visuals unique and used sparingly and effectively?

Know what you want and what you don't want. Then either design your Web site yourself, if you have the know-how, or seek the services of a designer. Shop around before you select a designer; always ask to see sample work. And educate yourself. Check out designer Steve Wirt's Web site for advice. His company, Inngenious, offers terrific pointers for innkeepers who are developing Web sites for their businesses.

For Web site design advice, visit: www.inngenious.com

For Web hosting resources, visit: www.tophosts.com

Provided later in this chapter as an example of an attractive Web site design is a print version of what you will find at www.taylorhouse.com. Designed by Dave Elliott, a computer software teacher and co-owner of Taylor House Bed & Breakfast in Boston, Massachusetts, the site is effective because it is uncluttered, easy to read, uses simple, clean layout of text and graphics, gives just enough information, and sets a warm, friendly tone.

Some hosts include an online reservation form on their Web sites, making it clear that the form is a request only and not an automatic confirmation. Many hosts like to follow up an online request with a telephone conversation. This allows a host to get "a feel" for the person through conversation and provides a secure method of payment. Some guests are still reluctant to provide too much information, especially credit card numbers, over the Internet.

Once you have your Web site constructed to your liking, you will need to hang it in cyberspace for others to see. Find out whether this can be done by your current Internet service provider (if you already have one for e-mail) for a reasonable fee. Some ISPs charge high fees to hang and maintain a customized domain name in cyberspace, so do some comparison shopping. As there are thousands of Web hosting services worldwide, start your research with a visit to TopHosts, a Web hosting resource that showcases the top twenty-five hosts each month. If you hired a designer to construct your Web site, ask for recommendations.

Blogging for Business

Lately, "blogs" are all the rage. A blog, or Web log, is an online forum located on your Web site where comments are posted at will. An active blog offers a B&B host some important marketing advantages. Hosts can use blogs to entice future guests with current postings about local attractions and upcoming events; to keep in touch with former guests with tidbits of news, recipes, and occasional snapshots; and to make their Web sites more prominent to search engines like Google (which gives placement favor to Web sites having new updates). If you decide to include a blog feature on your Web site, the best advice is to post entries a minimum of once a week; more is better. The more active the blog, the more visits your Web site will receive.

Learn to create a free blog at: www.blogger.com

For blog information, visit: www.blizzardinternet.com

For Web site accessibility guidelines, visit: www.w3.org/wai

For Web site accessibility tools, visit: http://webaim.org/products

Universal Design

Keeping in mind that people use the Internet in different ways, it is advisable to design a Web site that will work well for all users. Simply stated, that means presenting information in a way that people can access it regardless of the type of hardware or software they use and regardless of how they navigate through a site. This becomes especially important to B&B hosts as their guests, whose average age is around fifty according to an industry study, continue to age and perhaps develop various disabilities. Ideally, your Web site should be friendly to aging baby boomers and persons with disabilities. For example, a person with vision loss may want to navigate a Web site by using a screenreader, which reads the text aloud.

The Web Accessibility Initiative (WAI) makes specific recommendations for making a Web site accessible to everyone. Most are common sense, such as using headings, lists, and consistent structure in page organization; summarizing graphs and charts; and providing captions for photographs or other graphics. For guidelines and techniques, go to the WAI's Web site. If you want to test the accessibility of your Web site, visit the WebAIM Web site, which identifies access problems in Web sites. Just type in your Web site address. That's it. An analysis of your Web site will be provided right then and there. *Note:* The recommendations are written in technical language and may require consultation with a Web designer.

Taylor House Bed & Breakfast in Boston, Massachusetts

Taylor House B&B   E-mail

Taylor House, a gracious sixteen room Victorian home in Boston's Jamaica Plain section, was built around 1853 for George W. Taylor, an international merchant head-quartered in Boston. It is situated within the Monument Square Historic District, and lies in an area known as "Pondside", which contains some of Jamaica Plain's finest suburban architecture. The structure is predominantly Italianate in style, but retains some Greek Revival elements that reflect the earliest architectural style found in Jamaica Plain. A distinctive octagonal cupola sits atop the main house, and this shape is echoed in a number of ways within the interior of the structure.

A multi-stage restoration project was launched in 1996. The interior of the house is now complete and exterior renovations are the priority. The exterior was painted in the Summer of 2002. The next project is the addition of a porch to the right side of the house removed by previous owners. The house is surrounded by Victorian-inspired gardens and lies less than one block from a beautiful pond and a town centre that offers excellent dining.

Upon entering the main lobby through double arched doors, you will see a beautiful staircase leading to the second floor rooms. A continental plus breakfast that includes fresh baked bread and pastries as well as fresh cut fruit and cereals is served daily on the first floor. We offer a congenial, tasteful and serene environment that will enhance your visit to Boston, whether you are here for business or leisure. Three spacious guest rooms with private baths are available: the Taylor, Beaumont, and Haffenreffer rooms, named after former owners of the house.

The Taylor Room
Private Bath
Queen-size sleigh bed
Ornamental Fireplace
Front and side yard view

The Haffenreffer Room
Private Bath
Queen-size sleigh bed
Front and side yard view
Afternoon sun

The Beaumont Room
Private Bath
Queen-size sleigh bed
Front and side yard view
Afternoon sun

- Continental breakfast consisting of bread and pastries, cold cereals, fresh fruit, yogurt, juice, fresh ground coffee, teas
- Television sets with VCRs, hair dryers, irons, and other amenities
- Telephone, modem-access, Video Library
- A smoke-free environment
- *Wags (9) and Parker (4), the Taylor House Golden Retrievers are very friendly and never bark*
- Easy access to city buses and the "T" subway system
- Off-street parking

Your hosts, Dave Elliott and Daryl Bichel, will take delight in offering suggestions for enjoying all that Boston has to offer - whether it be the arts, historic attractions, fine dining, sports, outdoor activities, or other interests.

Taylor House is only a block from excellent restaurants, and lies adjacent to beautiful Jamaica Pond, a natural kettle hole formed by a pre-historic glacier. The pond is enjoyed daily by many residents and tourists using its boathouse and 1.5 mile paved trail for walking and running. For more spectacular beauty the incredible Arnold Arboretum is only 6 blocks away.

In addition to being located in a neighborhood of distinction and great beauty, the Taylor House site offers easy access to attractions through bus and subway transit. Taylor House is located two miles from the Longwood Medical Area, home to many hospitals, research facilities, and educational institutions. The Museum of Fine Arts, the Isabella Stewart Gardner Museum , Symphony Hall, and Fenway Park are also in this area. Just beyond that, the Back Bay, Charles River, and Boston Harbor offer beauty, history, unbelievable shopping, and fascinating restaurants.

Taylor House Bed & Breakfast
50 Burroughs Street
Boston, Massachusetts 02130
888-228-2956 (BBTAYLOR); (617) 983-9334; Fax: (617) 522-3852
email: taylorbnb@aol.com
Dave Elliott and Daryl Bichel, Innkeepers

Chapter Seven
The Perfect Guest

There are two main reasons to screen prospective guests before opening your home to any of them. One is to make sure that your bed and breakfast can meet their requirements; the other is to make sure they can meet yours. Bed and breakfast is not for everyone, and the screening process is as much an education as anything else. A number of people seek out bed and breakfast accommodations without really understanding what it's all about. Some people honestly would not enjoy staying in a bed and breakfast, and the screening process can help them discover this.

Screening Your Guests

If you choose to operate your bed and breakfast home independently, then the screening responsibility falls to you and you alone. If you list your home with a reservation service agency, the RSA will take care of screening for you. (See "Reservation Service Agencies" in chapter 4.) Either way, you should be knowledgeable about the process so that you can make it work to your best advantage. Following is a procedure for doing the screening yourself.

Meeting Your Guests' Needs

To ensure that your bed and breakfast can meet the needs of your prospective guests, you have to find out what kind of accommodations they are looking for, exactly. The information can be obtained by having them fill out a reservation request form (some independent hosts print such a form in their brochure or post it on their Web site), or the information can be taken over the telephone. More than one host has noted the importance of a telephone conversation as a way to get a "feel" for the prospective guest. For this reason many hosts will finalize a reservation by telephone.

A sample screening form is provided in this chapter as a guide for the kind of information you need to obtain from prospective guests. If you do the screening yourself, prepare your own checklist, adapting the items listed in the sample form to reflect what your bed and breakfast home is set up to provide. This form can then be used in your brochure, and copies can be kept by the telephone for easy access.

Always find out the reason a visitor is coming to your area because the location of your home could be an important factor. A teacher coming to attend a seminar at the university will want to be near the school. A couple coming to look at houses because they plan to relocate to the area will most likely want to stay in the neighborhood they are scouting. If your home is not in a good location for some of the people who contact you, tell them so. Then if they decide to stay at your B&B anyway, they will know what the situation is.

Your location could also be an issue if your home is not anywhere near public transportation. If this is the case, make it a point to find out whether guests will be bringing their own car or plan to rent one during their visit. If not, make sure they understand that transportation will be a problem if they choose to stay with you. At times like these it's good to be a part of a local network of bed and breakfast homes. The guests whose needs you cannot meet will appreciate a referral to another area B&B that can.

Finding out the reason guests will be visiting can also help you discover whether their activities will be compatible with your own routine. One host reports that she did not accept a guest who was coming to the area on a work assignment that meant he needed to sleep days. This schedule would have been disruptive to the normal routine of her home. And one Florida host whose home is located near a popular beach says she decided against hosting a group of people "who were obviously looking to party over Easter break." This activity would have disrupted her normally peaceful lifestyle, so she steered them, instead, to an area motel.

It is a good idea to keep on hand a list of alternative lodging for people who obviously would be more comfortable in a hotel or motel. Be aware, too, that it is not uncommon for bed and breakfast hosts to sometimes receive misdirected calls from people who are seeking a shelter or some sort of transient housing. If there are shelters, youth hostels, a YMCA or YWCA, or other low-cost temporary housing in your area, keep their numbers handy.

When prospective guests contact you, find out what the composition of the party will be—how many people, whether there are children (and if so, their ages), and whether they hope to bring along a pet. Use this information to determine whether you can accommodate the guests. If there is a party of six traveling together and you have accommodations for a maximum of four, then you should discuss the possibility of using the sofa bed or setting up cots in the rooms (some people will think this is fine; others won't). If necessary, refer them to another, larger bed and breakfast home. If there are children under the age of ten and you prefer children who are ten or older, be ready to suggest an alternative accommodation. (Handle this with care, as some guests have challenged the legality of refusing accommodation to children as a form of age discrimination.) If someone wants to bring a Doberman pinscher along on the trip and you have a cat that would object, explain that you cannot accommodate the pet; the guest will have to go elsewhere or leave the pet at home.

How many nights the party wishes to stay and the dates of the visit are additional pieces of information you must obtain not only to make your home "guest-ready" for their arrival but also so that you can block out those dates on your calendar in case other prospective guests inquire about those dates. If rooms are reserved, then this means no vacancy if others call. Be especially careful not to double-book a room or to overlap dates. You don't want to have one party of four still in residence when the next party of four shows up. Keep a good calendar!

Some hosts screen out guests who wish to stay for longer periods of time than the hosts would find comfortable. "A couple wanted to be here from three weeks to three months," says Marjorie Lindmark, owner of Bed 'n' Breakfast in Phoenix. That was too long, she felt, so she referred them elsewhere. For most hosts the pleasure in offering bed and breakfast comes largely from the variety of people who come and go, as well as the ability to schedule some time where there are no guests in residence at all. A guest who stays for a long time could begin to feel more like a roommate. So consider what your feelings are about long-term guests and then set a "maximum-stay" rule.

You will need to explain to prospective guests what kinds of beds are available in your bed and breakfast (twins, full, queen, or king) to see what they would prefer. And describe the bathroom facilities. If there is a shared bath only, expect that some people will immediately envision a line of guests going clear out the front door and down the block as they each wait their turn. Assure them that this is not the case by letting them know that the bathroom is shared by only one or two other people, that it is right next to the room they would be using, that there is a second bathroom available if necessary—any piece of information that would help dispel the image of long waits and lack of privacy. For those who still seem uncomfortable about the shared bath, don't press the issue. Some people really would be happier somewhere that offers a private bath.

If there are aspects of your bed and breakfast that could pose a problem to certain guests, be sure to bring them up: You have a cat or dog, which rules out guests who have allergies to animals. You have rooms on the second and third floors only, and no elevator, which rules out guests who have difficulty walking up stairs. You have a strictly nonsmoking household, which rules out any guests who want to be able to smoke wherever they stay. You have mattresses that are only 6 feet in length, a discomfort for anyone over 6 feet tall. Ask prospective guests if they have any special requirements that you should know about, such as diet restrictions or allergies. Be careful, though, not to pry into areas that are so personal that it makes the prospective guest uncomfortable. An open-ended question about "special requirements" should be sufficient to prompt the caller to supply whatever information is necessary.

The bottom line is that there should be no surprises. You should know exactly what prospective guests are looking for, and guests should know exactly what they'll be getting if they stay at your bed and breakfast. A good screening process will cover all the necessary information.

Meeting Your Own Needs

The screening process is intended not only to determine whether your bed and breakfast offers the kind of accommodations that a guest is seeking, it is also for the purpose of helping a host find out whether a prospective guest is a "bed and breakfast person." This refers to just about the most wonderful species of human being that ever walked the earth. People of this type stand out in a crowd: They smile at babies, say "thank you" to clerks and waiters, and hold doors for people who have their arms full of packages. They are kind to animals, they often give presents for no reason, and they love sunsets. Or in the words of one host from Indiana, bed and breakfast people are "the best in the world."

Now, how can you be sure that every person whom you allow to stay in your home is a "bed and breakfast person"? The truth is that you can't, no matter who does the screening—you or a reservation service agency—and no matter how carefully the process is followed. There is just no way to accurately assess someone's character through answers given on a form or through a telephone conversation. You can try, and you should try; just realize that no screening method is foolproof. Still, the guidelines given here should help you weed out the most obvious cases.

First of all, ask how the prospective guest heard about your bed and breakfast. This can tell you a lot. "My Aunt Gertrude stayed with you last summer" is a good piece of information. If you remember Aunt Gertrude fondly as the sweetest lady, then you can feel confident that she wouldn't refer her niece to you unless she, too, was just as sweet. On the other hand, if you found yourself counting the hours until Gertie's departure, then perhaps you should tell her niece that you have no vacancies for the weekend she would like to visit. The longer you are in business, the more you will be contacted by people who were referred to your bed and breakfast by friends and relatives who have already stayed with you. Accommodating "a friend of a friend" is usually safer for you because you already have a character reference.

Another piece of information you should ask for is a business address and telephone number, in addition to the prospective guest's home address and number. Anyone who is vague or evasive about his or her occupation or place of work, who gives incomplete information about a home residence, or who refuses to give you the names of all the members of the party should be screened out.

And some hosts will never, never take anyone who comes to the door without having first called to make a reservation. If you are advertising your bed and breakfast home (and its address) in directories and paid advertisements, you can expect this to happen every once in a while. It does mean that you have to turn away some business, but as long as yours is not a commercial enterprise but, rather, your private home, it's best to institute the safeguards that you can and adhere to them—with no exceptions.

Experienced hosts say that they try to draw out the people who contact them by telephone, getting them to talk about themselves a little bit so that the hosts can learn something about their personalities. Questions like "Have you ever visited our city before?" "Is this your first time staying in a bed and breakfast?" "Why are you coming to the area?" will

The owners of Blue's Bed & Breakfast in Cambridge, Massachusetts, enjoy hosting scientists who come to visit the nearby Harvard Observatory and never pass up an opportunity to learn about a guest's area of expertise. One guest, an astrophysicist, obligingly explained his work with radio waves in space. Finding the explanation somewhat beyond her ken, host Blue Magruder finally asked, "How many people in the world would really understand your work?" The physicist thought for a moment, then wryly replied, "Really only one, but perhaps a hundred would pretend to."

help get them talking. See how they handle themselves on the telephone. "Occasionally, I do not like the sound of a voice and we are magically full," says one Maine host. Anyone who is not friendly or seems too demanding or critical is not the "B&B person" that a host is looking for as a guest. You can simply say that you do not have a vacancy.

One Boston host does additional research before confirming a reservation: "I Google them! And I use anywho.com to do reverse look-ups of their e-mail addresses or phone numbers to obtain home or business addresses." The extra information she is able to sleuth out on the Internet helps her build a fuller picture of the people who are asking to stay in her home.

To research prospective guests, visit:
www.google.com
www.anywho.com

If you have a reservation request form online or in a print brochure, include a place for prospective guests to write down their interests or hobbies. Some hosts will add a note: "Tell me a little bit about yourself." This gives you something to talk about if you like to confirm the reservation by telephone, and it gives some insight into your guests' lives. The form is also a good place to request the license number of a guest's car (if he or she is bringing it). Some hosts report that they feel uncomfortable about asking for the license number because it gives the impression that they are suspicious of the guest; they will just make a note of it when the guest arrives, at a time when the guest will not notice. This is one more piece of information that is good for you to have on file in the unlikely event that the guest turns out to be of unsavory character.

One final note on the screening process: It should absolutely not be used as a form of discrimination against anyone on the basis of race, color, religion, sex, disability, familial status, national origin, or sexual preference. If you have irreconcilable differences with people for any of these reasons, you should think twice about becoming a host, and not just because you fear a lawsuit. To be a good host, you've got to love people in all their varieties. If a personal prejudice is going to interfere with your role as a friendly and hospitable host, then offering bed and breakfast is not a good idea.

Online Reservations

These days a number of B&B owners offer online reservations on their Web sites so that prospective guests can book right there and then, in cyberspace. This growing trend allows a host to snap up guests who are determined to make a quick booking, but it does not allow a host to screen guests at all.

To offer this service, a host can purchase and install special software. Before doing so, it would be wise to take a look at an online demonstration of how the software works. If you are satisfied that the process is user-friendly, and you are willing to accept unscreened guests, then you can turn the reservation process over to the software. Some B&B directories also offer their member hosts the option of online reservations. If you would like to try it, sign up with one of the directories (such as www.bedandbreakfast.com) and see how you like the results.

Some hosts, particularly those who offer bed and breakfast on a small scale in their family homes, are not comfortable forgoing guest screening altogether and prefer, instead, to offer a reservation request form on their Web sites. (A sample reservation request form appears in "Creating Your Own Web Site" in chapter 6.) This way, hosts can have some contact with prospective guests either through e-mail or phone calls before a reservation is finalized. Take a good look at your own comfort level, and then make your decision.

Confirming a Reservation

Once you and your prospective guest have decided to go ahead and make a reservation, there are a few matters to arrange, preferably by telephone. (*Note*: If you list your home with a reservation service agency, some or all of these details will be handled through the agency.)

Always settle on a definite arrival time that is convenient for both you and your guest and impress upon the guest that the arrival time is important to you. If the guest says that

Sample Screening Form

Name _____

Address _____

Home phone _____ Cell phone _____

E-mail _____

Occupation / job title _____

Employer's name _____

Work address _____

Work phone _____

Reservation Request Confirmed _____ Yes _____ No _____ Pending

Composition of party:

Adults (list names): _____

Children (list names and ages): _____

_____

Pets: _____

Number of nights _____

Date of arrival _____ Time of arrival _____

Date of departure _____ Expected time of departure _____

Accommodations desired:

_____ Single room   _____ Twin beds

_____ Double room   _____ Double bed

_____ Private bath   _____ Queen- or king-size bed

_____ Shared bath   _____ Extra cot in room

Location desired: _____

Arriving by:

_____ Air

_____ Bus

_____ Train

_____ Rental car

_____ Automobile (license number):

_____

_____ Desires pickup at airport or bus or train station (Note arrival time and identifying number of flight/bus/train)

_____ Needs parking for car

_____ Needs access to public transportation

Special requirements:

_____ Smoking/nonsmoking

_____ No stairs

_____ Other: _____

_____ Diet restrictions

_____ Allergies

Costs:

$ _____ room per night x _____ nights = $ _____

Deposit due in advance $ _____

Balance due upon arrival $ _____

Form of payment accepted:

_____ Cash

_____ Traveler's checks

_____ Personal check

_____ Credit card

Refund policy for cancellations: _____

_____

Purpose of visit: _____

_____

Where guest heard about this B&B: _____

_____

Has guest stayed in a B&B before? _____

_____

Guest's special interests/hobbies: _____

_____

he or she may be late, request a courtesy telephone call to let you know. If you are willing to pick up your guests at the airport or at the bus or train station, make plans to do this as you note the arrival time and flight/train/bus number.

Now is also the time to explain the prices and ask for a deposit to be sent to you in advance. Some hosts ask for an amount equal to that of one night's stay; others ask for a percentage of the total projected amount (usually 25 percent). Mention that the balance is due upon arrival and go over what forms of payment you accept. Cash and traveler's checks are the recommended forms of payment; personal checks are always a risk. Some hosts accept credit cards, but be warned that some credit card companies will support a guest's stop payment to a B&B for any reason, and fees can add up. Some hosts now use PayPal as a way to accept credit cards without the need to pay setup fees or monthly fees. PayPal is a secure payment system where you pay per transaction only. Billing and collecting is handled through e-mails.

For e-mail billing and collecting, visit: www.paypal.com

You will need to decide upon a cancellation policy because you will get cancellations, as well as no-shows. Generally, hosts will make a refund if a cancellation is made seven days prior to the originally planned date of arrival. A service charge is deducted from the refund (usually $15). This charge compensates you for your time and effort to process the reservation. Hosts generally do not refund the deposit for cancellations made at the last minute or for no-shows who later contact them. This is because they have had to hold the rooms, possibly turning away other guests.

To avoid conflicts over your cancellation policy, print it on your reservation request form or in a confirmation sent after a reservation has been made. This makes it the responsibility of the guest to notify you according to your guidelines if there is a problem and he or she cannot honor the reservation. (*Note*: If you list your home with an RSA, that agency will have a cancellation policy that guests must follow.)

A confirmation stating the dates that have been reserved and the prices, plus the expected time of arrival, is a good idea because it acts as a reminder to the guest about points you have already gone over. It can also act as an invoice in case the guest has not yet sent the deposit by the time the letter is received. Include with the letter a map and directions to your home. If the guest has a fax machine or e-mail, confirmation can be done almost instantaneously, but a friendly follow-up by "snail mail" is also recommended.

The Role of the RSA

A reservation service agency can make a host's life much easier when it comes to screening guests. You can literally let the RSA do all the work for you, taking calls from prospective guests, asking them the right questions, and obtaining the right information from them. (See "Reservation Service Agencies" in chapter 4.)

The managers of reservation service agencies take thousands of calls and, therefore, have considerable experience in weeding out those who do not fit the model of a "bed and breakfast person." "In dealing with people over the telephone day in and day out, you quickly learn to spot potential problems. Then we ask lots and lots of questions, and if we think there will be a problem, we don't place them," says the manager of a reservation service in Washington, D.C. The manager of a Florida reservation service says, "I have twenty years in personnel, know what to say and ask, and have a 'feel' for a good customer."

"We ask a lot of questions in order to find out what the caller is looking for," says the manager of a California reservation service agency. "We eliminate about 15 percent of potential guests and on the basis of nine years' experience know that it is foolhardy for any individual in a private home to try to do his or her own screening. Our credo is 'Our hosts are more important than the guests.'"

"Homeowners should find out how an agency screens their guests," says the manager of one reservation service agency in California. Is it typical for RSAs to turn away a percentage of the people who contact them looking for bed and breakfast accommodations? "Of course. It's our job," says one RSA manager. Some reasons prospective guests are turned away:

"Many people just call to find out prices," says the manager of a West Coast reservation service. "Those are the ones looking for a one-night cheap room, and we do not want those guests. They are better off in a cheap motel."

The manager of a reservation service in New York City has turned away those who were "too cranky" or whose address and telephone number did not check out. The manager of a Texas reservation service says, "I ask for references, business and personal, also credit card references. I *have called* the references!" The manager of a Boston reservation service has screened out those who "could not or would not provide information on an employer, occupation, reason for visit, full home address, work telephone number, home telephone number, and names of all members in their party."

"Chatting on the phone really helps you know the type of person," says the manager of a Wisconsin reservation service. The manager of a reservation service in Washington, D.C., says, "We make reservations by telephone only so that we may talk with potential guests. If they are polite, give personal information easily, and seem flexible, we'll book them. If they are rude, pushy, or demanding, we won't."

The manager of a New England RSA has turned away people who were "not wanting to have to meet people." A bed and breakfast is not for anyone who wishes to spend a few days in total privacy and anonymity. The manager of a Connecticut reservation service has turned away those who were "too fussy," and the manager of a Maine RSA turned away one caller who was "obviously intoxicated."

People who call at the last minute are not often placed. "With last-minute requests we do not have enough time to get background information," says the manager of a California reservation service.

Another manager lists a number of reasons for not placing some of the people who have contacted that RSA: Some wanted to have friends over for a party; some wanted to know "how liberal" the hosts were; some wanted to sneak people into their rooms; some had no idea what a bed and breakfast was.

If you list your home with a reservation service, find out how that agency screens the people who write or call looking for bed and breakfast accommodations. If you are going to relinquish this important process to someone else, you must be sure that the screening is done very carefully.

The reservation service agency provides an additional service for the hosts it represents—that of "matching" certain guests with certain hosts, based on mutual interests. This is a service that can help you enjoy offering bed and breakfast even more because guests with whom you share something in common will be directed to your home. One Boston host who loved to run especially enjoyed the visit of a woman who also loved to run. "We ran together every morning," she says. "It was hard to see her leave."

New hosts usually wonder how the placement process works and at what point they get involved in it when guests make their initial contact with the reservation service agency. RSAs keep on hand information about your bed and breakfast home based (usually) on a home visit. This is the same kind of information that you would include on your own screening checklist if you were to handle the process yourself: the bedroom and bathroom setups, the kinds of beds, special restrictions (such as no pets), special features (such as a swimming pool, or a fireplace in the bedroom), and potential problems (such as a pet in residence or stairway access only to second-floor rooms). With all this information, the RSA manager can easily answer the basic questions that a prospective guest will have about accommodations. Thus far you need not be involved in the process at all. If the guest decides that your bed and breakfast would be the best choice, and the RSA manager is satisfied with the reliability of the guest, the RSA will get in touch with you before confirming the reservation.

The RSA manager will tell you about the guest and the dates that he or she wishes to visit. "If a host has questions about a particular request, we will get the answers to their questions. We do drop or refuse reservations where the questions are not answered or are not answered to our or the host's satisfaction," says one RSA manager. This is fairly common among reservation service agencies; the host has final approval or refusal of a prospective guest. If the dates of the visit are not good for your schedule, you can turn down the guest, and the RSA will place the person elsewhere. If you choose not to host a single man because your husband will be away on business the particular days the guest wants to visit, you have the right to turn down the reservation and ask the RSA to place him somewhere else. Keep in mind, though, that even though each individual host does have the final say-so on each reservation, the RSA does expect a spirit of cooperation; if you wish to continue to list your home with the RSA, you've got to have a good reason for any reservation you do turn down.

One particular advantage enjoyed by hosts who list with a reservation service agency is the high number of guests who have used the services of the RSA before and who either come back again or refer their friends and relatives to the RSA. One Pennsylvania reservation service reports that approximately 50 percent of the guests placed by this RSA are repeat customers. And one reservation service agency on Cape Cod reports that more than 50 percent of its new guests have been referred by people who have been accommodated in the past. This is definitely an advantage for hosts who want to be sure that every guest is a "bed and breakfast person." One RSA even makes a point of placing some of its seasoned guests with brand-new hosts in order to make the hosts feel more comfortable in their new role! Guests who are personally known to be the right kind of persons for B&B are a treasured commodity. "Selected guests are notified on an annual basis of the new host directory," says one RSA manager. "A preferred-guest club is now being organized and will provide regular contact with selected guests."

Whether you choose to list with an RSA, which will handle the screening of guests for you, or whether you choose to stay independent and handle the screening yourself, the important thing is that it be done. As bed and breakfast becomes more and more popular in North America, more and more people are seeking out B&B accommodations, sometimes for the wrong reasons. The screening process can help educate prospective guests about bed and breakfast, making sure that the people who do come to visit your home understand the difference between a B&B and a hotel or motel. And those people who would honestly not enjoy the unique experience of bed and breakfast can be directed to another type of accommodation.

One-night Guests

There are many, many hosts out there who require a minimum stay of two nights for any guest who stays at their bed and breakfast home. There are good reasons for this, and they will become quite obvious to you once you start hosting. The main reason is that one-nighters are a lot more work than people who stay two or more nights.

Consider that you have to make both the guest room and the bathroom "guest-ready" between the departure of one guest and the arrival of the next. And consider that each guest uses an entire set of towels and an entire set of sheets and pillowcases—which means that the bed has to be stripped, the laundry done, and the bed remade. Someone staying two or three days can use the same towels and sheets during his or her visit, and the bathroom needs only a few touch-ups to keep it clean. For a series of one-nighters, the whole process of cleaning is a never-ending one. That's a lot of laundry and toilet bowls. The fact that you're doing this because you love people can get to be pretty remote under these circumstances.

Still, it is unlikely that your rooms will be booked every single night of the week by people who wish to stay only one night. Usually, they will be sprinkled among the number of guests who stay longer, giving you some respite from the amount of work that providing for a one-nighter causes. Keep this in mind before deciding to turn away all short-term guests.

A number of travelers want and need accommodations for only one night. People driving great distances could spend one night in Ohio and the next in Illinois and the one following who knows where. They have someplace to go and have no intention of lingering at a B&B just to fulfill the two-night minimum. Yet long-distance travelers sometimes prefer to stay in a bed and breakfast home just to have a little human contact on their trip. If no host will take them, they will end up in the nearest motel. Business travelers, too, sometimes need to be in town for only one or two days to have a meeting, go for a job interview, or attend a conference. They, too, will go elsewhere if no host will accept them for one night only.

If you are just starting out with your bed and breakfast or have trouble attracting as many guests as you would like even though you've been hosting for a while, do not be hasty in turning away one-nighters. Word-of-mouth is one of the most effective ways to publicize your bed and breakfast, so that one-night guest who was treated so well at your home means a lot more than just the laundry and cleanup time for you. The investment may be worth it for the future business you might enjoy as a result.

Some hosts do take steps to ensure that they don't end up losing money by taking a guest for just one night (think of the costs of detergent and electricity for the laundry, the breakfast ingredients that must be purchased, even gasoline if you offer a ride to or from the airport or train station). They ask for a surcharge as part of their system of pricing. (See "Pricing Your Bed and Breakfast" in chapter 3.) So if you normally charge $80 for a single room, you might add $10 or $15 to the cost for anyone who does not stay a minimum of two nights. This way, all your time and energy are counterbalanced to an extent, and the guest understands that you will make an exception under these terms.

Single Travelers

It has long been a tradition that people who travel alone are punished. They are given the smallest, most uncomfortable rooms in hotels and the worst tables in restaurants, and they are charged disproportionate prices for them. But more and more, travelers are evaluating the accommodations they use and are spreading the word—good or bad—faster and more efficiently than ever before. The point is that there are a lot of people who do travel alone for various reasons, and the kind of treatment they receive in your bed and breakfast will determine whether you win or lose their patronage.

As a host, you will be contacted by single travelers. They are drawn to bed and breakfast homes because of their reputation for atmosphere, comfort, safety, and friendliness—qualities that are sometimes valued by someone traveling alone even more than by those traveling with family or friends. Yet it is not unusual for a bed and breakfast host to fall into the same pattern of thinking that has been plaguing the single traveler for much too long. Consider the following incident:

Upon arrival at a bed and breakfast home, a woman was shown to a tiny bedroom (a "single") off the kitchen, with the bathroom down the hall. The tour of the house had included a peek at another, larger guest room that had a queen-size bed, a sitting area with a comfortable chair and table, and an adjoining private bath. This more comfortable room was vacant, and the woman would have much preferred that choice, but the host didn't even ask. Why? It was a "double." Surely no single person should have all that space to herself.

This is exactly the kind of thinking that could damage your B&B's reputation among single travelers. Of course, some people traveling alone are budget minded; they will find a tiny room with the bathroom down the hall just fine if the price is right. But many single travelers want to enjoy their accommodations. They are willing to pay a little more for a larger space and a private bath, perhaps even a more pleasing decor, a more comfortable bed, and a better view. (Unfortunately, these differences are too often the case when comparing singles with doubles.) This is not to say that people traveling alone are willing to pay the full price that would normally be charged for double occupancy. Many consider this another type of punishment for the single traveler, and you can bet that it will be duly noted.

Instead, think about the following compromise as a way to encourage single travelers to stay at your bed and breakfast home. Say you have a single room and a double room available for guests. No matter which room is used, you've still got to wash a set of sheets and clean the bathroom. Does it really matter whether the sheets are twin size or queen size? Does it really matter that one bathroom is off the hallway and the other adjoins the larger guest room? Of course, the answer is no. The work is essentially the same for you. The real difference is in the price. Let's say that your single room is priced at $80, your double at $100. This is only fair—more people, more money. And if the double is booked for two people at full price, so be it. But if it's not, why not give your single traveler a choice of rooms instead of assuming that he or she "should" automatically get the smaller room?

Now obviously the double room is worth more than the single room because it offers more. (See "Pricing Your Bed and Breakfast" in chapter 3.) So adjust your price accordingly. If the double is available, why not invite a single traveler to use it for a reduced rate, say $85 or $90? This way, your visitor makes the decision and will be much happier for the choice.

Realistically, this choice can be extended only at the time a guest arrives at your door, unless he or she does want to reserve the double room in advance, either at full price or at a small reduction that you determine. This keeps you from losing money if you get a call in the interim from someone else wanting to book the double at full cost and you have to turn them away.

Do your best to make the single rooms in your bed and breakfast comfortable and homey. For some reason single rooms end up on the bottom of the priority list for many hosts. This is just not good business sense. A guest will notice immediately and feel that you do not consider his or her comfort as important as the comfort of guests who are not alone. Make the quarters as spacious as possible by removing unnecessary furniture or rearranging what you have in a better way. Get rid of that big bookcase and install a few wall shelves on brackets instead. Put the floor lamp elsewhere in the house and substitute a space-saving fixture that hangs from the ceiling. Is that massive oak bureau the only one you've got, or can it be switched with a smaller bureau, maybe even one that fits neatly inside the closet?

Ask yourself if the room seems too dark—which will make it seem even smaller than it is. Paint the walls and ceiling white to open up the space. Take down the heavy, dark

"Did you hear about the host who married her very first guest?" asks Arline Kardasis, founder of Bed and Breakfast Associates, Bay Colony, Ltd., in Massachusetts. She tells the story of a host, whose home was located in an outlying area of Boston, who registered with her reservation service agency. Her inconvenient location and her restriction of "no single men" unfortunately meant no visitors. Then one day Arline was contacted by a company inquiring about housing for an executive coming from Sweden to do some consulting work for the firm. The host's home was very near the company, but the gentleman was unmarried. After some discussion, the host decided to relent on her rule about single men. Talk about the perfect guest. The couple was married within the year, and the host now lives in Sweden with her husband.

drapes and hang white or light-colored ones instead. Make sure that your lightbulbs have a high enough wattage to make the room feel bright and cheery. A small single room can be quite charming if you put the time and energy into making it that way.

Beyond making their accommodations as comfortable as possible, ask yourself whether you are being as hospitable to your single travelers as you are to couples or families. There is an unfortunate stigma attached to being alone, and sometimes the attitude that there is something wrong with anyone who is alone comes through unintentionally. Obvious discomfort when the single traveler joins a group of other guests who are in couples; different seating times at the breakfast table; a general feeling of being left out of activities that include other guests—you must guard against all of these. (But don't go overboard in the other direction either, making a single traveler uncomfortable by giving him or her too much attention.)

Some hosts who live alone do not want to accommodate single travelers of the opposite sex. If you live alone, this is a consideration, and you will have to make a decision. Some hosts are apprehensive about their personal safety or about how it might appear to the neighbors, or they are just plain uncomfortable about the idea of sharing a roof with a stranger of the opposite sex. Any of these reasons are good ones to screen out members of the opposite gender. It's your home, and you have a responsibility to yourself to feel comfortable and safe in it.

If your bed and breakfast is registered with a reservation service agency, ask the manager not to place any single traveler of the opposite sex with you. If you handle your own reservations, you need to come up with something to say when someone wants to make a reservation with you and you prefer not to accommodate that person because of the decision you've made. You can always say that you have personal plans for that particular night (or nights) that prevent you from accepting any bed and breakfast guests at that time and give your apologies graciously. (See "Screening Your Guests" earlier in this chapter.)

If you are set up to accept single travelers at your bed and breakfast, you can play an important part in extending the kind of hospitality to them that they have long been denied. And you can be sure that the good word will spread.

Hosting Children

If you're a parent, you are well aware of how disruptive and destructive children can be at times—but you also know how sweet and obedient they can be at others. They are not necessarily all terrors who should be unconditionally banned from bed and breakfast homes. Rather, children are guests of a special sort who need a different kind of hospitality. As a bed and breakfast host, you have to decide whether you wish to court a family market. Many people travel as a family, and if you choose to discourage parents from bringing their children to your home, then you will most certainly narrow your market. This is especially true if your home is well situated near an attraction geared toward young people—Sea World, Disneyland, amusement parks, special museums (such as the one devoted to Buffalo Bill)—or in an area where they can hike or swim. Note that recent studies indicate that up to 45 percent of guests have children living at home—not a small market. Consider the following points carefully before making your decision.

Some hosts feel that they are simply not set up to accommodate children as overnight guests, but others find they can make the necessary adjustments easily enough.

At Leftwich House in Graham, North Carolina, a small child can use the crib, and another older child can be accommodated in a small room with a bed that adjoins the parents' room. Patricia Boettcher, owner of 3B's Bed & Breakfast in Spring Valley, Ohio, puts older children right in the parents' room: "We can set up cots for children, as our rooms are spacious."

One couple traveling with a baby and a four-year-old child were happy to locate a bed and breakfast home in Mystic, Connecticut, that had adjoining bedrooms that shared a bath. The family could be together, bother no one else in the bed and breakfast, and have some privacy and space as well.

Some hosts prefer children of a certain age only—infants only, toddlers only, teens only—depending on what they're used to or what they think their home can best endure. How "childproof" is your home? Do you fear for your quilts, your antique furniture, the original paintings on the walls? Do you have a lot of knickknacks around, just the right size for a toddler to throw? If so, then you may wish to discourage children under the age of twelve.

But be aware that denying someone accommodation on the basis of age may be interpreted as a violation of civil rights. The Federal Public Accommodations Law, Title II of the Civil Rights Act of 1964, prohibits discrimination in public accommodations due to race, color, religion, sex, disability, national origin, and familial status. *Familial status* refers to children under eighteen living with a parent. This law has yet to be tested insofar as it applies to B&Bs; state law also exists in Maine, Michigan, and California. (A California case brought by a family denied B&B accommodation because of their child was settled out of court.) Therefore, it is wiser to adhere to the more negotiable guideline of "Children under twelve are discouraged because the premises are not child-safe," rather than the black-and-white rule of "No children allowed!" The latter shouts discrimination. Never, ever print a "no children" rule in your literature.

According to a B&B association representative, "during telephone conversations with prospective guests, many hosts have found it wise to no longer say they do not accept children. Instead, they take the time to explain that the B&B is not child-safe or that cribs or high chairs are not available because so few children visit. Then they let the guest determine whether the accommodation is suitable for the entire family. Under no circumstances should B&B owners refuse accommodations to guests with infants or children because the 'noise will disturb other guests' or 'the antiques might get damaged.'" Keep a list of other neighborhood B&Bs that are set up for accommodating children and be ready to recommend them to prospective guests as an alternative.

If you have a child yourself, chances are you've already made your house "safe" for little ones. This involves covering electrical outlets, putting up gates at the top and bottom of staircases, and locking cabinets, among other things. If you don't have a child but wish to host children, you've got to take whatever measures are necessary to ensure the well-being of your young guests. Take a close look at your home and evaluate its features in view of different age groups. Should you encourage young visitors of certain ages only, as some hosts do?

Of course, a lot depends on the parents. George and Barbara Painter, owners of Turkey Nest Rest in Gatlinburg, Tennessee, admit that "our town's a great place for children," but they enjoy young guests "only if parents can manage them." Ellen Madison, owner of Woody Hill Guest House in Westerly, Rhode Island, says she accepts children "reluctantly," based on "parents' assurances that other guests will not be disturbed." A frank talk with parents before they show up at your B&B, or when they first arrive, should be on your agenda.

Make it clear that the parents are expected to supervise their youngsters during their stay—that babysitting does not come with the price of the room.

If you wish, you can offer to babysit so that the parents can go out alone to dinner, shopping, or sightseeing. This is a terrific amenity to offer parents who are likely to be experiencing more family togetherness than they might be used to; a chance to get away by themselves for a while might be very welcome. Make it clear, though, that your babysitting services are *by arrangement only.* You can charge a fee for this service if you wish. (See "Pricing Your Bed and Breakfast" in chapter 3.)

Do your best to think of ways to entertain the children (bored children are often the ones who go looking for something to do that maybe they shouldn't). Meadowview Guest House in Lancaster, Pennsylvania, keeps toys and games on hand. At Leftwich House in Graham, North Carolina, "there is a playroom upstairs with toys." Ocean View House in Santa Barbara, California, even advertises its special "amenity" just for kids: "Children are delighted with the backyard playhouse." A San Diego man traveling with his young son was happy to find a swing set in the yard at a bed and breakfast home in Northern California.

"It was great to find children's books sitting on the nightstand next to the bed," said one mother traveling with her two small children. Books to read, or coloring books and a box of crayons, are good items to keep on hand for your young visitors. Consider preparing some "fun baskets" for children who will be indoors a lot during their visit—filled perhaps with old costume jewelry to play with; an assortment of old hats, purses, shawls, scarves, and other clothing with a lot of character (like a safari shirt or fancy dress with sequins and sparkles) for "dress up"; a variety of Tinkertoys, building blocks, and Erector set materials; stuffed animals; even a rock collection (fascinating for an older child, but hide this basket from younger kids).

It's a nice touch to give the child a farewell gift when the visit is over; if you see that a youngster is becoming especially attached to any item in a "fun basket," consider giving that item as a present—a string of beads from the costume jewelry, a small stuffed animal, a great-looking hunk of quartz—something small but valued by the child and appreciated by the parents for your thoughtfulness. (Be sure to check with the parents before giving an item to a child to keep.)

How will your other guests, the ones without children, react to sharing the bed and breakfast with youngsters? Chances are that there will be few problems if parents supervise their kids closely. Many people enjoy being around children and think of the opportunity as a highlight of their stay, rather than a liability.

One father who was staying at a B&B with his three-year-old son makes this report: "The other guests, rather than being put off by having kids present, responded more like grandparents and seemed to like it. Everyone was very supportive." The couple who owned this particular bed and breakfast home had two small children themselves, so there was already a family atmosphere. The home was already "childproof," and the kids all played together.

If you have children yourself, consider that they might enjoy the chance to meet a variety of kids their own age. This is one way to make bed and breakfast truly a family project; give your children some of the responsibility for hosting the younger members of a visiting family.

If you decide to go ahead with encouraging children to stay at your bed and breakfast, you will have to deal with the problem of preparing and serving food just for them. The welcome snack upon arrival and the evening snack should include milk, cookies, and fruit—items that adults usually enjoy as well. The parents of infants should supply their own formula (make this clear in advance), but you'll be responsible for the breakfast of children older than this. (See the section "Especially for Children" in chapter 9, "A Memorable Breakfast.")

Your success with hosting children has a lot to do with your feelings about them to begin with. If you really don't like kids, you probably shouldn't actively promote your B&B as a family accommodation, even if your location is a two-minute walk from Sea World and you'll be missing out on a lot of guests who are bringing their kids to see Shamu the Whale. One couple tried it but didn't like it: "Children want special food—they are fussy eaters, leave crumbs on the floor, and are noisy."

Yes, they are all of these things. But they are more as well, and you've got to be able to see this. One father sensed this right away about the hosts with whom he and his child stayed for a wonderful visit. "Mostly, it was more the attitude of really being glad to see kids at the place," he says. The hosts simply loved kids and enjoyed having them around. If you feel the same way, your bed and breakfast can reach out to the family market and make it work to your advantage.

Four-legged Guests

Hosting pets is not for everyone. There's no way you should allow a full set of paws to pad around your home if there are priceless Oriental rugs on the floor, heirloom crystal on the table, and museum-quality objets d'art on display. Of course, it's not worth the risk. There are plenty of guests who do not travel with their pets, and it's safer for your lovely home to host human beings exclusively on the assumption that they will be more careful. Remember, too, that some people are allergic to certain animals. All propective guests must be informed if animals (including any of your own) will be on the premises.

There are a large number of people who travel with their pets. These may be people who are relocating or just on vacation, but they want the whole family together—and this includes Bowzer. Pet owners do not have an easy time of it when trying to locate overnight accommodations. There are some hotels, motels, inns—and bed and breakfast homes, too—that accept pets, but most do not. "A problem we have is finding hosts who will take pets," says the manager of a Virginia reservation service. "Sorry, none of our hosts accept pets," reads the literature printed by one Massachusetts reservation service agency. Pet owners must go elsewhere.

One exception are service dogs, which are not considered "pets." Rather, they are highly trained assistants that act as guide dogs for people with visual impairments or in another service capacity. By law, you are obligated to accommodate a service animal that accompanies a guest. Be assured, though, that such animals are very well cared for, healthy, and under the control of the owner at all times. Indeed, you couldn't ask for a better exception to a "no pets" rule.

If you do choose to accept pets, you can definitely attract a market by offering this privilege. But before you decide, evaluate the space that would be used to accommodate the animals. It must be "petproof," able to handle the presence of animals with a minimum of wear and tear. Lincoln Alden, owner of Watercourse Way Bed & Breakfast in Stratford, Vermont, allows guests to house their dogs in the barn that is on his property. If you have a secure, separate space like this, you can easily accommodate the animals that your guests might want to bring with them. Keeping a dog outside on a leash, with no shelter, is not a good idea even in good weather. Little Fifi might never have been outdoors on her own in her entire life, and this will be uncomfortable for her. Never leave an animal outdoors in rain, snow, or subzero temperatures.

The ranch manager of Anchor Hill Ranch in Rogersville, Missouri, welcomes guests with horses. The place already has box stalls with runs to accommodate horses, so there is no problem. Guests are charged a small fee per horse per night. This rate includes hay and oats, stall cleaning, and watering.

Most of us don't have this kind of space, so if a guest wants to bring a pet, this means that the animal will have to stay inside the house. This rules out horses, but cats and dogs can work out fine if the individual guest room can be made petproof. Ideally, the floor should be tile or linoleum instead of wood, and there should not be wall-to-wall carpeting because it's too hard to clean thoroughly between visits. A throw rug next to the bed is nice for the owner's comfort, and it can be washed easily after each furry guest checks out. There should be no knickknacks on dresser or table tops (they can tempt even the most well-behaved pet into a game not unlike handball).

During your initial conversation with them on the telephone, ask guests to bring the animal's own feeding and watering dishes, food, a leash (for dogs), and a pooper-scooper if you wish to require that one be used for cleanups, and a kitty-litter box and litter. Ask where the animal usually sleeps and try to extract an honest answer. Some pet owners might be reluctant to tell you that their pet sleeps on the bed, but it's much better that you know this in advance. If Cuddles is used to being on the bed, that's probably where the little darling will end up no matter what you or his owner thinks about it. You're much better off just asking the owner to bring something along to protect the blankets you will be providing. Just in case this item is forgotten, keep on hand a washable cover that can be placed on top of the blankets to protect them from shedding hair.

Some animals are used to sleeping on their own special pillow or blanket; if your guest's furry friend usually sleeps alone on its own bedding, ask the owner to bring it along. (Janet Turley, owner of the House of Amacord in Buckland, Massachusetts, says she doesn't usually allow pets in her bed and breakfast, but she did agree to accept a dog once because he had his own sleeping bag!)

If the owner cannot bring along all the items you request for the pet's comfort (guests arriving by plane or bus might not be able to transport everything), find out what exactly you need to have on hand, such as the brand of food that the animal usually eats or kitty litter and a box (a sturdy cardboard one is fine if placed on top of a sheet of plastic). Add the cost of any items to the guest's bill, along with the surcharge you decide upon for the pet (usually $5.00–$10.00 per night).

Also ask the guests to clip the nails of their animals before arriving at your bed and breakfast. (It might be a good idea to invest in a pair of those special scissors available at pet stores just in case an owner forgets.) Then if the animal decides to scratch something, the damage will be limited.

Once guests arrive, tell them the "rules" for the pet: Never leave pets alone and unrestrained in any room of the house. (They might get overzealous in their exploration of new territory.) Never let cats roam the grounds. (They're very good at sneaking off and hiding.) Never let dogs roam the grounds unless they are accompanied by the owner and restrained on a leash. (They might get lost or run into a belligerent animal who thinks he owns the territory.) And point out to the owner where the dog may relieve itself.

If you wish, you can require that a guest confine a cat to the kennel most owners have to transport their animals. (Make sure you inform the guest of this in advance.) If the guest room has an adjoining petproof bathroom, you could also give the owner the option of putting Rambo in there if he becomes emotional (destructively so) about being in a new environment.

You might want to add your own rules to this list that are tailored to the needs of your own home—keep the dog away from the swimming pool, the pet ducks, and the flower bed. Keep the cat away from the fishbowl, the baby's toys, and the turkey defrosting in the kitchen. Make it clear to pet owners that it is their responsibility for supervising their animals at all times. So when the dog starts frantically scratching at the door to go outside, it's

A real case of puppy love is reported by Rita Duncan, owner of Blue Ridge Bed & Breakfast Reservation Service in Virginia. "One of my neighbor's dogs fell in love with a guest's dog. He slept on the hood of the guest's car and scratched it with his claws." The guest took his car to a Honda dealership, where they were able to buff the scratches out. "I paid for the buffing and gave the guest two more visits for free because he was so nice about it," says Rita.

the guest (and not the host) who takes the animal out to answer the call of nature. Most problems are caused because the host just didn't lay down the law right in the beginning. Don't make this mistake.

Every state requires a general health certificate for dogs and cats coming in from other states, and you must comply. In fact, you should require a health certificate even for pets that are traveling within the same state, just to be sure, according to veterinarian John Bujalski. Pets can carry communicable diseases and parasites, and you have a right to proof that any animal staying in your home is healthy.

At the time that pet owners are making reservations with you, inform them that you will expect them to produce a health certificate for their animal upon arrival. According to Dr. Bujalski, it should be issued by their own veterinarian within ten days prior to their visit with you, covering the following items: For dogs the animal must be current on its vaccinations against distemper, hepatitis, leptospirosis, bordatella, and parvovirus disease, as well as rabies. Dogs should also have a negative stool sample, ensuring that they carry no parasites, documented ten days before arrival. (Parasites deposited in stools can live more than a year in the ground.) If possible, prepare a separate area for owners to walk their pets to defecate. This area should ideally consist of 10 to 12 inches of pea gravel, which is deep enough so that parasite eggs will not surface after a heavy rain.

A health certificate for cats should show that inoculations are current for rabies, upper-respiratory viruses, and cat distemper (called feline panleukopenia). If the owner does not produce a health certificate, it's best to refuse the animal, especially if you have animals of your own that run the risk of picking up a parasite or contagious disease.

To be on the safe side, the guest room in which an animal has stayed should be thoroughly cleaned and disinfected after each use. Vacuum well to pick up any hair. To disinfect tile or linoleum floors, Dr. Bujalski recommends a solution of one part chlorine bleach and ten parts water. (Don't use the solution on wood, as the bleaching might affect it.) There is also a sanitizing spray called Asepticare that has been recommended to kill bacterial germs and viruses.

After disinfecting the room, use a "premise spray" containing the chemical methoprene (trademark name PRECOR) to kill flea eggs and larvae before they hatch. "Every animal potentially carries fleas," Dr. Bujalski says. The spray is colorless and water-based, so it can be used freely without harming furniture. Also recommend to your guests that they consult with their veterinarian about applying a product called Frontline Plus to their pet's coat five days before their scheduled arrival at your B&B. This product, available for both dogs and cats, kills fleas and ticks.

Dogs and cats are big on territorial rights, and their natural inclination is to "mark" new territory. This is a difficult problem to control, but you can take measures to discourage marking behavior. Dr. Bujalski suggests placing mothball flakes in the corners of the guest room (not enough for humans to detect the odor). Animals usually head for the corners first to begin exploration of a new environment. "They hate the smell of naphthalene," says Dr. Bujalski. Maybe, just maybe, they'll hate it enough to leave the room alone.

For information on interstate traveling regulations for pets, visit: www.aphis.usda.gov/vs/sregs

For an online directory of pet-friendly accommodations, visit: www.bring yourpet.com

Check current health department regulations meticulously before accepting pets. Hawaii and North Carolina in particular have historically applied strict regulations to animals from out of state.

If you have a pet yourself, you probably know that most pets are healthy most of the time and also fairly well behaved most of the time if they have been trained properly. Generally speaking, allowing guests to bring pets to your home will cause you no trouble at all. "They're very considerate of my home," says a Canadian host. Requiring a health certificate, cleaning and disinfecting the room after each use, and making the rules clear in advance will all provide that extra insurance for you that all will be well. Further precautions you might want to consider are limited stays for guests with animals, a restriction to small dogs only, a written statement that clearly spells out that the pet owner is liable for any damages caused by the pet (ask the guest to sign it), and a refundable deposit (payable in advance) that is in addition to the fee charged for accommodating the pet.

"We have found, being one of the few places in the area that allow pets, that we have met a lot of great (and grateful) people," says Sandra J. Conley of Applebrook in Jefferson, New Hampshire. "We started charging $5.00 per night per pet and donating half of that to the humane society. This has been very well received." One enterprising couple in Holland, Massachusetts, named their pet-friendly B&B "Restful Paws," and advertises with the slogan "where pets bring their owners to relax." The B&B offers doggie towels and massages, pet-sitting services, and even provides furry guests with their own swimming pool shaped like a bone!

To court business from pet owners, you can do several things: Include "cats and dogs welcome" on your business card or brochure. Make sure that your reservation service agency knows that you welcome pets. And mention this fact in the information you provide for any guidebook listing. Send information to authors of books devoted to pet-friendly accommodations, such as *Pets on the Go: The Definitive Pet Accommodation and Vacation Guide*. And list your B&B with online lodging directories geared toward travelers with pets.

Hosting International Visitors

People who live in Europe or who have traveled there from other countries around the world are familiar with the idea of bed and breakfast. They are delighted to find that B&B is available in North America, and when they plan their travels here, international visitors often seek out the type of accommodation that they have enjoyed so much elsewhere. A bed and breakfast host whose home is located in an area that attracts visitors from around the world (such as a large city, a popular resort, or a base for a large international corporation) is in a good position to reach out to this market.

You can expect that many visitors from other countries will speak English very well indeed, and many will have acquired enough English to communicate on a basic level. Still, there will be those who do not speak the English language well or at all. If you hope to attract the variety of international visitors who come to your area, it's a good idea to polish the language skills you might already have (remember high school French?) or work on acquiring a basic command of new languages so that you can make the most of your opportunities.

"We have multilingual host families, with French, German, and Spanish the major second languages. We believe this is not only more comfortable for foreign travelers but is also advantageous for those who are interested in other cultures," reads the brochure issued by a Florida a reservation service. By advertising the fact that some of its hosts speak other languages, the RSA can attract those visitors who are looking for that special amenity. An RSA located in Seattle, Washington, also advertises the language skills of its hosts. *"Wir sprechen Deutsch"* reads its brochure as a way to attract German-speaking guests. One Philadelphia host finds that people are especially attracted to her B&B because of her proficiency in languages: "I have traveled extensively, am familiar with various cultures, and speak several languages," says Marjorie Amrom, owner of Trade Winds. This has had a positive effect on her bed and breakfast business.

To make it easier for potential international guests to navigate your Web site, offer a link to an online translation service, such as Babel Fish. This service will convert your entire Web site into the requested language, plus translate e-mails.

> For language translations, visit: babel.altavista.com

If you already speak one or more languages besides English, you can start using this fact immediately to reach out to international visitors. If you list with an RSA, ask the agency to include a note on its brochure. If you print your own brochure as an independent host, make sure to include your language skill somewhere in the copy. (You might even want to print a bilingual brochure.) Then make your brochures available to tourist bureaus, embassies, consulates, international corporations, the chamber of commerce, car-rental companies, and any other places you can think of in your area that might have frequent contact with international visitors. And if your B&B is listed in any guidebook or online directory, be sure to include your language proficiency in the description.

An Accessible B&B

An estimated thirty-six million people in the United States have some kind of disability, and the number is growing as the population ages. As a result of legislation called the Americans with Disabilities Act (ADA), public accommodations such as hotels are required to follow rules for making bedrooms, bathrooms, common areas, entrances and exits, hallways, and parking facilities accessible to people with impairment of mobility, hearing, and vision. Guidelines provided by the ADA of 1990 (as amended in 2004) are reinforced by the Architectural Barriers Act to provide a consistent level of access. Make sure any architect or contractor you may hire is conversant on the newest regulations.

B&B consultant Kit Cassingham of Sage Blossom Consulting encourages hosts to recognize the advantages of ADA compliance. "From reactions I observe, it seems that many—if not most—innkeepers look at the ADA as something punitive, an expensive inconvenience. I think that reaction is missing the mark on how to respond to the law. Don't overlook the side benefit of making your B&B inn accessible as a way of also catering to people with temporary disabilities (say due to surgery or injury) and the aging population. If your inn is accessible, then any 'variously abled' person can enjoy your B&B, perhaps to your financial benefit, not detriment!"

Legal Requirements

Opening your home to the public as a B&B makes you subject to rules and regulations applied to public accommodations, so all B&B owners need to take special note of the Americans with Disability Act, which entitles people with disabilities to the same access as other Americans. Specifically, the ADA requires that a public accommodation shall remove architectural barriers in existing facilities where such removal is "readily achievable," that is, easily accomplishable and able to be carried out without much difficulty or expense. (Tax credits are available to small businesses to make these modifications. Contact the Internal Revenue Service for information on the Disabled Access Credit.) If barrier removal is not "readily achievable," a business is still obligated to provide goods, services, facilities, and accommodations through alternative methods. New construction is regulated by criteria in the ADA's appendix, which is called the Americans with Disabilities Act Accessibility Guidelines (ADAAG). New construction must be accessible if the building was opened for first occupancy after January 26, 1993. In new construction involving hotels with one to twenty-five guest rooms, one room must be wheelchair accessible and must also provide for people who are hearing impaired. The new guidelines also affect alterations or renovations of existing structures.

The law does allow an exemption for an establishment located within a building that contains not more than five rooms for rent or hire and that is occupied by the proprietor as his or her place of residence. This would seem to exempt owner-occupied B&Bs of five or fewer guest rooms; however, it would be prudent to undertake recommended modifications in your existing structure if they are "readily achievable" and to plan new construction with the ADA rules as your guide. This is crucial if you are remodeling with the intent to exceed five guest rooms.

One B&B consultant tells the story of one couple who borrowed money to add two rooms onto the third floor of their home because their financial projections needed seven guest rooms. Only when the construction was done did they discover that B&Bs with seven rooms were required to meet strict guidelines for accommodating people with disabilities. "Why didn't you check with us?" they were asked by town officials. "We could have warned you." The law covers the portions of the structure devoted to guest use exclusively, such as a guest bedroom, as well as those portions used by both guests and residents, such as entryways, hallways, and bathrooms.

Making Your B&B Accessible

What does it take to make a bed and breakfast home accessible? Clearly, some houses are structured so that they cannot easily be adapted for people with impairments in mobility. "I have a spiral staircase in a three-story town house in the city, which would be difficult for someone who cannot ambulate well," says a Philadelphia host. If this sounds like your own situation, making your B&B accessible is probably not "readily achievable." But if your home has a bedroom, a bathroom, and a dining room on the ground level (with no steps up or down between the areas), then making the necessary renovations to accommodate people who use wheelchairs to get around may not be prohibitively difficult or expensive.

How extensive would renovations be? Be advised that most houses are not constructed with anyone but the nondisabled in mind. Ground-floor accommodations could be enticement enough for some travelers who can get around with the aid of a cane, crutches, or a walker. But you may have to make major modifications if you want to accommodate travelers who use wheelchairs. If you intend to renovate your home anyway, these modifications should be included in your plans. Technical requirements can be found in those sections of the ADA referring to "transient lodging guests rooms," as well as those specific to certain areas, such as dining rooms and bathrooms.

A big problem for people without full mobility is getting through doorways that are too narrow—and in many private homes, they are. A person in a wheelchair needs more width to maneuver than typical doorways allow. How wide are yours? Measure the doors to the guest rooms, the bathroom, the dining area, and any common space that guests are invited to use (such as the living room or TV room), as well as the front door. Unless you've got French doors throughout the house, you very well might have to widen your doorways. And was your home built during the period when thresholds were in vogue? A threshold is a piece of wood positioned at the bottom of a doorframe as a cross piece—attractive maybe, but a hindrance to someone who needs a clear path. The thresholds will have to go.

A clear path is essential for people with an impairment of mobility or vision. Unnecessary furniture and decorations—extra chairs, tables, desks, pole lamps, throw rugs, knickknacks—should all be moved out of the guest room in favor of more floor space. Hallways, too, must be free of obstructions and wide enough to accommodate a wheelchair comfortably.

In the guest room, furniture should be arranged so that each piece has ample floor space near it to allow access by wheelchair. And remember that everything must be reachable from a sitting position. This includes light, heat, and air-conditioning switches. Hooks for robes should be placed low enough on doors or inside closets for your guests to reach easily. The horizontal pole in the closet should be lowered (or a second one added beneath the first) so that clothes can be hung on hangers and removed with no trouble.

Bathrooms tend to be small, which can pose a problem for someone who needs lots of floor space. Remove unnecessary furniture or decorations to make the area as roomy as possible. A person using a wheelchair should be able to turn around, open and close the door, and reach the sink and toilet easily. Grab-bars for the bathtub and shower are recommended for the safety of *all* your guests. In addition, an accessible bed and breakfast should have grab-bars at the toilet.

Getting in and out of your home needs to be as easy as getting around within it. The ADA specifically notes that any barriers at the entrance and on the sidewalk leading up to a public accommodation must be removed if doing so is "readily achievable." Steps up or down to the "ground level" can be a problem. The owners of Spindrift Bed & Breakfast in Bandon, Oregon, have installed a wheelchair ramp as a solution. If you need to install a ramp, have a professional builder do it so that it is sturdy, made of a nonskid material, rises at a *gradual* gradient, and is wide enough to allow ample clearance on each side of a wheelchair. If your bed and breakfast is located in a building that has an elevator, check to see if the buttons can be reached from a sitting position and if the doors are wide enough to facilitate wheelchairs; also check to see if there are Braille symbols to indicate floors.

The path to your B&B's entrance needs to be absolutely free of obstructions. Parking must be near the entrance, and parking spaces have to allow ample room for a guest to get in and out of a car easily.

Extensive renovations are not necessary to accommodate individuals with impairments in vision and hearing, but you will have to make some modifications for your guests' comfort and safety. Smoke alarms, for example, must be equipped with a flashing light as an emergency signal for those who are hearing impaired. Telephones must have volume controls and be compatible with adaptive equipment used by people with hearing impairments, such as a TTY. Use telephone interface jacks that allow both digital and analog signal use. The law also requires public accommodations to permit guide dogs or other service animals used by individuals with disabilities.

For detailed information about how the ADA affects lodging facilities, contact the Department of Justice and/or the U.S. Architectural and Transportation Barriers Compliance Board. In addition, each state and major city has an Office of Handicapped Affairs, as well as other agencies that specialize in the concerns of individuals with specific impairments. These offices can provide you with more information and perhaps even direct you to a local architectural center that has a program devoted to creating barrier-free environments for people with disabilities.

The government agencies mentioned earlier can be very helpful in spreading the word about your accessible bed and breakfast home. They sometimes publish an access guide to the area or collaborate with other organizations to provide information to both residents

> For ADA information, visit:
> www.usdoj.gov
> www.access-board.gov

and visitors about accessible lodging, restaurants, attractions, and transportation. Ideally, your B&B should be listed in updates of these guides. List your B&B with Access-Able Travel Source, which publishes a worldwide online directory of accessible lodging. Check the Web site of the Society for the Advancement of Travel and Hospitality for more marketing resources.

Be sure to include appropriate information on your brochure or Web site. If you have a TDD (also called a TTY) for the hearing impaired, list the number. If you are adept at

For an online directory of accessible lodging, visit: www.access-able.com

For marketing resources promoting accessible travel, visit: www.sath.org

sign language, mention this fact. If you have a ground-floor room, say so. If the bed and breakfast is wheel-chair accessible, publicize this information. Ask any reservation service agency that lists your B&B to include this important information in its literature or on its Web site.

Because smaller B&B operations—of five or fewer guest rooms—are typically exempt from ADA requirements, bed and breakfast homes that have already been adapted to accommodate a host or other resident with a disability are in an ideal position to court this specialized market. And any other B&B owner who takes the necessary steps to voluntarily comply with ADA recommendations will benefit from the increased business.

Chapter Eight
The Perfect Host

The Welcome

The front door was already open and the host was waving a welcome as my taxi stopped in front of her Hyannisport home, my bed and breakfast for the night. I was in a very bad humor, no question about it. I was tired after a three-hour ferry ride from Nantucket and exasperated by the confusion of bus schedules that had stranded me on Cape Cod until the next morning's bus to Boston. I was hot, my hair was sticky with ocean spray, I longed to wash my face, and I was worried about arriving on time for my midmorning appointment the next day. I had been very fortunate in finding a host registered with a Cape Cod reservation service who was willing to take a guest on such short notice (I had called from the bus station) and for one night only, but I sure didn't feel lucky. This was an emergency layover and no more. I was determined to be miserable.

My host showed me immediately to my room for the night and asked if I would like to have a glass of wine while I got settled. I suddenly realized that this was exactly what I wanted at that very moment. A chilled glass of chablis quickly appeared, and my host (who had heard my sad story already from the manager of the reservation service agency) quietly disappeared into another part of the house. A short time later—face scrubbed, hair combed, and clothes changed—I was following her directions to the nearby private beach to watch the sunset. Before long I found myself enjoying how peaceful it was there and thinking of little more than the plate of home-baked cookies waiting for me when I returned from my stroll.

As a bed and breakfast host, you'll be welcoming all sorts of people in all sorts of moods into your home. Some could very well be the way I was that evening in Hyannisport, wanting to be left alone but still needing just enough attention to bring me back to my normal, cheerful self. Other guests (most of them, we hope) will be in high spirits when they arrive.

If possible, you should find out in advance why your guests are visiting the area. You need not acknowledge the reason when you meet them for the first time, but it will help you tailor your welcome to the occasion. Those guests on vacation or celebrating a wedding, birthday, graduation, or anniversary will most likely be quite cheerful when they arrive at your doorstep. They will definitely contrast with those who are in town to visit a friend or relative who has taken ill, or to attend a funeral. And those who are relocating or traveling on business are in another category: They have business to take care of, and that is probably the first thing on their minds.

Although a smile and a warm handshake are always appropriate to welcome anyone under any circumstances, try to "read" how your guests are feeling when you open the front door—exuberant, sad, worried, rushed, joyful, tired, angry, happy, preoccupied. It's your job to make *all* your guests feel comfortable immediately, using your "antennae" to sense what should or should not be said and what should or should not be done in order to accomplish this. And leave your own problems behind when you open that door. You might have had a rough day, but don't let your guests see it on your face. It's time for a smile and a warm handshake, no matter what.

As a host, you will find that one of your major responsibilities is to make sure that you're home when your guests are scheduled to arrive. Always agree upon a definite arrival time when a guest is making a reservation. Then, when that day and time comes, be there waiting to welcome your visitors. It's incredibly disorienting for a guest to arrive at the right place at the right time and find no one home. A woman visiting the Big Apple reports such an unsettling experience: "The host was not home all day, so I was unable to gain access until dark—a little scary on my first solo trip to New York City."

Put yourself in your guests' shoes. You've just arrived in a strange city for the first time, and you're on your way to the private home of someone you've never seen before in your life. You're a little nervous about all this bed and breakfast stuff anyway, but your Aunt

Mavis has traveled the world over and swears that you'll love it. So the taxi leaves you and your two heavy suitcases off at the address you've been sent to. Right on time. But why is the house dark? Why does no one answer the doorbell? Should you run after the taxi? Should you sit down on the doorstep to wait, in the rain? Should you start looking for a phone to call the host just in case she really is in there but is asleep? Or too sick to come to the door? Or did she perhaps just forget about your reservation and fly to Switzerland to take in a little skiing?

This is no way to welcome a guest. Of course, things can come up unexpectedly, calling you away from home (to get your daughter's scraped knee checked after she fell off the swing; to pick up your spouse after the Volvo sputtered and died; to retrieve the purse you left on top of your desk when you ran out of your office so that you'd be home on time to welcome your guest). Whenever something like this occurs, try to find a friend or neighbor who is willing to come to your home and welcome your guests in your place. It's wonderful if you can find someone who loves people as much as you do and will invite your guests inside, offer them a cup of coffee or glass of wine, and even get them settled into their rooms if the delay will be lengthy. If a guest was referred to you through a reservation service agency, get in touch with the RSA manager if you have a problem finding someone to stand in for you. The RSA manager will help if possible because the problem reflects on that agency's service.

If you absolutely cannot find someone to welcome the guests who will be arriving while you're gone, do *not* leave the door unlocked with an open invitation to come inside pasted on the door. Your guests might very well be trustworthy, but who knows who else might come to your door while you're away and find the house empty and the door unlocked? Besides, new arrivals will feel uncomfortable about coming inside when no one is home, and you should really be there to satisfy the questions in your mind about any guest before you permit that person inside your home.

Some hosts leave a note on the door addressed to the expected guest by name. (If it's placed inside a sealed envelope, the contents will not be seen by anyone else who happens to come to the door.) In the note apologize for the inconvenience and say you'll be back shortly. You might also want to make a suggestion about how to spend the intervening time: "There's a lovely pond out back—please feel free to walk around and enjoy the scenery. And help yourself to the lemonade I've left in the thermos on the picnic table." Or: "There's a cafe at the end of the street that makes a terrific cappuccino. I've already told Tony to put it on my tab!" Do your best to turn the inconvenience into a pleasant experience.

If you are home when your guests arrive, open the door wide when you hear them coming, before they have to ring the doorbell. Opening the door not only resolves the question in their minds of whether they have indeed found the right place, but it's also just a friendly thing to do. It will give them a good feeling about your bed and breakfast.

To help your guests identify your home easily, display your house number clearly so that it is visible from the street. Some hosts affix a plate carrying their family name on or near the front door.

The difficulty that guests sometimes have in figuring out which home on the street is the bed and breakfast they're looking for prompted the owners of a bed and breakfast home in Michigan to design and sell flags that say "B&B" on them. A host can display the flag whenever guests are expected to help guide them to the right place easily. (For information on the B&B flags, contact the Parsonage, 6 East Twenty-fourth Street, Holland, MI 49423; 616–396–1316.) One note of caution: Check any regulations governing the use of signs and/or flags in your community; they could be prohibited in a residential area. Consider, too, that use of a sign or flag does declare in a public way that you are in the bed and breakfast business; some hosts prefer to protect their privacy more closely. Are you one of them?

> Ellen Madison has a pet in residence at the Woody Hill Guest House B&B in Westerly, Rhode Island. She recalls the day her furry friend decided to welcome some new guests. "I was not home when some of my guests arrived a bit early, and they were not sure that they had come to the right place. My fat, black, lazy cat ambled out for a pat. Very quickly my guests rushed back to the car, grabbed the book in which I am written up, consulted it, and found out that I had a cat named 'Treasure.' They tentatively addressed the cat by the name and were rewarded with an affirmative leg rub." Relieved, the guests immediately made themselves at home until their host arrived.

To make your home look inviting to a guest who is expected to arrive after dark, the director of a Colorado reservation service agency says, "The outside light must be on." (It's also a good safety measure to light the way to your door.) The owner of an RSA in Florida says that guests in residence appreciate "a light left burning outside while they are out at night." Even though they might no longer need assistance to locate your home, the light makes them feel more welcome to come back inside.

Leaving the light on as a warm welcome is a nice touch even if you will be picking up your guests at the airport, the bus station, or the train station. Many hosts are willing to do this if it's convenient for them. It's a wonderful amenity to offer guests who would otherwise have to take a taxi or public transportation to your home. This means that your first contact with some of your guests will be at the plane, bus, or train. Please don't be late. Finding that no one is there to meet you is just as unnerving as finding no one home at the bed and breakfast where you have a reservation. Make a good impression and be there waiting for your guest to disembark.

Have you ever been welcomed after a trip with a bouquet of flowers? Suddenly, the discomforts of traveling disappear. You will most likely be placing fresh flowers in your guests' room anyway; why not meet them with the bouquet when they arrive? (Of course, this gesture is appropriate only if a guest has no allergies to flowers.)

During the drive back to your home, use the time to find out a little more about your guests and their plans for their visit. It's very helpful to orient them to the area as much as possible during the drive; point out the landmarks as you pass them. If you arrive at your home during the evening hours, the light that you left on for the event will present a much cheerier welcome than will a dark house.

Once you have invited your guests inside your home, the best thing to do is show them directly to their room and point out where their bathroom is. Then if something is not as it should be (they expected twin beds; you have a double, for example), they can decide then and there whether they wish to leave. With luck, good communication between your guests and you at the time a reservation is made will have prevented misunderstandings from happening—but they do happen. For these times, you will need to have a clearly stated refund policy. (See "Confirming a Reservation" in chapter 7.)

If a guest does wish to leave, don't make a scene. Even though you may not think that the complaint is deserved, let this be your guide: "The customer is always right." Smile, say you're sorry that your bed and breakfast isn't quite what he or she was looking for, give any refund due according to your policy, and wave good-bye. It's just possible that what didn't work out for this guest would be perfect for that same guest's friend, acquaintance, or relative. For this reason, you want all of your guests (even the ones who decide to leave) to remember you kindly.

Once you're sure that the room is agreeable to your new guests, offer to help them with anything that might need to be taken care of immediately: Show them where they may leave their car for the night; help bring their belongings into the guest room; take their ice chest into the kitchen so that they may place perishables in your refrigerator after they've gotten settled. In the guest room itself, point out the light switches and explain how to operate the privacy lock on the door, window locks, the pull drapes, the heat, the air conditioner, the electric blanket, and anything else that might be there for their comfort. Show them where the extra pillows and blankets are kept.

Be aware that people who have been traveling will most likely want to freshen up a bit immediately after they arrive, so allow them this time before you start socializing. Always offer your guests a "welcome drink," but preface the offer with something like this: "You'll probably want a few minutes to get settled. Then I'd love for you to come join me for some coffee or a glass of wine. Why don't you just come into the living room when you're ready? Then I'll show you around the rest of the house and the grounds, too."

Make your living room as inviting as possible. Create an *atmosphere*, using your resources to *their* best advantage. Should you open the drapes so that your guests will have a view of the sunset over the beach? Should you close the drapes and light the two small lamps (instead of the overhead) to give the room a soft appearance? Should you open a window to let in a little fresh air? Should you put on some background music? Should you light a fire in the fireplace?

"It is incredible how many homes are fortunate enough to have a nice, homey fireplace and then neglect to use it," says one reservation service manager. She makes a comparison between two similar bed and breakfast homes. At the first one guests come out of the cold night and "they see a cheery fire burning in the fireplace." The host invites them to join him for a drink before the fire. At the other B&B home, however, "the fireplace is stone cold," which gives guests the impression that "they are not important enough for the host to go to the trouble. It's obvious which host has the best chance over the years of building up a steady repeat business and a lot of word-of-mouth recommendations. Keep in mind that some experienced travelers who use bed and breakfast have seen the best and the worst of B&Bs. Naturally, they will tell their friends about their best discoveries and the B&Bs to stay away from." Make yours a discovery that your guests will want to share.

Depending on the time of day and the season, offer your guests something to drink—hot chocolate, hot or cold cider, mulled wine, tea, hot or iced coffee, juice, soft drinks, a liqueur. Many hosts also offer a snack at the time of guests' arrival—cookies, cheese and fruit, cake, or a "dessert" type of bread such as banana or cranberry. A snack is always a good idea because your guests have most likely been traveling for a while, leaving them little time to eat. If it's late, they won't be able to go out to dinner before they retire; and if it's earlier in the day, it could take some time before they're ready to go out and look for a restaurant. Either way, some cookies or fruit would be very welcome indeed.

The occasion of a "welcome drink" also gives you and your guests a chance to get acquainted with one another. Here, you can find out a little more about your guests' plans and make suggestions to help make their visit more enjoyable. This can be a good time for "orientation"—directing your guests to the best that your area has to offer. (See "Orientation" later in this chapter.)

Afterward, take the time to show your guests the house and the grounds. As you do this, make it clear which areas of the house they are welcome to use: "This is the family room. Please feel free to come in here to watch television or select something to read from the bookcase. And we've got a deck of cards and Trivial Pursuit over there on the shelf."

At the same time point out (in a nice way) any parts of the house and grounds that are off-limits: "This is the bathroom that is used only by family members. The master bedroom is through that door. If there's some kind of emergency at night, that's where you can find me. Otherwise, once I'm in there for the night, I prefer not to be disturbed."

Your tour should include any other light switches or door locks that your guests will have to deal with. If you wish to give your guests keys to the front door or to their bedroom (see "Security" in chapter 5), now is the time to do it. And go over any "rules" that you expect your guests to follow: "After 11:00 P.M. we have 'quiet hours' so that the people who want to sleep aren't bothered by any kind of noise. And if you're the last one up, please turn off the light in the living room."

Introduce all family members and other guests in residence so that the new arrivals will feel at home. If someone is not home at the moment, at least mention that Sonny is at school and that the young couple staying in the Sunshine Room are out hiking. Also introduce your pets and explain any idiosyncrasies that they might have: "Foofie likes to nip toes, so be careful when she's in your room and you want to change your shoes."

The end of the tour is an opportune time for you to part company with your guests if you want to get on with other things, and it's a perfect time to take care of collecting the balance due. Bring it up now: "We like to get payment out of the way on the first night. This is the bill for the balance due on the three nights you've reserved. Why don't we do this now?"

Many hosts feel uncomfortable about asking for payment; it's like putting a price tag on hospitality and just doesn't feel right. Still, you've got to finance that hospitality. It's your responsibility to bring up the issue of payment and get it taken care of right away. Otherwise, you'll be suffering over it for days. If the bill is paid at the outset, you and your guests are free to proceed with one of the most enjoyable aspects of bed and breakfast—becoming friends.

Orientation

A New England woman visiting a town in Newfoundland for the first time decided to stay in a bed and breakfast home instead of a hotel or motel. Why? "In order to talk to a 'native,'" she says. The host answered her questions about the area and suggested some sights to see that she hadn't known about.

A medical worker from Wisconsin was relocating to Boston to take part in a one-year training program at a city hospital. "I wanted a human resource other than a front-desk clerk," he says. So he made arrangements to stay at a B&B registered with a Boston reservation service that was within walking distance of the hospital. He found the host a valuable source of information, advice, and comfort as he got oriented to a new city and located his own apartment. "Who better than a resident to help you out?" he asks.

"I'm not much of a tourist," says a woman from Pennsylvania who traveled the B&B way on a recent trip to Canada. "I wanted to visit a certain area and get a feeling for how it might be to live there. I wanted to meet people." It so happened that her hosts were involved in organizing a local festival that was to take place in the town during her stay. She was invited to help out and did just that. "I never had my thumbs in so many bowls of chowder in my life, but it was great," she says. "I found the people to be extraordinarily friendly."

These three guests are typical of people who prefer to stay at bed and breakfast homes instead of hotels and motels. They want an inside view of the area that they're visiting, something only a resident can give them. For your guests, a good orientation to the area is one of the key assets of staying in a bed and breakfast home, so be prepared to share your knowledge of local activities.

Gathering Information

Keep on hand any books written about your region to lend to your guests—a guidebook or two and books devoted to its history, architecture, or flora and fauna. Books suggesting interesting walks, hikes, or bicycle trips are also of interest to many people. And it's always fun for guests to read fictional stories set in the area they are visiting; these will make a welcome addition to your bookshelf.

Your guests will need to get around while they're staying with you, so stock up on schedules of buses, trains, subways, and ferries, and the business cards of any car-rental companies in the area. (It wouldn't hurt to inquire about obtaining rental discounts for your guests. Some hosts have successfully negotiated this benefit.) A good map that can be borrowed is always in demand. Check with your local tourist office or chamber of commerce about obtaining a supply of maps that can be given to your guests. Because both organizations are in the business of promoting the area, they will often make quantities available to bed and breakfast hosts at a discounted price or even for free. (It helps if you're a member.)

These organizations are also real gold mines when it comes to more general information directed to visitors. They produce brochures and pamphlets dealing with major tourist attractions as well as calendars of cultural and community events coming up. Get on their mailing lists and find out what the benefits of membership would be for your bed and breakfast.

Shopping is usually on the agenda for many tourists, so start collecting business cards from the various shops in your area that sell arts and crafts, clothing, souvenirs, and regional items. Keep track of sales so that whenever a guest wants to know where to get the best deal on an item, you can make some suggestions.

In addition to the business cards, start collecting brochures, pamphlets, and flyers that promote any type of event or service that could be of interest to your guests. Many stores, restaurants, and even supermarkets keep stacks of promotional literature from community businesses available to the public. Whenever you see something that looks appealing to a visitor, take a few copies. You'll soon be surprised at how quickly your collection of resources can grow.

The Orientation Basket

Now, where to keep them? One Boston host suggests placing all the information in a large basket and inviting guests to sift through it themselves. She also has an excellent suggestion for augmenting your basket's supplies. "I tell my guests that I'm trying to fill the basket and ask them to bring back extra literature from any of the places they'll be visiting," she says. Of course, many of her guests will be trekking off to the museums, the observatories, and the historical sites. The host has found her guests very cooperative about bringing back some extra brochures for other guests.

For those events that are here today and gone tomorrow, you might want to put all those notices inside a folder so that they can be sorted and thrown away easily whenever the event is over. These include those announcing films, museum exhibits, concerts, festivals, art exhibits, dance performances, theater presentations, and sporting events.

If you don't already subscribe to a daily newspaper, you should think about doing so for the benefit of your guests. It enables them to see what is going on around town for entertainment, and it helps keep them up with the news of the day. A subscription to any magazine published as a guide to the city, state, or region is also a good idea.

While your guests are staying with you, they might want to attend religious services or have a desire to get some exercise if these are a part of their usual routine. Obtain the schedules of services from the houses of worship in your neighborhood, as well as information about any drop-in classes or open exercise periods at local gyms, health clubs, and dance studios. Also keep on hand information regarding the rental of recreational equipment such as bicycles, roller or ice skates, skis, boats, or anything else that visitors would be likely to need.

Your guests will be seeking out their own lunch and dinner, so start collecting menus from restaurants that you like. The managers of most restaurants will be more than happy to give you a copy because your bed and breakfast could bring more business to their establishments. One host makes up his own personal restaurant guide for his guests. He calls it

"The Blue Wax Farm Zero Base Guide to Eating." It includes eight favorites in the East Burke, Vermont, area—how many miles away each is located from the farm and a short description of the food, the decor, the clientele, and the prices. (The owner of Blue Wax Farm also offers his own updates on the hiking trails in his area.) You don't have to produce anything as elaborate as this, but do take the trouble to point out the good restaurants when your guests are planning to go out to eat.

If there are any pizza parlors or delicatessens nearby that will deliver (especially any that are open late), make sure to have their menus on hand for the convenience of guests who arrive at your home after the usual dinner hour is over. At these times a large pizza to go, delivered right to your door, can be very welcome.

If you should notice that any restaurants or stores are advertising discount coupons for particular items, clip and save these, adding them to the basket. There's no reason your guests shouldn't enjoy their pizza at half price or buy their souvenirs at a two-for-one sale. They'll appreciate the thought.

Once you've got your "orientation basket" full of information, place it where all your guests have access to it, perhaps in the living room or family room or in the foyer between the guest rooms. You'll soon find that having your resources available in this way is a great time-saver for you. You won't have to draw the same little maps over and over again for different guests, and you won't have to check and double-check the hours of operation for that great restaurant down the street. For many questions dealing with orientation to your area, you can direct your guests right to the basket for the information they seek. You might even want to help them locate the right brochure or map, as you do not want to give the impression that they're annoying you with their questions and that's why you're pointing to a basket.

There will be times, though, when your guests will want information that is not contained in your trusty basket. One Boston host tells of spending an entire evening mapping out an itinerary for some guests who wanted to conduct their own walking tour of Boston's most notable Victorian houses. Expect that you will get requests like these for which you'll have to draw on your personal knowledge to give advice and make suggestions. If you enjoy pointing out what your neighborhood has to offer to visitors, you'll enjoy this aspect of your bed and breakfast business very much. This is exactly what will bring many guests to your door.

Orientation Checklist

- ☐ Books of interest
  - ☐ Guidebooks
  - ☐ History
  - ☐ Architecture
  - ☐ Flora and fauna
  - ☐ Fiction set in local area
  - ☐ Legends

- ☐ City/state/regional magazines

- ☐ Daily newspaper

- ☐ Calendar of events

- ☐ Business cards for local businesses

- ☐ Menus from restaurants

- ☐ Discount coupons for stores/ restaurants/rental cars/tours

- ☐ Sightseeing information
  - ☐ Tours
  - ☐ Brochures for tourist attractions

- ☐ Maps

- ☐ Car-rental information

- ☐ Equipment rentals
  - ☐ Skis
  - ☐ Boats
  - ☐ Bicycles
  - ☐ Roller/ice skates

- ☐ Brochures/flyers/schedules for current events
  - ☐ Theaters
  - ☐ Films
  - ☐ Museums
  - ☐ Concerts
  - ☐ Festivals
  - ☐ Art exhibits
  - ☐ Dance performances
  - ☐ Sports

- ☐ Transportation schedules
  - ☐ Subway
  - ☐ Bus
  - ☐ Train
  - ☐ Ferry

- ☐ Schedules
  - ☐ Religious services
  - ☐ Dance/exercise drop-in classes
  - ☐ Health clubs

Guest Letter

You have some decisions to make about how you wish your visitors to conduct themselves while they are guests in your home. And then you have the job of communicating these guidelines to your guests in a way that is "firm but nice," according to one host. The initial orientation tour of the house and grounds is an opportune time to point out some of the "rules" that you expect your guests to follow. Still, there will be some guidelines that will not come up naturally during the course of the tour. Also, you don't want to overwhelm your guests with a voluminous list of "dos and don'ts" when you first meet. A good way to outline what your guests need to know is to put your guidelines into a welcome letter. This is left inside the guest room, usually on the tray that contains the drinking glasses. This one-page letter (try not to make it longer) can be quickly scanned by your guests for the information that pertains to them. It can include the following items:

Welcome

Begin your letter by welcoming your guests to your home. A reservation service in Maine suggests this opening: "Welcome to your home away from home. I am pleased to have you as a guest and would like you to enjoy your stay. How can I help you? Do you need information about sightseeing? transportation? entertainment? Just ask. If I don't know the answer, I'll be glad to find out."

Breakfast

If you would like to establish a preferred time to serve breakfast, make this clear. A reservation service in Maine offers this model: "Breakfast will be served between 7:00 and 8:00 A.M. If that time is not convenient and you would like to serve yourself at a later time, please make arrangements with me before you retire."

Catherine Hatala, a Philadelphia host, includes this note about breakfast: "In most cases I will have the pleasure of eating with you. When I cannot and leave food warming in the toaster oven, kindly remember to push the lever down after you remove the food. If there is anything on the table that requires refrigeration, I would be grateful if you could return it to the fridge. Of course, I will take care of the dishes."

Food and Drink

Most hosts provide a snack (a fruit basket or other goodies) and complimentary drinks for their guests. Some guests will have no idea that these are available unless you tell them: "Please help yourself to some fresh fruit or a soft drink in the evening. Both can be found in the small refrigerator in the hallway just outside the kitchen door," reads the welcome letter provided as a model by a Maine reservation service.

Keys

You will have to decide whether you wish to give your guests house keys. The best advice for your own safety is *not* to do this if it can be avoided; however, there could be times when it's simply unavoidable given the incompatibility of your own schedule with your guests' comings and goings. An RSA in Massachusetts suggests to its hosts that they ask for a deposit for any house key that is lent to a guest. The deposit is refunded when the house key is returned.

You may have to explain how the lock works. One host with a tricky lock adds this note to her welcome letter: "On your tray you have probably found your set of keys. Please lock both the top and bottom locks when you leave. The bottom can be locked from the inside by simply putting the center piece in a vertical position."

Lights

Your guests will have to know what to do about the lights if they are the last ones up at night or if they leave the house, so an RSA located in Connecticut suggests covering this matter in the welcome letter. A simple "Please turn out the lights if you are the last one up at night" will make the responsibility clear to your guests.

Quiet Hours

It's a good idea to give guests some idea of the normal routine of the house so that they can fit themselves into it: "The hours between 11:00 P.M. and 7:00 A.M. are 'quiet hours' so that we can all get our rest. We ask that if you wish to use the radio or television between these hours, you keep the volume low."

If there are unusual hours kept by any member of the household on a regular basis, it's considerate to let your guests know this: "Our college-age son, Tommy, has a summer job with late hours. If you hear the back door opening at about midnight, it's Tommy. He is very quiet when he comes in, so unless you are already awake at this hour, you probably won't hear him at all."

The Telephone

Many people now carry cell phones, but this practice is not universal and, unfortunately, cell phones do not always work in every location. This means that a host can expect that a number of guests will want and need access to a telephone during their visit. Be *very* clear about what you expect from guests regarding local and long-distance telephone calls. Many hosts have been unpleasantly surprised by phone bills arriving a month after guests have let their fingers do the walking. It's especially important that you set guidelines for long-distance calls: "If you need to make long-distance calls, kindly charge them to your credit card or your telephone number," reads one host's welcome letter. Or you could request that guests use a telephone card with prepaid minutes.

Evaluate the type of local service that you now have to see if you need to add a similar note regarding message units for local calls that are out of the "unlimited call" area provided by your service. One host cuts out the page of the telephone book that explains how many message units are used for calls to nearby locales and asks her guests to leave the appropriate amount of change.

If you have an answering machine, explain how to disengage it if a guest wants to use the phone when you aren't around: "Because of my schedule, I must have an answering machine. You need not answer the phone when it rings. If you are expecting a call and do not reach the phone before the tape begins, push the 'Start/Stop' button when you pick up the phone. Upon completion of your call, depress the button again."

You can, if you wish, acquire telephone service that restricts outgoing calls to local areas. Another option is to offer long-distance service by credit card charges only. Special equipment is available for purchase that automatically adds a small amount for each call made as extra income for the host.

Keep in mind that if guests have access to your one and only phone line—your "money" line, in other words—you could be missing calls from prospective guests while the phone is in use. To avoid this, some hosts also have a cell phone and forward business calls to their cell as needed. Some opt to install expanded telephone service, providing guests with in-room telephones with a separate line not connected to the business phone. Another useful feature to consider is a built-in wake-up call, which helps relieve the host of the burden of awakening travelers, some in the wee hours of the morning.

A host should make it as easy as possible for guests to communicate with the outside world. For business travelers especially, telephone access is vital. Just be sure to weigh all the options and their costs.

House and Grounds

According to the manager of a New York reservation service, the biggest mistake that new hosts make is "giving guests the run of the entire apartment instead of setting reasonable limits." "Define 'your' territory and 'guest' territory, and guests will be more comfortable," adds the manager of a reservation service agency located in the Southwest. Your tour can point out some of the areas that guests are welcome to use or not to use; your welcome letter can clarify these further: "Feel free to use the pool and deck, and make yourself comfortable in the living room any evening after 8:00 P.M. to watch television or join us for conversation. Please walk around the farm if you wish, but we ask that you not go inside the barn or into the pasture."

Care of the Room

Because every host handles "care of the room" differently, you might want to explain what guests can expect from you regarding it while they are in residence. Some hosts will not enter a guest room during its occupancy. If the beds are left unmade, they'll stay that way. The idea here is that the room is like a private bedroom in their own home. A note in the welcome letter indicating this would be a good idea: "This room is 'yours' for your stay, and

I will not enter it except to change the linens every two days." Other hosts get right in there every day and change the sheets, make the bed, vacuum, dust, and water the plants. If you are this kind of host, your note can say: "I like to straighten the guest room after breakfast, so please make sure that any of your belongings are not left on the bed at this time."

Checkout Time

If you have an established checkout time (which is a good idea so that you can be sure that you'll be home when your guests will be leaving), a reminder in your welcome letter is not a bad idea: "We would appreciate your checking out by noon on your last day with us so that we can prepare the room for our next guests. If there is a problem, please let us know, and we'll be happy to work out an arrangement that suits your needs." Be flexible. Offer to store suitcases and invite use of common areas until later in the day.

Smoking

You have probably screened out any guests who are not compatible with your policy governing smoking in your home, but you still might want to include a reminder in your welcome letter: "We prefer that you do not smoke in the house, but you may smoke outdoors if you wish."

Alcohol

If you choose not to allow alcohol, specify this in your welcome letter: "We ask that you do not use alcoholic beverages while a guest in our home." Otherwise, a host sometimes provides complimentary wine as well as ice for those guests who wish to bring in their own alcoholic beverages.

Laundry

If you have laundry facilities and do not mind your guests using them, or if you are willing to do a load of dirty clothing for them, mention this in your welcome letter: "I will be glad to show you how to operate the laundry equipment if you should need to use it." If you wish to charge a small amount for the detergent, water, and electricity, specify it: "We ask for 50 cents per load to cover costs."

Pets in Residence

Always make an effort to introduce your pets to your guests when they arrive. If Frisky likes his afternoon romp and he's often not around when you're ready to make introductions, however, it might be a good idea to include a note about the little rascal in the welcome letter. This way, there will be no surprises for your guests when they find a large, furry creature curled up at the bottom of their bed. A Philadelphia host includes this note about her pet: "Our dog, which my son named at two, is Puppy. She is a lovely pet. Her only flaw is that she is too friendly. If she is bothersome to you, you may put her in the backyard for a bit. Actually, she has her own routine and will probably not disturb you at all."

Emergencies

Include "Emergencies" in your welcome letter so that your guests know what to do in case a serious problem arises. You might want to say something like this: "Should a problem of an emergency nature develop, there is a list of emergency telephone numbers right by the telephone. And should you need to reach me when I am out, my cell phone number is _____. Our next-door neighbor, Harry Jones, is a close friend of the family. He is usually home during the day and will be glad to help should the need arise. His phone number is _____."

The Closing

End your letter with something friendly, like "Wishing you a pleasant stay" or "I hope you enjoy your visit. Please let me know if there's anything else I can do to make your stay more enjoyable."

Tone and Format

In your letter include only those items that are absolutely necessary. Of the items discussed here, it's possible that you need mention only three or four, depending on how well you orient your guests to your house and grounds when they arrive. Again, keep the letter short—one page if possible. If it's too long, your guests won't take the time to read it, and they might also begin to feel that there are so many rules and regulations that maybe they should have just spent their vacation at Fort Dix.

Leave out the obvious information. Some hosts tell guests what they already know or what common sense would tell them anyway. "Your room is on the second floor." (No kidding. The guest had to get to his room on the second floor in order to read the welcome letter—which tells him that his room is on the second floor.) "If you smoke, please use the ashtray." (Are there other options?) "The bathroom adjoins the guest room." (It surely does, just as the host pointed out during the tour.)

There could be items that you need to add to your lists of "rules," tailored to your own household situation: "Please do not use the pool after dark. . . . Please do not leave your children unattended. . . . Please make sure that your pet is kept on a leash if you wish to take him outside." (One caution: Do not go overboard with rules. One guest who had made a trip specifically to enjoy a night of theater and clubbing was astounded when the host told him to be "home" by 10:00 P.M.! He opted for a hotel and put a stop payment on his credit card against the B&B.)

Keep the tone of the letter upbeat. Although you are laying down guidelines for guests to follow, you do not want to sound nasty, sarcastic, or patronizing—even when you're discussing your pet peeve. Pretend that you are writing the letter to your best friend, who will be staying with you for a few days. In fact you might want to give a draft of the letter to your best friend to see what he or she thinks of the tone and the content.

Check for spelling errors and then print multiple copies on good-quality paper or your own letterhead for a personal touch. Fold the letter in half and address it to each guest by name before placing it on the tray in the guest room.

Some hosts have gotten into the habit of leaving little notes in the guest room, the bathroom, and throughout the rest of the house to instruct their guests on what they can and cannot do. Other hosts feel that these detract from the homelike atmosphere of their bed and breakfast and interfere with the decor. A welcome letter keeps all the information together in one place and avoids all those sticky notes on the refrigerator, windows, doors. A welcome letter is definitely preferable—and much more friendly.

The Visit

Many new hosts wonder just how much time they are expected to spend with their guests. Strictly speaking, a host need see a guest only when that person arrives, when breakfast is served, and when it's time to check out. But the reality for most hosts is that they do see their guests more often than just at these times. This is by choice. Getting to know the people who visit you is one of the advantages of being a bed and breakfast host.

Try to arrange your day so that you can join your guests at the breakfast table. "Remember that the hospitality you extend will be more than repaid to you by the warm conversation and friendship that often develop at the breakfast table," says the founder of a reservation service agency in Boston.

For many guests, part of the attraction of staying at a bed and breakfast home is the opportunity to experience a life that is different from their own. Invite them to watch you milk the cows or help you pick blueberries. Show them how you refinish antique furniture or make a quilt. Your line of work or hobby could be very interesting to someone who knows little about what it involves. (Who knows? You might even get some help with your chores.)

As you carry out your daily activities, see if you can fit your guests into your routine somehow. If you're driving downtown to do a little shopping, consider asking your guests if they would like to come along for the ride. (They can explore while you're busy with errands.) If you're walking down to the drugstore for a newspaper, you might want to ask your guests if they would like to walk along with you. (They could need to purchase some personal items themselves, or maybe they would just enjoy a stroll around the neighborhood.) If you're planning to watch a movie on your DVD player in the evening, consider asking your guests to join you. (Maybe they'd prefer some company to spending the time in their room alone reading.)

Of course, you need not extend any of these invitations unless you want to. The idea is to allow yourself the freedom you need to go about your business but still be as helpful and hospitable to your guests as you can. In most cases you do want to leave yourself open to more social contact than what is possible over the breakfast table—provided that your guests want it as well. Some will, some won't, and some won't be sure. How much or how little a host gets involved can vary greatly, depending on the guest.

"Maybe it's meddling, but I love it," says one host who is registered with Bed and Breakfast Associates Bay Colony. To him being a good host means getting involved, "giving a guest more than breakfast and a smile." To illustrate his point, he tells of a woman from Toledo, Ohio, who was in Boston for a convention and away from her husband and children for the first time in her married life. She was clearly afraid to venture beyond the house, so the host decided to help her out, literally. "I sent her to the grocery store for milk," he says. Next came a trip together across town for fresh produce, at which point he left her with directions on how to use the city's subway system. Before two days had passed, the host found the guest confidently instructing a new arrival from Texas on how to get around in Boston. "If left to her own devices, she would have read those three library books she brought with her instead of exploring the city," the host says. Sometimes guests need a gentle nudge to get more out of their visit. A good host can help get things rolling, as did the "meddling" host who helped his rather timid visitor explore a new city and enjoy it, in spite of her apprehensions.

For some people in an unfamiliar area for reasons that are not at all pleasant—like visiting a relative in a hospital—be aware that they might want and need more social involvement than those guests who are merely interested in sightseeing. For these people the everyday activities of your household are comforting; they bring some semblance of normalcy back into their lives. One woman staying in a Boston B&B on such an occasion took it upon herself to wash the dishes every day. This is certainly

> "You might not have so much, but the plain simplicity of your life is what appeals to so many people who live the fast pace of the city," says Edna Shipe of Valley View Farm, a bed and breakfast in West Virginia. One guest who returns to the farm every so often is affectionately called "Manhattan Maude." She writes: "Edna, I am missing your pies. I also am missing the butterflies, the squirrels, the calves and sheep on the hill, the smell of the forest. I do not remember how many years since the last time I saw butterflies."

not a task that a host expects a guest to do, but the host let her alone. "It made her feel better to be busy," she says.

You'll find that you have a lot in common with some of your guests, and the desire to spend time together will be mutual. One gentleman tells of returning to the town where he had been born and raised to attend his fifty-year high school reunion. He felt lucky to find a bed and breakfast home ten minutes away from the high school where the reunion would be held. It so happened that the hosts remembered his father, who had been the county superintendent of schools when they had attended grade school. "We were able to compare memories about various mutual acquaintances and events," the guest recalls, even though they had not known one another as children. They indulged in long, nostalgic conversations that made the guest's return ("my last") to his hometown very special.

A young couple who spent their vacation in a rural coastal area found it enjoyable to be with their hosts a great deal of the time. "We spent a lot of time talking together and occasionally shared things like cooking and washing dishes. We ate all our meals together and spent most evenings together, chatting over wine or coffee." They also went sailing and hiking together.

This much togetherness is not the norm, but it's wonderful when it happens naturally and spontaneously, laying the groundwork for a lasting friendship. Just how much "togetherness" is the right amount is sometimes a difficult thing for a host to figure out, especially at first. There can be too much. Here is what some reservation service agency managers say about the biggest mistake that new hosts tend to make: "Trying to do too much and spending too much time with their guests. There is a middle ground and it takes a little while to find it," says the manager of a reservation service in Washington, D.C. "A few will suffocate the guests with attention," says the manager of Mi Casa Su Casa in Tempe, Arizona, or "hover over a guest, not leaving enough private space," as the former manager of a Seattle reservation service puts it. She goes on to advise new hosts to "be gracious, available, but know when to pull back. Don't talk a guest to death."

"New hosts, if anything, might try to do too much for their guests," says the manager of Greater Boston Hospitality. "If they are overly concerned for their guests' well-being, they could be perceived as intrusive and make their guests uncomfortable. A good feel for this comes with a little experience."

How do guests react to too much attention? "I like the helpfulness and friendliness of a local contact," says one California resident who enjoys traveling the B&B way. "But a few times I have encountered hosts who were too inquisitive. A friendly interest is one thing; being 'nosy' is something else. At one place I remember we were more or less asked to account for all our activities of the day: 'Where did you have dinner,' and so forth. Harmless but irritating."

An East Coast couple enjoyed their Canadian host (whom they describe as "a nice, talkative guy") very much, but they were quite tired upon arrival after their long trip and just wanted to rest. "Although we enjoyed his enthusiasm, he did hang out in 'our room'—which was clearly 'his room'—a bit too long. He didn't pick up on our weariness."

"You have to be able to tell when people want to visit and when they want privacy," says the manager of a Louisiana reservation service agency. When you aren't sure what they want, fish a little: "Would you like to join me for coffee, or are you tired? Maybe you'd just like to rest for a while?" Extend invitations, but don't come on too strong. Make yourself available, but let your guests seek you out.

There will be times when the shoe will be on the other foot, when you'll have an overly friendly guest who wants to spend a lot of time with you, but you just don't have the time or inclination for so much togetherness. At times like these you'll have to take it upon yourself to be firm but courteous to stop your guest from following you around. "I have to finish vacuuming the living room and then rush off to pick up Junior from baseball practice. Maybe we can get together for a glass of wine later this evening when the day is over"—this is one way of letting your guests know that you have other responsibilities at the moment but would be happy to resume the conversation later.

If you are expecting friends for a dinner party, you might want to announce the event to your guests ahead of time so that they understand that it is a private affair and that there is no open invitation: "Some of my friends will be coming over this evening for dinner, and I hope we won't disturb you. Please feel free to go into the family room and watch television if you wish and help yourself to some soft drinks from the refrigerator in the kitchen."

Discouraging lengthy conversations might be difficult at first, but it is a necessary skill to acquire so that you can balance your bed and breakfast business with your personal life. You might want to develop a few all-purpose ways to end conversations and practice role-playing with a friend: "I wish I could have a second cup of coffee and just sit here and relax for a while but I'm afraid I can't. Now, is there anything you'll be needing before I excuse myself?" One host admits to setting the timer on her clothes dryer for 10:00 A.M. so that when it rings she can excuse herself gracefully from lingering at the breakfast table.

The best advice is to recognize that no two guests are alike. Don't compare one with another. You'll like some more and others less. Some will like *you* more, others less. Each relationship between a host and a guest is unique. Try to let each one follow its natural course (making adjustments where necessary for both your privacy and your guests') and see where it leads. For many it's a lasting friendship.

The Farewell

"I can't believe that any motel or hotel manager would have hugged and kissed me good-bye and sent me away with a pint jar of rhubarb jam to take home with me," says a gentleman from California, describing the farewell he received from the couple who own a bed and breakfast home in Webster, South Dakota, called Lakeside Farm. These hosts made a lasting impression on their guest. "They are on my Christmas list for sure," he says.

How you say good-bye to your guests is just as important as how you say hello. A warm welcome can make your guests feel at home immediately and can even help to start a friendship; a hearty bon voyage confirms that your guests are welcome to come back and can help that budding friendship grow. You would take the time to say a personal good-bye to friends who had been visiting with you and who were about to take their leave; extend the same courtesy to your bed and breakfast guests. Be there, if you can, when they are packing their things and getting ready to drive off. If it is not possible for you to be home at this time (which could be the case if you have work or family responsibilities that take you out of the house), make it a point to say your farewells the last time you will be seeing your guests, perhaps the evening before their departure.

Many hosts like to give their guests a small gift when they leave. Food is always a good choice. Your guests will be traveling away from your home just as surely as they traveled to it. A box of your oatmeal cookies or a loaf of your zucchini bread will certainly help your guests to remember you fondly a few hours later when they're still on the road—and hungry. Attaching or enclosing the recipe has two advantages if you write it on the back of one of your brochures: It gives your guests a lasting memento of their visit (which they will enjoy over and over again each time they follow your directions), and it also leaves a permanent calling card with your guests (with your bed and breakfast's address and phone number on it) that you know they won't throw away!

If a guest especially enjoys something that you serve for breakfast or a snack, consider giving it as a gift. This is exactly how the Californian ended up with a pint of jam from his host at Lakeside Farm: "I raved about her homemade rhubarb jam, and so she had it on the table every morning," he recalls. When it came time to take his leave, what better remembrance of his happy visit could there possibly be?

A product of your region also makes a good gift—a small jar of honey, a bunch of red chili peppers, a corn-husk doll. The "city folk" who visit bed and breakfast homes in the country might especially appreciate seasonal produce from your garden—a container of strawberries, a pumpkin, a bag of apples, some ripe corn.

If you enjoy any type of arts or crafts, consider making small gifts for your guests—a ceramic bead, a pot holder, a postcard-size sketch or watercolor of your B&B.

If you do decide to give gifts, don't do anything elaborate, time consuming, or expensive. The gift should be a memento, nothing more. Think about your own resources and talents and see if you can come up with "a little something" that your guests would appreciate as a parting gift.

Before your guests make their final departure, conduct a last-minute inspection of their room and bathroom for forgotten items. "Shortly after opening I learned that one must always look under the bed when guests leave," says Lona Smith, owner of Summerwood in Richfield Springs, New York. "I have found quite an assortment of things—money, baby bottles, Cheerios." Under the bed, inside the drawers, in the closet, on the hooks in the bathroom, inside the medicine cabinet—all these places should be checked. Still, you won't find everything until it's too late, no matter how diligently you search.

Whenever you do find a lost item, follow the advice of one Colorado RSA, which suggests that hosts write a note to the guest who left the item behind, saying: "You left [specify the article] in your guest room during your recent stay with us. Please let me know how you would like to handle it. If you desire to have it sent by parcel post, or otherwise, I will prepare it for mailing and send you an estimate of the cost." One further suggestion to this good advice is to find out before you write the note how much it would cost to send the item parcel post and include that information in your communication. This way, you have to write only once, and the guest can send you a check in the right amount to cover the cost.

If you have lent anything to your guests during their stay, their checkout time is the right time to make sure you get it back. You can quickly lose a guidebook, your best map of the area, or your only umbrella when a forgetful guest makes a hurried departure. Your "inspection" of their room should tell you whether the borrowed items have been left for your future guests to use; if you don't see something, ask (tactfully, of course, or they might feel that you're accusing them of stealing). Also, if you gave your guests a house key or a key to the door of their bedroom, collect it at checkout time.

Perhaps your guests have extended their stay beyond their originally planned visit. (This is not uncommon.) This means that the "payment in full" that was taken care of upon arrival is no longer enough to cover everything that is now owed. The evening previous to their checkout is a good time to remind your guests about the balance due: "I've made up the bill for the extra two nights you added on to your visit. It might be hectic in the morning when you're trying to get packed and out of here in time to catch the train, so this evening might be a better time to take care of it." Some hosts prefer to place the final bill inside an envelope and set it near the guest's plate at his or her final morning meal with you.

Keep in mind that some of your guests need a ride to the airport or the bus or train station. Is it convenient for you to do this? Guests always appreciate the offer.

Just as your welcome is tailored to each guest's mood and reason for visiting, so should your farewell be tailored. In a way trying to say good-bye in an appropriate manner is easier because you've had some time to get to know your guests. There's not as much guesswork involved. For each farewell, follow your observations and intuitions about the person.

Don't embarrass a guest who spent most of her time in her room with little social contact during her one-night stay by producing a lavish show of affection and a gift upon her departure. Don't hug someone who is obviously not a "hugger." Don't give a gift to anyone with whom you simply did not hit it off. For these people a warm smile, a hearty handshake, and a word or two of goodwill are all it takes to leave them with a good feeling about your hospitality.

For those guests who did become friends, bring on the hugs and the gifts. Enjoy this precious benefit of being a bed and breakfast host to the fullest.

Guest Comments

So now you've done everything you thought possible to make your guests' visit comfortable and enjoyable. You cleaned like crazy, cooked up a veritable feast for breakfast, tried the right tests on the mattress and pillows to make sure that they weren't "dead," bought new designer sheets, and offered friendly conversation but did not intrude on your guests' privacy. So how did you do? Were you really a good host?

Was the bed and breakfast experience everything your guests expected?

There's one sure way to find out—ask. Not person to person, of course, because few guests will tell you straight out if anything was wrong. The best way to solicit honest comments from guests is to ask them to answer some questions on a form that you supply. They should do this before they leave—usually right before they leave so that they don't have to explain anything that they wrote, which is as it should be. No—what you want are the comments written down, short and to the point, so that you can evaluate the critique in your own way after your guests leave.

Various hosts have their own ways of devising evaluation forms that work for them. Some ask guests to rate the food, hospitality, cleanliness, comfort of the room, and other features on a scale of "Excellent," "Good," "Fair," or "Poor." Other hosts think that this kind of rating scale really does not give enough useful information to upgrade anything that is indicated as less than "Excellent." A better way to get what you need is to ask more open-ended questions that allow guests to say more clearly what's on their minds. A question like "If you could change one thing about this bed and breakfast, what would it be?" really provokes thought from both the guest who was dissatisfied with some aspect of your service as well as the one who was very satisfied but will think a little harder to come up with an observation that could help you improve your service and hospitality even more. This is what you want.

A sample evaluation form is provided here to use as a guide in developing your own form. Give a copy of the form to your guests the evening before they are scheduled to check out, or place a copy in their room. Ask them to leave the form in the guest room when they check out, or suggest that they mail it to you later. (It's nice to provide a stamped envelope for this purpose.)

Evaluation Form

You're important to us! We try hard to make every guest's stay comfortable and enjoyable. We would appreciate any suggestions you have to help us do our job well. Please take a few minutes to answer the questions below and leave this form for us when you check out. Thank you! We hope you enjoyed your visit!

What did you like most about staying at our bed and breakfast?

Were there any disappointments?

If you could change one thing about our bed and breakfast, what would it be?

Please add any comments that you wish.

If you are listed with a reservation service agency, it is possible that the RSA already has forms or postcards available for the purpose of soliciting comments from guests who were placed with you. Of course, the RSA needs to know that any guests placed with you found their accommodations satisfactory—and if not, why not. The quality of each bed and breakfast home it lists reflects upon the RSA itself. The manager of a reservation service agency in Maine supplies her hosts with copies of a short form to give their guests, who are asked to mail them directly to the RSA. The form includes the following method of evaluation: "Please rate our service, on a scale of 1 to 10, for promptness, courtesy, and efficiency." Other questions are: "Did you find your accommodations clean and attractive?" "Were your hosts congenial and helpful?" "Were there any surprises?"

Some RSAs give postcards to guests. (One even prestamps the cards to encourage guests to reply.) If your RSA does solicit comments from guests, ask that these be shared with you.

Remember that your bed and breakfast will be compared on the evaluation forms with any and all accommodations that your variety of guests has ever experienced. In a way this is good; you'll find out how you compare with hotels, motels, inns, even a weekend at the in-laws'. But you can also expect from guests who are still suffering from a bad case of "hotel mentality" comments about the problems of sharing a bathroom and lack of room service. Read them all and forget about the ones that don't apply, but take to heart those that do. For a new host especially, feedback from your guests will help you to improve upon the comfort and hospitality that you want to characterize your bed and breakfast.

Memories

"We stayed in the loveliest B&B last summer! (What *was* the name of that little town?) And we had the nicest hosts! (What *was* their name?)"

Few of us have a perfect memory. Nor are we as organized as we would like to be. While traveling, we certainly intend to write down all those important details that we want to remember for "next time"—mileage, rental costs, admission charges, names and addresses. Sometimes we don't. (Where *is* that pen when I need it?) Sometimes we do. (Have you seen my journal from last year's vacation anywhere?) And, of course, we collect brochures, maps, business cards, and postcards. (Are they in that box up in the attic?) The reality is that often we just can't remember the information we thought we would never forget.

This could mean trouble for a bed and breakfast host. As unbelievable as it might seem, a guest who had a wonderful visit at your B&B might very well have difficulty remembering your name six months hence. This very common and very human quirk can directly affect your business. There goes the possibility of a return visit in the near or distant future. If it is too much trouble to locate you again, a former guest could decide to try another B&B.

Worse, a guest's friends, associates, or relatives who might be planning to travel to your area will not be able to find you. A lead that consisted of no more than "I think her last name starts with a B and she lives somewhere on the Cape" would be a challenge for the best investigative reporter, never mind the average person trying to settle arrangements for a vacation that is supposed to make life easier for a while, not harder.

Return visits and personal recommendations from satisfied customers can bring you a considerable amount of business that could be lost to you unless you take steps to safeguard against it.

What's in a Name?

Name your B&B. A short, catchy name gives your B&B more of an identity, and it will be more likely to remain in a guest's memory long after your street and house number have been forgotten. There are, of course, no guarantees on this point, but it sure beats expecting former guests to come up with the right combination of details to locate you once again on the Internet or in the telephone directory. If you list with a reservation service agency, it will be a lot easier for its representatives to respond to an inquiry about "Hill House" than to pinpoint "some house on Beacon Hill—with black shutters, I think" as the certain B&B that the guest desires.

It is a good idea to adopt a designation that gives useful information about your B&B, but any name is better than none at all. Selecting a name like Jenny's Place or Maggie's Farm ensures that if they can remember your first name, former guests will have a good handle on your B&B's name. A surname can work effectively if it is not too long or too difficult. Using rhyme or alliteration will make it even easier to remember (Craven's Haven, for example, or the Henderson House). Some hosts opt for an abbreviation: Mrs. K's B&B in Kennett Square, Pennsylvania, is one of these.

Or consider including information about the location of your home. Identify the city or town where you reside, or specify a landmark nearby: Collegeville Digs, East Lake George House, Hill Pond House, the Old Forge. If former guests are able to recall the name of the landmark, then they'll remember your B&B as well.

Some hosts tie in the name of their B&Bs with the surroundings. Mention a special feature of the area, its geography, its flora or fauna: House on the Hill, House Among Trees, Rock Ledge Manor, Cliffside, the Lake House, the Beeches, Twin Maples, Corner Birches Guest House, Blueberry Bush, the Berry Patch.

Others refer to a special characteristic of their homes, such as the age, color, or architecture: Centennial House, A Century Old, Victorian Rose, Blue Shutters, the Yellow Cottage, Stone House Inn, the Farmhouse, the Four Gables, Widow's Walk, Mesa Manor, Georgian Guest House, Adobe Abode.

Or you could try to impart a sense of the general atmosphere of your B&B, as in Radnor Charm, Country Comfort, or Country Cupboard. But watch out for unintended references. Chestnut Hill Serenity and Fair Meadows may sound appealing for their tranquillity—but isn't Pleasant Acres the name of a cemetery out on Route 9? And Red Light Rooms could sound a little racy to someone who has no way of knowing that the name refers merely to the lovely scarlet-colored curtains in the guest rooms.

Still, do not be afraid to be innovative or playful with your selection. An unusual name, like A Doll's House, the Phoenix, or Mon Rêve, will raise questions about how you thought up the name in the first place. And the story behind it will make the name even more memorable for your guests.

Remember Me?

Within a month after a guest's visit, it is safe to assume that the person has either recorded and filed the necessary information about your B&B in a safe place or has hopelessly lost it despite all good intentions. A note from you, with your B&B's name and address on it, could be as welcome a sight as lost treasure that's been recovered.

Lona and George Smith recall the most embarrassing incident at their bed and breakfast home in Richfield Springs, New York, as perhaps also the funniest. It occurred when they were hosting their very first guests, three couples who were good friends. On their third night at Summerwood, the group returned home about 11:00 P.M., after their hosts had gone to bed. "Shortly, I heard a lot of running and laughter," says Lona. "Not wanting to embarrass them, I stayed put. Things settled down in fifteen or twenty minutes. The next morning when I got up, I found my house had been somewhat rearranged." Plants had been moved. Potatoes and onions, which were kept in baskets in the kitchen, were dumped on the kitchen table. And the baskets were in the dining room. Some kind of game? the host wondered.

The mystery was solved when the first guest came downstairs. There had been a bat in the house! The women had retreated upstairs and watched from the banister while the men (one a policeman), with baskets on their heads (they had heard that bats got into your hair), vanquished the bat with a broom. Quite an adventure to tell!

"They promised that with the telling, the tiny bat would grow into a large vampire with a 5-foot wingspread," says Lona.

Consider your note to follow up a guest's visit one of the most important elements of your hosting, even though the visit itself is over. If done well, it will leave a positive, final impression of your B&B with your guests and may perhaps help finally secure a place for your B&B in their permanent address books.

Although the note can be brief, under no circumstances should you send the same message to everyone indiscriminately. "Hope you enjoyed yourself while you were here!" may be fine for the couple on their second honeymoon, but it will not do for the man who came to visit his sister in the hospital. "We loved your company!" may be terrific for the aspiring comedian who liked to try out new jokes at the breakfast table, but it does not ring true for the rather shy young lady who spent most of her time alone in her room.

In your note try to reach out to address something in each guest's personal experience. Refer to a special interest or hobby: "I saw a program at the American Ballet Theatre last night, and it got me wondering how your dance classes are coming along." Recall a particular incident that occurred during the time a guest stayed with you: "Today was a beautiful sunny day, much like the day you went out into the fields with the neighbor's children to pick blackberries."

Keep the message upbeat, even when writing to someone who stayed with you under less than pleasant circumstances. You should not hesitate to show genuine concern about a guest suffering from an illness or recovering from the loss of a loved one: "I've been thinking about you and just wanted to drop you a note to send my best wishes." You might want to bring up a subject that would not act as a reminder of the problem: "Your favorite B&B companion, Fluffy, just had five wonderful little kittens yesterday!" If you find, however, that you have serious doubts about finding the right thing to say to people in these kinds of situations, then forget the note. Sometimes it is more sensitive and caring to say nothing at all.

Remembering the details of why different people visited you could be difficult, especially if you have a parade of guests all at once. So make sure that you record on your guests' reservation forms what you will need later—"here for computer programming seminar" or "attending niece's wedding." This way, when you write your notes a month afterward, you will not have to rely solely on your own faulty memory. "On the back of guests' registration cards, I will write special personal data to remind me of who they are—job information, hobbies, interests, anniversaries, et cetera," says the owner of Singleton House in Eureka Springs, Arkansas.

If you have the time and energy, jot down the contents of the follow-up message on the back of each guest's reservation form, along with the date it was sent (or input the information into the guest's computerized reservation form). It will serve as a handy reference in case you have further contact with the guest or need some inspiration before writing to someone else.

One final caution about content: Never, ever write a note that is not tailored to the person you are sending it to, or with the transparent purpose of drumming up more business. Your grace and style will attract more business than will appearing insistent, desperate, or insincere.

From the first moment a former guest lays eyes on it in the mailbox, your note should stand out as something special. It should not resemble a business communication, and it should give the feeling of being very personal. Purchase matching envelopes and note paper that in some way coordinate with the appearance or atmosphere of your B&B. If your home is painted blue, seek out blue paper near that shade. If your home is decorated with antiques, look for off-white or grained paper that looks like parchment. Keep an eye out for stationery sales and stock up in advance. Stock up on stamps, too. At the post office, request commemorative stamps. The designs change frequently and can make your envelope even more attractive. If you wish to go to the expense, personal stationery with your B&B's name and address imprinted on it can be made to order. This is not necessary, however. (See chapter 6, "Publicizing Your Bed & Breakfast.") Do not type your message, even if your best penmanship would not win any awards. A typed message is too formal. Your note should be a very personal communication.

Your Own Newsletter

If you belong to a reservation service agency, it's likely that it will take care of keeping in touch with your former guests by various means. (Be sure to ask how this is done.) This is one very important advantage of affiliating with a good RSA. A number of RSAs produce their own newsletters (in either print or electronic format) and send them to former guests of all their hosts.

There are some, however, that do not publish a newsletter or that do not maintain connections with your former guests to your satisfaction. If you find yourself in this situation, or if you are an independent host unaffiliated with an RSA, consider publishing your own newsletter.

If you've never done anything like this before, the idea can sound intimidating at first. But in this age of personal computers and desktop publishing, putting together a newsletter two or three times a year might be easier for you than writing all those personal notes.

The newsletter need not be elaborate—one page printed on both sides is all it takes. "News" items you could include are updates on yourself, your family, and your pets; favorite recipes; upcoming dates to remember (such as festivals, concerts, football games— whatever interests your guests); funny stories about your B&B; and facts about the area. Basically the newsletter should look and sound like you, giving former guests a fond remembrance of their visit.

If you have a Web site, post an electronic version of your newsletter or create a blog containing tidbits of news. This will allow former guests to keep abreast of what's new at your B&B and entice them back for a return visit. (See "Creating Your Own Web Site" in chapter 6.) It is an easy task to build an e-mail address book and send an electronic newsletter to former guests who choose to subscribe.

A Thousand Words

Some hosts like to take a photograph of each guest at some point during the visit and mail it with the follow-up notes as a memento. This is a great idea, provided that the timing and occasion of taking the picture are appropriate.

Choose the moment well: as your guests are happily loading up the station wagon with towels and picnic baskets for a day at the beach, for example, or donning their wraps for a night on the town. Toasting a successful job interview. Romping with the family dog in the yard. All of these are special memories that your guests would love to have captured on film.

On the other hand there are moments to avoid. When a guest is rushing to the airport, it is hardly the time to make him stop and pose for you. Or when someone has just come through the door after a grueling day of sales presentations. Or before breakfast—ever! If taking a picture seems forced, unnatural, or a problem in any way, don't do it. The last thing you want to do is make a guest uncomfortable.

Your photograph will be even more treasured if it comes in the mail as a surprise a month after the visit. So, if possible, keep your intention a secret from your guests. "Photography is a hobby of mine" and "We want to make a photo album of all our guests" are good lines, but if you have trouble making little white lies like these believable, then it is better to tell the truth and be done with it: "I'll send you a copy when I get the film developed." You could run the risk of giving the mistaken impression that what you are really doing is collecting mug shots just in case the family silver disappears. The photo should remind your guests of what a wonderful time they had at your B&B.

The photo you send to guests could be an especially appealing shot of the B&B itself, of course. Its potential use is strongest when imprinted on a postcard with your B&B's name and address. LesLee Solberg, owner of Denali View B&B in Talkeetna, Alaska, says, "The postcard is our greatest tool. We sell them five for a dollar and also use them as thank yous to all our guests. Upon their arrival home, they've received our postcard in the mail thanking them for staying with us and reminding them of how much they enjoyed our area." With the reduced cost of mailing at a postcard rate, a host saves on postage costs. "When you're talking about 600-plus guests a season, that's quite a savings," LesLee says.

A Book Exchange

Even people who do not read much in their normal, everyday lives often find themselves reaching for a book when they are on a trip. At last they have the time to read for pleasure over a leisurely breakfast, while relaxing at the beach, or before retiring for the night. And a good paperback seems to have become the universal solution for those long hours of waiting for bus, train, or airplane connections.

A good host will, of course, invite guests to use the family library and keep on hand guidebooks as a resource for guests. But a separate "book exchange" will not only indulge your guests' immediate desire for new reading material; it will also help your business once your guests have long since departed.

A good number of books read by people during their travels fall under the category of "light reading." Because of this, people are not inclined to keep these books once they have finished reading them. They would welcome the opportunity to trade them for other new or used, but unread, books. Your book exchange is the place to do just that.

Start your book exchange by seeding it with material that appeals to a wide variety of reading tastes—mysteries, science fiction, short stories, romance novels, and perhaps some plays or poetry. Stay away from anything too long, too dense, or too esoteric. It's not likely that many vacationers will feel like curling up with *War and Peace*. If your B&B accepts children, add some children's books and comic books as well.

All of these can be obtained inexpensively at flea markets, yard sales, thrift stores, and bookstores that have special discount sections. And you might be pleasantly surprised at what a request to friends for old, unwanted books can generate. One host found herself the happy recipient of a neighbor's entire library when he decided to retire, sell his house, and move to a sunnier climate!

Set aside a small bookcase or a few shelves for your book exchange, keeping the area separate from the library of books that you do not want leaving the house by mistake. You might even want to label it "Book Exchange," "Book Bar," or "Trading Post" just to designate clearly that these are the books that can be traded.

On the inside front cover of each book, write your B&B's name, address, and telephone number. Then, wherever a book may go, so does a calling card for your B&B.

Explain to guests that there is only one rule as far as the book exchange is concerned: For every book taken, one must be donated. Inside the cover of the donated book, in addition to the information about your B&B, a guest writes his or her name, the date of visit, home town, and any message he or she wants to pass along to future guests.

For those who protest that they do not know what kind of message to write, be ready with some suggestions based on their interests and activities while visiting you. A runner who just finished his first marathon might write a few words of advice for others who come to do the same thing next year. Someone who bravely faced and mastered the tangle of subway lines in the city might want to write down some helpful hints for someone else about to use mass transit for the first time. The key to interesting personal messages is imagination. For guests, thumbing through the books to read messages from all kinds of people can be part of the adventure of staying at your B&B. They will feel a part of the special community of people who have enjoyed your hospitality. A book taken from the book exchange will act as a memento of their visit, something they want to keep. And it's also something they can easily refer to when they want to locate your name and address once again.

Holiday Greetings

The end-of-year season of Christmas, Hanukkah, Kwanzaa, and New Year's is the time to get in touch with friends. A card from you at this time is a good way to keep in touch with your former guests.

If you buy holiday cards, stay away from those with religious themes, as your guests will undoubtedly be of a variety of faiths. "Seasons Greetings" and "Happy Holidays" are good, universal messages. Economize by purchasing cards right after the season is over, when there are half-price sales on leftover holiday merchandise. Thinking ahead for next year can save you money.

A photo card—with a picture of your B&B on it—is preferable to the regular cards. Obtainable at most photo-processing stores, photo cards do not cost significantly more than regular holiday cards bought in season, but they are much more personal.

Take a photo of your home, either inside or out. Better yet, have a friend take a photo so that you can be in the picture yourself. For former guests it will be fun to see their host all bundled up, standing ankle-deep in snow in front of the house they last saw in hot August sunshine, or sitting by the familiar living room fireplace, now decorated with pine boughs and holly berries.

The best type of photo card to purchase is the kind that has a cutout window where you can insert the photograph. It allows removal of the photo to be kept after the holiday season is over, which makes it preferable to those with the photo printed directly on them.

The Neighbors

New hosts usually wonder what kind of reception they're in for from the neighbors when they open their homes for bed and breakfast. They wonder if they should make some sort of public announcement. As a new host, should you take a full-page ad in the local paper, stage an open house, rent a loudspeaker? Need you do anything at all to let the neighbors know that you are now offering bed and breakfast to guests?

The answer is no. You need not parade up and down Main Street proclaiming that you operate a B&B any more than a writer, a seamstress, and a graphic designer do to herald the fact that they have opened home-based businesses. Bed and breakfast is the gentle art of hospitality, and as such is as unobtrusive as writing, sewing, or sketching. It will not bother anyone in the neighborhood. Possible problems arise only when neighbors don't under-stand that this is the case. Because of this, some hosts never mention their B&B operation to any of their neighbors.

You might find it hard to believe at first, but it's quite possible that your neighbors won't notice anything at all that might suggest to them that they are living next door to a bed and breakfast. One California host says this of her neighbors: "They don't know I'm a hostess. There's no indication that the couples who stay here are different from our own house guests and family members." "We are so low-key that many [neighbors] weren't even aware of it for over a year," says a Massachusetts host. A Florida host says, "I just say I have friends visiting." And hosts in rural areas report that their neighbors are so distant that they never notice a thing, or if they do, they don't care.

The key to keeping a low profile is to guard against anything that might bother the neighbors—such as noise or taking their parking spaces. "We try to get our guests' cars into our driveway so that the neighbors don't get a chance to complain. We did it for a year before I told anyone I was doing it," says a host from Kingston, Ontario. A Pennsylvania host says, "My driveway holds six cars, and there is ample parking in front of my house. Also, my guests cause no undue disturbance in the neighborhood."

If your neighbors do notice and you feel that an explanation is in order, or if you hope to use your community ties to draw visitors to your bed and breakfast, you can hardly keep the low profile that works best for some hosts. Or you will have to "go public" if you are required to appear before zoning board hearings in order to obtain permission to operate a B&B in your neighborhood. You'll have to tell people what you're doing, which means that you've got to be prepared to educate them in what bed and breakfast is all about— many will have no idea.

Lisa Hileman recalls her experience with the neighbors when she first opened Countryside in Summit Point, West Virginia: "Countryside was the first small B&B in the entire state of West Virginia. The local folks thought I was having an orgy—'Breakfast in Bed with Lisa.' They thought I was going to put up a flashing neon sign—'Eat and Sleep, Truckers Welcome!' We had to educate the local people and the tourists as to what we were doing here. In the beginning they were negative because it was something new and different. Now they accept us and see that we are not a blight on the neighborhood and that our guests are nice people."

Once your neighbors do understand what bed and breakfast is, chances are that they will be quite receptive. "They send their visiting relatives to stay with us, so it is a convenience for them," says Carol Emerick, owner of the Cottage in San Diego, California. "Several neighbors use me when they have out-of-town guests," says Robert Somaini of Woodruff House in Barre, Vermont. In fact, one of his neighbors takes his overflow in busy times. Another host reports that her neighbors love the idea of her having a B&B so much that they often come over to meet the guests!

Catherine Hatala, a Philadelphia host, says that one of her neighbors "will often walk a guest down and make him feel at home if I am not available at the guest's arrival time." She goes on to say that her neighbors are very kind and courteous to her guests when they encounter them anywhere in the neighborhood: "If my neighbors see my guests on the street, they greet them and sometimes answer questions for them and make recommendations," she says.

Because their bed and breakfast home is the only one in the village of Richfield Springs, New York, Lona and George Smith, the owners of Summerwood, have found that their neighbors "have been extremely supportive and encouraging to the point that they send us many guests who are out-of-town visitors coming for weddings, etc." Jeanne Gilbert, owner of Gilbert's Bed & Breakfast in Rehoboth, Massachusetts, says, "One of my neighbors was so supportive that she gave me some handmade rugs for the bedrooms."

Roy Mixon, too, has found that his neighbors more than accept the presence of Rockland Farm Retreat in Bumpass, Virginia. "They send guests, come to socials, and enjoy the benefits—the employment and the money the guests spend in the area," he says. Rockland is a former plantation that has been restored. In West Virginia the owner of a grand old house that she restored as a bed and breakfast also found that her neighbors approved of the project, viewing it as a contribution to the community: "They are very proud," she says. Another host, living in Eureka Springs, Arkansas, has had a similar experience with her neighbors. "They love it, since restoration improved the value of property," she says.

In one case it was the neighbors who suggested that the host open her home for bed and breakfast in the first place! For some years, the owner of a lovely home in Leaburg, Oregon, had allowed people to visit her extensive landscaped grounds with their many beautiful flowering plants. So that guests could enjoy the parklike atmosphere even more, as well as the home that was constructed especially to enhance the natural surroundings, both neighbors and guests urged the owner of Marjon, Margie Haas, to open her home for bed and breakfast. Eventually, she did just that.

The support of your neighbors can be especially important to you if you encounter any problems with zoning boards. (See "Zoning" in chapter 5.) A host in Graham, North Carolina, found her neighbors taking her side when she needed them. "I had to have their approval initially because the block had to be rezoned from residential," she says. She was glad she could count on their support.

If you decide that you wish to have a visible presence in your neighborhood, you've got to take steps to garner support for yourself and to foster the understanding of what bed and breakfast is and what kind of a contribution it can make to the community. An open house might not be a bad idea—invite some of the neighbors over for coffee and to meet a few of your guests. People seem to fear what they don't know, so take it upon yourself to dispel the mystery. Let your neighbors find out what a good neighbor a bed and breakfast can be.

Chapter Nine
A Memorable Breakfast

For many of us, eating breakfast is something we get through quickly so that we can move on to the more important business of the day. The setting doesn't really matter, as long as we have what we need on the table. Sometimes the food doesn't even seem to matter, as long as it can be prepared quickly and will hold us until lunch.

But there are days when we do make the time to have a leisurely morning meal with those special touches—a tablecloth, the "good" china, a vase of flowers, those terrific blueberry pancakes made from scratch. Sunday brunch—how wonderful it is! For your bed and breakfast guests, every day is Sunday. "We aim to spoil our guests!" says Mary Norton, owner of Norton's Green Bed and Breakfast in British Columbia. Let Mary be your role model. Your job as a host is to make the breakfast experience enjoyable not only with what you serve but also how you serve it.

Scenic Settings

Okay, we all learned that the fork goes to the left of the plate, on top of a plain white napkin that has been folded in half, then in thirds, and that the knife and spoon go to the right. The salt and pepper shakers go dead center, next to the sugar and cream.

This little lesson may have helped us set the table for our own meals throughout the years, but when it comes to bed and breakfast, it's not enough. Of course, there's nothing wrong with the common table setting we all use— but face it, it's so very ordinary. (When was the last time you sat down to eat in your own home and said, "Ooh! Just look at that setting!"?)

Think of the space where your guests will eat breakfast as an "environment." Everything in the area should contribute to the pleasure of the meal. You must first decide where the best place is for your guests to eat their breakfast. The dining room is an obvious choice, but there could be other options that would make the experience special.

Does your home have an area outdoors where guests could enjoy their meal in good weather—a patio, a balcony, a deck, a flower garden, a lawn? What would it take to set up a picnic table and chairs or patio furniture under the willow tree or next to the duck pond? Would it be easy enough to carry the food to the outdoor setting?

Moselle Schaffer, the owner of Camel Lot in Westfield, Indiana, offers bed and breakfast on her exotic-animal farm. Her brochure includes this note: "Breakfast is served on the terrace overlooking the tiger compound or in the sunroom or—on bleak days—beside a crackling fire in the library." Who could resist the chance to have a morning meal with a prince of the jungle?

Another alternative setting (for those of us who do not have a tiger compound) is the guest room itself, but only if the space is large enough and can be divided easily so that the sleeping area and the dining area do not interfere with each other. A suite or separate guesthouse is perfect for such an arrangement, but a small single or double room will not work—too cramped.

Keep in mind, too, that confining the dining area to the guest room does distance you from your visitors. Couples might enjoy the opportunity to have a more private breakfast, but single travelers might not want to eat alone in their room. Some hosts decide against setting up a separate breakfast area for guests for this reason; others do but let guests know that they're welcome in the dining room.

When asked if she had ever encountered a difficult guest, Elaine Dickson, owner of the Captain Ezra Nye House in Sandwich, Massachusetts, related the following tale: "Well, she wasn't difficult, but different. We have set times for breakfast, and our other guests at the table were waiting for a bride to come down for breakfast. They were having a lively conversation until she arrived—in her nightgown only. I was floored but carried on serving breakfast as if it were nothing unusual. The guests' conversation resumed, haltingly."

If you do want to set up a breakfast area in the guest room, first imagine that the room has no furniture at all in it. Then look at the shape of the room. Is there a particular section of it where a table and chairs would fit quite naturally? Next to the bay windows? In front of the fireplace? Near the sliding glass doors? Inside the alcove? What kind of a "view" would your guests have if you were to place the table and chairs where you think they would go best? (You don't want your guests staring straight at the unmade bed while they have their soufflé.) A window or fireplace will draw their attention; you can also create a view (of sorts) by placing an interesting piece of art near the table.

Now that you've identified where in the guest room a breakfast area would go best, take a look at the room in the morning during the hours (both early and late) that your guests will be having breakfast. From where does the light enter the room and from what angle? Can you position the table and chairs in your chosen spot without the strong morning sun shining directly into your guests' eyes? Can the window shade or curtain be adjusted to block the light but still offer a view?

Too little light is just as bad as too much. If the table and chairs would fit best inside a dark alcove or corner, is there an electrical outlet near enough to connect a small lamp? (A full or partial canopy of sheer or netted material can be draped above the dining area to separate it somewhat from the "bedroom." Don't use material that is opaque; it will make the environment feel too small and confined.)

Most hosts simply use their own dining room to serve their guests' breakfast. It's the most convenient place, requires no extra decorating, and provides a common area where hosts and guests can share breakfast and get to know one another—one of the treasured advantages of bed and breakfast.

Perhaps your dining room has been arranged the same way for years, but try to look at the room with new eyes. Evaluate it the same way you would if you were about to create a completely new dining area. Consider the shape of the room, the light source, the view, and the general comfort of the guests who will be joining you at the table. Should you make any changes? Perhaps the table and chairs actually go better over by the window or farther away from the kitchen door.

After you've determined the best place to serve breakfast, it's time to concentrate on how to make your table setting special. There are a few touches that make any table more appealing: a "real" tablecloth (instead of a plastic one), cloth napkins (instead of paper ones), and the "good" china and silver that you usually save for special occasions. Add to these a centerpiece and an interesting presentation for the napkin, and you're all set.

The main thing to remember is that you want the table to look attractive. For this, use your imagination. Maybe the fork, knife, and spoon should all go to the right of the plate in order to better display the beautifully folded napkin at the left. Or maybe the silverware looks best placed together at an angle on a napkin that has been folded end to end into a large, imposing triangle. Forget the rules we were taught about setting a table. Be daring. Experiment. And enjoy yourself.

The Centerpiece

Many of us get through life just fine with nothing more in the center of our dining room table than the salt and pepper shakers. And it's true that you need not go to the trouble of buying or creating a centerpiece just because you'll now be hosting bed and breakfast guests. But it's a nice gesture. The presence of a strong, imaginative centerpiece shows your guests that you consider breakfast a special event. This, they will remember.

A vase of flowers is a common centerpiece but always a very lovely one. Fresh flowers are especially attractive in season for their fragrance; a sprig of flowers from the arrangement can be placed on each napkin for a special touch that unifies the total table setting. (Be aware that some guests may suffer from hay fever, though. Do not place flowers on the table if you know this to be the case.) A permanent presentation of dried flowers is also appealing and has the advantages to a host of involving no work after the arrangement has been created and costing nothing beyond the initial expense. If you coordinate the colors in the flower arrangement with those in your tablecloth, placemats, napkins, and dishware, the most basic table setting can look quite elegant.

If you enjoy decorating and wish to do more than this, creating an unusual centerpiece can be a lot of fun for a host and can make the breakfast experience at your home quite memorable for your guests. You can develop an entire table theme around your centerpiece based on the season, a holiday or special occasion, or even your guests' personal interests.

For the fall season, consider a centerpiece of polished gourds piled high in a basket, along with a selection of dried flowers in autumn reds, golds, browns, and oranges. For the Christmas season, fill a basket or clear glass bowl with tiny wrapped packages. These can be empty, but it's fun to wrap matchboxes, scented soaps, or miniature candles; then a package can be placed on each napkin or plate as a gift and to unify the table setting. For New Year's, turn a large party hat on its side (or place it upside down, using a transparent vase for a base) and fill it with noisemakers, streaming ribbons (the kind that curl are good for this), and maybe a balloon or two; place a noisemaker on each plate or napkin as a gift (and, again, to unify the setting).

You should always try to coordinate any colors used in your centerpiece with those in the rest of your table setting. Of course, you're not going to run out and buy a whole new set of tablecloths, placemats, napkins, and dishware for every season and every holiday. This is not necessary to achieve the effect you want. You can change the entire look of your table quite inexpensively by choosing a white tablecloth that you can use year-in and year-out and merely changing the colors of your napkins or place mats. (If you sew, these can be made easily at a very reasonable cost.) Or buy napkin rings in a variety of colors and use those to accent the colors that dominate your centerpiece. (Doing this involves even less expense than buying or making several sets of napkins.)

If your dishware seems to clash with any of your seasonal color schemes, often all you need to do is simply add an accent of that color to the centerpiece (a dash of turquoise among the autumn colors), and the problem is solved. Or adapt the colors in the centerpiece to suit your dishware. (Sacrifice the "Valentine red" for a "Valentine pink," the color of the floral design on your dishes.)

If you want a real challenge but a very rewarding one, think of how you could tie in the theme of the breakfast table with some personal aspect of your guests' visits.

Many people travel on special occasions as a means of celebration—a birthday, anniversary, wedding, graduation. You will probably know this in advance from your reservation process; you can make the event especially memorable for your guests by taking the time to create a table setting just for the occasion. Now is the time to put that old mortarboard from college or dolls saved from atop your own wedding cake to good use as part of the centerpiece. And place a card with your good wishes on the plate of the visitor who is celebrating the event. (You might want to keep an assortment of cards on hand for this purpose.)

Some hosts have even surprised their guests by making a birthday cake. If the spirit moves you, by all means do it. There's no question that the thought (and the cake) will be greatly appreciated, but know that this is above and beyond what a bed and breakfast host is expected to provide.

For guests who are visiting you for other reasons, you might see where that leads you with centerpiece ideas. Are you hosting some fans who have come to cheer on their favorite team? (Maybe a pennant placed in a tall, slender vase would look better to these folks than any flower arrangement.) A few fishermen about to try their luck? (The goldfish bowl could be moved to the table for the morning.) A musician in town to give a concert? (What's to stop you from getting that old violin out of the attic, arranging a few flowers in its center, and placing it on the table on top of some sheet music?) A runner warming up for the big race? (Perhaps some new decorative shoelaces would make an appropriate napkin ring and a fun gift from you "for luck.") A teacher who's come to attend a conference on education? (How about your son's lunch box, with the lid open, filled with a couple of schoolbooks, some pencils, a box of chalk, and a few tall flowers towering over it all?)

You get the idea. You'll find that you can tailor-make centerpieces quite easily once you get started. Your guests will certainly remember you for highlighting their special moment. This works, of course, only when the reason for a guest's visit is an uplifting one. If a teacher has come to your bed and breakfast for a few days to escape from the schoolbooks and the pencils and the chalk, she probably won't want to be reminded of them at her breakfast table. Use your good judgment about when to go for something out of the ordinary in a centerpiece and when to use just a nice vase of flowers.

Always try to draw from what you already have instead of spending extra money to create individualized centerpieces. Yet, if your location happens to draw a certain type of visitor (football fans, skiers, honeymooners, fishermen), it's easier to plan ahead for the "unusual" centerpieces. In this case you can use the items over and over again. Maybe a goldfish wouldn't be such a bad investment.

Especially for Children

No one needs to tell you that children usually can't wait to get away from the table. There are too many rules ("Don't talk with your mouth full!"), too many things that can break ("Be careful with that glass!") or spill ("Watch out for the milk!"). Eating may be necessary, but it's sure not much fun when Mom and Dad are worried about your every move. It's even worse in someone else's house, where parents are more concerned than ever that their children behave.

If you accept children at your bed and breakfast, there are some things you can do to help cut the tension so that both the kids and their parents can relax and have a good time.

You are most likely using your best china and crystal for the adults. Do not feel that you are obligated to use these for a child who is old enough to sit at the table but still likely to break and spill. It will be a big relief all around (for you, for the parents, and for the child, too) if the youngster's place setting contains attractive, but unbreakable, dishware. (Take care, though, not to insult a well-behaved guest who is eleven or twelve years old with the kid stuff.)

This doesn't mean merely trotting out the "old" plastic dishes imprinted with designs of fronds and rosettes. Doing this will make it embarrassingly obvious that you fear for the safety of your "good" things. (They may not be safe, but parents can sometimes be sensitive about this.) Instead, give some attention to creating a special place setting for the child.

Brightly colored dishes, and perhaps a colored or patterned napkin as well, are a good start. You can make the setting interesting by folding the napkin in a way a child might enjoy or by placing it in the arms of a small stuffed animal.

Do you have any toy soldiers, monsters, superheroes? Why not give Godzilla a fork to hold or put Spiderman in charge of the spoon? Do you have a small train set? Why not put three or four cars in a half-circle above the child's plate and load them up with the silverware, the napkin, and the salt and pepper shakers?

If you are hosting more than one child, or if you have children yourself who will be eating breakfast with the guests, it might be fun to set up a "children's table" near the "adults' table," where they can be watched but can still enjoy their breakfast in peace. Just as for the adult table, you'll need a centerpiece and a theme for the table setting. You can do this easily with stuffed animals. Set up a few extra chairs at the table with Teddy in one and Garfield in the other with their own place settings. If you have some plastic fruit, place a selection on each plate. (As a centerpiece, how about an empty honey pot with a small bear poking his nose inside?)

Other ideas: Place a tiny table-and-chairs set from a dollhouse on the table as a centerpiece. Or display a toy tea-party set. Or create a miniature farm right in the center of the table and use some of the pieces for the place setting: Put a cow next to the glass of milk. A tractor can haul the spoon. (Maybe a large green place mat would make a good field for the tractor.) Or think about a jungle theme, with toy lions, tigers, bears, elephants, and maybe a Tarzan model. (And how about a napkin made of black and yellow tiger-striped material?) Or perhaps a prehistoric theme would be fun, with a few dinosaurs roaming the table.

If a holiday is near, work it into the child's place setting. For a Halloween centerpiece put a mask on the teddy bear and a toy jack-o'-lantern in his lap. For Christmas try a Santa's hat on Teddy and place the silverware inside a red stocking, along with a candy cane.

The child should be able to touch the things that you place on the table for his or her amusement and, yes, even play with them. For this reason all items you use should be touchable—that is, unbreakable. And of course, you must always take a child's age into consideration when planning a place setting. Some very small children would get so totally distracted by the toys that they forget to eat altogether, or Raggedy Ann ends up face-down in the oatmeal. Use your judgment about what's possible and appropriate for youngsters of various ages. And consult with a child's parents the evening before as you plan the breakfast. Respect their wishes regarding their youngster's meal.

You shouldn't spend a lot of money buying stuffed animals and other toys for the table setting. Look at what you might already have and use your imagination. Your own children's toys are your greatest resource. (Ask them to help you design and set up place settings for visiting children—it's a good way to make them feel part of the family B&B business.) Remember that a child's table setting does not have to be elaborate, just something that says, "This is for you!"

One more thing to keep in mind is that if kids like what they see, they might want to take it home with them. Plan for this. Check with the parents first; then have a little something on the table that the youngsters can take with them—a monster of their choice, one of the plastic farm animals, the Christmas stocking, the toy jack-o'-lantern, the Halloween mask—something that does not cost you a lot of money and that will make them happy. The children who visit you will be sure to remember their special breakfast. And their parents will appreciate the trouble you took for their children. If you want to attract families with children to your bed and breakfast, this is absolutely one way to do it. The good word will spread.

The Coffee

If the development of the bed and breakfast industry in this part of the world is any indication that people here are becoming more interested in enjoying the finer things in life, so is the parallel development of a more refined taste in another area—coffee. What we were satisfied with at the breakfast table fifteen or twenty years ago no longer satisfies. As a nation, we've collectively developed an educated palate. Today there's no excuse for serving anything but a great cup of coffee. We know it, and so do our guests. "Better coffee" went at the top of the list of desired improvements suggested by one guest for the bed and breakfast home she had visited. This is how your guests will be judging you. Can you make your coffee any better than it is now? If you are not a coffee drinker yourself, ask for the honest opinion of several coffee-drinking friends.

The quality of your coffee depends on a number of things. The first is the method you use to brew it (and I do mean "brew"—never use an instant coffee for your guests). If you are using an electric percolator, it's time to unplug it, permanently. Why? Because the pot has more control over the brewing process than you do. This type of pot can produce under-brewed or overbrewed coffee, depending on the temperature of the water—which you cannot control. So if you're looking to make "the perfect cup," you've got to look elsewhere.

A number of people have been turning in their percolators for an electric drip pot. (The type with an automatic timer to start the coffee brewing even before you get up can make a host's life a little easier, but do check to see which models have a good track record for safety before you buy.) This type of pot matches the advantage of the percolator in keeping the coffee hot while you linger at the breakfast table, but it brews a better cup of coffee if used correctly. This is due in part to the filtration method of brewing. Here, hot water is poured over drip grind coffee that has been placed in a filter (usually made of paper). The water goes through the coffee once, unlike in a percolator, which pumps the same water over the same grounds again and again. This is considered the crucial factor in the superiority of a drip pot over a percolator. There is at least one auto-timed electric drip pot on the market that drips the brewed coffee directly into a carafe, which keeps the coffee fresh and hot.

Nonelectric drip pots make excellent coffee but present a problem in keeping it hot. You can put the pot over a low flame to heat, but this must be done no later than fifteen minutes after the coffee has been brewed and no longer than thirty minutes at a stretch, or the flavor will be altered. As a rule, "old" coffee should never be reheated. It's just not the same.

Another brewing method that has taken hold in this country is steeping in a French Melior pot. This method involves adding freshly boiled water directly to ground coffee and steeping the mixture for five full minutes (no more and no less). The grounds are then separated from the finished brew by means of a plunger device. This method is favored by some because the resulting coffee is rich and flavorful, and it can be brewed fresh right at the table. A disadvantage is that the coffee can cool off during the steeping process, but you can now buy a "coffee cozy" modeled after the traditional "tea cozy" but designed to fit snugly over the Melior's glass cylinder to help trap the heat inside. (A cozy—which is sort of a jacket for the pot of hot liquid—is easy enough to make out of quilted material.) The pot (with or without its cozy) is so attractive that it makes a nice addition to the breakfast table or an early morning wake-up tray.

A more elaborate (and more expensive) pot that employs steam pressure to produce espresso or cappuccino is wonderful if you already happen to have one, and it provides a good amenity for your guests, but it's not necessary to buy one just for this purpose. An exception is if you run a restaurant as part of your B&B operation. In this context, where you sell coffee, an espresso machine has been compared to a gold mine, generating considerable revenue for very little investment.

The best advice for small B&Bs without a restaurant is to make sure you have a good, basic pot (drip is really the most reliable for the quality it produces) and care for it well. If you are buying a new pot, select one made of glass, as a metallic surface will alter the taste of the brew somewhat (stainless steel is the best choice of the metals). The pot must be scrubbed clean after each use; a quick rinse will not remove the oils that form an invisible film on the pot's surface—and this film will change the taste of the coffee.

The size of your coffeepot also affects the taste. An eight-cup pot is designed to brew eight cups of coffee to its peak aroma and taste. If you use this same pot to brew only one or two cups of coffee, you won't get the same quality. You should not brew less than three-quarters of a pot's maximum capacity. So for an eight-cup pot, don't make any less than six or your brew will lose some of its flavor.

If you're buying a new pot, don't select one that will produce more coffee than you need at any one time. (Remember, you lose quality when you reheat. It's better to make several smaller pots of coffee throughout the day than one large pot in the morning.) You might want to have two pots, one small and one large, that you can alternate depending on the number of guests you have staying with you.

The choice of the coffee itself is another major factor when it comes to creating the best possible cup of coffee. Find out which is the proper grind of coffee suited to your particular coffeemaker (look in the directions or ask someone in a gourmet store). If the grind is too fine or too coarse for your pot, the quality of the coffee will diminish. It's best to pass by the shelf in the local grocery store that contains all those cans of vacuum-packed, preground coffee and head instead to the specialty section or to a gourmet store where you can see and smell the coffee beans you are buying.

Yes, a good cup of coffee typically costs slightly more than what you find in vacuum-sealed cans, but the extra pennies ensure that your guests will enjoy

For mail-order coffee, visit: www.greatcoffee.com

their first waking moments in your B&B. To put the expense in perspective, Ron Walters, an inngoer for many years and president of Great Estates Coffee Company, reminds us that a pound of coffee is equal to a case of wine in volume.

The best coffee is made from newly roasted beans (some stores guarantee that theirs have been roasted within twenty-four hours of sale) that are ground immediately before brewing. You may wish to purchase a small grinder to use at home; devices that will do this can usually be purchased at the same place you find whole coffee beans. If you don't choose to become this much of a purist about the coffee you serve, you can have the beans ground to the right consistency for your pot right at the store. Even decaffeinated coffee beans are available for purchase this way. (It's a good idea to keep some decaf on hand for those guests who like coffee but not the effects of caffeine.)

If you store it properly, the coffee you have had ground just right for your pot will not lose any of its taste. Coffee can become stale. You wouldn't think of serving bread that has lost is freshness; neither should you serve coffee that has suffered a similar fate. To guard its freshness, store your coffee in an airtight container in the freezer compartment of your refrigerator. It can be used directly from the freezer (it won't crystallize, so you don't have to "thaw" it). It will keep here about a month, compared with ten days (tops) in the regular part of the refrigerator. Do not use coffee that has been stored in the freezer to make espresso, however, as it will affect the taste. Keep the coffee away from moisture and food odors, as these will destroy its flavor.

Do not buy large quantities of coffee in advance and store it because it will lose its freshness the longer you keep it. Estimate one and one-half pounds of coffee per room per month. If you have four guest rooms, then you can estimate six pounds per month and purchase only what you will need.

When serving your delicious coffee, do it justice by providing whole milk or cream along with the choice of 2-percent or skim milk. Never use an imitation cream or a powdered substitute. Offer sugar and a good low-calorie sweetener for those who prefer it. These items are most attractive when served in a creamer and bowl instead of the cartons in which they were originally packaged.

Although there are many flavored coffees on the market today, these are not the best choice for first thing in the morning. Someone looking forward to that initial cup of basic, steaming java may be less than thrilled with the exotic taste of some hazelnut-raspberry blend before fully waking up. You might want to consider a variation for the coffee you serve in the afternoon or evening. This can be done easily by adding any number of flavorings to the finished brew: a few cinnamon sticks, chocolate syrup, or even a little hot chocolate and an orange slice mixed with the coffee. A topping of whipped cream is a favorite touch. This can be sprinkled with a little nutmeg, shaved chocolate, grated orange rind, or cinnamon.

Iced coffee is a wonderful drink to serve on hot, lazy afternoons or evenings. Too many people have given up on making iced coffee after one or two bad experiences—too watery, not cold enough, not enough taste. There are a few tricks to creating good iced coffee. First, always brew double-strength coffee if you plan to pour it over ice cubes (the ice dilutes the coffee to regular strength). Or freeze some newly made coffee in the ice-cube tray and use the cubes instead of ice (less dilution, more taste). Freshly brewed coffee whipped with a few scoops of a good, creamy brand of coffee ice cream, with maybe a little chocolate syrup, and topped with whipped cream, if you wish, makes a terrific drink. Where most people have made their mistake with iced coffee in the past is using leftover coffee to make it. Coffee that has been chilled in the refrigerator or that has even been standing at room temperature for a few hours just does not have the taste that freshly brewed coffee has. When you're making iced coffee, start at the beginning with a new brew, just as you would if you were preparing to serve your guests hot coffee. It makes a world of difference in the finished product.

The serious coffee drinkers among your guests will thank you for a good cup of coffee in the morning even more if you offer to bring a wake-up tray to their room before they have to face anyone across the breakfast table. Some people really rely on that first cup to get them on their feet at the beginning of the day. Ask your guests before they retire if they would like their coffee in the privacy of their room. If so, prepare the tray with a small Thermos or an insulated carafe, cups, spoons, napkins, milk or cream, sugar and sugar substitute, and perhaps a small vase with a flower in it. For this your guests will always remember you fondly.

For Tea Drinkers

Expect that some of your guests will not want coffee at all but a nice cup of tea instead. Keep various kinds of teas on hand to suit the varying tastes of your guests. Include some decaffeinated brands among your selections.

There are some helpful hints for making the perfect cup of tea, just as there are with coffee. One of the most common mistakes is that we tend to use up whatever water might already be standing in the teakettle. Boiling this water might ensure that it's safe to drink, certainly, but "old" water gets flat, just as your soft drink does if you leave its bottle or can open for a while. You can't notice the deaeration as much with water, but it's still there, and your tea will suffer for it. Always start with fresh, cold water brought to the boiling point.

An earthenware or porcelain teapot is superior to any made of metal (as with coffee, a metallic surface affects the taste). Preheat the teapot by rinsing it with some of the boiling water. This will help maintain the temperature of the tea once the brewing begins. Some people claim that loose tea mixed directly with the water, or contained within a tea ball or leaf basket, is superior to using tea bags; some say it doesn't matter. Let your own taste buds guide your choice.

Don't judge the finished brew by its color; rather, time the brewing to determine when it's ready. Most teas should be left for at least three minutes and usually no more than five, or you run the risk of bitterness. (Note that the popular green tea brews in about one minute.) Then remove the tea bags or the tea ball or leaf basket to stop the brewing process. Never reuse teabags or leaves.

To keep the tea hot while your guests enjoy lingering over a few cups, place the pot inside a tea cozy to trap the heat. Some people love their tea served with a little honey, lemon, sugar, or milk. A wake-up tray containing these and a teapot with freshly brewed tea is a considerate amenity to offer your guests in the morning.

The Food

When it comes to food, everyone's a critic. We're always evaluating what we eat, judging its merits for taste ("This is a teeny bit overcooked"), amount ("It was great but I'm still hungry"), nutrition ("Does this have sugar in it?"), price ("I expected something better than this for what I paid"), calories ("This is much too fattening"), and eye appeal ("What in the world is this green stuff?"). As a bed and breakfast host, you not only have to be aware that your guests are judging the food you serve according to these criteria, but also that the meal you're responsible for happens to carry with it the reputation of being the most important meal of the day. As if this weren't enough, it has to be "special" in keeping with the bed and breakfast tradition. The pressure's on. How are you going to make your guests (*all* of them) happy when they join you at the breakfast table?

First of all give them a choice—but not too much of a choice. According to the former director of a reservation service agency in Texas, the biggest mistake made by new hosts is asking, "What would you like for breakfast?" An open-ended question like this could get requests for anything from fried ostrich eggs to oatmeal. You decide what the options will be and list them for your guests. It's a good idea to leave a copy of this "menu" in the guest room. Ask your guests to note which items they prefer and to give the menu back to you before they retire for the night. A query at the bottom of the page—"Any dietary restrictions?"—allows

> "In the big-city B&Bs, hosts generally lead a hectic life between work, play, and interpersonal relations," says the manager of a reservation service agency in New York City. "One host reported hearing a tiny voice from the bedroom about 11:00 A.M. saying, "Please, I'm still waiting for my breakfast."

the guest to let you know if modification of menu choices or ingredients may be necessary. Many hosts also include this question in the reservation process as a way to do advance menu planning.

Some hosts print menu choices on their brochures so that prospective guests know exactly what to expect. Prentice Strong, owner of Penury Hall in Southwest Harbor, Maine, lists these items on his brochure: juice, fruit compote, melon, seasonal fruit, eggs Benedict, blueberry pancakes, "penurious" omelet, date-walnut French toast, poached eggs 'n' hash, "favorite eggs" and muffins, plus homemade jams and jellies, pure maple syrup, and coffee, tea, or milk. This sure lets guests know that they're in for quite a gastronomical treat if they decide to stay at Penury Hall. An interesting, varied menu like this can be used, as Prentice Strong does, to attract people to his B&B.

The brochure for Dairy Hollow House in Eureka Springs, Arkansas, also describes the pleasures of eating a delicious "from scratch" breakfast: "A Dairy Hollow House Breakfast is a leisurely affair. Coffee, tea, herb tea, or café au lait, in your room if you like (the morning paper is by your door), is followed by fresh fruit in season or just-squeezed orange juice served in our sunny parlour. Next comes a basket of fresh-baked whole-wheat butterhorns and a loaf of sweet bread, or a generous helping of our famous German baked pancakes, puffy and golden, hot from the oven. Of course, there's more coffee (or whatever) to go with the meal, as well as homemade jam and real butter."

For breakfast recipes, try:
www.bbonline.com
www.lanierbb.com
www.epicurious.com

Notice that the choices at Dairy Hollow House are limited to basically two—one a "continental" type of breakfast, the other a "full" breakfast. Here, a guest can decide how much or how little he or she wants to eat. And because there's a set menu, the host does not have to scramble to buy ingredients and prepare a variety of items for breakfast. This is especially important if you have a number of guests staying with you at one time and you give them too wide a choice. You could end up spending hours in the kitchen preparing an assortment of omelets, oatmeal, quiche, and pancakes.

Some hosts choose to serve a continental breakfast only or are required to do so by health department regulations. Check to see if there are food-preparation restrictions in your region before you plan your menu. (Check "Health and Safety" in chapter 5.) A continental breakfast is fine as long as guests are told in advance that this is the case. According to the manager of a reservation service agency called Greater Boston Hospitality, a continental breakfast usually includes fruit, juice, rolls or muffins with butter and jam and honey, and fresh coffee, tea, and/or milk. Some hosts also offer croissants and individual cold cereals. The owners of a Massachusetts RSA suggest adding to the selection small containers of assorted yogurts, foil-wrapped wedges of cheese or any type of quality cheese, and a package of cream cheese that can be used on bagels, toast, or bread.

Serving a continental breakfast appeals to many hosts because it's less trouble and generally less expensive than preparing a "full" breakfast. It's a great alternative for hosts who have to leave for work early in the morning, often before their guests have gotten out of bed. A continental breakfast can be prepared the night before and left for guests to help themselves. Be advised, though, that some of your guests may not be satisfied with a continental breakfast unless you have made the effort to make it hearty enough for those who consider breakfast an important meal of the day. "If you want repeat business and word-of-mouth praise, you'll not be able to get away with the skimpy continental breakfast of low-cost rolls, doughnuts, coffee, and canned juice," say the owners of one RSA.

All items served in a continental breakfast must be of high quality and plentiful: Your own home-baked breads, muffins, or scones (if regulations allow) or products from a good bakery are absolutely necessary. (Stay away from those quickie, prepackaged mixes. Your guests will no doubt recognize them for what they are and will not be impressed.) And provide real butter, fresh-squeezed juice (if allowed), and brewed coffee (not instant) with real milk or cream. A toaster oven or microwave oven that guests can operate themselves in your absence to heat their croissants or muffins is a nice touch if your schedule does not allow you to serve the breakfast yourself. (Be sure to select a toaster oven that meets the highest safety standards, with a timer and an automatic shutoff.)

Including an offer of a continental breakfast as a choice on your menu is a good way of accommodating those guests who prefer to eat lightly in the morning. If at all possible, though, you should also offer the option of a full breakfast—which could include a main dish like quiche, omelets, casseroles, French toast, blintzes, soufflés, waffles, or pancakes—as well as servings of ham, bacon, or sausage and other side dishes if you wish—and items that normally constitute a continental breakfast. Offering a full breakfast is especially important if your bed and breakfast business is based in a resort area where your guests will be leaving for some kind of demanding physical activity afterwards, such as skiing, boating, or hiking. They need that hearty breakfast and will most likely choose to stay at a B&B that will provide it, assuming that health department regulations do not prohibit the serving of anything but a continental menu.

The best advice is to settle on a few main dishes that you're particularly good at preparing and offer those on your menu. One couple always offers a baked apple pancake because it's a sure hit every time. Some of the items that guests have reported that they particularly enjoyed while staying at bed and breakfast homes are "good coffee cake" (from a Pennsylvania couple), "homemade sourdough biscuits and fresh blueberries" (from a Canadian woman), "homemade breads, muffins, Scotch ham, oatmeal pancakes, Swedish pancakes, and quiche" (from an Ohio woman), "delicious scrambled eggs and Danish that came from a special bakery" (from a Pennsylvania woman), "small fresh tomatoes in season" (from an Ontario woman), and "raspberries with real cream" (from a New Mexico couple).

For guests staying longer than one night, you will need to vary your menu so that your guests don't get tired of eating the same thing all the time. A California man reports enjoying a variety of food during his extended stay at a bed and breakfast home: "Other than a nice slice of cold, fresh cantaloupe, the menu changed every day—scrambled eggs with sausage, homemade bread toasted, homemade cinnamon rolls, hot cereal." His hosts kept him quite happy with the selection.

Hot cereal is always a good option. It's inexpensive, easy to make, and great on a cold winter morning. One New York host likes to serve hot oatmeal with grated apples and raisins in it. A little milk and brown sugar, "and everyone loves it," she says.

Include some regional specialties among your selections if you can. Many of your guests will be visiting your area because of its special sights, sounds, smells, and tastes. They are very interested in what it has to offer, what makes it unique. For someone who doesn't live in the South, chances are that grits exist only in the imagination. Why not let your guests sample them with the rest of their meal? And what visitor to the Southwest hasn't heard about the use of chili peppers in *everything?* Maybe they'd like to try your green chili quiche—just issue the appropriate warnings well in advance. It will surely give them something to talk about when they get back home. And there's a lot of talk about those famous Boston baked beans. Maybe a side dish at breakfast isn't a bad idea.

As you plan your menu, include items that you yourself enjoy eating—just in case you've overestimated the number of cantaloupes you'll be needing for this weekend's guests or the number of banana-walnut muffins it takes to feed a family of four. And try any new recipes first yourself, before you experiment on guests at the breakfast table.

Be advised to take into consideration how much you should be spending for each guest's breakfast based on your room price. According to the manager of a Pennsylvania reservation service, the number-one mistake that new hosts make is "spending too much money on breakfast." If your bed and breakfast offers rooms at a low to moderate price, you should not be serving seafood soufflé with fresh crab flown in specially from the coast. You need to economize, or buying your breakfast ingredients will eat up all your profits. On the other hand, if yours can be considered luxurious accommodations, fresh crab soufflé would not be unexpected by guests who have paid a pretty penny for the privilege of staying at your B&B.

Try to cost out the ingredients for preparing one serving of a full breakfast (this means dividing the cost of a dozen eggs by twelve, cutting the cost of one grapefruit in half, and so forth), and see if you can come up with a total cost per person for breakfast. The figure could vary quite a bit depending on what you serve and how wisely you shop. (You can keep costs down by buying in bulk and watching for sales.) If the figure exceeds 25 percent of a guest's share of a room's cost, you're spending too much on breakfast. And 25 percent is high; most hosts spend far less than this.

In order to save money, and to prevent breakfast from becoming a major undertaking every time you have guests, think ahead. Buy what food you can in advance and even prepare it in advance, then freeze it. This way you don't have to run out and buy fresh ingredients each time you're expecting guests; you can serve foods that are regional specialties but are out of season; and you can take advantage of sales and special prices on bulk quantities. Even if you've never tried to freeze anything before in your life, be assured that it is a simple process to learn and well worth the effort for what it saves you in time, trouble, and expense.

Whatever you serve, it should be done in as attractive a way as possible. This means no jars, cans, or boxes on the table. Instead use pretty bowls or dishes, little wicker baskets lined with colorful cloth, small ceramic or wooden boxes, or even glasses that are intended for liqueurs or wine. Lacy paper doilies on platters for serving dry foods (rolls, bread, cookies) add a special touch. Place cereals inside clear Mason jars (perhaps an assortment of small Mason jars containing individual-size portions could be arranged in a basket lined with a cloth that is color coordinated with the tablecloth). For jam and honey, place single servings in small dishes (cut glass is especially attractive). It's possible to buy jam in small two-ounce containers. Placing an assortment of these inside a basket is a good way to give your guests a choice without having to open a number of large jars of jam.

Even the most ordinary food can be presented in an especially appealing way. Hard-boiled eggs, for example, are great to have on hand because they're nutritious, low in calories, delicious, and very easy to prepare and keep. Why not dress them up a little with a stenciled design on the shell, or one of the many types of sticky decals now available in different shapes and colors (stars, hearts, flowers)? Decorated or dyed eggs are especially fun for any children who might be staying at your bed and breakfast.

Butter is a staple at the breakfast table for rolls, toast, or muffins. Instead of just setting out a stick of butter on a dish, consider molding the butter into individual pats shaped into flowerettes, shells, or other shapes. To your guests it will look as if you've spent hours hand-sculpting the butter for them to enjoy, when actually it takes only a few minutes of your time. The mold does all the work. Various kinds of molds are available in most housewares departments or stores; if you can't find those intended just for butter, small cookie molds are fine for the job. Soften the butter at room temperature (do *not* melt it on the stove), and then press it into the molds. Refrigerate until the butter hardens inside the molds; then pop the shapes out. They will keep their form as long as they are refrigerated, but if you wish to stack one on top of the other, place squares of waxed paper in between them. Do keep some margarine in the refrigerator for guests who prefer it.

If you enjoy baking your own bread, experiment with a variety of shapes. Bread dough can be braided, shaped into a wreath, or even used to hand-build a snowman, a cat, a dinosaur, a guitar, even an entire tool set with hammer and nails. Use the dough as you would children's clay, shaping and poking and pinching it to create the designs you want. Then bake it. All you need is a good, basic recipe for bread (dessert breads won't hold the shapes) and your imagination. (Children especially enjoy the chance to eat a dinosaur for breakfast.)

Be sure to seek out menu items for those guests who are strict vegetarians (no milk products, eggs, meat, or fish), as well as those who have food allergies (wheat, milk products, and nuts are common triggers). Some guests may have other dietary restrictions and therefore minimize their consumption of sugar, fats, or high-calorie items in general. It is always good advice to consider your options ahead of time and be prepared, so that every guest will enjoy a flavorful, creative breakfast menu.

If you wish, invite your guests to join you and your family for lunch or dinner, or offer to prepare a picnic basket for their lunch if they're going for an outing. Of course, this is an extra that is not included in the price set for bed and breakfast. Some hosts do extend this kind of invitation, and it is often most welcome.

Be aware, though, that some would consider adding an extra charge for lunch or dinner "selling" food—which might bring your bed and breakfast under the scrutiny of agencies that govern the sanitation of food served in restaurants. (By offering breakfast as "complimentary," a host usually encounters no problem. After all, no one regulates how you prepare and serve a meal in your own home—on a gratis basis—to friends, family, or business associates.) Of course, a bed and breakfast in a private home is *not* a restaurant. Sometimes there is confusion, which grows when a host starts offering lunches and dinners—and attaching prices to them. So proceed with caution if you wish to offer more than the "free" breakfast; talk first with other bed and breakfast hosts, as well as representatives from B&B associations and managers of reservation service agencies in your area who might have some experience with this issue. If you plan to open a full-time inn, where a restaurant is part of your operation, it's a different story altogether. Here, there is no question that your "restaurant" is indeed a restaurant; you will, of course, have to comply with any regulations governing such commercial enterprises. (See "Health and Safety" in chapter 5.)

Where alcohol is concerned, there is no confusion. No one can sell alcoholic beverages without first obtaining a license to do so. Because of this, bed and breakfast hosts simply do not *sell* liquor to their guests. Some offer a complimentary drink to their guests upon arrival or in the evening before bed, but it is advisable not to advertise this amenity in your literature. Others allow guests to bring in their own liquor if they wish; ice and mixers can be provided by the host. Be aware that offering or permitting alcohol could affect insurance coverage for your B&B, as it is considered an additional risk.

In some states a permit may be required to serve even complimentary alcoholic beverages. Owners of a B&B in Colorado were instrumental in helping enact state legislation (Colorado House Bill 94-1111) that allows B&B owners to obtain such a permit for a small fee. Californians can obtain a similar permit. Be sure to check your state's policy before offering complimentary drinks.

Especially for Children

Creamed eggs are yucky. So are fried tomatoes, a Brie and spinach omelet, and salmon roulade. Ask any five-year-old child. If you're going to be hosting children at your bed and breakfast, you've got to think about what to serve them as a breakfast that they will actually agree to eat. As a group, children are just not very adventurous when it comes to food. It seems as if somewhere along the line, all the children under twelve had a meeting and decided not to eat anything that they had not already tried. The gourmet items that their parents love will most likely remain untouched on the plates of your young visitors.

When the parents are making the reservation with you, ask what their children like to eat. "I have Cheerios. Will they like that? Or will they eat scrambled eggs and toast?" If the child is a fussy eater, the parents can make a few suggestions: "He eats Wheaties, loves raisin toast, and adores pancakes." An advance tip like this can help you plan the menu for the whole family: Go with the creamed eggs and fried tomatoes for the adults, but get a box of Wheaties next time you're at the supermarket; plan to serve raisin toast (and a lot of it) with the quiche; or make pancakes for everyone.

If you don't have the occasion to question the parent about a child's usual diet, you can't go wrong by stocking up on small individual packages of assorted cereals. There's bound to be something in the snack-pack that the child likes, and the other boxes will keep until your next young visitors arrive. Try to stay away from those cereals that are coated with sugar or chocolate, as many parents can be just as fussy about the nutritional value of what their children eat.

Fresh fruit is also a good bet for young people—bananas, apples, oranges. Many children also enjoy hard-boiled eggs (especially if they're decorated with decals or stencils or are dyed). And the old standby—peanut butter and jelly sandwiches—can often get a fussy but hungry child through breakfast. Indeed, it's very hard to predict what children of any age will be willing to eat at the breakfast table. All you can do is try. Who knows? They might even eat the creamed eggs.

B&B Consulting Services

The list is annotated as follows: Code letter "W" indicates workshops, which could be anything from an hour-long class to a seminar that lasts for several days. Code letter "I" refers to individual, private consultations, arranged at a time convenient for both the instructor and the client. Code letter "A" identifies those consultants who offer apprenticeships, where aspiring innkeepers can receive on-the-job training and experience. And code letter "O" indicates consultants who offer online instruction on the Internet.

Arkansas

Eureka Springs: Barbara Gavron, Singleton House B&B, 11 Singleton Street, 72632; (800) 833–3394 or (479) 253–9111; www.singletonhouse.com. *Specialties:* interior design, decorating, business. I A

California

Berkeley: G. Michael Yovino-Young, MAI, 2716 Telegraph Avenue, 94705; (510) 548–1210; www.yovino.com. *Specialty:* inn appraisals. I

Napa: Bed & Breakfast Innstitute of Learning, 1045 Easum Drive, 94558; (800) 631–9080; www.bbinnstitute.com. *Specialties:* start-ups, innsitting, B&B management. I W

Palm Springs: Michael Diaz, 255 North El Cielo Road, Suite 140-136, 92262; (760) 202–3188. *Specialties:* setups, makeovers, marketing, Internet tweaking, telephone sales training. I W

Colorado

Colorado Springs: Sallie and Welling Clark, Holden House 1902 B&B Inn, 1102 West Pikes Peak Avenue, 80904; (719) 471–3980, (888) 565–3980; www.holdenhouse.com. *Specialties*: marketing, finances, operations, industry research, business management. I W

Glenwood Springs: Trent and Susan Blizzard, 1001 Grand Avenue, Suite 203, 81601; (970) 928–7875, (888) 840–5893; www.blizzardinternet.com. *Specialties*: marketing, Web site design, blogs. I

Ridgway: Kit Cassingham, Sage Blossom Consulting, P.O. Box 668, 81432; (970) 626–2277; www.thebandblady.com. *Specialties*: marketing, customer service, valuation, real estate. I W O

Florida

Amelia Island: David Caples and Helen Cook, Lodging Resources Workshops, 98 South Fletcher Avenue, 32034; (800) 500–9625; www.lodgingresources.com. *Specialties:* start-up assistance, marketing plans, business plans, valuation and feasibility studies, financing, real estate. I W A

Kentucky

Louisville: Merle Meyer, Central Park Bed & Breakfast, 1353 South Fourth Street, 40208; (502) 638–1505, (877) 922–1505; www.centralparkbandb.com. *Specialties*: marketing, operations, interim innkeeping. I W A

Maine

Fryeburg: Hilary Jones, Inngenium, Admiral Peary House, 27 Elm Street, 04037; (207) 935–3365; www.inngenium.com. *Specialty*: business plans. I W

Portland: Don Johnson, Inn Your Dreams, 290 Baxter Blvd., #G2, 04101; (207) 775–5818; www.innyourdreams.com. *Specialties*: real estate, financing, marketing. W

Massachusetts

Brewster: Carol and Tom Edmondson, Innkeeping Specialists, P.O. Box 2408, 51 Captain Dunbar Road, 02631; (800) 585–4011; www.innseminars.com. *Specialties*: purchase, business plans, marketing, start-up. I W

New York

Croton-on-Hudson: Barbara Notarius, Alexander Hamilton House, 49 Van Wyck Street, 10520; (914) 271–6737; www .alexanderhamiltonhouse.com. *Specialties:* real estate, zoning, operations. I W A

Lodi: Steve Wirt, Inngenious, 8744 Lower Lake Spur, 14860; (607) 582–7025; www.inn genious.com. *Specialties*: Web site design and promotion. I

Pennsylvania

New Hope: Carl Glassman, The Inn School, Wedgwood Inn, 111 West Bridge Street, 18938; (215) 862–2570; www.wedgwoodinn.com. *Specialties:* real estate, marketing, zoning, financing, operations, upscaling your inn. I W A

Vermont

Brattleboro: Oates & Bredfeldt, P.O. Box 1162, 05302; (802) 254–5931, (866) 720–4667; www.oatesbredfeldt.com. *Specialties:* country inns, real estate purchase, financing. I W

Johnsbury: New England B&B Consultants, 215 Underclyffe Road, 05819; (802) 748 6321; www.nebbc.com. *Specialties*: start-up assistance, assessments, feasibility studies, buying/selling, innsitting. I W

Wisconsin

Siren: Lynn and Del Mottaz, Meadows B&B Seminars, 7209 County Road B, 54872; (520) 625–5726; www.bbonline .com/innkeeper/meadows. *Specialties*: zoning, licensing, business plans, policies, taxes, market niche. I W

Canada

Courtenay, British Columbia: Bruce and Mary Jaffary, Bruman Books & B&B Seminars, 2611A First Street, V9N 8Z3; (250) 338–8045, (877) 883–6579; www.bbbookinfo.com. *Specialties*: planning and operations. I W O

Niagara on the Lake, Ontario: Niagara College of Applied Arts & Technology, Department of Continuing Education, Glendale Campus, 135 Taylor Road, L0S IJ0; (905) 641–2252; www.niagarac.on.ca. *Specialty*: 12-week course, fall semester, covering all aspects of operating a B&B, including business plan. W

St. Catharines, Ontario: Barbara Knight-Woodward, Niagara Bed and Breakfast Reservation Service, (905) 641–9866, (866) 646–8866; www.bandbniagara.com. *Specialty*: all aspects of opening and operating a B&B. I

Appendix 2

Reservation Service Agencies

The following list contains a selection of reservation service agencies (RSAs) throughout the United States and Canada. Please note that many have Web sites, but some still do not at this time. Some states have no reservation services. B&Bs in those areas operate independently. For current information about reservation services in your locality, check the Yellow Pages, your local tourist office, or take a look at the Web sites that provide listings. As a service, the manager of Advance Reservations Inn Arizona / Mi Casa Su Casa maintains a nationwide listing on her own RSA's Web site (www.azres.com). Members of Bed & Breakfast, the National Network (TNN), an association of reservation services, post information on TNN's Web site (www.go-lodging.com).

Alabama

See:

Mississippi: Lincoln Ltd. Bed & Breakfast Mississippi

Tennessee: Natchez Trace Bed & Breakfast Reservation Service

Alaska

Alaska Private Lodgings: Stay with a Friend
P.O. Box 200047
Anchorage 99520
(907) 235–2148
www.alaskangetaways.net
Southcentral and Southeastern Alaska

Alaska Travelers Accommodations
4672 South Tongass Highway
Ketchikan 99901
(907) 247–7117
(800) 928–3308
www.alaskatravelers.com
Southeast Alaska

Ketchikan Reservation Service
412 D-1 Loop Road
Ketchikan 99901
(907) 247–5337
(800) 987–5337
www.ketchikan-lodging.com
Ketchikan area

Arizona

Advance Reservations Inn Arizona/
    Mi Casa Su Casa
P.O. Box 950
Tempe 85280
(480) 990–0682
(800) 456–0682
www.azres.com
Statewide, plus Utah, New Mexico,
    Nevada, and Southern California

Arizona Trails Travel Services
P.O. Box 18998
Fountain Hills 85269
(480) 837–4284
(888) 799–4284
www.arizonatrails.com

Statewide, plus Utah, Southern California,
    and Las Vegas

Arkansas

See:
Missouri: Ozark Mountain Bed & Break-
    fast Service

California

Bed and Breakfast Exchange of Marin
45 Entrata Avenue
San Anselmo 94960
(415) 485–1971
www.bedandbreakfastmarin.com
Sausalito, San Anselmo, Fairfax, Mill
    Valley, and Woodacre

Bed & Breakfast San Francisco
P.O. Box 420009
San Francisco 94142
(415) 899–0060
www.bbsf.com
Greater San Francisco wine and gold
    country, Monterey, and Carmel

See also:
Arizona: Arizona Trails Travel Services;
    Advance Reservations Inn Arizona/Mi
    Casa Su Casa
Washington: A Pacific Reservation
    Service

Colorado

Colorado Bed and Breakfast "On the
   Web"
1534 Stoneleigh Court, #1029
Arlington, TX 76011
(817) 462–0289
http://colorado-bnb.com

Connecticut

See:
Massachusetts: Berkshire Bed & Breakfast
   Reservation Service

Delaware

Bed & Breakfast of Delaware
2701 Landon Drive, Suite 200
Wilmington 19810
(302) 479–9500
Statewide, plus Maryland, Pennsylvania,
   and Virginia

District of Columbia

Bed & Breakfast Accommodations, Ltd.
P.O. Box 12011
Washington, DC 20005
(413) 582–9888
(877) 893–3233
www.bedandbreakfastdc.com
Washington, D.C., and nearby Maryland
   and Virginia suburbs

Georgia

Bed & Breakfast Atlanta
790 North Avenue NE
Atlanta 30306
(404) 875–0525
(800) 967–3224
www.bedandbreakfastatlanta.com
Metro Atlanta and nearby suburbs

Hawaii

Affordable Accommodations Maui
2825 Kauhale Street
Kihei 96753
(808) 879–7865
(888) 333–9747
www.affordablemaui.com
Maui area

All Islands Bed & Breakfast
(808) 263–2342
(800) 542–0344
www.all-islands.com
Statewide

Bed & Breakfast Hawaii
P.O. Box 449
Kapaa 96746
(808) 822–7771
(800) 733–1632
www.bandb-hawaii.com
Statewide

Bed & Breakfast Honolulu (Statewide)
3242 Kaohinani Drive
Honolulu 96817
(808) 595–7533
(800) 288–4666
www.hawaiibnb.com
Statewide

The Chalet Kilauea Collection
P.O. Box 998
Volcano 96785
(808) 967–7786
(800) 937–7786
www.volcano-hawaii.com
Statewide

Hawaii's Best Bed & Breakfasts
571 Pauku Street
Kailua 96734
(808) 263–3100
(800) 262–9912
www.bestbnb.com
Statewide

See also:
Washington: A Pacific Reservation
Service

Illinois

At Home Inn Chicago, Inc.
P.O. Box 14088
Chicago 60614
(312) 640–1050
(800) 375–7084

www.athomeinnchicago.com
Downtown Chicago and nearby
neighborhoods

Kentucky

Bluegrass Bed & Breakfast Reservation
Service
2785 McGowans Ferry Pike
Versailles 40383
(859) 873–3208
Central Kentucky

Louisiana

Bed & Breakfast, Inc. Reservation Service
1021 Moss Street, Box 52257
New Orleans 70152
(504) 342–4861
(800) 729–4640
www.historiclodging.com
New Orleans

New Orleans Bed & Breakfast and French
Quarter Accommodations
828 Rue Royal, Suite 259
New Orleans 70116
(504) 561–0447
(888) 240–0070
www.neworleansbandb.com
Greater New Orleans

See also:
Mississippi: Lincoln Ltd. Bed & Breakfast
Mississippi

Maryland

See:

Delaware: Bed & Breakfast of Delaware
District of Columbia: Bed & Breakfast
Accommodations, Ltd.
Virginia: Blue Ridge Bed & Breakfast

Massachusetts

Bed and Breakfast Agency of Boston
47 Commercial Wharf
Boston 02110
(617) 720–3540
(800) 248–9262
www.boston-bnbagency.com
Boston and vicinity, Cape Cod

Bed and Breakfast Associates Bay Colony
P.O. Box 57166
Boston 02457
(781) 449–5302
(888) 486–6018
www.bnbboston.com
Boston and suburbs, plus Cape Cod and
the islands

Bed and Breakfast Cambridge & Greater
Boston
P.O. Box 626
Boston 02128
(617) 720–1492
(800) 888–0178
Boston, Cambridge, and nearby towns

Bed and Breakfast Cape Cod
P.O. Box 1312
Orleans 02653
(508) 255–3824
(800) 541–6226
www.bedandbreakfastcapecod.com
Cape Cod and the islands

Bed & Breakfast Reservations—North
Shore/Greater Boston/Cape Cod
11A Beach Road
Gloucester 01930
(617) 964–1606
(978) 281–9505
(800) 832–2632
www.bbreserve.com
North Shore, Greater Boston, and Cape
Cod (mainland)

Berkshire Bed & Breakfast Reservation
Service
(800) 762–2751
Berkshire mountains area, central Massachusetts, northern Connecticut, and
eastern New York

Greater Boston Hospitality
P.O. Box 525
Newton 02456
(617) 393–1548
www.bostonbedandbreakfast.com
Boston and suburbs

Host Homes of Boston
P.O. Box 117, Waban Branch
Boston 02468
(617) 244–1308
(800) 600–1308
Web site: www.hosthomesofboston.com
Boston and Greater Boston area

Nantucket Accommodations
P.O. Box 217
Nantucket 02554
(508) 228–9559
www.nantucketaccommodation.com
Nantucket

See also:
New York: American Country Collection
  of Bed & Breakfast Homes

Mississippi

Lincoln Ltd. Bed & Breakfast Mississippi
P.O. Box 3459
Meridian 39303
(601) 482–5483
(800) 633–6477
www.bandbmississippi.com
Statewide, plus Alabama, Louisiana, and
  Tennessee

See also:
Tennessee: Natchez Trace Bed & Breakfast
  Reservation Service

Missouri

Ozark Mountain Bed & Breakfast Service
P.O. Box 295
Branson 65615
(417) 334–4720
(800) 933–8529
www.ozarkbedandbreakfast.com
Southern Missouri and northern
  Arkansas

Nevada

See:
Arizona: Advance Reservations Inn
  Arizona/Mi Casa Su Casa; Arizona
  Trails Travel Services

New Mexico

Bed and Breakfast of New Mexico
369 Montezuma #167
Santa Fe 87501
(505) 982–3332
(888) 511–2200
www.santafebnb.com
Statewide

See also:
Arizona: Advance Reservations Inn
  Arizona/Mi Casa Su Casa

New York

All Around The Town
270 Lafayette Street, Suite 804
New York 10012
(212) 334–2655
(800) 443–3800
www.newyorkcitybestbb.com
New York City

American Country Collection of Bed &
    Breakfast Homes
1353 Union Street
Schenectady 12308
(518) 370–4948
(800) 810–4948
www.bandbreservations.com
Eastern New York State, western Massa-
    chusetts, and Vermont

At Home in New York
P.O. Box 407
New York 10185
(212) 956–3125
(800) 692–4262
www.athomeny.com
New York City boroughs

Bed & Breakfast Network of New York
130 Barrow Street, Suite 508
New York 10014
(212) 645–8134
(800) 900–8134
www.bedandbreakfastnetny.com
New York City

City Lights Bed & Breakfast
P.O. Box 244
1562 First Avenue
New York 10028
(212) 737–7049
www.citylightsnewyork.com
New York City

Manhattan Getaways
P.O. Box 1994
New York 10101
(212) 956–2010
www.manhattangetaways.com
New York City

A Reasonable Alternative (Long Island)
117 Spring Street
Port Jefferson 11777
(631) 928–4034
www.areasonablealternative.com
Long Island area

See also:
Massachusetts: Berkshire Bed & Breakfast
    Reservation Service

Ohio

Private Lodgings
P.O. Box 18557
Cleveland 44118
(216) 291–1209
www.privatelodgings.com
Greater Cleveland area

Oregon

See:

Washington: A Pacific Reservation
  Service

Pennsylvania

Bed & Breakfast Connections of
  Philadelphia
P.O. Box 21
Devon 19333
(610) 687–3565
(800) 448–3619
www.bnbphiladelphia.com
Philadelphia and suburbs, eastern Pennsylvania, Susquehanna River Valley,
  and Lancaster County

Rest and Repast
P.O. Box 179
Boalsburg 16827
(814) 238–1484
(800) 262–2655
www.restandrepast.com
Central Pennsylvania, Penn State area,
  and selected statewide listings

See also:

Delaware: Bed & Breakfast of Delaware

Rhode Island

Bed & Breakfast Newport, Ltd.
7 Park Street
Newport 02840
(401) 846–5408
(800) 800–8765
www.bbnewport.com
Newport

Rhode Island Getaways
76 Armstrong Avenue, 1R
Providence 02903
(401) 486–2021
www.rigetaways.com
Statewide

South Carolina

Historic Charleston Bed & Breakfast
57 Broad Street
Charleston 29401
(843) 722–6606
(800) 743–3583
www.historiccharlestonbedandbreakfast
  .com
Charleston and vicinity

Tennessee

Natchez Trace Bed & Breakfast Reservation Service
P.O. Box 193
Hampshire 38461
(931) 285–2777
(800) 377–2770
www.bbonline.com/natcheztrace
Natchez Trace Parkway area, Alabama, and Mississippi

See also:
Mississippi: Lincoln Ltd. Bed & Breakfast Mississippi

Texas

Bed & Breakfast Texas Style
6374 Ivanhoe Lane
Beaumont 77706
(409) 860–9100
(800) 899–4538
www.bnbtexasstyle.com
Statewide

First Class Bed & Breakfast Reservation Service
P.O. Box 631
Fredericksburg 78624
(888) 991–6749
www.fredericksburg-lodging.com
Fredericksburg and surrounding Hill Country area

Gästehaus Schmidt Fredericksburg Lodging Company
231 West Main
Fredericksburg 78624
(830) 997–5612
(866) 427–8374
www.fbglodging.com
Fredericksburg and Hill Country area

Main Street Bed and Breakfast Reservation Service
337 East Main Street
Fredericksburg 78624
(830) 997–0153
(888) 559–8555
www.travelmainstreet.com
Fredericksburg and Central Texas Hill Country

Utah

See:
Arizona: Advance Reservations Inn Arizona/Mi Casa Su Casa; Arizona Trails Travel Services

Vermont

See:
New York: American Country Collection of Bed & Breakfast Homes

Virginia

Blue Ridge Bed & Breakfast
2458 Castleman Road
Berryville 22611
(540) 955–1246
(800) 296–1246
www.blueridgebb.com
Statewide, plus Maryland and West
Virginia

Guesthouses Bed & Breakfast
P.O. Box 5737
Charlottesville 22905
(434) 979–7264
www.va-guesthouses.com
Greater Charlottesville and Albemarle
County

See also:
Delaware: Bed & Breakfast of Delaware
District of Columbia: Bed & Breakfast
Accommodations, Ltd.

Washington

A Greater Tacoma Bed & Breakfast
Reservation Service
619 North K Street
Tacoma 98403
(253) 627–6916
(888) 627–1920
www.plumduff.com
Tacoma and suburbs

A Pacific Reservation Service
2040 Westlake Avenue North, #301
Seattle 98019
(206) 439–7677
(800) 684–2932
www.seattlebedandbreakfast.com
Seattle and statewide, plus Oregon, California, Hawaii, and British Columbia

West Virginia

See:
Virginia: Blue Ridge Bed & Breakfast

British Columbia

Garden City Bed and Breakfast
    Reservation Service
660 Jones Terrace
Victoria V8Z 2L7
(250) 479–1986
(866) 247–2421
www.bc-bed-breakfast.com
Vancouver and Victoria

Old English Bed & Breakfast Registry
1226 Silverwood Crescent
North Vancouver V7P 1J3
(604) 986–5069
www.bandbinn.com
Vancouver and Victoria

See also:
Washington: A Pacific Reservation
Service

Ontario

Downtown Toronto Association of Bed
    and Breakfast Guesthouses
P.O. Box 190 Station B
Toronto M5T 2W1
(416) 410–3938
(888) 559–5515
www.bnbinfo.com
Toronto area

Niagara Bed & Breakfast Reservation
    Service
(905) 641–9866
Web site: www.bandbniagara.com

The Niagara-on-the-Lake Bed & Breakfast
    Service
(866) 739–4445
www.vaxxine.com/bb
Niagara lake region

Toronto Bed & Breakfast Reservation
    Service
253 College Street, Box 269
Toronto M5T 1R5
(705) 738–9449
(877) 922–6522
www.torontobandb.com
Toronto area

Quebec

Downtown B&B Network in Montreal
3458 Laval Avenue
Montreal H2X 3C8
(514) 289–9749
(800) 267–5180
www.bbmontreal.qc.ca
Montreal

Appendix 3
State Bed and Breakfast Associations

Below is a list of selected bed and breakfast associations for the United States and Canada. Please note that some states and provinces have no associations, while others may have multiple associations, usually covering a specific region or city. Some associations are "virtual," that is, a number of B&Bs have joined together to maintain a Web site but do not have an office address, phone number, and/or an association e-mail address. To locate the most current information about local associations, check the following Web sites: www.bbonline .com, www.lanierbb.com, and www.bedandbreakfast.com. Canadian B&B associations are listed at www.bbcanada.com.

Alabama

Bed & Breakfast Association of Alabama
P.O. Box 707
Montgomery 36101
www.bedandbreakfastalabama.com

Alaska

Alaska's Mat-Su Bed & Breakfast Association
P.O. Box 873507
Wasilla 99687
www.alaskabnbhosts.com

Anchorage Alaska Bed & Breakfast Association
P.O. Box 242623
Anchorage 99524
(907) 272–5909
(888) 584–5147
www.anchorage-bnb.com

Bed and Breakfast Association of Alaska
7800 North Lucky Shot Lane
Palmer 99645
www.alaskabba.com

Arizona

Arizona Association of Bed & Breakfast
  Inns
11770 East Rambling Trail
Tucson 85747
(800) 752–1912
www.arizona-bed-breakfast.com

Bed and Breakfast Sedona Guild
65 Piki Drive
Sedona 86336
(800) 915–4442
www.bbsedona.net

Arkansas

Bed & Breakfast Association of Arkansas
17221 Highway 9
Mountain View 72560
www.bedandbreakfastarkansas.com

California

Bed and Breakfast Association of Sonoma
  Valley
3250 Trinity Road
Glen Ellen 95442
(800) 969–4667
www.sonomabb.com

California Association of Bed & Breakfast
  Inns
2715 Porter Street
Soquel 95073

(800) 373–9251
www.cabbi.com

Gold Country Bed & Breakfast Inns of
  Tuolumne County
P.O. Box 462
Sonora 95370
www.goldbnbs.com

Lake Tahoe Bed and Breakfast Association
(800) 562–1292
www.bedandbreakfasts.com

San Diego Bed & Breakfast Guild
(800) 619–7666
www.bandbguildsandiego.org

Colorado

Bed & Breakfast Innkeepers of Colorado
P.O. Box 38416
Colorado Springs 80937
(800) 265–7696
www.innsofcolorado.org

Distinctive Inns of Colorado
P.O. Box 4113
Boulder 80306
(800) 866–0621
(303) 665–0974
www.bedandbreakfastinns.org

Connecticut

Bed and Breakfasts of the Mystic Coast
P.O. Box 555

Old Mystic 06372
(800) 886–6059
www.thebbmc.com

Delaware

Association of Delaware Shore Inns & Bed
and Breakfasts
(302) 684–5166
www.deshorebnbs.com

Florida

Florida Bed & Breakfast Inns
c/o Association Management Services
P.O. Box 2147
Stafford, TX 77497
(800) 524–1880
www.florida-inns.com

Georgia

Georgia Innkeepers Association
1789 Bear Gap Road
Clarkesville 30523
(706) 754–7295
www.georgiainnkeepersassociation.com

Hawaii

Hawaii Island Bed & Breakfast Association
P.O. Box 1890
Honokaa 96727
www.stayhawaii.com

Kaua'i Bed and Breakfast Association
1470 Wana'ao Road
Kapa'a 96746
(800) 533–9316
www.kauaibb.com

Maui Bed & Breakfast Association
www.bedbreakfastmaui.com

Idaho

The North Idaho Bed and Breakfast
Association
www.bb-cda.com

Illinois

Illinois Bed & Breakfast Association
6130 Old Highway 50
Aviston 62216
(618) 228–7068
www.go-illinois.com

Indiana

Amish Country Bed and Breakfast Group
219 Caravan Drive
Elkhart 46514
(800) 377–3579
www.amishcountrybb.org

Indiana Bed & Breakfast Association
P.O. Box 354
Salem 47167
(877) 846–4222
www.indianabedandbreakfast.org

Iowa

Iowa Bed & Breakfast Guild
9001 Hickman Road, Suite 220
Des Moines 50322
(800) 743–4692
www.ia-bednbreakfast-inns.com

Iowa Bed & Breakfast Innkeepers
    Association
P.O. Box 171
Spencer 51301
(800) 888–4667
www.iabedandbreakfast.com

Kansas

Kansas Bed & Breakfast Association
221 Arch Street
Leavenworth 66048
(888) 572–2632
www.kbba.com

Kentucky

Bed & Breakfast Association of Kentucky
2941 Perryville Road
Highway 150 East
Springfield 40069
(888) 281–8188
www.kentuckybb.com

Louisiana

Louisiana Bed & Breakfast Association
1165 South Foster Drive
Baton Rouge 70806
(225) 346–1857
www.louisianabandb.com

Maine

Maine Innkeepers Association
304 US Route 1
Freeport 04032
(207) 865–6100
www.maineinns.com

Maryland

Maryland Bed & Breakfast Association
1001 Atlantic Avenue
Ocean City 21842
(410) 289–8894
(888) 226–6223
www.marylandbb.com

Massachusetts

Five College Area Bed and Breakfast
    Association
P.O. Box 215
Northampton 01060
www.fivecollegebb.com

Hampshire Hills B&B Association
P.O. Box 211
Williamsburg 01096
(888) 414–7664
www.hhbba.com

Massachusetts Lodging Association
7 Liberty Square
Boston 02109
(617) 720–1776
www.masslodging.com

Michigan

The Bed & Breakfast Association of
    Southern Michigan
58138 M-40 North
Jones 49061
(800) 249–5910
www.getaway2smi.com

Michigan Lake to Lake Bed & Breakfast
    Association
P.O. Box 863
Harrison 48625
(989) 539–7935
www.laketolake.com

Minnesota

Minnesota Bed & Breakfast Association
620 Ramsey Street
Hastings 55033
(651) 438–7499
www.minnesotabedandbreakfasts.org

Mississippi

Bed & Breakfast Association of
    Mississippi
212 Walnut Street
Port Gibson 39150
(601) 437–2843
www.missbab.com

Missouri

Bed & Breakfast Inns of Missouri
204 East High Street
Jefferson City 65101
(800) 213–5642
www.bbim.org

Montana

Montana Bed & Breakfast Association
c/o MTBBA President
Fox Hollow B&B
545 Mary Road
Bozeman 59718
(406) 582–8440
www.mtbba.com

Nebraska

Nebraska Association of Bed & Breakfasts
2730 Manse Avenue
Lincoln 68502
(877) 223–6222
www.nabb1.com

New Hampshire

Bed and Breakfast Association of New
  Hampshire
100 Lower Bay Road
Sanbornton 03269
(603) 524–0087
www.nhbba.com

Monadnock Lodging Association
P.O. Box 1088
Keene 03431
(603) 924–6543
www.nhlodging.org

New England Inns & Resorts Association
P.O. Box 1089
44 Lafayette Road, Unit 6
North Hampton 03862
(603) 964–6689
www.newenglandinns.com

New Hampshire Lodging & Restaurant
  Association
P.O. Box 1175
14 Dixon Avenue, Suite 208
Concord 03302
(603) 228–9585
www.nhlra.com

New Jersey

Bed & Breakfast Innkeepers Association of
  New Jersey
P.O. Box 108

Spring Lake 07762
(732) 449–3535
www.bbianj.com

New Mexico

New Mexico Bed & Breakfast Association
P.O. Box 70454
Albuquerque 87157
(800) 661–6649
www.nmbba.org

New York

Central New York Bed & Breakfast
  Association
www.cnybb.com

Empire State Bed & Breakfast Association
www.esbba.com

Finger Lakes Bed & Breakfast Association
4610 State Route 14
Rock Stream 14878
(877) 422–6327
www.flbba.org

North Carolina

North Carolina Bed & Breakfasts and Inns
9650 Strickland Road, Suite 103-254
Raleigh 27615
(800) 849–5392
www.ncbbi.org

North Dakota

North Dakota Bed & Breakfast Association
423 8th Street South
Fargo 58103
(888) 273–3380
www.ndbba.com

Ohio

Bed & Breakfast Council of OH&LA
Ohio Hotel & Lodging Association
692 North High Street, Suite 212
Columbus 43215
(614) 461–6462
(800) 589–6462
www.ohla.org

Ohio Bed & Breakfast Association
5310 East Main Street, Suite 104
Columbus 43213
(614) 868–5567
www.ohiobba.com

Oklahoma

Oklahoma Bed & Breakfast Association
328 East First Street
Edmond 73034
(866) 676–5522
www.oklabedandbreakfast.com

Oregon

Central Oregon Bed & Breakfast
 Association
www.centraloregonbedandbreakfasts.com

Oregon Bed & Breakfast Guild
P.O. Box 3187
Ashland 97520
(800) 944–6196
www.obbg.org

Pennsylvania

Authentic Bed & Breakfasts of Lancaster
 County
(800) 552–2632
www.authenticbandb.com

Brandywine Valley Bed & Breakfasts
www.bvbb.com

North Central Pennsylvania Bed & Breakfast Association
c/o Larry Emery
80 Eagle Mill Lane
Williamsport 17701
www.pa-bedandbreakfast.com

Pennsylvania Mid-State Bed and Breakfast
 Association
P.O. Box 336
Boalsburg 16827
www.bedandbreakfastpa.com

Pennsylvania Tourism & Lodging
Association
128 Walnut Street
Harrisburg 17101
(717) 232–8880
www.patourism.org

Pittsburgh Bed & Breakfast Association
www.pittsburghbnb.com

Rhode Island

Newport Inns and Bed & Breakfast
Association, Inc.
P.O. Box 1063
Newport 02840
www.newportinns.com

South Carolina

South Carolina Bed & Breakfast
Association
P.O. Box 2020
Georgetown 29442
(888) 599–1234
www.southcarolinabedandbreakfast.com

South Dakota

Bed & Breakfast Innkeepers of South
Dakota
P.O. Box 7682
Rapid City 57709
(888) 500–4667
www.southdakotabb.com

Tennessee

Tennessee Bed & Breakfast Innkeepers
Association
5341 Mountain View Road, Suite 150
Antioch 37013
(800) 820–8144
www.tennessee-inns.com

Texas

Historic Accommodations of Texas
P.O. Box 301596
Austin 78703
(512) 371–9884
(800) 428–0368
www.hat.org

The Heart of Texas Bed & Breakfast
Owners Association
http://heartoftexasbb.com

Utah

Bed & Breakfast Inns of Utah, Inc.
P.O. Box 3066
Park City 84060
www.bbiu.org

Vermont

Chester Innkeepers Association
P.O. Box 788
Chester 05143
www.chesterlodging.com

Heart of Vermont Lodging Association
P.O. Box 711
Middlebury 05753
www.vermontinns.com

Virginia

Bed & Breakfast Association of Virginia
P.O. Box 1077
Standardsville 22973
(888) 660–2228
www.innvirginia.com

Virginia's Eastern Shore Bed and Breakfast Association
www.virginiabedbreakfasts.com

Washington

Washington Bed & Breakfast Guild
2442 Northwest Market Street, #355
Seattle 98017
(800) 647–2918
www.wbbg.com

West Virginia

Mountainstate Association of Bed & Breakfasts
www.wvbnbs.com

Wisconsin

Madison Wisconsin Area Bed and Breakfast Inns Association
1090 Severson Road
Belleville 53508
www.madisoninns.com

Wisconsin Bed & Breakfast Association
108 South Cleveland Street
Merrill 54452
(715) 539–9222
www.wbba.org

Wisconsin Bed and Breakfast Inns of Distinction Association
1090 Severson Road
Belleville 53508
www.innwisconsin.com

Wyoming

Bed & Breakfast Inns and Ranches of Wyoming
671 Steinle Ranch Road
Douglas 82633
(307) 359–1289
www.wyomingbnb-ranchrec.com

Cody Country Bed and Breakfast Association
P.O. Box 1943
Cody 82414
www.codybedandbreakfast.com

Canadian Provincial B&B Associations
(Alphabetical by Province or Territory)

Alberta

Alberta Bed & Breakfast Association
www.bbalberta.com

Bed and Breakfast Association of Calgary
111 Sun Canyon Park SE
Calgary T2X 2W4
(403) 286–0777
www.bbcalgary.com

Bed & Breakfast Association of Greater
   Edmonton
(780) 432–7116
www.bbedmonton.com

Canmore Bow Valley Bed & Breakfast
   Association
P.O. Box 8005
Canmore T1W 2T8
www.bbcanmore.com

British Columbia

Association of North Vancouver Bed and
   Breakfast Accommodations
www.bbvancouverbc.com

Western Canada Bed & Breakfast
   Innkeepers Association
P.O. Box 182
Parksville V9P 2G4
www.wcbbia.com

Manitoba

Bed and Breakfast of Manitoba
893 Dorchester Avenue
Winnipeg R3M 0T7
(204) 661–0300
www.bedandbreakfast.mb.ca

New Brunswick

New Brunswick Bed and Breakfast
   Association
(506) 488–8989
www.bbcanada.com/associations/new
   brunswick

Newfoundland and Labrador

Bed & Breakfast/Country Inns Association
   of Newfoundland and Labrador
187 Kenmount Road, ICON Building
St. John's A1B 3P9
(709) 722–2000
(800) 563–0700
bandb.hnl.ca

Nova Scotia

Nova Scotia Bed and Breakfast
   Association
1099 Marginal Road

Halifax B3H 4P7

(902) 423–4480

www.bbcanada.com/associations/
  novascotia

Ontario

Canadian Bed and Breakfast Hosts
  Toronto Downtown Bed and Breakfast
57 Chicora Avenue
Toronto M5R 1T7
(877) 950–6200
www.canadabbhosts.com

Federation of Ontario Bed & Breakfast
  Accommodation
95 King Street West
Gananoque K7G 2G2
www.fobba.com

Prince Edward Island

Bed & Breakfast and Country Inns
  Association of Prince Edward Island
Box 2551
Charlottetown C1A 8C2
www.bandbpei.com

Quebec

Quebec Provincial Association of B&Bs
(418) 522–6354
www.bbbonjourquebec.com

Saskatchewan

Saskatchewan Bed and Breakfast
  Association
Box 694
Lumsden S0G 3C0
(306) 731–2646
www.bbsask.ca

Yukon

Bed & Breakfast Association of the Yukon
Box 31518
Whitehorse Y1A 6K8
www.yukonbandb.com

Tourist Offices

Alabama

Alabama Bureau of Tourism & Travel
401 Adams Avenue, Suite 126
P.O. Box 4927
Montgomery 36103
(334) 242–4546
(800) 252–2262
www.touralabama.org

Alaska

Alaska Travel Industry Association
2600 Cordova Street, Suite 201
Anchorage 99503
(800) 327–9372
www.travelalaska.com

Arizona

Arizona Office of Tourism
1110 West Washington Street, Suite 155
Phoenix 85007
(602) 364–3700
(888) 520–3434
www.arizonaguide.com

Arkansas

Arkansas Department of Parks & Tourism
One Capitol Mall
Little Rock 72201
(501) 682–7777
(800) 628–8725
www.arkansas.com

California

California Division of Tourism
P.O. Box 1499
Sacramento 95812
(916) 444–4429
(800) 862 2543
www.gocalif.ca.gov

Colorado

Colorado Tourism Office
1625 Broadway, Suite 1700
Denver 80202
(303) 892–3840
(800) 265–6723
www.colorado.com

Connecticut

Connecticut Commission on Culture and
    Tourism
Tourism Division
505 Hudson Street
Hartford 06106
(860) 270–8080
(800) 282–6863
www.tourism.state.ct.us

Delaware

Delaware Tourism Office
99 Kings Highway
Dover 19901
(302) 739–4271
(866) 284–7483
www.visitdelaware.net

District of Columbia

Washington, D.C., Convention & Tourism
    Corporation
901 7th Street NW, 4th Floor
Washington 20001
(202) 789–7000
(800) 422–8644
www.washington.org

Florida

Visit Florida
661 East Jefferson Street, Suite 300
Tallahassee 32301
(850) 488–5607
(888) 735–2872
www.visitflorida.com

Georgia

Georgia Department of Industry, Trade &
    Tourism
75 Fifth Street
Atlanta 30308
(404) 656–3590
(800) 847–4842
www.georgia.org/travel

Hawaii

Hawaii Visitors and Convention Bureau
2270 Kalakaua Avenue, Suite 801
Honolulu 96815
(808) 923–1811
(800) 924–0266
www.visit.hawaii.org

Idaho

Idaho Division of Tourism Development
700 West State Street
P.O. Box 83720
Boise 83720
(208) 334–2470
(800) 847–4843
www.visitid.org

Illinois

Illinois Bureau of Tourism
James R. Thompson Center
100 West Randolph Street
Chicago 60601
(800) 406–6418
(800) 226–6632
www.enjoyillinois.com

Indiana

Indiana Office of Tourism Development
One North Capitol, Suite 100
Indianapolis 46204
(317) 232–8860
(800) 677–9800
www.visitindiana.com

Iowa

Iowa Tourism Office
200 East Grand Avenue
Des Moines 50309
(515) 242–4705
(888) 472–6035
www.traveliowa.com

Kansas

Kansas Travel and Tourism
1000 South Jackson Street, Suite 100
Topeka 66612
(785) 296–8478
(800) 252–6727
www.travelks.com

Kentucky

Kentucky Department of Tourism
Capital Plaza Tower, 22nd Floor
500 Mero Street
Frankfort 40601
(502) 564–4930
(800) 225–8747
www.kentuckytourism.com

Louisiana

Louisiana Office of Tourism
P.O. Box 94291
Baton Rouge 70804
(225) 342–8100
(800) 227–4386
www.louisianatravel.com

Maine

Maine Office of Tourism
59 State House Station
Augusta 04333
(207) 287–5711
(888) 624–6345
www.visitmaine.com

Maryland

Maryland Office of Tourism Development
217 East Redwood Street, Ninth Floor
Baltimore 21202
(866) 639–3526
www.mdisfun.org

Massachusetts

Massachusetts Office of Travel & Tourism
10 Park Plaza, Suite 4510
Boston 02116
(617) 973–8500
(800) 277–6277
www.mass-vacation.com

Michigan

Travel Michigan
P.O. Box 30226
Lansing 48909
(517) 373–0670
(888) 784–7328
www.michigan.org

Minnesota

Explore Minnesota Tourism
121 Seventh Place East
Metro Square, Suite 100
Saint Paul 55101
(651) 296–5029
(888) 868–7476
www.exploreminnesota.com

Mississippi

Mississippi Division of Tourism
     Development
P.O. Box 849
Jackson 39205

(601) 359–3297
(866) 733–6477
www.visitmississippi.org

Missouri

Missouri Division of Tourism
P.O. Box 1055
Jefferson City 65102
(573) 751–4133
(800) 519–2100
www.missouritourism.org

Montana

Travel Montana
301 South Park
P.O. Box 200533
Helena 59620
(406) 841–2870
(800) 847–4868
www.visitmt.com

Nebraska

Nebraska Division of Travel and Tourism
P.O. Box 98907
Lincoln 68509
(402) 471–3791
(877) 632–7275
www.visitnebraska.org

Nevada

Nevada Commission on Tourism
410 North Carson Street
Carson City 89710
(775) 687–4322
(800) 638–2328
www.travelnevada.com

New Hampshire

New Hampshire Division of Travel and
    Tourism Development
172 Pembroke Road
P.O. Box 1856
Concord 03302
(603) 271–2665
(800) 386–4664
www.visitnh.gov

New Jersey

New Jersey Commerce, Economic
    Growth, & Tourism Commission
P.O. Box 820
Trenton 08625
(609) 777–0885
(800) 847–4865
www.visitnj.org

New Mexico

New Mexico Tourism Department
491 Old Santa Fe Trail

Santa Fe 87503
(505) 827–7400
(800) 545–2070
www.newmexico.org

New York

I Love New York Tourism
30 South Pearl Street
Albany 12245
(518) 474–4116
(800) 225–5697
www.iloveny.com

North Carolina

North Carolina Division of Tourism, Film
    and Sports Development
301 North Wilmington Street
Raleigh 27601
(919) 733–8372
(800) 847–4862
www.visitnc.com

North Dakota

North Dakota Tourism Division Century
    Center
1600 East Century Avenue, Suite 2
P.O. Box 2057
Bismarck 58502
(701) 328–2525
(800) 435–5663
www.ndtourism.com

Ohio

Ohio Division of Travel & Tourism
77 South High Street
P.O. Box 1001
Columbus 43216
(614) 466–8844
(800) 282–5393
www.ohiotourism.com

Oklahoma

Oklahoma Travel & Tourism Division
P.O. Box 52002
Oklahoma City 73152
(405) 230–8400
(800) 652–6552
www.travelok.com

Oregon

Oregon Tourism Commission
670 Hawthorne SE, Suite 240
Salem 97301
(503) 378–8850
(800) 547–7842
www.traveloregon.com

Pennsylvania

Pennsylvania Tourism Office
Department of Community and
    Economic Development
Commonwealth Keystone Building, 4th
Floor

400 North Street
Harrisburg 17120
(717) 787–5453
(800) 237–4363
www.experiencepa.com

Rhode Island

Rhode Island Tourism Division
1 West Exchange Street
Providence 02903
(401) 222–2601
(800) 556–2484
www.visitrhodeisland.com

South Carolina

South Carolina Department of Parks,
    Recreation, and Tourism
1205 Pendleton Street, Room 505
Columbia 29201
(803) 734–1700
(800) 346–3634
www.discoversouthcarolina.com

South Dakota

South Dakota Department of Tourism
    and State Development
711 East Wells Avenue
Capitol Lake Plaza
c/o 500 East Capitol Avenue
Pierre 57501
(605) 773–3301

(800) 732–5682

www.travelsd.com

Tennessee

Tennessee Department of Tourism
　Development
Wm. Snodgrass/Tennessee Tower
312 8th Avenue North, 28th Floor
Nashville 37243
(615) 741–2159
(800) 836–6200
www.tnvacation.com

Texas

Texas Tourism Division
P.O. Box 141009
Austin 78714
(512) 936–0101
(800) 888–8839
www.traveltex.com

Utah

Utah Travel Council
300 North State Street
Salt Lake City 84114
(801) 538–1030
(800) 200–1160
www.utah.com

Vermont

Vermont Department of Tourism and
　Marketing
6 Baldwin Street, Drawer 33
Montpelier 05633
(802) 828–3676
(800) 837–6668
www.vermontvacation.com

Virginia

Virginia Tourism Corporation
901 East Byrd Street
Richmond 23219
(804) 786–2051
(800) 847–4882
www.virginia.org

Washington

Washington State Tourism
P.O. Box 42500
Olympia 98504
(800) 544–1800
www.experiencewashington.com

West Virginia

West Virginia Division of Tourism
90 MacCorkle Avenue SW
South Charleston 25303
(304) 558–2200
(800) 225–5982
www.callwva.com

Wisconsin

Wisconsin Department of Tourism
201 West Washington Avenue
P.O. Box 8690
Madison 53708
(608) 266–2161
(800) 432–8747
www.travelwisconsin.com

Wyoming

Wyoming Travel & Tourism
Interstate 25 at College Drive
Cheyenne 82002
(307) 777–7777
(800) 225–5996
www.wyomingtourism.org

Alberta

Travel Alberta
500–900 8th Street SW
Calgary T2R 1J5
(403) 297–2700
(800) 252–3782
www1.travelalberta.com

British Columbia

Tourism British Columbia Marketing
    Office
865 Homby Street, Suite 802
Vancouver V6Z 2G3
(604) 660–2861
(800) 436–6622
www.hellobc.com

Manitoba

Travel Manitoba
155 Carlton Street, Seventh Floor
Winnipeg R3C 3H8
(800) 665–0040
www.travelmanitoba.com

New Brunswick

Tourism and Parks New Brunswick
P.O. Box 12345, Main Station
Campbellton E3N 3T6

(800) 561–0123
www.tourismnbcanada.com

Newfoundland and Labrador

Newfoundland and Labrador Tourism
P.O. Box 8700
St. John's, Newfoundland A1B 4J6
(709) 729–2831
(800) 563–6353
www.gov.nf.ca/tourism

Northwest Territories

Travel Canada's Northwest Territories
NWT Tourism
P.O. Box 610
Yellowknife X1A 2N5
(800) 661–0788
www.explorenwt.com

Nova Scotia

Nova Scotia Department of Tourism,
    Culture, and Heritage
P.O. Box 456
Halifax B3J 2R5
(902) 425–5781
(800) 565–0000
www.novascotia.com

Nunavut

Nunavut Tourism
Box 1450
Iqaluit X0A 0H0
(767) 979–6551
(866) 686–2888
www.nunavuttourism.com

Ontario

Ontario Tourism Marketing Partnership
   Corporation
900 Bay Street
Hearst Block, Tenth Floor
Toronto M7A 2E1
(416) 325–9823
(800) 668–2746
www.ontariotravel.net

Prince Edward Island

Tourism PEI
P.O. Box 2000
Charlottetown C1A 7N8
(902) 368–5540
(800) 463–4734
www.peiplay.com

Quebec

Tourisme Québec
P.O. Box 979
Montreal H3C 2W3
(514) 873–2015
(877) 266–5687
www.bonjourquebec.com

Saskatchewan

Tourism Saskatchewan
1922 Park Street
Regina S4N 7M4
(306) 787–9600
(877) 237–2273
www.sasktourism.com

Yukon

Department of Tourism and Culture
Government of Yukon
P.O. Box 2703
Whitehorse Y1A 2C6
(867) 661–0494
www.touryukon.com

Appendix 5
Bed and Breakfast Book List

Following is a selection of books that feature bed and breakfast accommodations. Check your local bookstores for current editions of the titles that interest you. If a publisher is a B&B association or other industry representative, contact the publisher directly; some bookstores may not carry titles published independently. To mail-order books, an excellent resource for current titles is the Web site www.amazon.com.

United States

Nationwide

Bed & Breakfasts and Country Inns, by Deborah Edwards Sakach (American Historic Inns).

The Complete Guide to Bed & Breakfasts, Inns & Guesthouses International, by Pamela Lanier (Lanier Publishing).

Good Bed & Breakfast Guide, by Elsie Dillard (Pelican).

The Official Bed & Breakfast Guide and Cookbook: United States, Canada & the Caribbean, by Phyllis Featherston and Barbara Ostler (National Bed & Breakfast Association).

The Official Guide to American Historic Inns, by Deborah Edwards Sakach (American Historic Inns).

Pelican's Select Guide to American Bed and Breakfasts, by Judi Russell (Pelican).

Pets on the Go: The Definitive Pet Accommodation and Vacation Guide, by Dawn and Robert Habgood (Dawbert Press).

New England

Bed, Breakfast & Bike Northeast, by Cynthia Reeder (Anacus Press).

The Berkshire Hills and Pioneer Valley of Western Massachusetts: An Explorer's Guide, by Christine Tree and Williams Davis (Countryman Press).

Best Places to Stay: New England, by Christina Tree and Kim Grant (Houghton Mifflin).

Cape Cod, Martha's Vineyard and Nantucket: An Explorer's Guide, by Kim Grant (Countryman Press).

Compass American Guides: Boston, by Patricia Harris, David Lyon, Robert Holmes, and Joel Satore (Fodor's).

Compass American Guides: Cape Cod (Fodor's).

Compass American Guides: Maine, by Charles Calhoun and Thomas Mark Szelog (Fodor's).

Compass American Guides: Massachusetts, by Patricia Harris, David Lyon, Anna Mundow, and Lisa Oppenheimer (Fodor's).

Compass American Guides: New Hampshire (Fodor's).

Compass American Guides: Vermont, by Don Mitchell and Luke Powell (Fodor's).

Connecticut: An Explorer's Guide, by Barnett D. Laschever and Andi Marie Fusco (Countryman Press).

Dog-friendly New England, by Trisha Blanchet (Countryman Press).

Inn Spots & Special Places in New England, by Nancy and Richard Woodworth (Wood Pond Press).

Maine: An Explorer's Guide, by Christina Tree and Nancy English (Countryman Press).

Massachusetts: An Explorer's Guide, by Christina Tree and William Davis (Countryman Press).

Mobil Travel Guide: New England (Globe Pequot Press).

New Hampshire: An Explorer's Guide, by Christina Tree and Christine Hamm (Countryman Press).

Quick Escapes Boston, by Sandy MacDonald (Globe Pequot Press).

Recommended Bed & Breakfasts New England, by Eleanor Berman (Globe Pequot Press).

Recommended Country Inns New England, by Elizabeth Squier (Globe Pequot Press).

Rhode Island: An Explorer's Guide, by Phyllis Meras and Katherine Imbrie (Countryman Press).

Vermont: An Explorer's Guide, by Christina Tree and Diane E. Foulds (Countryman Press).

Waterside Escapes in the Northeast: Great Getaways by Lake, River & Sea, by Nancy and Richard Woodworth (Countryman Press).

Mid-Atlantic

Compass American Guides: Manhattan, by Gil Reavill and Michael Yamashita (Fodor's).

Compass American Guides: Pennsylvania, by Douglas L. Root and Jerry Irwin (Fodor's).

Dog-friendly New York, by Trisha Blanchet (Countryman Press).

Dog-friendly Washington, D.C,. & the Mid-Atlantic States, by Trisha Blanchet (Countryman Press).

The Hudson Valley & Catskill Mountains: An Explorer's Guide, by Joanne Michaels (Countryman Press).

Inn Spots & Special Places in the Mid-Atlantic (Wood Pond Press).

Maryland: An Explorer's Guide, by Leonard M. Adkins (Countryman Press).

Mobil Travel Guide: Mid-Atlantic (Globe Pequot Press).

Mobil Travel Guide: New York (Globe Pequot Press).

New Jersey: An Explorer's Guide, by Andi Marie Cantele (Countryman Press).

New York City: An Explorer's Guide, by Paul Karr (Countryman Press).

Quick Escapes New York City, by Susan Farwell (Globe Pequot Press).

Quick Escapes Philadelphia, by Marilyn Odesser-Torpey (Globe Pequot Press).

Quick Escapes Pittsburgh, by Michelle Pilecki (Globe Pequot Press).

Quick Escapes Washington, D.C., by John Fitzpatrick and Holly J. Burkhalter (Globe Pequot Press).

Western New York: An Explorer's Guide, by Christine Smyczynski (Countryman Press).

Southeast

Baldwin's Guide to Inns of Louisiana, by Jack and Winnie Baldwin (Pelican).

Bed, Breakfast & Bike Florida, by Dale V. Lally (Anacus Press).

Bed, Breakfast & Bike Mississippi Valley, by Dale Lally (Anacus Press).

Best Places to Stay: Florida, by Christine Davidson and Bruce Shaw (Houghton Mifflin).

Blue Ridge and Smoky Mountains: An Explorer's Guide, by Jim Hargan (Countryman Press).

Compass American Guides: Florida, by Chelle Walton and Tony Arruza (Fodor's).

Compass American Guides: Kentucky, by Susan H. Reigler (Fodor's).

Compass American Guides: North Carolina, by Sheila Turnage and Jim Hargan (Fodor's).

Compass American Guides: Virginia, by K.M. Kostyal and David M. Doody (Fodor's).

Exploring South Carolina's Islands, by Terrance Zepke (Pineapple Press).

Florida's Finest Inns and Bed & Breakfasts, by Bruce Hunt (Pineapple Press).

Georgia: An Explorer's Guide, by Carol and Dan Thalimer (Countryman Press).

Inn Spots & Special Places in the Southeast, by Nancy and Richard Woodworth (Wood Pond Press).

Inn-to-Inn Walking Guide: Virginia and West Virginia, by Su Clauson-Wicker (Menasha Ridge Press).

Mobil Travel Guide: Coastal Southeast (Globe Pequot Press).

Mobil Travel Guide: Florida (Globe Pequot Press).

Mobil Travel Guide: South (Globe Pequot Press).

Orlando, Central & North Florida: An Explorer's Guide, by Sandra Friend and Kathy Wolf (Countryman Press).

Quick Escapes Atlanta, by Carol and Dan Thalimer (Globe Pequot Press).

Quick Escapes Florida, by W. Lynn Seldon Jr. (Globe Pequot Press).

Quick Escapes Washington, D.C., by John Fitzpatrick and Holly Burkhalter (Globe Pequot Press).

The Shenandoah Valley & Mountains of the Virginias: An Explorer's Guide, by Jim Harrigan (Countryman Press).

South Florida: An Explorer's Guide, by Sandra Friend and Kathy Wolf (Countryman Press).

Midwest

Bed, Breakfast & Bike Midwest, by Robert and Theresa Russell (Anacus Press).

Bed, Breakfast & Bike Western Great Lakes, by Byron Glick and Michele Gast (Anacus Press).

Compass American Guides: Chicago, by Jack Schnedler (Fodor's).

Compass American Guides: Michigan, by Dixie Franklin and Dennis Cox (Fodor's).

Compass American Guides: South Dakota, by T. D. Griffith and Paul Horsted (Fodor's).

Compass American Guides: Wisconsin, by Tracy Will (Fodor's).

Michigan Vacation Guide: Cottages, Chalets, Condos & B&Bs, by Kathleen R. Tedsen, Beverlee Rydel, and Clara M. Rydel (TR Desktop Publishing).

Mobil Travel Guide: Great Plains (Globe Pequot Press).

Mobil Travel Guide: Northern Great Lakes (Globe Pequot Press).

Mobil Travel Guide: Southern Great Lakes (Globe Pequot Press).

Quick Escapes Chicago, by Bonnie Miller Rubin and Marcy Mason (Globe Pequot Press).

Quick Escapes Cleveland, by Marcia Schonberg (Globe Pequot Press).

Quick Escapes Detroit, by Khristi Sigurdson Zimmeth (Globe Pequot Press).

Quick Escapes Minneapolis/St. Paul, by Mark R. Weinberger (Globe Pequot Press).

Southwest

Absolutely Every* Bed & Breakfast in Texas (*Almost), by Carl Hanson (Sasquatch Books).

Compass American Guides: Arizona (Fodor's).

Compass American Guides: New Mexico (Fodor's).

Compass American Guides: Texas, by Mary G. Ramos, Dick Reavis, and Kevin Vandivier (Fodor's).

Mobil Travel Guide: Southwest (Globe Pequot Press).

Mobil Travel Guide: Texas (Globe Pequot Press).

Quick Escapes Dallas/Ft. Worth, by June Naylor (Globe Pequot Press).

West

Best Places: California Wine Country Destinations, by Erika Lenkert (Sasquatch Books).

Best Places: Central California Coast Destinations, by Judith Babcock Wylie (Sasquatch Books).

Best Places: Destinations Marin, by Joanne Miller (Sasquatch Books).

Best Places: Las Vegas, by James Reza (Sasquatch Books).

Best Places: Northern California, by Matthew R. Poole (Sasquatch Books).

Best Places: Northern California Coast Destinations, by Matthew R. Poole (Sasquatch Books).

Best Places: Palm Springs and the Desert Communities, by Robin Kleven (Sasquatch Books).

Best Places: San Diego, by Maribeth Mellin (Sasquatch Books).

Best Places: Southern California, by Stephani Avnet Yates (Sasquatch Books).

Best Places to Kiss in Northern California, by Kate Chynoweth (Sasquatch Books).

Best Places to Kiss in Southern California, by Bonnie Steele (Sasquatch Books).

California Coast, by John J. Osborn Jr. (Countryman Press).

Compass American Guides: Coastal California, by John Doerper and Galen Rowell (Fodor's).

Compass American Guides: Colorado, by Jon Klusmire and Paul Chesley (Fodor's).

Compass American Guides: Hawaii, by Moana Tregaskis, Wayne Levin, and Paul Chesley (Fodor's).

Compass American Guides: Montana, by Norma Tirrell and John Reddy (Fodor's).

Compass American Guides: Nevada, by Deke Castleman (Fodor's).

Compass American Guides: Santa Fe (Fodor's).

Compass American Guides: Utah, by Tom Wharton (Fodor's).

Dog Lover's Companion to California, by Maria Goodavage (Avalon Travel Publishing).

Hawaii: An Explorer's Guide, by Kim Grant (Countryman Press).

Karen Brown's California: Charming Inns & Itineraries, by Clare Brown (Fodor's).

Mobil Travel Guide: Hawaii (Globe Pequot Press).

Mobil Travel Guide: Northern California (Globe Pequot Press).

Mobil Travel Guide: Southern California (Globe Pequot Press).

Montana & Wyoming: An Explorer's Guide, by Alli Rainey Wendling (Countryman Press).

Quick Escapes Denver, by Sherry Spitsnaugle (Globe Pequot Press).

Quick Escapes Las Vegas, by Heidi Knapp Rinella (Globe Pequot Press).

Quick Escapes Los Angeles, by Eleanor Harris and Claudia Harris Lichtig (Globe Pequot Press).

Quick Escapes San Francisco, by Karen Misuraca (Globe Pequot Press).

Recommended Bed & Breakfasts California, by Kathy Strong (Globe Pequot Press).

Northwest

Best Places: Alaska, by Kate Ripley (Sasquatch Books).

Best Places: Destinations Oregon Coast, by Stephanie Irving (Sasquatch Books).

Best Places: Northwest, by Giselle Smith (Sasquatch Books).

Best Places: Olympic Peninsula Destinations, by Ruth Kirk (Sasquatch Books).

Best Places: Portland, by John Guttberg (Sasquatch Books).

Best Places: Seattle, by Shannon O'Leary (Sasquatch Books).

Best Places to Kiss in the Northwest, by Kate Chynoweth (Sasquatch Books).

Best Places to Stay: Pacific Northwest, by Marilyn McFarlane (Houghton Mifflin).

Compass American Guides: Alaska, by John A. Murray (Fodor's).

Compass American Guides: Oregon, by Judy Jewell and Greg Vaughn (Fodor's).

Compass American Guides: Pacific Northwest, by John Doerper and Greg Vaughn (Fodor's).

Compass American Guides: Washington, by John Doerper and Greg Vaughn (Fodor's).

Mobil Travel Guide: Northwest and Alaska (Globe Pequot Press).

Oregon: An Explorer's Guide, by Mark Highberger (Countryman Press).

Quick Escapes Pacific Northwest, by Marilyn McFarlane and Christine A. Cunningham (Globe Pequot Press).

Canada

Best Places: Vancouver, by Kasey Wilson (Sasquatch Books).

British Columbia Bed & Breakfast Guide, by Sarah Bell (Gordon Soules).

Compass American Guides: Montreal (Fodor's).

The Complete Guide to Bed & Breakfasts, Inns & Guesthouses International, by Pamela Lanier (Lanier Publishing).

Exploring Nova Scotia, by Dale Dunlop and Alison Scott (Formac Publishing).

Historic Inns of Canada's East Coast, by Julian Beveridge, Norman Munroe, and Wayne Chase (Formac Publishing).

Inns and Bed & Breakfasts in Quebec, by Federation Des Agricotours Du Quebec (Ulysses Travel Guides).

Manitoba: A Colourguide, by Marilyn Morton (Formac Publishing).

Mobil Travel Guide: Canada (Globe Pequot Press).

Montreal and Quebec City Colourguide, by Emma McKay (Formac Publishing).

Niagara & Southwestern Ontario: A Colourguide, by Paul Knowles (Formac Publishing).

Nova Scotia Colourguide, by Stephen Poole and Colleen Abdullah (Formac Publishing).

The Official Bed & Breakfast Guide and Cookbook: United States, Canada & the Caribbean, by Phyllis Featherston and Barbara Ostler (National Bed & Breakfast Association).

Prince Edward Island Colourguide, by Laurie Brinklow (Formac Publishing).

Toronto Colourguide, by Nicholas Dinka (Formac Publishing).

Ulysses Bed & Breakfasts in Ontario, by Julia Roles (Ulysses Travel Guides).

Vancouver and Victoria Colourguide, by Constance Brissenden (Formac Publishing).

Waterside Escapes in the Northeast: Great Getaways by Lake, River & Sea, by Nancy and Richard Woodworth (Countryman Press).

Worksheets

Activity Worksheet for Opening a B&B

Activities	Task Done	Action Items	Progress Notes

1. Collect information
   Publications
   Workshops / apprenticeships
   Consultants
   Associations / reservation services
   Internet			

2. Examine lifestyle
   Personality
   Skills
   Work
   Family
   Support networks			

3. Evaluate home and surroundings
   Location
   Suitability
   Available space
   Appeal / atmosphere			

4. Identify market
   Visitor demographics
   Area attractions / activities			

5. Develop a business plan
   Goals
   Financial resources / needs
   Competition
   Your B&B image / description
   Statistics
   Letters of support			

6. Comply with regulations
   Zoning
   Fire
   Americans with Disabilities Act
   Insurance
   Health and safety
   Taxes

7. Develop a marketing plan
   Materials
   Distribution
   Memberships
   Advertising

8. Prepare a budget
   Start-up expenses
   Ongoing expenses
   Optional expenses
   Projected income
   Room rates
   Break-even point

9. Set up business systems
   Telephone / voice mail
   Fax
   E-mail / Internet access
   Record keeping
   Computer system

10. Refurbish and decorate
    Repairs
    Furniture
    Plumbing
    Electricity
    Amenities

Marketing Plan for the Year

Three Primary Objectives:

A. _____

B. _____

C. _____

Month	Type of Marketing Activity	Projected Expenses	Actual Expenses
January			
February			
March			
April			
May			

Marketing Plan for the Year

Month	Type of Marketing Activity	Projected Expenses	Actual Expenses
June			
July			
August			
September			
October			
November			
December			

Marketing Projection Worksheet

Calendar	Marketing Activity or Local Attraction	Projected Room Nights Sold	Actual Room Nights Sold
January			
February			
March			
April			
May			
June			

Marketing Projection Worksheet

Calendar	Marketing Activity or Local Attraction	Projected Room Nights Sold	Actual Room Nights Sold
July			
August			
September			
October			
November			
December			

Projected Expenses Worksheet

Onetime Start-up Expenses	Amount
Moving costs (if purchasing a B&B)	$
Down payment (if purchasing a B&B)	$
Closing costs (if purchasing a B&B)	$
Web site design	$
Accountant	$
Attorney	$
B&B consultants	$
Computer hardware/software	$
Brochures/stationery	$
Business cards	$
Licenses/permits	$
Office supplies	$
New furniture	$
Mattresses	$
Linens/towels	$
Repairs	$
Renovations	$
Business books/workshops	$
Plumbing upgrade	$
Electrical upgrade	$
Smoke/carbon monoxide detectors	$
New kitchen appliances	$

Serving trays/ice buckets/coffee carafes	$
New dishware/cutlery	$
Painting supplies/labor	$
Guidebook/local attraction library	$
DVD library	$
Guest room wastebaskets	$
Night-lights	$
Clock radios	$
Soap dispensers	$
Locks/keys	$
Fans/air conditioners	$
Small guest refrigerators	$
Lamps/lightbulbs	$
Televisions/DVD players	$
Luggage racks	$
Landscaping	$
Deposits	$
Miscellaneous	$
Total projected start-up costs	$

Monthly Operating Expenses	Amount
Mortgage	$
Loan payments	$
Insurance	$
Professional fees	$
Taxes	$
Memberships	$
Advertising	$
Dues	$
Subscriptions	$
Cleaning supplies	$
Food and beverages	$
Telephone service	$
Internet service	$
Laundry supplies	$
Trash/recycling pickup	$
Landscaping maintenance	$
Maintenance	$
Utilities (electricity/gas)	$
Heat	$
Water and sewer	$

Reservation service commissions	$
Postage/deliveries	$
Employee wages	$
Employee benefits	$
Owner's salary or draw	$
Owner's health insurance	$
Office supplies	$
Housekeeping supplies	$
Gas/mileage	$
Facial/toilet tissue	$
Soap	$
Lotions/shampoos	$
Other amenities	$
Sundry supplies/services	$
Miscellaneous	$
Total projected monthly costs	$
Monthly costs x 12 months = annual costs	$
Total start-up costs	$
+ Annual costs	$
= First-year costs	$

Index

About the Author

Jan Stankus writes about subjects that inspire her, with travel, bed and breakfast, and her home city of Boston at the top of the list. Much of her expertise in these areas comes from her ten years as the director of the Traveler's Information Exchange. She now works full-time writing film and television program description for people who are blind or visually impaired. For more information, visit openabedandbreakfast.com.